Kate ~ ...ry ~ K.
I'm ver...
for the loss...
mom. I underst...
both love and heart...
This book is about
both and how

the Gift

God was with me
through it all. I
look forward to
getting to know you,
Shelley

the Gift

And we lived

HAPPILY...

In God's

perfect timing

comes the

EVER AFTER

SHELLEY BAKER

HIS BOOKS
PUBLISHING

The Gift

ISBN: 978-0-578-79844-8

Published by His Books Publishing

Edited by Dana L. Cobb

Cover and interior design by TLC Book Design, *TLCBookDesign.com.* Cover by: Tamara Dever; Interior by Monica Thomas

Cover image by DepositPhotos @natis76/Nataliia Natykach. Interior heart drawings by Brittney Mae Nunes.

Printed in the United States of America

To Mary—my mother-in-law, friend, and Naomi.
My life is better because you are in it.
I love you so very much.

Contents

Preface

WRITING A BOOK—a memoir—is like letting someone read your diary. It's so private, yet I have an undeniable feeling of joy to share my story with you. I haven't journaled much in my life, but if I had, this is what would have been in there. This is my life story. So much of what lives in my heart is now on the pages of my book, The Gift. Kind of funny how someone who was never much interested in reading is now an author. Me, an author? Really? Yes, I am the author of this book, but God, however, is the author of my life story. I simply wrote down the love story He blessed me with, the trials and tribulations He helped me to endure, and the hope that He gives me about my future.

God's plan for my life story was being set in motion when, one afternoon, I noticed my dad slowly walking in the large field behind our house. What was he doing? Immediately, I had a feeling that something wasn't right. Intrigued, I stood there watching him out of the window of my upstairs bedroom. Within days, the announcement was made that we would be moving to Salinas, California. We would be leaving Santa Maria—my hometown of 15 years—to live in a place I had never been.

After a going away party, taking pictures and hugging friends goodbye, I found our family en route to our new home in a new town. We spent the next few weeks unpacking and getting settled. I had a new room, but even though all my belongings were there, my heart was not. My summer of turning *Sweet 16* was anything but sweet.

My junior year of high school soon started with sounds of locker doors shutting, and the chatter of students and friends reuniting from summer break filling the hallways—the same hallways I was walking through alone. I enviously looked at them and imagined what my friends back in Santa Maria were doing.

I pleaded with my mom to let us go back home. All my friends would start driving soon and everyone would be graduating together the next year. I didn't know anybody in Salinas, and I didn't want to be there! Although my mom let me vent, and was empathetic toward my distress, moving back was not an option.

Although I didn't understand the bigger picture in the summer of 1984, looking back I can see God—who had already written my life story—was strategically putting all of the pieces in place. Little did I know, in less than two years I would meet the love of my life, Nate Baker. A year after meeting, Nate would ask me to be his wife. I came to realize that moving to Salinas was the best idea my parents ever had!

Today, if you were to ask me where my hometown is, I would answer Salinas. It is where Nate and I met, fell in love, and got married. It is where we began our college days in pursuit of our chosen careers. It is where, a few years after saying *"I do!"* we started our family. Our daughter Brittney Mae and our son Justin Ryan were born close by on the Monterey Peninsula. The Salinas Valley overflows with memories and it is where many lifelong friends still reside. This picturesque urban town, nestled between two mountain ranges, will also be the final resting place for Nate and me.

Section 7, Row 1, plot number 113. These are the numbers of the land that I purchased at *The Garden of Memories* soon after Nate passed away.

Once again, I am in the position of not understanding. This time, however, I choose to look at the bigger picture and trust that God is in control of my life.

This book is about my personal journey through both love and grief, and how God was right there with me through both. It's a reminder that when you say, "I am a Christian; I am yours, God; Your will be done, not mine," then you better be ready to stand by those words when God does just that. This is a book about how I made the choice to continue to trust my Lord and Savior, Jesus Christ, unconditionally regardless of the situation. My love for God remains the same, whether it be when I am loving life, laughing with family and friends, or when I am in the fetal position, lying on the floor, sobbing with a broken heart.

Psalm 34:18 (NASB) says, "The Lord is near to the brokenhearted. And saves those who are crushed in spirit." Crushed. That was me. The pain was so deep I felt paralyzed. Breathing was hard. Eating was a chore. Sleeping was a struggle, and being awake was even more of a struggle. There have been countless times when I have said, "I can't do this!" and in reality this was true. I really can't! However, Jesus can. He can do all things. Matthew 19:26 (NASB) says, "And looking at them, Jesus said to them, 'With people this is impossible, but with God all things are possible.' "

And as promised, time and time again, I could feel Him close in my brokenness. There were so many miracles that happened to me after losing Nate that had God's signature written all over them.

I don't know what hardships you may be going through, or what your future holds, but God does. And He wants to experience them with you. God is love and He will never leave you. John 16:33

(NASB) "These things I have spoken to you, so that in Me you may have peace. In the world you have tribulation, but take courage; I have overcome the world." The Lord has written a life story for each of us, and someday at the end of life, we will each look back and see how He put all the pieces together.

That closeness with God, and the authentic, romantic comedy of Nate's and my love story are what this book is about. It's a Nicholas Sparks meets Billy Graham kind of love story. Because it is not only the love story of Nate and me, but also the love story of Jesus and me. I open my heart now to share with you, and show how God both gives and takes away—becoming a bride at 19 and a widow at 42.

These days my life is filled with joy for my many blessings. Happiness is circumstantial; joy is a choice. And while I don't yet know exactly what my future holds, that's okay. In God I trust.

Chapter 1

"Heaven" by Bryan Adams

"IS THIS WHERE THE PROM IS?"

My boyfriend Nate, so striking in a tuxedo, politely stood waiting for an answer. The front desk clerks exchanged confused glances and began chatting amongst themselves. Standing next to Nate, in my eighties-sort-of little black dress, I was just as puzzled as the employees. We certainly looked the part for a prom, right down to the corsage I was wearing. However, nothing else in this situation made any sense. We had graduated high school over a year ago...and I was certain our junior college didn't have an unannounced prom. I looked around the elegant lobby of the Monterey Beach Hotel and wondered what on earth we were doing here!

Uh-huh-ing into the phone, the lady clerk continued to smile at us while another clicked through event bookings. My look of confusion matched that of the receptionist at the front desk as I tried to figure out what was going on. It wasn't prom...it was July 24th, my nineteenth birthday. Just moments before, we had been on our way to dinner in Monterey when Nate had randomly pulled over at this beachside hotel off Highway 1. As if we were late for something, he grabbed my hand and led me into the hotel.

The clerk hung up the phone and her co-worker ceased her search. She shook her head with a baffled, yet polite, expression, "I'm very sorry, but unfortunately, there is no prom scheduled here for tonight."

"Ah, no problem. Thank you very much for checking," Nate smiled, and with a subtle nod of his head, squeezed my hand gently. By the look of intent and amusement on his face, something told me that he already knew that.

Within minutes, we were back in the hotel parking lot. My heels click-clacked as I made my way around Nate's blue Ford EXP where he was holding the door open for me. He had a twisted expression on his face as if he were trying his very best to resist laughing out loud. Catching a glimpse of his custom license plate that read "IMKRAZE," I chuckled and agreed whole-heartedly.

The more time I spent with Nate, the more those seven letters proved to be true. He had a way of making me laugh and always kept me guessing. As I got into the car, I could see in that familiar, mischievous gleam in his eyes that he was having fun tonight. His smile was contagious. I returned a happy smile and softly shook my head, silently thanking God and telling Him how much I loved this crazy man.

As Nate started the car, I looked over at Spike, the Gremlin hanging upside down from the rearview mirror. Funny how Spike's crazed expression was so appropriate in this scenario. It was almost as if the two of them had secretly planned our odd little detour.

"What just happened?!" I laughed in my perplexed amusement.

Nate, highly pleased with himself, smiled as he leaned over for a quick kiss, "C'mon Princess, let's eat!"

Back on the highway, Nate shifted the car into fourth gear and reached for my hand. His warmth radiated through my entire body as we listened to Billy Joel's voice serenading us from the cassette player. Nate exited the highway where we were welcomed by rows of moored sailboats, their masts rising with the waters as if waving at our arrival. As we passed Fisherman's Wharf, I cracked open the window to take in the salty air.

I could feel the enchantment of the evening as we drove through the tunnel on Lighthouse Avenue and then back out again. Looking out the window, I thought about the many times Nate and I had driven to Monterey over the past year that we had been dating. There were memories scattered all over this town — like feeding the squirrels at Lover's Point, making out at the top of a rocket ship at Dennis the Menace Park, dinner and movie nights, and even ignoring the NO TRESPASSING sign posted on the island in the middle of Lake El Estero when on a paddle boat one night. We turned toward Cannery Row and into a beachside parking lot. I could hear the rumble of the surf as Nate turned off the engine and leaned over for a kiss.

The restaurant was made to impress. It was built in a pier-like style with strong wooden pillars anchored into the ground that were being constantly challenged by the crashing waves. As we entered through the oversized wooden door of the Chart House, the savory aroma of the cuisine filled the air. We were welcomed by a smiling hostess dressed in black. After looking in the reservation book, she guided us to our table. We passed candlelit tables where other couples dressed up for a night out clinked their glasses, and waiters carried trays of entrees that looked like works of art. We followed her past the bar amply supplied with all the bottles of liquor we were too young to drink, and were seated at a table in front of a windowed wall that opened up the restaurant to the sea's moonlit horizon.

Menu in hand, Nate studied the many choices. Deciding on the lobster tail, he rubbed his hands together in mouth-watering anticipation. I, however, opened the menu, skipped over every sea creature listed and found the chicken teriyaki with garlic mashed potatoes. Nate was a fan of everything under the sea, whereas I was not. I enjoyed chicken or beef entrees — extra well done.

Nate held my hand over the table as we waited for our food. Looking at him sitting across from me made my heart race. My boyfriend was so handsome with his blonde hair that curled at the back of his neck. I loved running my fingers through the curls, but I liked his eyebrows the most. He could be anybody with those eyebrows. He could wrinkle his forehead into a crazy Chris Farley, or form a narrow V as the unpredictable Jack Nicholson. But when he looked at me, his eyebrows eased into place and he was just Nate, my Nate, dashing green eyes and all.

Our food arrived. I circled the savory teriyaki sauce into the mashed potatoes, while at the same time, Nate was in seafood heaven. He dipped his lobster in melted butter and grinned between bites like a happy child.

"Here, try this." Nate held out a piece of lobster meat at the end of his fork that he had just extracted from the bright red tail.

"No way!" I waved my hands as if creating a barrier.

"C'mon, you know you want to try it," he teased, popping it into his mouth, "It's delicious!"

"Sorry, seafood is just too much information and besides, it isn't cooked enough," I responded in defense. He knew I preferred my meat extremely well-done, almost to the point of being jerky. "You can eat all the seafood you want. I'll just watch *you* enjoy it," I said as I wrinkled my nose. He raised a brow playfully at me.

We topped off our delicious dinner by sharing a slice of mud pie with two forks. I took in a deep breath, as if I could taste these moments, savoring them as long as I could.

After dinner, Nate took me to Carmel where we walked on the beach. I carried my strappy heels in one hand and held Nate's hand with the other. The sand was cool, and so was the air. Nate gave me his jacket, my body swam in the fabric and the fragrance of his Brut aftershave. As the evening progressed, it seemed as though Nate had every detail of my birthday night planned so perfectly.

"You look very debonair," I teased, complimenting his neat, white shirt and red bow tie. He teased back, his eyebrows jumping flirtatiously.

Under a blanket of stars in the sky, we sat on the sand. I nuzzled into Nate's arm, watching the waves curl and crash. This night was incredible and romantic—and completely serene. With no one around, it was as if the beach existed only for this moment. Nate leaned in for a kiss. His tender, warm lips melted every inch of me. My boyfriend was amazing, and I was completely in love. I could have stayed there forever, but he kissed my forehead signaling that it was time to head home.

Back in the car, I leaned my head onto his shoulder—my head rocked in unison with each shift of the gears. He had exchanged Billy Joel for Bryan Adams on our return to Salinas. Nate's car was never without music. My thoughts and dreams, intertwining with Bryan's guitar solo, were interrupted by a clicking turn signal. Feeling the car change lanes, I lifted my head to see where we were going.

"One more stop," Nate said, as he took the turn toward Jack's Peak. As the car was winding up the mountain, I looked around at the beauty of a park I had never been to before. With the scent of pine in the air and the feeling of sand still between my toes from our walk, I looked out into the forest wishing this night would never end.

Reaching the summit of Jack's Peak, Nate parked. We sat there enjoying the view of the ocean reflecting the lights of the cities on the bay. When we got out of the car, we smiled at how good we were at fogging up windows. Surrounded by pine and oak trees, we stood there, hand in hand, taking in the twilight view of the Monterey coastline. We pointed out the places we had been tonight: the Monterey Beach Hotel, the Chart House, and Carmel Beach. Nate and I had a way of being lost in our own world. My favorite place had become wherever Nate was, and he always made me feel like he felt the same.

"I have a gift for you," Nate said, almost bashfully.

"A gift? Really?" I asked in surprise. After such a dream night, how could he possibly have more to give me? The surprises just kept coming.

With the crickets chirping—like a drum roll of anticipation—I watched as Nate stepped back to the car and returned with a nicely wrapped box. I sighed in disbelief, and reached out for the gift wondering what it could be. As my fingertips brushed the silky red ribbon, Nate pulled back his arm and flung my gift off the mountainside!

Shocked, I watched the gift fly through the air as if in slow motion. The beautiful red bow seemed to wave goodbye to me as its ribbons rippled from the force of Nate's throw. My eyes stayed fixated on my present as it tumbled and disappeared into the darkness of the summer night.

What? My birthday gift was gone! I turned back around to Nate, wanting some answers for his unique behavior tonight. First, we had gone into a hotel and asked about a mystery prom, and now, he just threw my birthday present off the top of the mountain!

As I turned to get some answers, he wasn't where I had last seen him. This time he was on one knee, holding open a little black box with a diamond ring inside.

The whole forest hushed.

"I love you, Princess," he said. "Will you marry me?" A proud smile formed across the lips I had been kissing all night. His eyebrows were high, awaiting an answer.

My eyes welled up with emotion and excitement as I immediately answered, "Yes!"

Nate placed the engagement ring on my finger. As he stood up, I embraced him to confirm my answer. "I love you, Nate," I cried with tears filling my eyes as we continued our embrace. I had never been this happy in my entire life.

Nate took my hand and we looked at the beautiful engagement ring. "I can't wait to tell my parents!" I exclaimed.

"They already know," Nate replied. "I met with them earlier to ask for your hand in marriage."

My eyes left the glistening diamond, and I asked incredulously, "My parents knew when I left tonight that you were going to propose to me?!" I was still trying to piece together this night, a night that would live forever in my heart.

Nate smiled, as if he could see the wheels spinning inside my head and opened the car door for me. I got in, and practicing what all engaged girls do, held out my hand. I even showed Spike my engagement ring! I was nineteen, in love, and on my way to becoming Mrs. Nathan Andrew Baker.

Somewhere on that mountainside was an empty, wrapped box. And on my hand was a beautiful engagement ring from Nate, my fiancé.

Chapter 2

"Love Walks In" by Van Halen

ONE YEAR EARLIER...

The summer after high school graduation was the summer of parties. It's that small amount of time in between graduating from both school and childhood, but not quite being part of the adult world yet. That was all just around the corner, but for now, at this moment in time, I had just turned eighteen and was enjoying every minute of the summer of '86.

My friends and I were at a party, and there was a lot to celebrate. It was the typical scenario with friends, and friends of friends, gathering at a home where the parents were out of town. Empty bottles of Bartles and Jaymes wine coolers of various flavors and beer cans cluttered the counters. Sounds of laughter, conversation, and '80s hits playing on MTV filled the air.

Sitting at the kitchen table playing poker with friends, I waited for Chris to play his hand. Chris was one of the first friends I had made after I moved to Salinas from Santa Maria the summer before my junior year. It had been a difficult transition, but he had made it so much easier. A social soul at heart, with a lifetime spent growing up in Salinas, Chris knew a lot of people.

"Hey, Shelley, you want a drink?" Chris asked. He took off his glasses and folded his cards with a sigh of defeat.

I looked down at my cards with confidence. With no intention of throwing my hand in yet, I nodded, "Sure, I'll have whatever you're having."

He got up and made his way into the kitchen as I continued to focus on the game. As I threw in a few more chips to the center of the table, the front door opened. My attention was instantly captured by a handsome guy smoking a pipe who was walking in with a couple of friends. I focused on the pipe. There was no smoke—no puffing either. Strange, yet oddly charming. The group of guys was talking and joking as they made their way into the kitchen.

"Steiny!" the blonde guy with the pipe called out in a playful voice as he greeted Chris.

Steiny? That's a new one! I chuckled to myself as I made sense of it. *Chris's last name… Steinbruner.*

The way they all greeted each other made it obvious that they had been friends for a long time. After knowing Chris for almost a year now, it was surprising to me that I'd never seen these friends of his. Chris handed a can of Coors Light to one of the other guys in the group who had dark hair and was wearing a pair of 501 jeans and a T-shirt. His hair was thick in the front and longer in the back—a mullet almost.

While they continued chatting, I tried to keep focused on my hand of cards. I became preoccupied as I took subtle glances at the guy with the pipe while trying to concentrate on my game of poker. As I took another look at him, our eyes met. My heart jumped in surprise. I quickly looked away feeling my cheeks turn warm. I sat there awkwardly wondering if he had noticed.

He came over and sat in the chair next to me, and I could feel butterflies take flight in my stomach. Out of the handful of empty chairs around the table, he decided to sit in the one next to me.

"Hey," he said, his pipe bouncing lazily in his mouth as he spoke to me.

I looked at him sitting there in his brown leather jacket trying very hard not to let my eyes linger, which was difficult, very difficult. I managed to reply with a "Hi" and a smile, maintaining my poker face not so much for the sake of the game, but to mask my stomach from doing flips.

We began to chat a little as the game continued. Everything about this guy with the pipe was drawing me in. The grip on my hand of cards tightened to cope with my struggle to keep it cool.

Chris came back to join the game, giving me a slight sense of relief as the tension inside of me eased. He handed me a drink and sat down. I was hoping for an introduction to finally get to know this guy's name, but of course teenagers aren't very good with proper introductions.

"Paul, come on over here!" Chris called out. The guy with the mullet walked out of the kitchen to join us at the poker table.

"Here's to no late shoppers tonight," Paul said, as he held up his beer and took a gulp.

"How's everything going at Star?" Chris asked.

"Nate and I had the closing shift tonight," Paul answered, looking over at his friend with the pipe. "Some lady was giving me crap for not double bagging the milk," he groaned, laughing it off.

The guy with the pipe smirked, "C'mon Grothe, you should know by now to double bag milk, especially for Mrs. Gleason."

"You and your photographic memory, Nate," Paul chuckled. "It's going to take her bustin' my ass a few more times before I'll remember."

Chris, with his buzzed laugh, finished off his beer. "Bagging milk sounds SUPER difficult ... at least one of you has it down."

"Shut up, Chris!" Paul laughed.

As they continued talking and joking around, I was busy silently piecing together their conversation. Nate. The captivating guy with the pipe sitting next to me was Nate. I knew that Star Market was a local, family-owned grocery store, which is where Nate and Paul apparently worked bagging groceries. Not too long after their chat, the guys said goodbye to Chris.

Nate glanced at me briefly before joining his friends as they left the party. Although they hadn't stayed long, my life had changed forever during that game of poker. Our story began that night.

I had all the symptoms: insomnia, light-headedness, and loss of appetite. I could smell my dad's coffee brewing in the kitchen. It smelled amazing, and I don't even like coffee. My eyes scanned the walls of my bedroom. Have they always been this purple? I could hear my mom cleaning the house, and began humming along to the record she was playing. Her painfully twangy country album sounded almost pleasant this morning.

I zipped up my blue jeans and pulled a T-shirt over my head. As I headed toward the door, my eyes met Bruce Springsteen's gaze from the poster pinned to my wall. I was instantly taken back to last night when Nate's and my eyes met from across the room. Nate. I *had* to see him again, and I knew just where to find him!

I pulled my long, brunette hair back into a ponytail and headed out to the kitchen. I felt amazing—alive and vibrant—like I was on top of a mountain that no one else could reach. With a rhythm in my walk, I energetically turned the corner into the dining room, grinning with excitement.

My dad, in his robe with a mug of coffee in his hand, sat at his usual spot at the kitchen table reading the morning paper. He took slow sips as he thumbed through the pages. Catching my mom's attention as I entered the room, I immediately made a U-turn to escape the inevitable Saturday morning chores.

"Oh good, you're up," my mom said. "Shelley, the frying pans have spots on the bottoms again. Go ahead and clean them off."

With no time to object, I found myself in front of the sink with soapy hands scrubbing the same spots from last Saturday that I knew would never come off. This was a complete waste of time. I had something really important to do. Irritated, I aggressively scrubbed the old pans. An emptied box of Cheerios on the counter next to me caught my attention. We were out of cereal!

"Hey, Mom..." I called from the kitchen, the grin returning to my face, "we're out of Cheerios... we need to go to the grocery store."

"No, it's okay," she called back as she dusted another picture in the living room, "I'll go later this week."

"But we always have Cheerios in the morning. What are we supposed to eat for breakfast?" I asked.

My dad lifted his head from the paper, "I can scramble up some eggs."

Upset with Dad's offer, I opened the fridge. My eyes lit up when I found that the egg carton was almost empty, too. Trying to contain my excitement at the lack of food in the house, I answered, "There's only one egg in here!"

"Why don't you just eat dumb?" my mom suggested.

I tapped my foot thinking of another reply. *Eating dumb* was my family's made up phrase for making a meal out of leftovers or basically whatever you could find in the kitchen to eat. It was always the back-up plan.

"I don't want to eat dumb. We need to go grocery shopping," I insisted.

She put her dusting cloth down and looked across the room at me. "We have plenty of food in the house. Why are you so interested in grocery shopping all of a sudden?"

Parents! They always have a way of knowing. My attempt to keep last night private wasn't working. "Okay, so I met this guy last night," I confessed. "He works at Star Market and I just *have* to see him again."

My dad stopped reading and glanced over at my mom. She smirked, satisfied to know my real reason, and gave him a nod.

"Well ... I have the day off. I'll go *grocery shopping* with you," my dad said, playing along. "I'm going to have to check this guy out," he said in a fatherly tone.

"Okay, Dad, here's the thing—I don't want Nate to see me. I hardly even know him." I looked at my dad making sure he understood the game plan. I had never made such a request, but then again, no one had ever captured my attention the way Nate had. Together we drove to the store.

Once parked, my dad took the keys out of the ignition and looked at the big blue star at the top of the grocery store. "What ... we're not here for Cheerios?" he teased. He looked at me, seemingly excited to be a part of the mission at hand.

After trying all morning to get here, I was now in the parking lot but couldn't seem to even get out of the car. I felt my heart racing. What if he sees me? What would I say?

Flat out nervous, I walked through the front door of Star Market with my dad. As we stepped in, I tried to keep my composure and refrained from running back out the door. The anxiety of trying to see him, while keeping myself unseen, was almost too much to handle.

"What does he look like?" my dad asked. "I'll keep an eye out for him."

"He looks like Joe Montana," I replied with a starry-eyed smile.

My dad puffed up proudly. Being a huge football fan, he was on high alert for someone who resembled one of his favorite 49ers.

We walked up and down a few aisles with our full attention on catching a glimpse of Nate. Midway through the store, my dad and I rounded a corner into the next aisle and my eyes widened. There he was!

I could see Nate from a distance bagging groceries. His handsomeness made my knees weak as I watched him bag the customer's groceries with such finesse. I held my hand out to stop my dad from searching any longer. Nate was in sight. I stayed planted at the end of the bread aisle, pointing him out to my dad. Dad seemed to approve as he remained shushed and hidden amongst the bread. I responded with a nod and a smile as I stared ahead. With our mission accomplished, we left the store unseen by Nate.

For teens, every night is a Friday night during summer break. As the days went by, I would see Nate at parties. We would always seem to find one another. Each time I talked with him, the more interested I became.

One night we were hanging out on the street with a group of friends. Nate and I were talking when the group decided to relocate to another friend's house.

"Baker!" Nate turned his head to see Paul waving him over. "Let's go!" Paul called out.

Nate had a gleam in his eyes as he looked at me with a mischievous smile. He walked over to Paul and they began talking. Nate made gestures toward the car. Paul snickered, nodded his head, and popped the trunk of the car open. Piqued with curiosity, I watched Paul give Nate a friendly punch on the shoulder as he jumped in. Nate sat proudly in the trunk and gave a valiant salute to Paul before he sank down for him to shut the lid. Paul laughed as he got in the driver's seat. His door shut and the car started down the road.

"What is he doing?!" I asked Chris in a confused tone as I rejoined the rest of the group.

Chris laughed and shook his head. "He's just like that, always doing crazy things," he explained.

With Nate no longer in sight, I rushed over to Chris's car pulling him along with me. He seemed calm and in no rush to follow along. Anxious and concerned, I fastened my seatbelt hoping we would catch up quickly.

As we followed behind in the dark, our headlights illuminated their car. I cringed at every bump in the road imagining Nate bouncing around in the dark trunk. What if something went wrong? He could be in trouble and no one would even know! Is there even enough air in there for him? With my eyes glued to the back of the car, we carpooled our group to the next house. "Why can't he sit *inside* the car like a normal person?" I asked out loud.

Chris noticed my anxious finger tapping, "This is nothing compared to the time he rode his skateboard down the huge hill by our cabin. He crashed so hard! We used an entire box of bandaids for all the bleeding... I'm surprised he still has a face." I hit Chris on the shoulder for not making me feel better, but I couldn't help laughing along with him.

When we arrived, the trunk popped open and Nate jumped out playfully with a smile. Paul walked over and gave him a high five. Nate looked over at me, and I sighed with relief. No bandaids were required for this stunt. That night was when I found out that *antics* was one of Nate's endearing qualities. Now I had fallen for him even more.

"Where's the party tonight?" I asked Chris, who was driving me along with a few other friends.

"Nate's house," he answered.

"Nate's house? Cool." I sat back trying my very best to mask my pure excitement. I smiled thinking, *This is good, really good!* I anxiously ran my fingers through my hair.

We pulled up to the house. My friends and I walked through the courtyard to the front door. There were a bunch of people scattered around the house. Most of the people I knew, but some I didn't. As my eyes scanned the people at the party, I looked over and there was Nate.

I could feel my face get warm as I got a little shy. I hadn't known Nate for very long, but I was definitely interested. I wondered what he thought about me. He smiled as he came toward us to say hi, and his eyes seemed to linger on me. Chris had been to Nate's house countless times, but this was the first visit for a few of us. Nate gave us the tour. We walked around the one story, four bedroom house where he lived with his mom and two younger brothers.

I usually didn't pay much attention to the houses where parties were held, but this time it was different. This was Nate's house which made it special. My eyes took in all the little details of his home, and eventually he led us to the last room down the hall ... his room.

Nate's bedroom was clean, organized, and simple. Posters of baseball and football players, as well as some Van Halen decor, were neatly hung on the walls. A metal Chargers trash can sat on the floor along with a big cushioned chair that was next to a TV by the side of his bed. After a few minutes of talking in Nate's room, Chris and the others left to hang out with more friends. I stayed with Nate.

You can tell a lot about a person based on their room. Nate liked sports, rock music, organization, and ... fish? My eyes focused on the fish swimming around the medium-sized tank. I walked over to get a closer look. There were silver barbs and black mollies swimming mindlessly around the tank. Whenever they would pass by a plastic log in the middle of the tank, a small, fresh water shark with a gray body and red tail would rush out from the log and chase them around. He was reminding the other fish who was the boss. He would then dash back into the log he'd claimed as his own. I watched the shark do this a few times. Nate came over and stood beside me, making me feel all tingly inside. He could tell I was amused by his bully, pet shark.

"That's Bruno!" He paused, watching the shark chase another fish away. "He's a rogue, like me."

A rogue? What an interesting way to describe himself. I looked up at Nate, who was now close enough that we were almost touching. Our eyes lingered for a long moment. Everything about him had my attention—the sound of his voice, his dashing smile, his cologne, and the blue and ivory striped sweater he was wearing with the sleeves rolled up to his elbows. The party was buzzing around us, but as Nate and I watched Bruno, it was like we were in our own little world.

"Nate! Get your ass in here!" Paul's voice echoed from down the hall, over the sound of music and chatter from the living room.

Nate kept his eyes on me, then smiled. He ran his hand through his blonde hair as he moved toward the door. I exhaled slowly. Had I been holding my breath that whole time? I took one last look at Bruno and then followed Nate out to the kitchen.

A group of friends was gathered in Nate's kitchen. I was still in awe of the fact that Nate lived here. This is where he ate with his family—his family that I was thankful for being away tonight. I lifted myself up onto the kitchen counter, and Nate and I continued talking with a couple of friends. Friends came in and out of the kitchen as Nate and I stayed there talking. After a while, I looked around and noticed a piano in the front room. I jumped down and walked toward it grinning as Nate followed me.

The piano was sitting against the wall facing the front door entrance. I thought back to all the piano lessons I had taken as a child. I had practiced almost daily, and had even been in a few recitals, but it had been years since I had played. I sat down on the piano bench and let my fingers linger over the keys. Would I remember any of the songs? As my fingers gently touched the keys, Nate came behind me and started playing the piano along with me, his arms wrapping around me, his head resting next to mine. I could feel his large, solid body gently leaning against my back as we played some notes. His arms were warm and covered with blonde hair. The intimacy of that moment was enough to make me completely forget everything I had ever learned about playing the piano. I blushed and could feel my heart racing as we got up. With the party interrupting our moment alone, we walked back into the dining room.

There were people gathered all around the house talking, drinking, and having a good time. Chris and Paul had taken Nate's attention elsewhere in the house, and I remained standing in the family room dreamily thinking of Nate and the music we had just played together. Within moments, Nate came up behind me one more time. This time, he took my hand and led me out to the deck in the backyard to get away from the crowd. My heart raced, yet at the same time, I felt so comfortable. I could feel his warmth as we stepped out into the night air. The noises from the party became muted as Nate closed the sliding glass door behind us. He turned toward me with a tenderness in his eyes. Without saying a word, he wrapped his arms around me and pulled me in close. I felt the strength of his body as our lips met. Our eyes closed and Nate kissed me. Our first kiss.

The intensity of our kiss made my knees feel like they, too, had a heartbeat. Our first kiss led to our second, third, fourth, and so on. We had now found our way onto the patio lounge chair.

Even though we had the deck to ourselves, the only thing separating us from the party was the sliding glass door. Wanting some time to ourselves, Nate took my hand again, and we walked over to the back door entrance into the garage. The porch light was dimly spilling in through a small window, lighting our way to a couch against the wall of the dark garage. We sat down on the couch and picked up where we had left off. We were out there, just the two of us, for the entire rest of the party.

Eventually, we returned and joined everyone sitting at the kitchen table. Our friends began teasing and making comments about us being gone so long. Evidence that a party had happened was scattered all over; empty beer cans, wine cooler, bottles, and remnants of snacks covered the table. I noticed a half-eaten box of crackers. It was getting late, and I still had a curfew to meet. I really had to go, but had to find a way to have another night like this with Nate. I grabbed the box of crackers, wrote my phone number all over the box, gave Nate a smile, and I left.

I was in another world as I sat in the car with Chris and some friends as we drove home. A permanent smile was plastered on my face as I melted into the seat. Chris looked over at me and smiled. By then, everyone knew how I felt about Nate. I began to ask Chris a little bit about him and his dating life.

"I've known Nate my whole life," Chris said, as he turned the steering wheel. "Great, great guy, but he's never really dated. He's kind of a loner in that way."

I understood what Chris was saying, and thought about Bruno. Nate seemed to relate to that red-finned rogue. Nate, just a few hours ago, had described himself that same way. Nate, also, just a few hours ago, had wanted me with him. From the front seat of the car, I smiled and looked out the window. Nate had invited me into his rogue life tonight... maybe this loner was changing his ways.

The box of crackers led to daily phone calls—our young love connected by a coiled cord. If we weren't together, we were talking on the phone, finding it impossible to hang up. It seemed almost unfair to end our conversations with a click when there was so much more we wanted to learn about each other. We talked about everything—our families, our jobs, music, concerts, God, our dreams, and our goals for the future. The more I got to know Nate, the more I realized how special he was. He was old fashioned, yet spontaneous and unpredictable at the same time. His unique sense of humor was a big part of his personality, making our conversations highly entertaining. I loved how much Nate made me laugh. He never told jokes to be funny—he just was.

We would be on the phone for so long that, resisting hanging up, I would fall asleep with the phone still in my hand. Sometimes, I would wake up with the phone lying next to me still off the hook with Nate asleep on the other end. It was easier for me to hang up when I knew that he was sleeping. Funny how a simple box of crackers was not only the beginning of our daily phone calls, but also the start of Nate and I going to parties together.

It was one of the last parties before summer ended, and everyone was drinking down their farewells. We were no longer gathering to celebrate our high school diplomas, but instead, we were holding onto the little time we had left before everything changed. While some friends, like Chris, would be packing their bags to leave for college, others either planned on jumping straight into the working world or attending the local junior college like Nate and me. After we had visited with friends, we decided to break away for some time to ourselves.

The sun began setting a little earlier each night and the warm air began to have a slight chill to it. Music pulsed through the windows as we rounded the corner of the country home. We walked past neglected rose bushes and found a lawn chair on a grassy hill. Glad to see only one chair instead of two, I sat on Nate's lap, his hand settled comfortably on my leg. I reclined sideways next to Nate, admiring the stars. It was quiet, except for Madonna's voice in the background singing "Crazy For You."

"Hey, Shelley," Nate patted my leg for attention. I turned my gaze toward him in response. "Will you be my girlfriend?"

"Yes," I nodded. "I'm crazy for you." I smiled, looking into his eyes, as *Madonna* seemed to join in repeating those same words in her love song.

Nate pulled out a gold bracelet from his pocket and carefully fastened the chain around my wrist. The bracelet was light and delicate and lovely. I was touched by the thought he had put into giving me the bracelet and blushed.

"I want to take you out on a date Wednesday night. Are you free?"

I nodded. Of course I was. Nate handed me a folded piece of paper, and even through the darkness, I could make out the words, *Eddie and The Tide*, as I opened the flyer. He told me we were going to The Paragon in Old Town Salinas where *Eddie and the Tide* would be playing. I couldn't wait!

People came and left the party that night, but for the rest of our time together, my boyfriend and I stayed right there, on the chair, up on the grassy hill.

I energetically rushed back and forth from my bedroom to the bathroom, hopping along as I managed to brush my teeth, and pull on my heels at the same time. My gold bracelet bounced along to my upbeat steps around the house. With a dash of fuchsia lip gloss, I completed my look and joined my parents in the dining room. They had heard so much about Nate, and tonight they would finally be meeting him before our first official date to the concert. Dad had been the only one who had actually seen him, but only from down the bread aisle at the grocery store.

Nate, being very punctual, pulled into the driveway right on time. I could hear the engine of his car turn off as I walked out to meet him in the courtyard. My heart skipped a beat as we met. His eyebrows lifted as he saw me in a denim mini skirt and big hooped earrings. Nate was so good looking all dressed up, and he always smelled as good as he looked.

Nate smiled and took my hand as we walked into the house together. I introduced Nate to my mom and dad who were very welcoming, wanting to get to know the young man who was about to take their daughter out. They shook hands, and we took a seat around the dining room table. Nate seemed slightly nervous as he looked across the table at my parents, his fingers anxiously drumming his leg. By the expression on their faces as we talked, I could tell that they liked him. We talked for a while, and my parents laughed when I told them about Nate's license plate, "IMKRAZE."

"I don't know about this guy," my dad teased.

"Yeah, his license plate has me worried too," Mom agreed as they exchanged a playful glance of parental disapproval.

Nate grinned at their remarks, as his leg bounced underneath the table. My parents held on to their little joke as they walked us out to the car.

"Alright, we'll let Shelley go, but that license plate better not be taken literally," Dad said with a smirk. "Take good care of her, Mr. Nate."

"I will," Nate promised, as he held the car door open for me.

It was a short drive to Main Street in Old Town Salinas. We barely had time to listen to a few *Eddie and The Tide* songs to get all fired up for the show before we parked the car along the street. The Paragon, an old renovated white brick building on Main Street, was surrounded by small family-owned shops, restaurants, and quaint boutiques. During the day, all the businesses along Main Street were open and bustling with people. Old Town at night, however, told a completely different story. All the shops seemed to be peacefully sleeping as the *Paragon Night Club* boomed with bright lights and music. On the front overhang of the building, a bright sign announced *Eddie and The Tide* in large red letters.

The sidewalk was lined with teenagers eager for the doors of the club to open. Although *The Paragon* was usually a place that only allowed people twenty-one and over, *Eddie and The Tide* had two shows tonight—the first one open to teenagers too young to legally order a drink. We waited in line surrounded by colorful '80s outfits and big hair, heavy on the hairspray. The energy of the crowd only made the event all the more exciting.

The large double doors opened, and the line of people poured in. Nate took my hand, eager to get us the best spot. We moved past teens clustered in the main entry way, through another set of double doors to the left, and down a set of stairs to the basement.

The bartender slushed soda into cups as we passed by the bar. We found an open table, the closest we could find to the dance floor, and sat down. The stage, right in front of the dance floor, was still draped with a thick curtain. The theatre buzzed with commotion and we could hear the mics being checked behind the covered stage.

"Check. Check. One. Two."

I bounced slightly in my seat, and then looked across the table at Nate. He had his eyes on me. He looked at me in a way that made me feel like he knew exactly what he wanted, and it was me. That look—it was a look of complete confidence, and, at the same time, a little bashful. The activity in the room seemed to slow down around us. All the noises began to blend together into nothing more than a soft hum. His gaze created a new warmth inside of me that encompassed my whole body. I could feel the energy between us like some kind of gravitational presence moving from within. There was something different in this moment, something special that, if I could, I would stay forever just like this. This ineffable interconnection and wonder of falling in love had captured my heart. Nate's soft smile from across the table melted me. I exhaled slowly as I continued to look into his eyes. The lights of the night club dimmed. Nate took his gaze off me and looked toward the stage. All the noise and color around me returned, reminding me of where I was. The concert was starting. Girls screamed as the curtain rose from the stage, revealing the local band, *Eddie and The Tide*.

As the music started, the crowd began cheering. Nate took my hand and led me onto the dance floor. We got so close to the stage that I could almost reach out and touch the hem of the singer's tight pants. All the girls swooned over Eddie—the lead singer of the band—who was in his half-buttoned white shirt and blue jean vest. His black and white electric guitar hung from his neck as he leaned forward singing into the mic to the dancing fans in front of him.

With the music's energy filling the room, and this new sensation of being in love, I had every reason to take it all in and dance! Everyone's attention was on the band, but my attention was on Nate. He danced with me, banging his head along to the beat. It was like our cassette tape had come to life—we knew every word to every song. The band was all in for showing their underaged fans a great time.

As the concert was nearing its end, the band slowed it down with their hit song *One in a Million*. Nate wrapped his arms around my waist. He felt so good. I could feel the heat from his body as we slow danced. I followed his steps, swaying along with him to the rhythm of this love song. I could hear Nate softly singing the words as if they were written just for me. My heart raced as I ran my hands gently down his shoulders and rested them against the deep curve of his back, enjoying every second of this night that felt like a dream. As we continued to dance, I noticed Nate looking over at the stage with a grin. I turned my attention toward the stage. Eddie was looking at us through the crowd of fans. He was smiling and giving us a thumbs up as he sang! I gasped in excitement and looked up at Nate. He gave Eddie a nod as he held on to me.

The song ended and the curtain fell back onto the stage. Nate sealed the night, and my love, with a kiss right there on the dance floor. It was love at first concert!

Our college days were upon us, leaving behind treasured memories of the best summer of my life. Nate and I were enjoying our time at Hartnell Junior College. Both of us were taking a full load—fifteen units. We took a lot of classes together, but for those times when we were apart, I always looked forward to him meeting me at the door after class.

Nate invited me over to his house for dinner—he wanted me to meet his family. As I walked into the courtyard and up to the front door, I took in a deep breath, releasing it to calm my nerves. The cool October breeze carried the scent of buttered garlic bread and zesty tomato sauce from the Baker's kitchen. The garden window of the kitchen looked out onto the courtyard and I could see Nate standing at the stove shaking spices into a large pot. He set the spice jars down on the counter and looked up, smiling as he saw me.

My nerves matched my excitement—I was about to meet Nate's family for the first time. I had heard so much about them and wanted to learn more about what Nate's life was like at home. The brass knob turned and Nate grinned at me as he opened the door and saw me standing on the front porch.

"Smells amazing," I smiled.

He kissed me in the doorway, "Come on in, I'm cooking spaghetti."

Each time I was in Nate's house, I noticed something I hadn't seen before. I smiled at a section of fraying brown and gold grass-cloth wallpaper in the hallway. I'll bet that has a story. A macrame owl hung from the ceiling in the corner of the dining room that was, like, totally from the '70s. I grew up with my mom's homemade macrame decorations around my old house in Santa Maria. Seeing the smiling owl brought back familiar memories and made me feel right at home. The oval oak table had already been set with plates, napkins, and forks with a bowl of grated parmesan cheese in the center. Nate returned to the stove as I set my purse down.

The door right next to the kitchen opened, and Nate's mom came in from the garage with a laundry basket full of clean clothes. As she shut the door behind her, I caught a quick glimpse of the couch where Nate and I had spent the majority of our time kissing during his party. Her eyes lit up with excitement as she saw me,

"Oh! Shelley's here!" She rested the basket on her hip and shook my hand. "Hi, I'm Mary. It's so nice to finally meet you!"

Mary's friendly smile matched the warm tone of her voice. Her shoulder length hair was a couple of shades darker than Nate's, and the dangling gold earrings she was wearing matched her outfit. She made her way to the adjoining family room and placed the basket of laundry on the sofa before waving me over to sit at the dinner table with her.

"How was your trip to Washington?" I asked as I sat down.

"Oh, it was really nice. We drive up every summer to visit my family, but Nate couldn't go this year because he had to work."

I looked up from the table to share a quick smile with Nate. Although he had worked a lot, he and I both knew that more than work had happened while his family had been away.

"Nate didn't tell me that he was dating." She looked over at Nate and gave him a look that only a mother can deliver. "I had to find out from a girl, named Sylvia, who was working at one of the department stores in the mall when I took Jonathan and Justin shopping for school clothes. She noticed the name on my check, and asked me if I was Nate Baker's mom. I told her yes, and that's when she told me that Nate was dating her good friend. She had a picture of you and her together on a keychain. I guess a lot happened while we were in Washington." Her voice trailed off, giving Nate another motherly glance. I looked at Nate and agreed with a smile.

A few thumps and thuds echoed from down the hallway. I looked at both Mary and Nate, who either didn't hear the commotion or didn't pay any attention to it.

"Give it back, Jon!," a young voice called out.

"C'mon J, just take it from me. It's not that hard," another voice playfully taunted.

I could hear jumping and grunting and soon the boys made their way out of the hallway. All three boys were blonde, set five years apart like the stages of manhood. The youngest brother, Justin, who also went by "J," was jumping for a basketball that his older brother was holding over his head. Jon, the middle child, seemed to tower over Justin as his lengthy arm almost touched the ceiling while he held the ball. Justin's blonde hair bounced as he tried to grab for it.

"Jonathan, will you stop teasing your brother and pick up your things? We have company for dinner," Mary said, shaking her head.

Jon dropped it and the orange ball bounced on the brown carpet a few times before Justin finally snatched it. Jon smiled and shook my hand as Mary introduced us. He went over and picked up his things from underneath the countertop. My mouth almost dropped open as I saw the size of his shoes, easily doubling the size of my own. Justin held the basketball tightly to his chest as Jon passed by. J gave me a quick, shy smile before walking to the counter. As he stood up on his tip toes, he rested himself on the ball, leaning over the counter toward Nate.

"Is dinner almost ready?" Justin asked as he rolled back and forth on the ball.

"What's it matter to you, you hardly eat anyway?" Nate teased.

"I do too!" Justin rebutted as the ball slipped out from under him, rolling off the counter and bouncing on the ground toward Nate.

Without taking his attention off the stove, Nate picked up the basketball and tossed it back to his brother. "It's never going to be done if you keep bugging me," he said.

"Maybe that's a good thing," Justin giggled.

"Shut your pie-hole and sit down!" Nate smirked, as he poured the sauce over the pasta.

I sat back and laughed, humored by all of their teasing and how it seemed to be very loving—in a brotherly sort of way. Mary got up from the table and began carefully placing each piece of garlic bread into a basket while Nate carried the bowl of spaghetti to the table. Justin poured everyone a large glass of milk, tossing another empty carton into the trash can. Everyone gathered around the table and Nate sat down in the high-backed chair next to mine.

Mary smiled, "Looks delicious, Honey. Thank you."

Nate waved off her praise as he took my plate to serve me first, and then scooped himself a hefty pile of noodles.

Unlike her boys, Mary took slow, thoughtful bites. She seemed to savor each mouthful as much as the memories she was making, chewing at a slow pace to prolong these moments just a little while longer.

"So tell me about yourself," Mary asked. Her interest in me was genuine and heartwarming.

Between bites, I told her about how my family had moved here from Santa Maria because of my dad's new job. "He's a principal at an elementary school nearby," I said. "Lincoln Elementary," I added.

Mary sat with a stunned look on her face. "I can't believe it! That's where my brothers and sister went to school. And that's where one of my best friends, Jean Steinbruner, teaches. You know what, that's where I'm going to be doing my student teaching in a few weeks! So, I'll get to meet your dad soon."

"Chris's mom is one of your best friends? He's how Nate and I met," I continued. "Oh my gosh, wait till I tell my dad that you're going to be one of his teachers!"

"So, where did you and Nate meet?" Mary asked. "The boys didn't go to the same school." She sat there trying to figure it all out.

"We met at a party," I answered. "Chris and I went to Salinas High together. And now Nate and I go to Hartnell together," I smiled over at Nate. "We even have some classes together." I held out my hand to show Mary the bracelet that Nate had given me.

Whenever I talked about my relationship with Nate, Mary would lean in, excited for the new information. Nate's nose would scrunch if it got too mushy. We shared stories and laughed as we ate dinner together. Jon reached over for a second helping of spaghetti and a couple more pieces of bread as I told them about *Eddie and the Tide*.

Nate seemed to purposely interrupt as I was telling them about the concert, "Oh yeah, Mom, can I have my *Van Halen* tape back? Shelley and I are going to see them next month."

"Oh sure, I'll get it out of my car after dinner," she answered.

"I can't believe you listen to *Van Halen*, that's so cool! I didn't even know parents knew who *Van Halen* was!" I chimed in.

Mary chortled.

I looked over at Justin's plate, still full of spaghetti as he twirled the noodles with his fork.

"If Nate had made quesadillas for dinner, I know your plate would be empty by now," Mary commented.

"I'm full, really," Justin replied.

Mary looked at me. "The boys take turns cooking when I have class or when I work Bingo at night, and Justin always makes quesadillas."

"You work Bingo too? I asked.

"Yeah, I've been working there once a week for the past few years. The principal at Palma is letting me work off some of the boys' tuition."

"Wow, you do a lot. Taking classes…working Bingo…three boys…" I exclaimed.

"Oh, thank you," she blushed. "After the divorce, I wanted to fulfill my dream of becoming a teacher. Oh! That reminds me, Jerry is coming next week to watch Jonathan's next basketball game. Why don't you go with the boys? It'll give you a chance to meet their dad."

"He's coming down from Seattle? Yeah sure, I would love to meet him," I responded.

I helped as the boys cleared the table, even though Mary told me not to. She made me feel like their special guest. With no leftovers to put in the fridge, clean up was simply bringing all of the emptied dishes to the sink.

"I really like your family," I said, handing Nate another bowl.

Nate smiled and winked, "Yeah, they're alright."

Mary came in from the garage and handed me *Van Halen's 5150* tape. "Here you go." She smiled at me with a look of sincerity. "I'm so glad you could join us for dinner. You can come over any time. It's nice to have another girl around here."

I smiled and gave her a hug, "Thanks, I'm sure I'll be seeing you again real soon."

The Baker house soon became my second home. It was interesting being around brothers; I only had one sibling—a younger sister. Brothers thought differently, and would do things like climb up on the roof of the house to scare people as they came up to the front door. When it was me, I'd be startled, and they would laugh. Brothers liked to make up games like *Hallway Football*, which explained the scuffs and fraying on the hallway wallpaper. As Nate's and my relationship continued, it was like I had an up close and personal place in their boy world.

Although Mary was home as much as possible for the boys, on occasion, there were still those times when she needed to be gone. Her busy schedule of commuting to San Jose State for her teaching credential, working Bingo, and volunteering at church would lead to the boys being creative in the kitchen. When preparing a meal, they began foraging through the cupboards. Jon's favorite quick meal was a plate full of Vienna sausages and dill pickles, while Justin, a simple eater, stuck to cheese quesadillas. If ingredients ran low from ravenous male hunger, there was always cereal, poured to the brim of a mixing bowl.

One night, Nate showed me his favorite concoction, something he called *Macaroni Surprise*. I boosted myself up on the kitchen counter and watched as Nate grabbed a few handfuls of uncooked macaroni from the bag. He then dropped the raw noodles onto an empty plate.

"Want me to get a pot?" I offered.

"No, no. Watch this," he said, opening a can of olives. After draining the juice into the sink, he poured nearly the entire can into his bare hand. The ones that dropped onto the counter, he popped in his mouth. He then squished the black mass of olives into pieces with his fist, olive juice running down his fingers onto the noodles. On top of the uncooked macaroni and olives, Nate added mounds of shredded cheddar cheese until his meal was a mass of orange. It was like the Frankenstein version of macaroni and cheese. I watched in confusion as he put the plate straight into the microwave.

"It's burning, Babe," I informed him, peeking through the microwave door as the plate rotated.

He smiled at my bewildered concern. "It's supposed to do that," he replied. By the time the microwave beeped, the air smelled burnt. I watched in disbelief as Nate contentedly ate his meal with the olive can lid as his spoon. "Wanna try it?" he asked between mouthfuls.

Cautiously, I took a bite. It was like crunching down on hard, sharp noodle flavored shards of glass. The soft cheese and olives saved my teeth from needing dental work. "Umm, I think I'll stick to your spaghetti...where the pasta is cooked in water, like how normal people eat!" I laughed. I kept crunching the hard noodles until they were soft enough to swallow. "Do you know how bad this is for your teeth?! You're lucky I work in a dental office!"

"This?" *CRUNCH. CRUNCH. CRUNCH.* "How could this possibly be bad for your teeth?" he smirked facetiously.

I pushed him and laughed, "I'll just eat dumb when I get home."

It was true. Macaroni Surprise really was bad for Nate's teeth, but how could I resist his natural charm that had me smitten.

A couple of hours later, Mary came in the front door holding paper bags from Star Market filled with groceries. The boys grabbed the bags to both help their mom and to see what treasures were inside. Mary always let the boys request one treat each for her weekly shopping trip. Nate's pick was *Captain Crunch*, Jon asked for Shoe String Potatoes, and Justin liked beef jerky. All these were as good as gold in the Baker house.

Nate and I were watching a show on TV when I heard a sizzling sound coming from the kitchen.

I tugged Nate's shirt. "What's your mom doing?" I asked.

"Making dinner. I think fajitas," he answered, his gaze returning to the screen.

"But it's 9:00."

Nate shrugged. At my house, a late dinner was served at 7:00, but the Bakers were night owls. Making fajitas at nine for dinner was normal, and midnight snacks were practically a regular meal of the day. I set my head back on Nate's shoulder and smiled, thinking of my own parents who, by now, were flicking the lights off for bedtime.

Nate was standing at his usual spot on campus waiting for me to arrive. I wasn't early, but I wasn't late either—somehow I always seemed to arrive without a minute to spare. I smiled at him as I crossed the street and walked right into his good morning hug. My favorite part of school was spending time with Nate.

He took the backpack from my shoulder and carried it for me as we walked hand in hand past the oak trees, gardens, and brick buildings of Hartnell's campus. We talked about the *Genesis* concert coming up in Oakland, and how we would make a stop in Santa Clara to see Chris on our way. We arrived at the lower level of the science building, and Nate walked with me right to the door of my Chemistry Lab. Before leaving for his own class across the campus, he handed me a folded note.

Beakers and test tubes were set up at each sink for today's lab experiment. I grabbed a stool and unfolded the paper. For the classes that we didn't have together, we passed the time by writing notes and poetry to each other. Writing poems was our way of being together when we were separated. As always, his poem was dated at the top, signed on the bottom, and written in blue, orderly, capitalized letters. The fact that he shared his deepest thoughts and feelings on paper was a complete anomaly. I had come to the realization that I was the exception to Nate's rogue tendencies.

Nate wrote many things in his notes to me—sometimes a poem, sometimes a love letter, and other times song lyrics. In this poem, he was contemplating doorways and spiders and power. He symbolically compared his hand to that of God's when he saw a spider in the doorway of his bedroom. Nate understood that he had the power to smash the spider or to let it live. He thought about the power that God has when we show up at His doorway—the power of life in His hands.

"Hi, Shelley!" My reading was interrupted by my lab partner, Carrie, as she scooted her stool up to the table across from me. She placed her backpack on the floor.

I could always recognize Carrie just by her voice. Her soft spoken tone made each word linger ever so slightly. Just the sound of her voice made you feel comfortable, like you could tell her anything and she'd listen and care.

I looked at her and smiled.

"Oooh, is that from Nate?" Carrie asked, as she gave a nod to the note in my hands.

"Yeah, how'd you know?" I asked, tucking the paper into my jeans pocket.

"You look *way* too happy to be in Organic Chemistry," she answered. She was right. I wanted to read every word of Nate's note, and had forgotten that class was about to start.

"I want you to meet him before he goes on his trip to Seattle."

"Yeah, after everything I've heard about him, I'd love to!"

"Okay, great! You can meet him after class."

The dark-haired instructor walked into the room to get class started with the day's lab experiment. Carrie pulled her blonde hair back into a ponytail and put on her safety glasses.

"What in the world is this?" she laughed, holding up a bag of purple powder that was sitting on our table, her white teeth standing out against the deep purple.

Carrie had great teeth. Of course she had great teeth; she was a dental assistant just like me. The cross that hung from her neck reminded me that it wasn't coincidence that had brought us together. Out of all the places in the entire classroom to sit, we ended up sitting right across from each other. This led to us becoming lab partners. Turns out, we had a lot in common, including sharing the same goals of getting accepted into dental hygiene school. She had become an instant friend through our lab experiments together—like today's assignment of observing the reaction of iodine and zinc causing purple smoke to puff from our table.

"Hey, would you be interested in working in my dental office? The doctors are really cool and they're looking for another dental assistant. Then we can work together!" Carrie asked, enthusiastically.

"Really? That would be great! I'll need a general office," I replied. My RDA exam is coming soon. I'll miss where I am now, but once I pass the exam, I'm gonna need to move on from root canals."

She laughed, "Okay, I'll talk with them when I get to work this afternoon."

Once class ended, we headed out to the parking lot, walking between the cars, with the sun beaming off the glass and metal. I spotted my red Renault Fuego parked next to the fence. Nate wasn't at my car yet—his 6' 2" height and blonde hair usually gave him away. I slung my backpack around, searching for my keys in the midst of pens and lecture notes. Keys finally in hand, we were nearing my car chatting about Carrie's boyfriend and how he was going to bring her Taco Bell for lunch when suddenly Nate popped out from behind a Buick.

We screamed.

"Nate!" I yelled, "That's not funny!" I ran after him, playfully chasing him through the parked cars and slapping his arm.

Nate laughed, mocking our girly screams. We circled a car and returned to Carrie. She stood there, completely amused by Nate's first impression.

"Carrie," I said, exhaling with a laugh, "this is Nate. And Babe, this is Carrie."

"Nice to meet you," Carrie said, still laughing. She finally had a face to my amazing boyfriend whose old-fashioned charm matched his very humorous idiosyncrasies.

My family lived in John Steinbeck country on the outskirts of town right off the hills, roads, and lettuce fields written about in his books. Somewhere behind the trees and mounds of grass, the Salinas River flowed. The rolling hills rose in their mighty green splendor as Nate and I drove into town for pizza.

We were heading down River Road to catch Highway 68 when Nate drove right past the onramp. I turned my head in confusion, wondering if maybe he hadn't seen it. But how could he not? It's the only highway that leads straight into town.

Just beyond our missed turn, the car slowed. We transitioned from asphalt onto dirt that surrounded a small country home. Loose gravel crackled underneath the tires as we pulled up to a large yard surrounded by a wire fence.

"Aw yeah, new kids!" Nate snickered, as he put the car in neutral and pulled up the brake. With an excited smile, he leaned over me and rolled down the window.

Captivated by the sweet baby goats playing and grazing in the grass, I was all smiles and understood that this was just another one of Nate's spontaneous detours. One baby goat nuzzled against his mother. Another bounced along the wire fence, his legs springing out from underneath him. Goats of many sizes and colors were scattered all around the front yard, but it was the babies that had our attention.

"Look at their little bitty horns!" I said, leaning into the door. My hunger for pizza subsided momentarily as I gushed over a tan and white baby with floppy ears standing closest to the fence. His little gray nubs had yet to grow into powerful curled horns. Other goats, with mature long white beards, lazily chewed at the ground or snoozed in the shade of the porch.

"Watch this," Nate said with a playful grin. He took in a deep breath, and let out an all-convincing *"BAHAHAHA!"*

In a chain reaction, the baby goats whipped their heads toward us. Their alert ears were perked up, shifting from side to side, as they watched Nate call out from inside of our idling car. Even the mother lifted her gaze, curious about this man who spoke their language. One of the kids marched bravely to the fence, his little pink tongue quivered along with his spirited reply. It wasn't long before other goats had joined in to create a bleating chorus that echoed throughout the yard. Nate held his stomach as he laughed, getting exactly the reaction he had planned.

"Bahaha!" Nate continued, his deep breaths compromised by laughter. Nate nodded and snickered as if each head-whip scored a point in this game of his. Nate's laughter was contagious, and the innocent reactions from the baby goats only made the situation more comical.

Who does this? Who even thinks to do this!? I shook my head in both amusement and admiration as they bleated back and forth.

The goat's mother stood attentive, as if eavesdropping on their exchange. I wondered if all the commotion would catch the attention of the homeowners, and hoped that if they were inside, they were as amused as I was.

Satisfied, Nate delivered his final *"bah,"* and rolled my window back up. Putting the car into first gear, we made our way back to the highway to pick up our pizza. I sat back and looked at Nate, as our laughter calmed into big smiles. Everything I was thinking seemed to reflect in his eyes.

We watched as the busy employees rushed to and from ovens with floured dough or freshly baked pizzas. With pepper spicing the air, I could almost taste the half pepperoni and half Hawaiian pizza baking just for us as we sat on the bench waiting for our take-out order. In the corner, a juke box shuffled through hit songs and "Endless Love" began to play. I began humming along to the tune as we waited for our pizza to show up in the take-out window. Nate reached over and took my hand, lifting me up off the bench.

"What are we doing?" I asked, as he began to lead me toward the juke box.

"Dancing," he answered matter-of-factly.

"Here!?" my voice cracked, as Nate led me to the dance floor. The only thing was...there was no dance floor, just a bit of space between the tables in the middle of the restaurant. Nate pulled me in close with a smile as he clasped his fingers between mine, his other hand wrapped around my waist. I held onto Nate as we began to sway gently back and forth.

We were surrounded by people eating their dinners and drinking from clear plastic cups, eyes obviously staring. I could feel their attention on us. I didn't look at anyone. I just kept my focus on Nate, lost in the moment.

"Look at them dancing," I could hear amongst the chatter buzzing around the restaurant.

I followed Nate's lead as we glided on top of breadcrumbs and straw wrappers scattered on the orange tiled floor. Blushed from adrenaline as we danced in circles, I glanced up at my boyfriend, who was seemingly unbothered by all the attention we were drawing. How was he so calm? Nate usually avoided being the center of attention, but here he was, ignoring the curious glances of the crowd—not even paying attention at all to our order number being called from the counter.

I let his confident swaying sweep away my shyness as people watched. With my fingers intertwined with Nate's and my other arm wrapped around his shoulder, I soaked it all in. I knew that we were creating a profound memory at this very moment.

A couple of weeks later, Nate and I were in the parking lot behind the campus. Thanksgiving break had arrived. Nate was ready to brave his solo road trip to the Pacific Northwest. His car was packed with a large duffle bag of clothes, hair band cassettes in the glovebox, and a full tank of gas. I didn't want to say goodbye, but I was happy for Nate to be able to spend some time with his dad.

"I'm going to miss you," I sighed, as we got to my car. I leaned against the door, delaying our kiss goodbye.

"Before I leave, there's something I want to tell you," Nate said, stepping forward to take my hands. His hands were warm, always warm, even in the autumn cold. He paused, looking down for a moment, clearly deep in thought. More leaves scattered across the parking lot. He tightened his grip and looked directly at me. "I love you, Princess. I didn't want to leave without telling you that."

I could feel his love for me as we stood there holding hands. The intimacy of this moment reached the deepest parts of my heart, making me feel as if I were glowing. I felt blanketed in Nate's love, and with his words, I knew I would never be the same. I softly responded, "I love you, too," releasing the words that I had been feeling, but hadn't said out loud yet.

"I've never told anyone that before," he confessed.

"Me either," I responded, leaning into his brown leather jacket. We held each other, squeezing out the goodbyes. I got in my car and wished him a safe trip. He stood in the parking lot watching me until I drove onto the main road. I missed him already.

As the days went by, I kept myself busy. At work, I daydreamed about Nate while assisting the doctor, and cleaning cement off the endless endodontic hand files back in the sterilization room. I had met the doctors at Carrie's office, accepted the job, and gave my two weeks' notice to Dr. Cohen. When I wasn't at work, I celebrated Thanksgiving with my family, hung out with friends, and played some tennis with my dad. At night, I wrote more poetry. I felt closer to Nate, somehow, as if the pen on the page allowed my love to bridge the gap between Salinas and Seattle.

I was assisting the doctor with a root canal, making the best of my last two weeks, when the receptionist stuck her head through the doorway. "Shelley, you have a visitor," she said.

I passed the doctor another endo file. He nodded at me, giving his okay to leave. I slipped off my gloves and walked into the lobby where I was greeted by a handsome man in a sombrero. Nate was back and was making me laugh already.

"Did you go to Mexico, too?!" I asked, giving him a big hug in front of our three o'clock patient with an abscess.

He smiled. "Yeah. While I was checking out San Diego State, I decided to check out Mexico, too. He shrugged his shoulders like it was no big deal. "I just wanted to let you know I'm back." His eyes danced under the orange brim of the sombrero. "How about I pick you up after work?"

"I can't wait! I missed you and want to hear all about your trip."

"Same here, Princess," he said, sneaking a kiss on my cheek. The secretary pretended to be filing papers at her desk.

"I'll see you after work." I watched Nate, still wearing his sombrero, walk out the glass door and out to the parking lot.

"Hey, Mr. Nate," my dad said with a welcoming smile as he opened the front door. The cold winter air disturbed the warmth coming from the fireplace. Multicolored outdoor Christmas lights illuminated Nate as he walked into the house. "You see this?" my dad gestured to the life-sized Santa taped to the inside of the front door as he shut it behind him.

Nate nodded, his nose scrunching slightly at the sight of Santa's rosy red cheeks and jolly smile.

Dad continued, "It used to be a tradition for the girls to kiss Santa every Christmas. They were so young, I would have to lift them up for them to give him a kiss so their mom could take a picture."

I rushed up the steps from the living room into the entry-way and greeted Nate with a hug.

"If you can lift me, I'll give him a kiss, too," Nate teased.

My dad laughed as he looked at my boyfriend's size. Nate hung his brown leather jacket on the hall tree and waved to my mom who was in the kitchen busily preparing our favorite once-a-year Christmas Eve snacks. I took Nate's hand and we walked down into the living room, joining my sister on the couch.

"The Iowa box arrived yesterday!" I said, happy to share our family traditions with Nate. Spread out on the table were plates filled with homemade cookies and Grandma's chocolate fudge. The centerpiece was a large, two-piece white Tupperware decoration that had been a part of Christmas for as far back as I could remember. The bottom had circular divots that were filled with alternating apples and oranges surrounded by a variety of unshelled nuts. In the middle was a vase for plastic poinsettias.

"Ooohhh," Nate's eyes widened as he grabbed a couple of peanut butter cookies.

As he happily chewed, his eyes began to narrow, taking in all the cute decorations that surrounded him. Nate looked over at the ceramic hand-painted Santa that was sitting on the table holding a yellow sack filled with candy canes. Nate grunted. He then noticed our beautiful artificial Christmas tree, festooned in all of its tinsel and twinkling glory. A smiling wooden reindeer stood on each side. With Christmas music filling the air, his attention was now on the hand-painted words on the window wishing anyone who passed by a Merry Christmas.

By the time Mom had finished slicing the salami, all the Christmas decorations were rearranged—small elves that were once scattered around the house were now half buried upside down in a bowl of Christmas colored M & M's; the snowman was missing his carrot nose; and several reindeer were turned backwards with their rear ends welcoming everyone to the living room. Although I knew Nate liked Christmas, he didn't like *cute*, and deemed all holiday decor useless.

"Lame, lame, lame," he chanted, as he rearranged each decoration in the room. He even hung my red and white homemade stocking by its toes! My sister and I giggled, knowing that our Mom was in for a big surprise.

"Nate, what are you doing?!" my mom gasped as she entered the room with a tray of crackers, sliced salami, and cheese.

"Whaaat? I was just *fixing* it," he laughed, looking pleased with himself for causing trouble.

The Christmas decorations became almost a game for Nate and my mom. As presents were being unwrapped, my mom would undo some of Nate's destruction. One by one, she rescued her Christmas decorations and returned them to their original positions. Satisfied, she would then go back to her chair near the fire. Nate *corrected* her mistakes the next time it was her turn to open a gift. My family seemed to be amused at their game.

With the floor now covered with wrapping paper and bows, Nate stood up. "I have one for Shelley now. It's in my car, I'll be right back." As he made his way to the front door, he looked back to make sure my parents weren't watching, and then flicked his fingers from under his chin at Santa Claus as he let himself out. I covered my mouth laughing, glad that my parents didn't catch that one.

Nate had his arms stretched out in front of him as he carried in a large rectangular object that seemed to be a bird cage under a blanket. He brought it down carefully into the sunken living room and slowly sat it down next to the tree. I went over to the covered present and sat down on the floor next to it.

"Did you get me a bird?" I asked, looking at the large gift in front of me. I never quite knew what to expect from Nate.

Careful not to disturb whatever was inside, I cautiously removed the blanket. His gift was indeed a birdcage, but there was no bird behind its metal bars. Sitting on the bottom of the cage was a nicely wrapped Christmas present. The room was quiet, I could feel my family trying to figure out Nate's unique style of present giving. I gently took the present out from the cage and began unwrapping it.

My eyes widened as I looked down at a beautiful porcelain music box. I had never seen one like it. It had a round base, and on top was a carefully molded scene with two blue jays looking at each other from a curved tree branch. Below the base was a flat knob that you could twist. This would cause the scene to rotate along to the theme song of Doctor Zhivago. On the side was a golden plate with an inscription that read: *Shelley, All my love-Nate*.

Carefully, I traced my fingertips over all of the delicate details. Each green leaf and pink flower was individually crafted. Every aspect of this music box was finely detailed. I had never been given anything so beautiful.

"I love it," I said, almost in a whisper.

Nate shrugged it off as if his present was no more special than anything else I had received. He grabbed for another cookie.

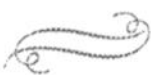

I gazed at the clock on the microwave and smiled as I saw how late it was getting. While my family went to the early church service *before* opening presents on Christmas Eve, Nate's family would go to Midnight Mass *after* they opened presents. Long after my family had gone to bed for the night, Nate's family festivities were just beginning.

I sipped on a mug of hot chocolate as I looked around the Baker house. Most of the house looked the same as it did any other time of year. Unlike my family's excessive Christmas decorating, Mary wasn't one for decorations. The only evidence of Christmas was in the living room. As I rounded the corner, my eyes widened at the size of the tree. It was tall, and no doubt brought in the house with the help of the boys. A few bent branches told the story of its journey from the tree farm to inside the Baker house. The tree was a deep green and made the whole house smell like pine. Dried pine needles sprinkled the carpet around the presents underneath the tree.

I walked over to the tree admiring the many homemade ornaments that hung from every branch—they all seemed to tell a story. I smiled, noticing Nate's small handprint in paint on a felt ornament from kindergarten. The ornaments showed their age. I noticed some had missing parts and colors were fading.

"That's my favorite part of Christmas, putting up the kids' ornaments," Mary smiled as she knelt down to pour water into the steel Christmas tree stand. "Look at this one," she said as she stood back up. "Justin made this one in class."

"Can we start now?" Justin begged, as he sat on the floor, his legs drumming the carpet. He knew right where his presents were located under the tree.

It was new and exciting for me to be celebrating Christmas with Nate this way. Sharing in each other's Christmas Eve traditions was special. Mary ushered me to the couch where a few presents were waiting for me. The tags all read "From: Santa" in Mary's neat handwriting.

“Aww, Mary, you didn’t have to get me anything,” I told her.

“I don’t know what you are talking about,” she said, shrugging her shoulders, “They’re from Santa. He knew you were coming over.”

Justin went over to the tree and knelt on the ground to get close to the many presents to be opened. This year he would be the one to hand out the gifts. As the presents were being exchanged and opened one by one, Mary snapped some photos of the boys holding up their gifts from Santa, Rudolph, or Mrs. Claus—which always meant it was from Mary. Although the boys could rip off Christmas paper in a matter of seconds, Mary did things slowly and deliberately, reading each tag and carefully pulling the scotch tape off the decorative bows.

“Come on, Mom,” Nate teased. “We ain’t got time for that!”

Nate was happily piecing together the telescope I had just given him. Jon was reading the manual, intrigued by the planets and stars.

“There’s one more present under the tree for you, Nate,” Mary smiled.

He eyed his gift from “Santa,” and pulled the long rectangular box out from behind the tree. He eagerly tore off the paper.

“Yeah!” Nate said, as he pulled a red electric guitar out of the box. He immediately put the strap over his shoulder and tested out the strings.

“After watching you play air guitar for years, I guess Santa thought you needed a real one,” Mary joked.

Nate got up and gave his mom a big hug, lifting her feet slightly off the carpet.

Although Nate and I had only been dating for six months, I felt comfortable and happy as I shared Christmas Eve with the Baker family. I smiled as I watched Nate strum his new guitar.

Classes were finished for the day. Well, they were finished for *me* anyway. Nate still had a class he called *Talks for Jocks* to attend, but he decided to skip it today so we could leave and have a little time together before work. After a late lunch in town, Nate drove us over to his house to hang out for a while.

We walked through the front door and set our things down on the dining room table. As I took off my jacket, I noticed how quiet it was in the house.

"Where's your family?" I asked, as Nate walked into the kitchen. He didn't answer. I looked over at him to see if he heard me, and watched as he reached for a couple of glasses in the cupboard and filled them with water.

He handed me a glass of water and then leaned into the counter facing me as he took a drink. I smiled at him, "Thank you," I said. I took a few sips and asked again where everyone was.

"They're still at school," Nate answered. In the stillness of the house, our eyes met. We stood there with only the counter between us. There was a lot in Nate's eyes as I looked at him—his usual charm and vitality, but still, there was something else. Nate's lips, wet from his drink, caught my eye. My gaze lingered ever so slightly before I slowly looked away. I took in a deep breath. He set his glass down on the counter and walked over to me.

Nate reached for my hands and pulled me in close right there in the dining room.

Saying nothing at all, we began to sway back and forth. As we held each other, Nate leaned his head down close to my ear. "I wrote a song for you," he said softly.

His whispered words made me tingle with goosebumps. I stopped moving. "You wrote a song for me?" I asked, stepping back just enough to see his face fully. I could tell by his expression and the vibe between us that he meant what he said. “What, really Babe? You wrote a song for me?”

Nate responded by taking my hand and leading me down the hallway. I followed him to his bedroom where he ushered me to his bed for a front row seat. Captivated, I sat there watching him as he adjusted the guitar strap around his neck. Like a rock star about to take the stage, he began plucking each chord and tuning the six strings to find just the right pitch. Nate pulled out a piece of paper from his nightstand and set it on his bed. He paused for a moment, giving me a tender smile before the first strum of his guitar.

I reveled in the melody of Nate’s song as I sat on his bed. He continued to strum as he looked over at the paper on his bed and began singing. I sat there mesmerized by his voice as he sang to me. Nate had taken his poetry and upped it to a musical ballad.

With a rhythmic easy tempo, he sang about our love. The lyrics journeyed through our six months of dating. I smiled at all the fun and unforgettable times we had shared. The song then evolved into our future. I watched him, fully immersed in the words and harmony of his song. As he continued, he began to sing about our future children. Oh my gosh! I knew that Nate loved me, but this song was the first time kids had come up. Nate saw me as the future mother of his children—someone to share his whole life with. With each word that he sang about our life, it was as if he had taken every dream I had ever had about our relationship and put it into a song. My throat tightened with emotion. His sincerity was tender-hearted and real, because I knew that Nate was *not* big on sharing his feelings. No one else knew Nate this way, which made me love him even more.

His voice lulled into a hum until his fingers plucked the last note. My enthusiasm could barely be contained as I stood up and wrapped my arms around Nate really tight.

With the guitar pressed between us as we embraced, I told him how much I loved his song and how much I loved him. Anything Nate did, he did exceptionally well, and his song was just that. I tenderly kissed Nate, and then released my arms from around him.

As he returned his guitar to the wall, I glanced down at the fringed piece of paper torn from a spiraled notebook. A drawing next to the handwritten lyrics caught my attention. Sketched in blue ink was a small child standing next to a car in a driveway. I stood there, awestruck. The drawing was our child—our future sketched on a piece of paper. As my fingers traced the drawing, Nate set his hand gently on top of mine. With my heart thumping, I continued to stare at our child. I knew that Nate's touching song, inspired by true love, would be a melody that would never fade—a musical ballad set on repeat in my heart for the rest of my life.

Chapter 3

"Endless Love" by Diana Ross & Lionel Richie

MY BODY GENTLY SWAYED back and forth as the words of the hymn spoke to me. Music, in general, usually did. Every word passionately sung by the choir on the stage before us seemed to grab hold of my heart and fill me with even more happiness and excitement than I was already feeling. I looked down at my engagement ring and then at Nate standing next to me. He was all dressed up for Sunday morning church service. It meant so much to me that Nate would join my family and me at our small church on the hill. Having him beside me in church made everything feel right.

The organ stopped playing and the pastor, dressed in his usual black robe, walked up to the pulpit facing his congregation. We all took a seat on the pews with the hymnal books still in our hands. As he began his sermon, my mind wandered. I imagined Nate and me, just months down the road, standing in front of Pastor Jim as he married us right here on this very stage.

Nate's warmth and love radiated from his hand into mine as the pastor spoke God's Word to his congregation. The cross standing tall behind him grabbed my attention and became my focus. Its rugged wooden surface stirred something deep within my heart. I began thinking about God and how much I loved Him. My personal relationship with Jesus had been strong for as long as I could remember. I could feel His presence with me wherever I was. I then thought about how much I loved Nate. The feelings we shared for each other were more intense and more powerful than I ever knew existed. My mind drifted off on thoughts of how much time Nate and I were spending together. As I sat there in the pew, I told Jesus how He would always remain number one in my life. I knew that Nate felt the same way because we talked about God a lot.

Nate was a Christian as well, and I loved how much he knew about the Bible. I would ask him questions about God all the time, and he usually knew the answer. Neither one of us had our own Bibles, but we could always find the answers to our questions about God. I was raised in a Christian family that always loved God, but didn't always go to church on Sundays. Nate, on the other hand, attended church with his mom and brothers every week. He also attended a private Catholic school where Theology was a daily class.

With Nate's and my love growing each day, I decided to step up my walk with The Lord even more. The pastor's gentle voice became bold, and snapped my focus back as he began reading Isaiah 14:24. *"The Lord of hosts has sworn saying, 'Surely, just as I have intended so it has happened, and just as I have planned so it will stand.' "* My Amen echoed with the congregation. Nate squeezed my hand and I smiled at him. The experience of being in church together, and sharing our love for God, brought our relationship to an even higher level.

We bowed our heads in closing prayer, and I silently thanked God for His guidance in my life. Even when I had begged Him to let me go back to Santa Maria after we had moved, His unanswered prayer guided me to exactly where He wanted me to be. He led me to Nate, and my life was now better than I could ever have imagined. I asked God to keep leading me, and promised Him that I would continue to love Him more than *anything* in life—including Nate.

After the service, Nate and I followed my family back to the house for some lunch. As Nate drove, I started thinking about the long list of things we needed to do before the wedding. "We need to pick out a picture to use for our engagement announcement. Chris's dad is gonna put it in the newspaper while he's at work. Hey, what about that picture we took a few months ago? You know, the one we took out on the deck?" I asked.

"Yeah, that'll work," Nate replied.

"Great! That corsage you got me was so beautiful."

"Eeeehhhh..." he grumbled, as if my compliment caused him pain.

I shoved him playfully and laughed. "I love the wedding date we picked out," I said, as I leaned over to grab the wedding *To Do List* out of my purse. February 13th. It was perfect—different and a little quirky with it being the day before Valentine's Day.

Enthusiastically, I checked *engagement picture* off of the list and noticed all of the empty boxes of things yet to do. I wasn't a picky bride who planned every detail. My only *must have* was Nate, and we were more than ready to say, "I do."

"Oooh, look Honey, this will be perfect for our wedding picture!" I said, holding up a beautiful frame.

Nate gave a grin and took another bite of cake. I knew his smile was coming from the buttercream frosting and not the frame I was holding up. I set the frame down next to the pile of colorful paper and bows and the gifts we had already unwrapped. I sat on the family room couch next to Nate and admired all of the presents we were given. Mary was busily offering drinks to the guests at our Engagement Party, as my parents went around snapping pictures on their Kodak camera. Mary's house was filled with our family and close friends celebrating our upcoming wedding.

The parents of Chris, Paul, and Matt—another one of Nate's childhood friends—stood together as they handed Nate and me an envelope. "This one's from all of us parents." The four families were more like family than friends.

I excitedly opened the envelope as Nate watched me pull out a brochure and gift certificate from the card. Unsure of what we were just given, I read the papers trying to figure it out.

"It's an Engagement Encounter," Chris's mom said excitedly.

"Yeah, you guys are so young. We thought it would be a good experience to learn more about each other before getting married," Paul's mom added.

Mary brought her hand to her heart with a thoughtful sigh, "What a good idea!"

"Oh, thank you," I said, trying to understand more about this uncommon gift. "To question, examine, and deepen our relationship to one another..." I read out loud from the brochure. I looked over at Nate to see his nose scrunched as he focused on the logo of a computer drawn heart balanced on top of a cross.

I watched as Nate looked across the room at Chris who was shaking his head, almost like an apology. Paul smirked at the thought of Nate expressing his feelings to a bunch of strangers for an entire weekend.

"This is great," I told the thoughtful parents who were watching us with warm smiles. "We can't wait to go!"

Although I wasn't fond of the idea of sharing feelings with people I didn't know either, I was willing to give the Encounter a try. If nothing else, at least it was a ticket out of town for a weekend alone with Nate.

The weekend of our Engagement Encounter had arrived. Nate picked me up Friday afternoon, Van Halen belting from the cassette player. The short drive up Highway 101 was like a preview of our upcoming marital adventures—traveling free of curfews and parental agendas. This weekend, however, had a full itinerary of relationship exercises and guest speakers sharing experiences of marital issues packed into every hour.

Nate parked the car at the St. Francis Retreat Center in San Juan Bautista, its clay roof a deep red in the setting sun. *Intended for privacy and a distraction-free atmosphere* I read from the brochure as I got our gift certificate ready for check in. We spent a few minutes wandering around the grounds which had been built in a quiet, grassy field surrounded by trees. Scattered throughout the grounds were benches under live oaks positioned for couples to initiate deep, relationship-building conversations.

Nate and I walked into the lobby and were greeted by enthusiastic group leaders handing us *Hello, my name is* tags as we checked ourselves in. A peppy, blonde, middle-aged woman gave us a very fast and spirited run down of the welcoming ceremony that would be starting soon. I sighed as we were separated into the women's and men's wings to get settled before the night's events began.

With hallways structured similar to that of a hotel, everyone was assigned a roommate. Mine was especially chatty, already sharing her fiancé's flaws and their relationship goals for the weekend. I unpacked my bag, glad to have nothing to add to the conversation. I politely listened until the women's leader marched through the hall and directed our group to the main building where we would reunite with our mates.

I entered through the doors and noticed how many people there were in the room. Wow! I didn't realize Engagement Encounters were so popular. While most couples headed to the front for a good seat, I noticed Nate saving me a spot in the very back row. Relieved, I joined him as he greeted me with a, "Hey, Princess!" and a kiss to my forehead.

I looked around. We were the youngest couple by far. I leaned toward Nate and whispered, "So ... what do you think?"

His smile switched to a snarl as he began a low growl. I chuckled and shook my head—without words, Nate had just said it all. The men's leader began the welcoming ceremony by introducing the counselors, each one flicking a wave as their names were called. With each enthusiastic introduction, Nate would either growl or scrunch his face, which in turn caused me to go from chuckling, to laughing, and then straight into an uncontrollable giggle fit. With my eyes filling with laugh-induced tears, Nate seemed to feed off my reaction, and upped his humor even more.

A few of the couples began whispering, while some slightly turned their heads, disturbed by our commotion behind them. I squeezed Nate's hand, and held my stomach, as I concentrated on trying to get myself under control. I gave Nate *the look*. With a pleased look on his face, he settled down and waited for my laughter to run its course.

The leader explained that the weekend was dedicated to discussing God, love, money, sex, and the future. With no TVs, no radios, and no distractions, he assured us that this tranquil environment would encourage good communication that would strengthen our bond. I patted Nate's leg, hoping it would get better.

It didn't.

We were separated again. The ladies followed in a single-file line into a side room which I hesitantly followed. I sat on a couch and watched as the leader passed out our first worksheet. It had one writing exercise meant to dig deep into character. *Write about a selfless act of your fiancé.*

I sighed. The weekend felt long already. My roommate studied the paper seriously—her eyes flitting back and forth over the question. Others jotted down notes, full paragraphs, or looked out the window pondering their fiancé in silence. I had known Nate for well over a year now. How could I possibly choose one memory? I had so many, but I picked one and began to write.

We regrouped in the main room where each couple was instructed to sit and share their answers in private. Nate's face said it all—his green eyes bugged out in an *"are you serious?"* plea. I covered my mouth, but the giggles escaped through my fingers. We walked our disruptive selves outside where we climbed up a cement wall and sat with our feet dangling in the chilly night air.

"So what did you write about?" I asked, amused by how much Nate disliked these exercises.

"I didn't write anything. This is lame," he grumbled.

I laughed again, totally understanding his private heart. "You know, it was hard for me to decide. Our memories are countless!" I said, leaning into him. The sounds of nature surrounding us meshed harmoniously with Nate's growling. "But I wrote one. Do you want to hear it?"

"No-Kay," Nate answered—No-Kay was his word for combining humor and discomfort. He aggressively scratched his arm, as if he were allergic to this place.

I nudged him to stop as I began to read in a carefree and spirited voice. "I was in the hospital when my fiancé completed an entire art appreciation report for me..."

Nate drummed his leg, eyes on the trees.

"The doctor diagnosed me with 'burning the candle at both ends' induced mono." Full-time college, a packed work schedule, topped with homework, and late nights with Nate had taken its toll on my body. I didn't ask Nate for help—I couldn't—I was too sick. The doctor advised me to do nothing but sleep, so he kept me in the hospital for three days to make sure I did just that. Nate did everything I couldn't, including my Art Appreciation project, which accounted for a third of my semester grade. He wandered the city snapping photos of anything artsy Salinas could offer—murals, graffiti, and bronze statues."

Nate looked at the ground—or his shoes—anything other than the paper I was reading from. I continued reading.

"He had even cut the Quaker Oats man from an oatmeal box and taped it to one of the pages. Beneath the iconic blue coat was Nate's typed explanation of Puritan influences on modern art. He had met the project's deadline, and showed up at the hospital with a finished typed report and flowers."

When I finished reading, Nate replied, "Ahh, it was nothing," and dramatically started to scratch again.

The next morning, we were awakened at an early hour for our planned day of Engagement Encounter lectures and activities. We sat at a table eating our breakfast. Nate's eyebrows were expressionless as he filled his mug with coffee. We couldn't do this for two more days! Nate's skin would be scratched raw by Sunday night, and I didn't think I could handle one more story of my roommate's relationship drama. There was nothing in our relationship to fix, nothing to revisit, or nothing to rekindle. Our future was not completely figured out yet, but we knew what we wanted in life. And right now, all we wanted was to get married!

Nate looked up at me. Our eyes met, lingering there. People finished breakfast and started making their way to the first meeting of the day. As the group walked one way, Nate grabbed my hand and we fled in the opposite direction. The glint had returned to Nate's eyes as he said, "Grab your stuff and let's get out of here!"

We hurried down our separate hallways. My heart began racing as I kept an eye out for wandering counselors who would helpfully guide us to where we were supposed to be. I threw all of my things in the bag and jumped in the car—Van Halen picking up where they had left off. As we drove away, I watched the retreat center shrink in the side-view mirror. We didn't tell anyone—we hadn't told the counselors, our roommates, and our parents definitely weren't informed of our escape. We were young, on the run, and not expected home until Sunday!

Nate flung the encounter brochure to the back seat and let out an excited holler. I squealed with adrenaline, "I can't believe we're doing this!" I clapped my hand onto his as he shifted gears. "Where are we going to go?!" I asked, not caring where we went as long as we were together.

"Apartment?"

"Apartment!" I confirmed with a wide grin. I had a feeling he was going to say that.

We had just signed the papers earlier in the week for our very first apartment, which was waiting for us to move into as soon as we were married. Other than a hand-me-down table, it was all walls and newly cleaned carpet. Due to Nate getting promoted to the produce department at Star Market—which included benefits and a raise—and with me passing the Registered Dental Assistant exam in San Francisco, rent was manageable.

As we were nearing Highway 101, a Christmas tree sign caught my attention and I immediately asked if we could stop. This was a big deal. It would be our first tree in our first apartment. Even though decorating—*especially* holiday decorating—wasn't Nate's thing, he didn't put up much of a fuss as he strapped our chosen tree onto the roof of the car. We drove south — the trees outside our windows eventually changed to banks and department stores as we arrived back in Salinas.

Being back in our small town made us nervous about being spotted. Nate's IMKRAZE license plate would surely give us away if anyone we knew saw it. We cautiously stopped at Tico's Tacos to grab some take out, followed by a quick run into a nearby Chevron station for a few snacks.

We parked in front of our empty apartment. Nate unstrapped the tree from the top of his EXP, and displayed his strength by carrying our chosen tree over his shoulder and through the doorway. As Nate set the tree up in the living room, I began unpacking our array of chosen foods — tacos, chips and salsa, corn nuts, and candy. With our new apartment being just a block away from my dad's work, we couldn't take the risk of staying parked in the driveway. To be safe, we parked a couple of miles away from any parental suspicions and walked back to the apartment to eat lunch.

We took a picture in front of the tree with Le Mutt, my mom's favorite stuffed animal. Nate had taken him without asking — just to tease her. He sat on the dog, for the sake of the photo, Le Mutt's ivory colored head sticking out from under Nate's blue jeans. Nate had a love-hate relationship with Le Mutt, and it was my job to keep the dog from getting destuffed — any further — or completely destroyed. He got up from the poor pup and caught him by the felt collar.

"What are you doing?" I asked.

"Hanging him from the fan. He'll be our first decoration," Nate laughed.

"Uh, no," I said matter-of-factly.

"No?" Nate looked at me playfully. His eyebrows wrinkled forward in determination as he held Le Mutt inches from the unmoving fan blades.

"Maybe you should be nice to Le Mutt and return him to my mom in one piece," I suggested. It was hard for me to be serious—my mouth going awry from fighting off a smile.

Like a statue street performer, Nate remained frozen as if contemplating his next move. I crossed my arms in pretend stubbornness. Le Mutt dangled in Nate's grip, his body limp with the little stuffing he had left. Nate made his move. He let go of Le Mutt. His eyes were on me. Le Mutt's soft body landed on the carpet—safe. I, however, wasn't! Nate dropped to his hands and knees, growling like a predator about to chase down its prey. I backed up toward the kitchen, my mind mapping out an escape route.

He charged.

I ran.

Full speed into the kitchen, I used the table to barricade myself from Nate. He chased after me. I ran out the other side and down the hallway. I screamed dramatically as he gained more ground. In my spirited attempt to escape capture, Nate took a brief pause in his pursuit due to laughing at the ridiculousness of it all. Just like a boy pulling a girl's hair in secret admiration, this was Nate's way of pulling my hair. Although I knew it was all in fun, it still made my heart race as Nate came at me on all fours!

Nate tackled me in the empty room that would soon become our bedroom, his hands searching for my tickle spots. Once his lips met mine, the growls and tickling subsided between kisses.

Side-by-side, we laid on our bedroom floor listening to Bon Jovi's *Slippery When Wet* from a portable cassette player as we stared at the popcorn ceiling with our backs against the carpet. In less than twenty-four hours, we would be expected home—refreshed from a weekend of nature and soulful journaling. I wanted to hold onto our freedom—not wanting this to end—but I knew in a couple of months, this would be our home and we would have many more moments like this.

We were at our apartment washing borrowed dishes from Chris's parents. We didn't live there yet, but our apartment had become a place to hang out in the meantime. It had been a fun night of hosting our first dinner party for a few friends. The kitchen still had the lingering smell of Chris's Chicken Cordon Bleu. His cooking had impressed everyone—I didn't know he could cook like that! Until last night, I had never even tasted Chicken Cordon Bleu. Even its name made me feel all grown up. A dinner party, a sophisticated meal, and an apartment that I could call my own made me realize that I was becoming more of an adult with each passing day.

"There's something I want to get for you so bad I'd sell my car for it," Nate said, as he handed me a pan to dry.

"I'm very attached to your car, I responded jokingly. And where would Spike hang if you sold it?"

"Good point," he played along. But I could tell that whatever Nate was thinking about was still on his mind.

A few weeks later, we stopped by the apartment to feed Bruno. Feeding the fish was the perfect ongoing excuse for us to stop by—sometimes sticking around for a while. Every time we had to leave, I would drag my feet in protest.

Besides the '70s style kitchen table from my parents, and a few old dining chairs, the only other piece of furniture we had in our apartment was the brown couch from Mary's garage.

As I passed our future bedroom to feed the fish, I halted, noticing our room was no longer empty. There, against the wall, sat a beautiful vanity set. Nate watched me hurry over to it and sit on the cushioned seat. The vanity set was solid oak, its carvings swirled into vines of leaves and flowery blooms. With my fingertips, I traced a rose and then a tulip along the edge. Its trifold mirror displayed my face of giddiness in three different angles. I opened and closed each drawer, imagining my make-up brushes, lip gloss, Forever Krystal perfume, mascara, and all the girly splendor a vanity set could hold. It was the utmost stunning piece of furniture I had ever seen, and I couldn't believe it was mine!

I got up and swiftly walked over to my fiancé. "I love it, Baby. Thank you!" I gushed, my arms wrapping around him.

He was grinning modestly, "I'm glad you like it."

"I love it!" I replied. "I love it, I love it, I love it!"

I walked over to the window and leaned my head against the glass. "Wow, you were able to buy this *and* keep your car?" I asked, impressed.

"My mom let me borrow the money, and I almost have her paid back already," Nate responded humbly.

It was a heartfelt gift that I already cherished. Not only did I love the gift, but I loved how much Nate wanted me to have it.

There was a church on a hill, a bride adorned in white, a groom more handsome than anyone on the planet, and a pastor with a Bible in his hands.

When the music began with *Here Comes the Bride,* I knew that was my cue to link arms with my dad and walk down the aisle. Everyone we loved was there, together in one room, for the most important day that Nate and I had ever had. I walked fast, causing poor Dad to quicken his steps. At the altar, he embraced me before bestowing his nineteen-year-old daughter to the man she loved.

Through my veil, I looked at Nate in his red bow tie and matching cummerbund. A row of groomsmen lined up beside him, their complimentary pink bow ties made to match the color of my bridesmaids' dresses. Since our wedding was on the day before Valentine's Day, we kept to the traditional colors of red, pink, and white.

Two singers from our church choir began their duet of *Endless Love* as we stood facing each other at the altar. Memories of this song made my eyes glow. Nate smiled lovingly at me. I could tell he was thinking of our dance at Round Table Pizza, too. After the wedding singers finished the last stanza, the pastor opened the Bible and the church was quiet—except for a few coughs and creaking pews.

We listened to the pastor's message as he made Biblical references to the sanctity of marriage. He deemed Christ the center of our marriage, uniting two hearts and two souls together as one. We bowed our heads as we knelt to receive the blessing. The pastor spoke of strength, protection, commitment, and love for each other in marriage. He prayed for us to not only explore the depths of our love for one another, but also for us to explore the depths of our love for Jesus Christ. After the prayer, Nate helped me up as my bridesmaids fixed the train of my dress. With our hands clasped, we watched our moms light the unity candle.

It was our turn to speak. With the pastor guiding our words, we made our vows to each other and to our Lord in Heaven. Everything we said, we meant. My heart pounded with excitement as the pastor reached the end of the ceremony. There were only two words left to say. "I do!"

"You may now kiss the bride," the pastor announced as we leaned toward each other.

With one kiss it was official, we were married!

After our limo drive along the scenic 17-Mile Drive, Nate and I entered the ballroom at the Hyatt Regency Hotel as husband and wife. Everyone cheered, raising their glasses of wine and soft drinks. The ballroom looked like it could be Saint Valentine's birthday party with red and white balloons as floating centerpieces at each table. My mom had used her passion for balloon art to create a floor-to-ceiling heart of red balloons nearly stealing the spotlight from our wedding cake with buttercream frosting — Nate's one and only request.

The ballroom was packed with proud parents, relatives, friends, neighbors, co-workers, and a live band called *The American Express*. The lead singer congratulated our marriage followed by more cheers and shouts from our loved ones. He strummed his guitar, the drummer tapped his cymbals and we shared our first dance to *You Are The Sunshine Of My Life*. By the end of the song, the dance floor was packed with all of our loved ones ready to dance the night away in a sea of red and white balloons.

Nate and I followed all of the wedding traditions, except for the garter toss. He was very protective of me and the physical intimacy of our marriage.

Our wedding celebration was ending. After months of preparation, I couldn't believe that it had gone by so quickly. Nate and I said our goodbyes to everyone as we left the reception and walked hand in hand to our hotel room. Nate carried me over the threshold into our room and we spent our first night together. I couldn't believe it — this was real! We had each other, as husband and wife, to have and to hold ... so long as we both shall live.

Our honeymoon destination was in Long Beach, California, where we would board a cruise ship at noon the following day — its posted ports in San Diego, Catalina, and Mexico. Nate started the car to begin our five hour trip as our family and friends waved us off. My parents' house fell behind Dad's handwritten *Just Married*—painted in white on the back window of our car.

I loved being in the car with Nate. Most of our dates had happened on the road and now we were driving into the beginning of our married life with *Guns and Roses* playing on the cassette. We talked for hours about our wedding, the dancing, the gifts, and all the kisses encouraged by clinking glasses. It had been a perfect wedding day and we were feeling high as we soaked in all of the excitement. I sat back, caught up in a dreamy exhale.

Well after the freeway had turned dark, we checked into a hotel just off the Grapevine. We were an hour and a half from Long Beach, where our cruise ship waited for us in the harbor. The front desk clerk addressed us as "Mr. and Mrs. Baker," and I almost dropped my luggage. We weren't the kids asking about a fictitious prom anymore—we had a credit card and real reservations. Nate took the key and we walked together down the hall. Our room was the basic layout—a bed, a desk, and a woven chair angled toward the view of the moonlit parking lot. As I closed the curtains, I watched the headlights of cars off in the distance make their way up and down the surrounding hills of the Grapevine. Complete paradise.

Nate stripped down to his boxers. "What's the matter, Babe?" he asked, searching for a towel.

I lay down on the bed. "It's nothing…I just feel like I forgot something," I answered. There was something nagging at the back of my mind. What was I forgetting? I had everything I ever wanted and he was shirtless.

"Okay, let me know if you need anything," Nate said and disappeared into the bathroom. I heard the water turn on in the sink as my husband washed up for the night.

I nestled my head into one of the pillows, and everything sunk in. My whole life had changed. I looked at the clock, its hands nearing midnight. That was it! My curfew was the *something*! The strict rule of being home by midnight had been all I had known during my teenage years, but I didn't have to do that anymore. I held up my left hand and examined the beautiful wedding ring on my finger. I wasn't in danger of being grounded, I was Nate's wife, Shelley Baker.

"Hey, Baby!" I yelled at the ceiling.

"Yeah?" Nate asked, as he walked out of the bathroom drying his face with a hand towel.

I sat up and exclaimed, "I don't have a curfew tonight!"

"What?!" he gasped dramatically and tossed the towel like a frisbee at me.

I smiled, coming to the realization that we were no longer bound to such rules, but instead bound to one another. Nate walked toward me with a look of intent. He leaned over the bed and kissed me, slowly shifting his weight onto mine.

My face reflected my newlywed glow as I prepared to highlight it with makeup. Even though I had only used my new vanity set a few times, I already had my morning routine of getting ready for the day. My eyes traced the vines and flowers carved into the oak frame and I thought about how, just weeks ago, this had been the only piece of furniture in our bedroom. Now, through my mirrored image, I could see our room set up with all of the furniture from Nate's bedroom. Our new teal patterned bedsheets smelled of fresh cotton. A flyer from the *Eddie and the Tide* concert was taped to the side of the armoire—facing our bed—a fond remembrance of our first date. I smiled with contentment, loving the fact that this was Nate's and my bedroom.

As I flossed my teeth, I adjusted the right mirror and let out a loud shriek. There in the reflection was a horrifying skeleton mask staring at me.

"NATE!" I yelled out.

Grunts and tackle sounds from the boys' game of *Hallway Football* echoed through the apartment, followed by a "Yeah? What's up, Princess?"

"Must we have this in our room!?" I questioned, as I pointed to the styrofoam head wearing the scary skeleton mask displayed on top of our armoire.

I could hear Justin laughing and teasing Nate for getting in trouble as they made another play. With each crash and bang, I cringed. I had witnessed firsthand how this game was notorious for breaking things, and knew it was only a matter of time before their rough housing led to holes in the walls.

Nate poked his head into the bedroom, "What thing?"

I pointed to his *decoration*—the sickly, yellow, rubber mask with brownish coloring around sunken eyes.

Nate snickered, "I love that thing! Paul and I used to put it on the dummies we'd make to scare the neighbors."

"Well, it startles me every time I see it!"

Justin threw the football at Nate, hitting him on the shoulder. "Doh!" Nate responded as he looked at his little brother with a mischievous gleam in his eyes. "You have five seconds. Four! Three! Two! One!" he called out as he went after Justin.

"Ugh, boys!" I turned back around shaking my head with a smile.

I applied moisturizing lotion to my face hoping to ease the rosy cheeks that I had brought back from our honeymoon—it had been an unusually warm February this year. Although my back was to the hallway, I could see Nate and Justin in the mirror as they passed by. Curious, they looked at me and then stopped what they were doing. The football dropped to the floor as they walked into the room. Mumbling to each other, they sat down on the edge of the bed right behind me. After an awkward moment of silence, they looked at each other, both confused and humored, as if I were doing some strange ritual they had never seen. Through my reflection in the mirror, I smiled and opened a tube of foundation.

"What's that? It looks like Spackle," Nate teased, then looked at Justin as he snickered.

Justin snorted.

"It's makeup," I said, trying not to laugh. I smoothed a touch of foundation on my face, and then I switched over to a powder compact. Once again, Nate and Justin looked at each other in confusion.

"What's that goop for?" Nate asked. I ignored him and brought out the pinkish blush with a hint of sparkles.

"What do you do with that one?" Justin snickered, following Nate's lead. Nate flopped backwards onto the bed, holding his stomach as he laughed. They were quite amused with themselves.

"Okay, that's enough out of you two!" I called out, turning away from the mirror. The towel toppled forward and slid off my wet head which amplified their hilarity. "You two, go! You can continue destroying the hallway while I finish getting ready without boys!" I said as I escorted them out and shut the door.

I could hear their laughter on the other side of the door. I smiled at their amusement as I returned to my vanity and I picked up where I had left off.

It was late. Returning home tired from a night class, I flicked on the lights, kicked off my shoes, and walked over to the kitchen to get a

Coke. As ice cubes clinked into the glass, my mind buzzed with all the things I had fit into the day. On top of both my morning and night classes, with work shoved in between, I was able to squeeze in a few errands. I even managed to pull off a good grade on the pop quiz in Microbiology. I noticed all the dishes that I did not have the energy to wash. Not a problem, I'll just do them in the morning. Oh wait…that would be a problem. Even though Nate and I were newlyweds, I knew him. Without a doubt, I knew that once I went to bed, Nate would do the dishes. While most wives wouldn't consider that a problem—I did. I preferred to do the dishes in the morning with daybreak's sun shining through the kitchen window. Nate, on the other hand, would fit washing dishes into his long nights of studying. I was tired and didn't want to clean the kitchen. I also didn't want the dishes to interrupt Nate's study time tonight either.

For the past few days, the routine for both Nate and me had been school, work, school again, study. Repeat. When Nate and I would finally return home for the day, all we wanted was to spend our last bit of time with each other. I had just plopped down on the couch when I heard Nate's car pull into the parking lot right outside our living room window. Even though I had just sat down, I was instantly re-energized by the sound of Nate arriving home. Rushing over to my vanity set, I powdered my nose and walked over to welcome him at the front door. He greeted me with his usual smiling eyes, a kiss, and a take-out bag from Tico's Tacos. While Nate changed out of his white polo work shirt and khaki pants, I unpacked our dinner of chili verde and rice, and set it on the coffee table in front of the television. I walked over to the fridge to pour Nate a glass of unsweetened iced tea. Ready for some dinner, he walked over in his boxers and a T-shirt to join me.

Full and content from our late dinner, we sat on the couch with empty containers in front of us. I rested my head on Nate's lap as he took over the remote. He had a habit of bouncing his leg up and down, which I found oddly comforting—my head bobbed in rhythm along with his motion. I was already tired, but after a tasty meal and being gently rocked by Nate's leg, my eyes were heavy and I was ready for some sleep. The sight of our dinner mess reminded me of the dishes... ugh, the dishes.

I slowly got up and threw away the empty containers in the trash can. I stood in the doorway noting all the cleaning to be done. The kitchen counter was sprinkled with bread crumbs retelling the story of our morning routine of a quick breakfast and packing lunches. An empty popcorn bag with leftover kernels rested next to the unwashed dishes, a couple of crushed Coke cans waited to be recycled, a pan crusted in eggs sat on the stove, and abandoned tea bags drooped over the side of the iced tea maker from freshly brewed iced tea. I looked at the dishes and they looked back at me.

"I'll wash you tomorrow," I told them and readied myself for bed by *degooping* (as Nate called it), brushing my teeth, and slipping on Nate's XL Def Leppard T-shirt. I loved being wrapped up in the manly scent of my husband. It was rare for us to go to sleep at the same time—Nate was a total night owl who was due for his second wind any minute now. We walked to our room and he got in with me to tuck me in for the night. I always felt so loved by Nate. He loved me in every way a man could love a woman: his heart, his body, his time, his fun, and even his help around the house.

"Please don't do the dishes tonight," I told Nate as he played air guitar on my arm and hummed a tune.

"It's not a big deal, Babe," he objected. Nothing was ever a problem for Nate.

"I mean it. I'll wash them in the morning," my voice was firm now. "You'll be up late enough studying."

"But—"

"Don't!" I interrupted, "Don't so much as lift a spoon. Promise?"

He smiled tenderly, "Okay, I promise."

I awoke the next morning to Nate fast asleep, his head resting on *Conker*—my lifelong pillow—formed into a very tight wad tucked under his head. How in the world can that be comfortable? I smiled as his shoulders rose and fell in deep sighs. Seeing Nate next to me in bed was my favorite part of the morning. I looked over at him, his lips smooshed against the pillow, and thanked God for blessing me with this man.

I got up quietly and shut the door behind me as I walked down the short hallway and through the living room. We were so young. Our home decor consisted mostly of hand-me-downs, posters, and wedding gifts. Nate's humor made me laugh as I looked at our new picture that he had been more than eager to hang up on the wall. We had just bought a print of a cartoon duck sunbathing while unknowingly being surrounded by smiling alligators. I smiled as I turned into the kitchen to get some breakfast. Stunned, I stopped.

I stood there dumbfounded as I looked at the kitchen in front of me. The entire kitchen had been wiped spotlessly clean. The sink was empty, and so was the stove, along with an emptied trash can to match. Spoons, however, were everywhere! Spoons on the countertops, spoons huddled at the bottom of the sink, the thick ice cream scoop, and even the wooden spoon from stirring the eggs was left untouched. All the spoons remained in the exact location they were in when I had gone to bed last night. As promised, Nate had managed to clean the entire kitchen without lifting a spoon!

I turned the key in the mailbox and pulled out the cluster of envelopes and papers. Fumbling through the usual mail, my eyes lit up as I came across what I had been waiting for—my application to Dental Hygiene school! Although the acceptance process was competitive, my heart soared with the possibility of being selected. I skimmed over the paperwork, smiling as I walked into our study to grab a pen so I could start filling out the application right away.

A small glimpse of red caught my eye. "Bruno!" I gasped, lifting my hands to my mouth at the sight of our little shark floating at the top of the aquarium. I instantly turned and looked away. "Oh no..." I stood there for a moment and then turned back around to make sure what I saw was true. I watched Bruno's lifeless body drift in the ripples of the water filter. It was true, Bruno had died.

Although Nate was not big on pets, he was very fond of his bully fish. I knew he would be upset. It made me sad that I had to be the one to break the news to him when he got home from work. I didn't like seeing Bruno like this, and didn't have the heart to be the one to flush him. I sighed, thinking back to Nate's party the night of our first kiss. Bruno had helped me to understand my husband's rogue personality. I left the study and shut the door behind me.

A few hours later, Nate walked in the door. I was always excited to see Nate, but tonight I felt a bit sad about the news I had for him. I kissed him and asked about his day as I followed him into our room so he could change out of his work clothes. I then told him about Bruno.

"Oh... okay," he said and continued pulling on a fresh T-shirt.

"Okay?" I asked, a little confused at his unexpected reaction.

"It's just a fish," Nate responded calmly as he walked into the study.

"He's still in the tank," I said, "I didn't want to get rid of him."

Nate grabbed the tiny green net out of the drawer, scooped up Bruno, and walked over to the bathroom. I waited in the hallway. My heart sank a little with the sound of the toilet flushing. Nate walked back in, "What's for dinner?"

Dinner was normal with a slight tinge of melancholy as we ate. “I was sad to tell you about Bruno when you got home. I know even though you don’t care much for animals, he was still your favorite fish in the tank.”

Nate got up to grab the salt shaker, “It’s not a big deal, really. Fish die all the time.”

“He wasn’t just a fish. He was special. He was your red finned rogue.”

“Even rogues die eventually.” He gave me a reassuring smile.

“Maybe we can look into getting another pet someday,” I said cheering up.

“No way! We have a good thing going. You’re allergic and I don’t like animals. It’s perfect,” he said with a teasing smile. Nate called my sensitive nose and asthma a *bonus* and a solid excuse for refusing to get a pet for our future kids.

“I’m serious, Babe, I want a pet.”

“No-Kay,” Nate smiled and sat back down next to me.

“I can’t believe we actually did this!” I squealed, as Nate drove us home.

“I can’t believe you talked me into this,” he growled, looking down at the gray baby cockatiel in its cage on my lap.

My smile beamed as I focused on his bright orange cheeks. His tiny body was covered more in fluff than feathers, and hints of white and yellow peeked out from underneath his gray wings. His crest feathers on top of his head perked up to all the unfamiliar noises. I named him Bo, short for Beauregard Aurelius Brady, a character on my favorite soap opera *Days of Our Lives.*

“He’s so cute!” I gushed as I hugged the cage.

“Eeeee...” Nate grumbled as we pulled back into the apartment parking lot. He carried the cage of our new pet through the front door and set it down on the end table next to the couch in the living room.

Bo looked around wide-eyed at his new surroundings and at my face smiling at him through the bars. I rested my head on Nate's shoulder and intertwined my fingers with his. He kissed the top of my head. We stayed in the living room with Bo for the rest of the day as he settled into his new home. Every now and then I would look over at Nate who, although he had put up a fuss, was enjoying our newest family member.

"*Dew!*" Bo shrieked.

Although he was settled into his new surroundings, poor Bo didn't understand Nate's teasing. Nate would stick his finger through the cage and point at Bo's orange cheeks causing his crest feathers to rise in response to the intrusion. Nate would snigger at the reaction of our flustered bird. Sometimes Bo seemed to like the *play time*, puffing up his feathers as he aggressively pecked the tip of Nate's finger without actually biting.

"Dew!" Nate mimicked Bo's pathetic avian chirp.

"Nate! Would you two knock it off? I'm trying to study here," I laughed as I shook my head. Bo ruffled his feathers as Nate pulled back his finger. "Just put him down here. He can help me study."

The pitter patter of little bird feet trailed across the scattered books and papers on the floor as he walked over to me. As usual, I was lying on my stomach on the living room carpet while I did my homework. Bo busied himself by chewing the erasers off all my pencils.

After a few hours of studying, I picked up Bo and put him in his cage for the night. His cute baby bird beeps made me smile as I started collecting my papers off the floor. Before leaving the room, Nate couldn't resist poking his finger through the cage one last time.

"*Dew*!" Bo squealed. Nate laughed, getting just the reaction he wanted.

I laughed, "Ya know... I think Bo actually likes all the attention you give him."

As we walked into the bedroom, I caught a glimpse of a small yellow piece of paper that I had tossed on the bed earlier. I gave a frustrated sigh.

In an attempt to console me, Nate said, "People get speeding tickets all the time, Babe, we'll take care of it."

"Well it happens to us A LOT... !" I paced the floor and fell onto the covers of the bed. "It was like he was just waiting for me at the bottom of the hill! Maybe I should get rid of my red car," I groaned. "It's like I'm a moving target for the cops."

Nate laid next to me on his side, his weight supported by his elbow. "Are you a Dew?" he asked calmly.

"Am I a what??" I lifted my face from my pillow, almost irritated at Nate's odd question. This was *not* the comfort I was looking for. It took me a few seconds, but then I got it. "Yes!" I said, crossing my eyes like a distressed Bo. "Dew!"

We both laughed as I got up to *degoop*.

I sat at my vanity set and sarcastically commented, "Well, I guess both of our days involved the police, only *yours* was a good thing. Catching a shoplifter is way better than getting a speeding ticket!"

"Ha, yeah," he agreed. "You should have seen the guy's face when they snapped his picture for the *Wall of Shame*."

I almost sympathized with the shoplifter. Nate chased me around the house all the time—normally on all fours—but I couldn't imagine what it would feel like being actually chased across the parking lot by a tall, husky man running at full speed.

"Did you handcuff him?"

Nate's eyes were bright with excitement. "Yep, I handcuffed him to the dumpster out back."

I laughed at his enthusiasm as he acted out the scene. "Any day involving a *Check-Stand-Ten* is a good day," I chuckled, referring to Star Market's code phrase for shoplifter.

"Yeah, it's definitely more exciting than rotating produce all day." After a quiet moment, Nate rolled over onto his back. "You're lucky you know what you want to do for your career. I don't know what I want to do yet."

"You still have time, Honey. We're still in junior college," I said softly. I finished *degooping* and laid down next to him. "What about your wanting to be a pediatrician? You're so good with kids."

Nate sighed, "I don't know... I think my dad's idea of majoring in business will be good — it covers a lot of career options for me."

"Hmmm, yeah, business classes will buy you some time to figure things out."

I closed my eyes and snuggled into Nate. In the quiet, I started to think about the upcoming year with Nate starting at San Jose State and me starting dental hygiene school in Aptos. Our schedules would be different and involve commuting for us both.

"I'm going to miss us going to school together next year," I said, as I rested my head on his shoulder. "We won't be able to pass notes to each other or ditch class together."

Nate smiled, "Yeah, like the time— "

Brring, Brring.

Nate got up and walked to the kitchen to answer the phone. From down the hall I could hear a few "uh huhs" followed by a "Really? That would be great. I'll talk to Shelley about it and let you know."

Nate hung up the phone and came back with a surprised smile as he stood in the doorway. “The tenants at my mom’s rental just gave their notice. She offered us the house!”

“Really?!” I asked, and immediately sat up.

“Really,” Nate answered, “What do you think?”

“Our own house? Yes!” Suddenly I wasn’t tired anymore. “Wow, I guess lots of things are changing.” My energetic mind was already starting to pack our apartment into boxes. “One suggestion…can we leave that skeleton mask here?” I teased.

Chapter 4

"Sweet Child O' Mine" by Guns N' Roses

THE ZIP, STICK, AND TEAR of packing tape secured another box as Mary held the cardboard flaps together for me to fasten. I tossed another emptied roll into the trash pile. This weekend had been spent with unpinning posters from the walls and covering dishes in bubble wrap. How, in two years, had we collected so much stuff?

"Hey Mom, is there another roll of tape somewhere over there?" I called out from the living room floor.

"Hang on, I'll look for some," she said, as she took a break from emptying the drawers in the kitchen.

The front door opened and my dad poked his head in. "The truck is here."

I stood up to see the orange and white U-Haul pull into the driveway. Nate got out of the truck and started opening the back doors, while Justin jumped out of the passenger seat with a big smile on his face.

Seeing the U-Haul, and everything we owned stuffed into brown boxes, brought reality to what was actually happening—we were moving into a house. A house! We would have two bathrooms, a dishwasher, a fireplace, a backyard, and a garage with our own washer and dryer. No more waiting for an available machine or collecting quarters for each load of laundry.

As I looked around, the bare walls and emptied rooms turned my smile into a bittersweet sigh. This apartment was our first home together, our newlywed home, where life had gone from curfews to paying rent and utility bills. I will forever cherish the memories we made here. Memories of dinner parties with friends, roasting my first Thanksgiving turkey, and the many times I practiced my dental hygiene instruments on Nate as he laid on the couch with his mouth wide open. We had even survived the 6.9 magnitude Loma Prieta earthquake here together last year. The power was out all over Salinas. By candlelight, Nate and I listened to the news updates on the transistor radio. With the power still out the next morning, we cooked breakfast on our Weber BBQ Grill in the courtyard.

I was used to what we had, and even though I was excited, having this new house would mean that things would change. Change was always difficult for me because change usually leads to goodbyes, and moving would mean saying goodbye to our apartment.

Jon's black Nissan pulled up next to the U-Haul, and I was thankful for the additional muscle power to load our furniture and boxes into the truck. Jon walked in the front door, his blonde hair almost long enough to pull back into a ponytail now. I greeted him with a hug and thanked him for coming over to help with the heavy lifting. Nate's grunting echoed down the hall as he tried to ambitiously carry the mattress out by himself.

"Jonathan, help your brother with that, would you please? He's going to break his back trying to lift that mattress!" Mary said as she shook her head at Nate.

With every box we carried out to the truck, Bo would raise his crest feathers and let out a pathetic avian chirp. Even with all the commotion of the move, Nate still found time to poke his finger at poor Bo and tease him for "being a Dew." Protecting Bo from Nate's teasing, I went over and picked up his cage.

"Okay, Bo is the last thing we need to load up," I said with excitement, as I looked around the empty apartment.

"Or, we can just leave him here," Nate suggested with a playful snicker.

"Nate!" I laughed, pushing him with my shoulder as I walked to the car and put Bo in the back seat. "Are you sure we have everything?" I asked, shutting the door.

"Yep, we have it all. Let's lock up and turn in the keys. Everyone's going to be waiting for us over at the house."

"I'm so excited! And ... a little bit sad at the same time," I admitted, as I took the key off my key chain. I could tell he noticed the mixture of emotions in my voice as we left the landlord's office and walked toward the car.

Nate held my hand gently as we looked back at the apartment one last time before leaving. "We've definitely had some good times here, but things are changing, like they do all the time," he said, with a soft smile. Nate started the car, and we drove away.

For the past week, our house had been Box City, but after days of unpacking and decorating, all the emptied boxes were flattened and piled up in the garage. Nate and Justin began loading up Nate's car with Goodwill items to be donated. Even though we had only been married for a couple of years, we were already getting rid of some things that we didn't need. Nate and I both got a lot of satisfaction out of throwing things away—clutter was pretty much non-existent in our house.

Excited to do some cooking in our new kitchen, I started making some chili. As the meat was browning, and the chopped tomatoes were warming, I searched the spice rack for the cumin. I started reading each label one by one. "Thyme, no…coriander, no…rosemary, no…where the heck is the cumin?" I went back to the stove to stir the ground beef. I wasn't the most organized person. The spice bottles had no particular order and I had forgotten what cumin even looked like. *Was it ground like cinnamon? Did it look like grass?* The beef sizzled and I returned to the spice rack for the missing ingredient. "Nutmeg, no…" I groaned as I continued down the line of bottles. They all looked the same.

"What's going on in there, Nice Lady?" Nate called out, as he and Justin started following the scent of dinner. I had a lot of nicknames—this one came from a scene from the movie *Smokey and the Bandit*. I was pretty sure that Nate remembered my *actual* name, but he had his own style of addressing me. I was usually *Princess* or *Nice Lady*—sometimes *Crazy Lady*, sometimes *Dew*, but never Shelley. Oh, Nate. I sure do love him.

I smiled as I continued lifting each little bottle and returned it to the shelf. "How long can it take to find the dang cumin? Where is it? Can you find it for me, Honey? I need to stir the dinner."

"Why don't you put the labels in front where you can read them?" Nate asked. This piece of advice was coming from a man who organized everything—even his candy! A bag of *Skittles* would be separated by color, groups of greens and oranges on the table like a kindergarten lesson. Then he would rub his hands together, ready to enjoy his candy, now that the bag was "fixed."

“I don’t have time for that,” I answered, returning to the meat.

Nate used a chair as a stool and took my place at the rack. He handed me the cumin.

“I dare you to try this,” Nate challenged Justin as he handed him one of the spice bottles and began alphabetizing them.

Justin didn’t hesitate. He twisted the top and shook its red spice into his palm and took a brave lick. Justin shrugged, unimpressed by Nate’s dare. Then the spice competition began. Nate selected two bottles this time and handed them over. Justin challenged the same for Nate, adding a third bottle to the mix. They opened their bottles, shook, licked, and grimaced.

The “Ugggghhhs,” “Ewes” and “Hot! Hot! Hots!” grew louder as I continued cooking dinner, completely entertained. I poured the cooked meat into the warming pot of tomatoes and beans, laughing at their dramatic expressions of disgust. The winner of this game was obviously the inventor of the worst taste. Nate’s inner child was never really *inner*. When he played, the possibilities were endless.

Life was moving along quickly. I had made it to my senior year of hygiene school where the days were hectic and the classes were more intense. One of the classes this year was Local Anesthetic. Today we would learn our last new injection. We spent the afternoon in the clinic both giving and receiving the final injection. For weeks now, we had been learning the correct placement of the needle by practicing on each other. After today, injections would be given on patients instead of fellow students! I don’t know what was more intimidating—getting someone numb for the first time, or having someone get *me* numb for *their* first time. Although our nerves had settled down over the past few months, it was still nerve-racking getting an injection by someone who was learning. Our teacher assured us that she would be right there watching, as usual, to make sure that we directed the needle at just the right angle so that we didn't make a mistake.

There were a lot of graduation requirements to meet, but I was working really hard and getting good grades. I was optimistic about passing all my classes and taking the written National Board Exam in the spring.

When I finally got home after a long day at school, I saw Nate's car in the garage and gave a semi-lopsided smile—a result of lingering anesthesia. Some days Nate would go right to work after he got home from San Jose State, but tonight, he was off. After our long school day, tonight we could eat some dinner and just relax together before starting our homework.

I walked in the house and immediately noticed that the house was quiet. Nate and I had been married well over two years now—long enough to know that living with Nate was never really quiet.

"Babe? Are you here?" I asked cautiously, as I walked down the hall to our room. I couldn't wait to get out of my clinic clothes. Within seconds, the silence was broken and my question was answered.

Commotion erupted as loud sirens began to fill the air.

"Put your hands up in the air!" Nate came barreling out of our bedroom and instantly forced me against the wall. He took my arms down and began handcuffing my wrists together behind my back. Although Nate didn't really have handcuffs, he made such convincing clicking noises that I would swear that I really was under arrest... again. With my head turned sideways and half of my face pressed to the wall, I started in with my own sound effects.

"Naaate!" I squealed in a boisterous response. But instead of stopping, he went on to read me my Miranda rights.

"Dew!" Bo's shriek echoed down the fall from the living room.

"You have the right to remain silent. Anything you say can and will be used against you in a court of law..."

Although I was annoyed at being arrested, Nate, with his playful charm, just ended up making me laugh. "Nate, do you know what a long day I have had? I had to get shots today, shots, Babe! In fact, I'm still kinda numb."

As I talked, he began the weapons search, which I knew was his favorite part. He patted down my body—just to make sure I wasn't hiding any weapons—which got me giggling, "That, ha ha ha, that tickles! Stop it, ha ha, stop it Nate!"

"Okay, you're clear," he declared sternly.

I rolled my eyes.

He then escorted me, with my hands still behind my back, down the hall into our room. Once we got to the edge of the bed, he turned me around to face him, where he was met with my annoyed—yet very entertained—expression.

"Is this *really* necessary? Can't you study for your classes by reading your text books like normal people?"

Nate gave me a look of satisfaction and gently pushed me back on the bed. My handcuffs seemed to magically disappear as we got comfortable on the bed.

"I'm glad that you love your classes so much," I exhaled with a chuckle. "It all makes sense now. You've loved catching shoplifters at Star for years."

"Yeah, I'm glad I switched my major to Criminal Justice; I'm really liking it a lot." Nate acknowledged, and began kissing my neck as we talked.

"I can tell," I responded with a smile, "It sounds like you have those Miranda rights down pretty good. You'll get an A on that test for sure," I teased, completely enjoying the moment.

"You're going to make a great prosecutor," I said, feeling the strength of Nate's arms as he held me.

"You know what I think?" Nate paused for a moment, "I think you're going to make a great mom."

...As I took in Nate's words, I could feel the busy day melt away as our bodies began to intertwine. Last summer we had talked about starting a family, but we had decided to wait a little while longer until we were closer to graduation. With only six months left, we were definitely close to my being finished with school.

"Well..." I whispered playfully, "Maybe when I get out of jail, we can make that happen. Will you wait for me?"

I began pacing back and forth. My heart beat faster and louder, each second seemed to take forever. I waited. I hate waiting. Ugh, can time just go faster?!

Why is this towel on the floor? Our toothbrushes don't go there, they go here. No, here. No. Here. Does Nate chew his toothbrush? These bristles are all frayed. Whatever, I'm just going to get us new ones.

I picked up the tiny rectangular box on the side of the sink and read the directions once again. Did I even do this right?

I looked for a sign.

Nothing yet.

God, this is the plan, right? I like this plan. Do You like this plan?

I looked at myself in the mirror and smiled.

Are you ready for this?

I'm ready for this. So ready for this.

I took in a deep breath and looked down. Holding the stick, I watched without blinking as its light red message slowly surfaced from the blank circle. In an instant, bliss and pure joy began to rise inside of me, making me feel like I was glowing.

I rushed out the door, shouting, "I'm pregnant! We're having a baby!"

Nate froze mid-step in the living room and his pacing came to a standstill. His eyes lit up and darted from side to side as his mind took in this amazing news.

He rushed over to me and gently held me as if I had suddenly become fragile. Riding the waves of emotion, we stared at the stick as proof of our parenthood. It seemed almost surreal that our future included a plus one. Somewhere behind my belly button, was a little ball of life that would soon grow into our first child.

Nate got on his knees, hands cupped to my flat tummy. "Hello in there. I am your Faaaaaatherrrr," he told the baby. He held his ear against my stomach as if listening for a response. I laughed as my fingers caressed his thick blonde hair.

I looked up and noticed our backpacks leaning against the front door, ready for yet another morning commute. I had momentarily forgotten that we had a whole day of school ahead of us.

"I wish we could stay home together and celebrate," I said not wanting to leave, "I can't wait to tell everyone!"

"I know, me neither! We can tell them this weekend." He stood up and gently held my shoulders looking me over. "Are you going to be okay? Do you feel okay? Do you need anything?" Nate asked, trying to find something to do for me.

I smiled at his protectiveness. "I feel fine, Honey, great actually!" I started counting on my fingers "...December, January, February,...wow, I'm barely going to be graduated before the baby is born! I kind of thought it would take a little longer than one month!"

Nate smiled.

Nate and I had already discussed the time frame. We were at the end of our fall semester with the year 1990 coming to a close. Nine months would bring us into next year's summer break as college graduates. I would finish my senior year of hygiene school with a big belly, giving my childhood nickname, Shelley Belly, a whole new meaning, and Nate would, God willing, be accepted into law school.

I swung my backpack over my shoulder and kissed him goodbye.

"I'll see you both tonight," Nate grinned.

Bo was getting used to my new homework position. For years, I had done my homework on the floor laying on my stomach with a *Big Gulp* sized Coke with extra ice. Bo would be there keeping me company as he explored the ground. My growing tummy prevented me from that old habit and now I had my new spot sitting at the kitchen table with a much less satisfying glass of water. Bo was sitting on top of his cage next to the table that was scattered with books, papers, and a borrowed computer that I needed for my project.

I perked up at the sound of the garage door lifting and got up to meet Nate as he came home from his long day of back-to-back school and work. I was craving fruit and Nate's job working produce at Star Market was perfect for fulfilling my early pregnancy cravings. I walked into the garage as Nate leaned over to pick up a cardboard box from the passenger seat. He got out and tossed his apron back in the car.

"Hey, Crazy Lady," he said, greeting me with a kiss. I grabbed for the box, but Nate didn't allow me to carry anything—not even his backpack abandoned in the backseat. "I've got it," he insisted. I held the door open for him and watched with my fructose craving eyes.

"Yay, Daddy's home!" I rubbed my stomach, "fresh fruit!"

"Okay, Babe, these are for you." Nate set the box on the kitchen counter.

I eagerly opened the flaps and gazed at my juicy treasures. All the apples, tangerines, pears, and oranges had slight dings and bruises, unusable to Star Market, but not to me. Nate's nightly deliveries were like opening a Christmas present.

"Oh! Blueberries!" I squealed, popping a few in my mouth. Fruit tasted different now, sweeter, and surprisingly more addicting than Coke. Not only had I taken nutrition in junior college, but by common sense alone, I knew that soda was deemed *bad* for the baby, along with raw meat — no problem with that one! It had been three months, two weeks, and five days since my last sip of Coke.

I started rinsing the fruit at the sink. Nate placed his hands on his hips like Superman, "Need anything else, Pretty Lady?"

I hesitated mid-rinse.

"What is it?" he asked as he moved in closer.

"It's nothing, Babe... just thinking," I smiled, setting the blueberries on a dry towel.

"Tell me," he said, as he gently traced the outline of my belly.

"Peach cobbler," I admitted. The craving had distracted me all day. Its golden crumbly crust, filled with gooey, warm sliced peaches swirled with cinnamon had taunted my every thought during my class lectures.

"Peach cobbler?" Nate repeated.

I felt bad for even bringing it up, but pregnancy cravings, you just gotta have them when they hit! Forget the pickles! I wanted — no, I somehow *needed* — peach cobbler. Before I had even finished the thought, Nate was on it, grabbing his keys from the kitchen counter.

"Babe, it's okay, I'll just pick some up tomorrow after school. You're still in your work clothes."

"I'll go get it now, so you can have a piece tonight," he assured me. My hero made his way back to the car. I watched him back out of the garage, his headlights disappearing into the dark as he began his search for peach cobbler.

Our growing baby seemed to cause contagious excitement in everyone. After surprising Mary, Justin, and my parents with the news that we were expecting, my dad had instantly reacted by pulling out a comfortable chair for me to sit down on. A couple of days later, while Nate and I were away at school, my mom had covered our kitchen table with pregnancy approved snacks—nuts, peanut butter and crackers, colorful veggies, and lots of fruit. Mary even had flowers delivered with a card packed with X's and O's.

I returned to the table and continued working on my homework. My senior project was taking over my life. For the last year, a classmate and I had studied a small group of students from Mary's fifth grade class. We had to monitor and evaluate the oral hygiene of these chosen students from the beginning to the end of the school year.

I can't wait until Nate gets back with the peach cobbler!

We had weekly meetings with them, teaching them how to take care of their teeth and even graded their performance.

Peach cobbler.

One of the perks of my dad being a principal was that I got to borrow one of the school's computers. I continued to type away on the project, summing up all of the data so far, trying to meet all of the requirements so I could pass this class and graduate.

MMMMMM, peach cobbler.

"I found some!" Nate said in triumph as he walked in. He held a box of frozen peach cobbler above his head like a trophy. "It took three stores, but I finally found it!"

"Three stores?!" I gawked at him from the computer.

He read the instructions and slid the cobbler in the oven, "Thirty minutes, Babe," and left to change his clothes.

I turned the computer off and the television on as I found a comfortable spot on the couch. Picking up the remote, I flicked through the channels. Nate took his usual spot on the couch next to me in his T-shirt, boxers, and socks. He began talking into my baby bump, "Don't worry, your peach cobbler will be in there real soon."

"Thank you for finding it, Sweetheart," I said, laughing at Nate's nightly conversation with the baby.

The half hour was worth the wait. Fresh out of the oven, Nate brought the entire cobbler over on a cookie sheet with two spoons. I took my first bite. The bursts of peaches and cinnamon were everything I had been dreaming of all day. I savored every gooey spoonful. Nate sat back with a proud look on his face; he had satisfied the primal instinct of venturing out to hunt for food to bring back home for his mate. As he joined in, the satisfaction of his success was as good as the taste of the cobbler.

We sat back, comfortably sprawled out on the couch, as we watched a rerun of *All in the Family* before bed. Nate laughed at Archie Bunker's rude comment to his ditzy, loving wife Edith as he rubbed my feet. I smiled at Nate's belly laugh.

"You really like this show, don't you?" I chuckled.

"Yeah. I've seen every episode. Well, all except one," he clarified.

"Really?" I asked, a little confused as to why he hadn't seen them all. "Why don't you just watch the last one?"

Nate paused. "It's the one where Edith dies," Nate answered as he continued rubbing my feet. From time to time I would be taken aback by his unexpected answers, this being one of those times. His tender response left me at a loss for words.

The emptied cobbler tin sat on the coffee table in front of us. Only scraps of the crust remained, but the house still smelled of cinnamon. I sat there feeling content and very loved.

The pressure was on. With only a month left until graduation, finals were looming. The pages of my senior project were growing by the day, as was my tummy!

"Squawk! Squawk! Squaawwkk!" Bo shrieked as his wings were flapping, almost in a panic.

I looked over at Bo. He must be feeling the pressure too.

"What's up, Bo?" I asked, as I went over to the cage to settle him down. His eyes were wide, his crown feathers were up as he panted in short breaths. That's odd, Nate wasn't even here teasing him.

"Settle down, big guy," I said as I went over to pick him up. Maybe a cat outside had spooked him. "Come over here with me. We have a lot of work ahead of us to meet these deadlines and pass these classes!" He sat on my shoulder as I tried to calm him down. "You can't act like that once the baby gets here, you'll scare him ... or her." I smiled. I couldn't wait to find out if we were having a boy or a girl, *but* we had decided for the gender to be announced by the doctor in the delivery room. The girls from hygiene school had surprised me with a baby shower a couple of weeks ago—their gifts mostly a neutral yellow.

"Squawk! Squawk! Squaawwkk!" Bo flapped his wings once again as he flew from my shoulder into the living room.

"Bo! What's gotten into you today?" I walked over and picked him up off the floor. "I really don't have time for this. You know Nate would call you a Dew if he were home right now," I told Bo as I put him into his cage to calm down.

I looked over at the array of homework and papers on the table and took in a deep breath. At least Carrie was coming over to quiz me with the Head and Neck Anatomy flashcards I had made. There was so much to memorize! Although Carrie and I had taken chemistry together, she was a year ahead of me, which worked out to my benefit because Carrie was an awesome "Big Sister." Every senior adopts a junior in hygiene school, so I was Carrie's "Little Sister." She had already gone through all of this stress last year. Now, she had a year of experience in the working world, making her the perfect person to quiz me on this pile of flash cards. I couldn't wait for the day where, instead of working as assistants together, we would be working as *hygienists* together.

Ding Dong.

"Squawk! Squawk! Squaawwkk!" Once again, Bo was in a tizzy.

"Ugghhh," I groaned as I went to open the door. "Hey, Carrie! So glad you're here. Bo's acting weird today. I don't know what's gotten into him." Bo continued to throw a fit as she walked in.

"Maybe he's getting jealous of the baby. It's getting so close!" She smiled in excitement. "Wow, Shelley, you have so much happening right now. I remember how stressed I felt last year with finals and the State Board, and you have a *baby* to add to all of that!" She grabbed the stack of flash cards from the table. "Are you ready for the State Board?"

"Yeah, I found a great patient to work on, thank God! But first comes finals," I said, crossing my eyes to intermix some humor with the stress.

"Well, let's get to testing you on these flash cards then," Carrie laughed. "Where's Nate? Is he at work?"

"Yeah, he's been working all day. He works full shifts on the weekends these days due to him being in San Jose a lot during the week. Star Market has been so good about working around Nate's classes."

"That's too bad he has to work on Sunday mornings. Is that why I haven't seen you and Nate around church lately?"

I paused at Carrie's question. "Yeah, our schedules are kind of nuts right now and I don't want to go without Nate. He'll be starting law school in the fall; the baby will be born this summer; and everything is just too busy right now. We will though. Really. We both want to. It's just so hard keeping up with it all."

"I totally understand. But I miss seeing you guys there, and staying connected with God can really help you through this busy time," Carrie said in her soft, caring tone. "Being at church can really bring you some peace and guidance at this time of *craziness,"* she accentuated, as she flipped through the cards and began organizing them. "I know church really helped me when I was going through all of this. Maybe you can see if Nate can start work after church so you guys can go."

I smiled at Carrie, knowing she was right. I really looked up to her, not only as a Big Sister, but also as a great Christian friend.

"I'll talk to Nate about it. We'll see what we can work out. Lord knows, I will be praying to Him non-stop as I'm taking that State Board!" We laughed.

Long after Carrie had left and the sun had gone down for the night, I put the flashcards away and started cooking dinner.

"Heellloo, Nice Lady," Nate smiled as he walked in the door.

"How was work?" I asked as I gave him a kiss.

"Wooorrrrkkk wwwaaassss gooood," he talked into my belly like *Darth Vader*.

I laughed as I walked back to the stove to scoop up dinner while Nate set his keys in the basket and went over to the sink to wash his hands.

"Bo sure has been acting weird today," I said, setting a plate down for him at the table.

"He's always weird!" Nate laughed as he sat down and took a bite.

"Very funny, Nate. No really. The last few days I've noticed his chirp sounds different…and then today he's been kind of psycho. I think I'm going to call the vet."

Nate nodded as he looked over at Bo. "Ahhh, BoBo. What's going on over there?" he asked him, and continued eating his dinner.

Between work and school the next week, I was able to schedule an appointment for Bo. Nate drove us to the vet on South Main Street. "Maybe he just needs some medicine," I said, as I tried to figure out what was going on.

Nate and I were used to going to doctor appointments together for the baby, so we knew the drill when it came to filling out paperwork in the lobby. It felt strange answering bird-related questions instead of answering baby-related questions though. It also felt strange being at a veterinarian's office in general since I've always been allergic to animals my whole life.

After filling out the paperwork, we got called back and I could already feel my ears getting itchy from all the cat and dog hair around the office. I wanted to make this quick—just get the medication and leave. I didn't want to even start in with my allergies because I didn't want to take any allergy meds being pregnant.

The doctor came in. A few paw prints marked his otherwise perfectly white lab coat. He looked at Bo. "So what's going on with this little guy?" he asked, picking him up on his index finger.

"The last week or so his chirp has been sounding different. Do birds get colds? Maybe he's sick?" I asked.

"I'll take him in the back room and we can run a couple of tests," the doctor explained.

Thankful for some help, Nate and I sat back in the chairs, letting the vet figure things out.

Nate and I used this time to catch up with each other. We talked about everything from criminals to cadavers. Although I was not having fun working on cadavers—a mandatory part of hygiene school—Nate was loving studying Criminal Justice. I was so proud of him. He had been accepted into the Monterey College of Law, and would start in the fall. Before that though, he had finals of his own to pass, and we had a baby to bring into this world!

"Achoo!" I grabbed a tissue out of my purse as we continued talking.

The door opened and I noticed the solemn look on the doctor's face as he handed Bo over to me.

"Mr. and Mrs. Baker," the tone in his voice made my stomach tighten, "... I'm sorry to have to tell you this. Bo has a tumor. There is no medication I can prescribe to help this situation. In fact, this particular type of tumor is inoperable.

I looked over at Nate, stunned by this unexpected news, "What should we do?" I asked, in shock and confusion.

"This tumor is causing Bo a lot of pain, which explains his chirp sounding different. It will only get bigger and become more painful. My recommendation is for you to put him down ... I'm so sorry." The doctor looked down slightly.

Blinking back tears, I looked at Bo, who was sitting on my finger.

"I will give you a few minutes to discuss it and to spend some time with Bo. When I come back ... if you would like me to take him ... I will." He assured us that the procedure to end Bo's life would be pain free. He once again told us he was sorry before walking out to give us some time to say our goodbyes.

The door shut behind the doctor and I started tearing up. I could feel Nate's arm around me as an overload of thoughts went through my mind. This is not what I thought was going to happen! If we put Bo down, he wouldn't even have a chance to meet the baby. Bo was only a few years old…he's too young to have a tumor! How could I possibly hand him over to the doctor knowing what they were going to do?

Although Nate handled his emotions differently than I did, I could tell he was sad. He was quiet, his face was still and somber. I wept as Nate held me, trying his best to give me some comfort, knowing the inevitable was just moments away.

We sat there looking at Bo as he sat on my outstretched hand. He cleaned his feathers and puffed up. He was so innocent, unaware he was living his last few moments of life. Besides the echo of a few barks and people walking in the hallway, the room was silent. I looked at Bo and tried to hand him over to Nate, but couldn't get myself to do it.

God…This is so sad…Bo hasn't even met the baby yet…I just want You to make him better so we can take him back home…This is not what was supposed to happen today. I could feel the tears running down my cheek.

Bo let out a weak little chirp.

I said, "goodbye," closed my eyes, and handed him over to Nate.

Nate went over with Bo to the door to get the doctor who was waiting nearby. He walked in, then took our little bird gently in his hands. As Nate and I walked out of the room, I turned around for one last look at Bo. Nate put his arm around me and we left.

I grabbed another tissue out of the glove box, "What are we going to do with the cage and all of Bo's toys?" I asked as we neared the house. "I don't want to see an empty cage when we get inside."

"I'll take care of it, Honey. You just go and get some rest."

I avoided looking at Bo's cage in the living room as I walked to our bedroom and shut the door. I could hear Nate removing all of Bo's things from the house. How could life change so fast? One moment we were on our way to the vet to get some medicine...and now Bo was gone—forever.

I slowed my car to a stop and waited as the red light allowed the cars around me to have their turn through the intersection. I looked down at the little piece of paper sitting on the passenger seat, a receipt for my first pair of glasses. My normally good vision had been having a lot of trouble lately. Everything seemed to be blurring together—even the white letters of the street signs were barely legible against the green. I strained my eyes. *Man, I must be going blind.* Not only were my eyes not cooperating, but my feet were sore and very puffy. *I've got to get myself together in time for the State Board. I can't believe it's only a few weeks away. One test away from my career!*

By the time I pulled into the garage, I felt like the seams of my shoes were going to burst wide open from the pressure of my swollen feet. *I'll ask the doctor at my next appointment if he has any ideas on how to reduce this swelling. Until then, maybe I'll just walk around barefoot. Or maybe I'll start wearing Nate's shoes!* I smiled, amused at the thought of me walking around in his size twelve tennis shoes.

I opened the door and looked ahead to the far wall. Even though it had been a couple of months now, I still wasn't used to coming through the door and not seeing Bo on his cage. It hurt to see an empty space where he used to be, and I missed his excited chirping welcoming us home. Nate came around the corner and I felt better as we sat down on the couch together.

"Look, Honey, you can't even see my ankles or any of the bones in my feet," I complained. "Oh, by the way, I can't see anymore either," I half smiled at Nate.

"Awww Dew... here, give me your feet," Nate said, as he began giving me a relieving foot massage.

We both chuckled, a bittersweet reminder that although Bo was gone, he lived on through Nate's humor. With Nate massaging my feet, I closed my tired eyes, and began melting into the couch.

"Your doctor's on television," Nate joked. I opened my eyes slightly to see Mr. Spock in his blue shirt on the screen.

I laughed. My OBGYN was like a clone of the Vulcan character from Star Trek. Although his ears and eyebrows were not pointed, his dark hairline, fair skin tone, and angular face made for a remarkable resemblance to the character from the show. Nate appropriately referred to him as Doctor Spock.

I lifted my arm for the nurse to take my blood pressure. As she pumped air into the sleeve, I looked down at my feet to see if the swelling had gone down. Nope, not even a little bit. I can't wait until I can wear normal shoes again—and normal clothes too! Unfortunately, Nate had to miss this appointment because of work. He had been to almost all of them. It was always so exciting for us to listen to the baby's heartbeat. My appointments were getting closer together now that I was only a month away from the big day. The sleeve deflated and the nurse jotted down a number. I wondered if she knew if the baby was a boy or a girl. We had told "Dr. Spock" to write down in my chart that we wanted the gender of our baby to be a surprise, but I always wondered if only he knew or if all the nurses knew as well. It was like being left out of my own secret, but somehow that made it even more exciting.

The nurse excused herself from the room. A poster of a fetus growing larger at each trimester hung on the wall. I sat there imagining what our baby must look like at this point and comparing it to the timeline on the poster. I couldn't wait for the next part of my exam; I thought it was so cute how the baby's heartbeat sounded like a dog barking.

There was a knock on the door, but instead of the nurse returning, the doctor walked in and greeted me. That's different... usually I didn't see the doctor until later in the appointment. The nurse handed him her clipboard and I instantly got the feeling that something was wrong.

My stomach knotted up. "Is everything okay?" I asked.

"Hello, Shelley. I don't want to alarm you, but you are showing symptoms of having pre-eclampsia. I need to check you and the baby. Go ahead and lay back for me," the doctor said as he placed the stethoscope in his ears. "Have you noticed a difference in your eyesight lately?"

My mind began racing, "Um, yeah. I have actually... but what do my eyes have to do with..."

"Pre-eclampsia?" the doctor finished my sentence as he helped me sit back up. He began examining my hands and feet to check the swelling. I told him about my recent ophthalmologist appointment, and how I had just ordered glasses.

"You don't need glasses," he said, in a matter of fact tone. He pulled up a chair close to me, which made my heart race. What was he about to tell me? Why was he sitting so close?

"The baby is fine."

I let out a deep sigh of relief.

"You have pre-eclampsia, which is often referred to as toxemia. It is a hypertensive disorder that pregnant women can get, usually during their last trimester. It's not common, but it's one of the most common complications during pregnancy."

Complication? That word seemed to knock the wind right out of me.

"But I feel fine. I was just here a couple of weeks ago, and everything was okay. I don't feel sick at all. Are you sure?" I asked, hoping there was some kind of mistake.

"Yes. I'm sure. Your blood pressure has abruptly elevated, which is unusual, especially for you. Your chart indicated that you normally have low blood pressure. Your urine test came back with albuminuria, which is high levels of protein in your urine, you're having difficulty seeing, and you have edema — excessive swelling," he explained, as he pressed on the tops of my swollen feet. These are all key symptoms of toxemia."

I sat there in a daze, my heart pounding. A million questions ran through my mind. "Well, can you give me some medicine, or a shot of something to fix it?"

"Unfortunately, no. There is no cure for toxemia other than delivery. When you have your baby, the toxemia will go away on its own."

"But... I'm still not due for another month," I responded.

"Sometimes with toxemia patients, we end up needing to deliver the baby early. When we do that, the baby is delivered before it has finished growing, which can lead to other complications. So, if you can make it to full term, or at least thirty-seven weeks, you and the baby should be fine. We need to get you on bed rest and monitor you closely, so I am sending you to the hospital. The nurse is making the arrangements as we speak."

"Whoa, whoa, whoa, I can't go to the hospital. If the baby is fine and I don't feel sick, then I shouldn't *need* to go to the hospital, right? I take the State Board Exam in less than two weeks! And... I have my baby shower in, like, five days."

"Shelley, you have to go to the hospital. Pre-eclampsia can develop into eclampsia, which can cause you to have a seizure. If this gets worse, it can seriously affect you and the baby."

I couldn't believe this was happening. As the doctor began filling out the paperwork, he asked, "Do you have someone who can drive you to the hospital?"

"No, I drove myself today. My husband's at work."

I walked out of the room with an admission form to CHOMP—Community Hospital of the Monterey Peninsula—in my hand. How could I be so sick but feel totally fine? The doctor said he would meet me over there after I got settled. The receptionist handed me the phone from behind the counter and I dialed Star Market's number. Trying hard to contain my emotions, I waited for Nate to pick up the phone.

"Nate...something's wrong...the doctor's sending me to the hospital and I need someone to drive me there," I said, my voice cracking.

"What's wrong, Princess?" I could tell that he was trying to remain calm for the both of us. I could picture his eyebrows pulling together in concern.

"I have pre-eclampsia or toxemia, I guess, whatever it's called. My blood pressure is super high and my urine test showed something...I don't know. Can you come and get me?"

"I'm on my way," Nate assured me. "Just sit down and try to stay calm. I'll be right there."

Other than the sound of water trickling from the fountain in the courtyard, the surroundings were quiet. Although there were plenty of open benches, I restlessly stood in the shade of the massive Monterey Pine trees that surrounded the parking lot while I waited for Nate. I needed him to tell me that everything was going to be okay.

"Don't worry, baby, we'll get through this," I said, as I looked down and began rubbing my belly. With a lump in my throat, I gave a soft smile. I love this baby so much and can't bear the thought of something going wrong.

Please, please, please, God, keep our baby safe. I've been working so hard to do everything right. There is so much going on right now, God. I do not have time for this. I really don't have time for this.

After a while of waiting and praying, Nate's car pulled into the parking lot and up to the curb. I got in and began explaining the situation. Nate's face was serious but comforting.

The hospital was expecting me, and within minutes, I was taken to a single-bed room and hooked up to a number of machines. The IV took two tries to get in. A blood pressure cuff was strapped around my arm to regularly take my blood pressure. Nate stood right beside me for everything. As the nurse was writing in my chart, I asked her questions.

"How long am I going to be here?"

"As long as it takes to get your blood pressure down and get you healthy again. Your doctor will make that call. In the meantime, you just need to rest," the nurse answered, in a gentle tone.

Nate came in from the hallway. He had been busy making phone calls and letting people know what was going on. Your mom's on her way over. She says if you're still in the hospital this weekend, she'll find a way to have the baby shower here for you."

"Ugh, is she worried?"

"Well, she's not NOT worried," he smiled, and sat down next to me.

"I don't want to be here," I grumbled. "I want to go home with you. We were going to paint the nursery this week before the baby shower."

"That's okay, Honey, I can take care of it. You just rest. I don't want you breathing in the paint fumes anyway," Nate said, trying to comfort me. "You need to stay here and take care of yourself and the baby. Just get better, Princess."

Nate stayed with me until well past visiting hours. He would have stayed with me the entire time if he could, but he had to continue his work schedule and help prepare for the baby. As the days went by, Nate was there with me as much as possible, as were our family and friends, but there were some times when I was by myself. I was practically chained to the bed by IV lines, blood pressure cuffs, and fetal monitors. Sometimes, nurses and visitors would tell me how lucky I was to have doctor's orders to rest. But to me, resting was like being confined to a jail cell. I didn't want to rest. I had so much to do before the baby was born.

After a few days, I had somewhat accepted the fact that I was stuck here, so I decided to put all of my effort and energy into getting better. I did everything I could to rest by watching TV, reading, and taking naps. Like clockwork, the nurses would bring me a tray of hospital food three times a day. Although most people would enjoy having food brought to them in bed, the alternating colors of jello and lack of salt and seasonings left me missing home all the more. The cuff that was permanently strapped to my arm would regularly begin inflating to take my latest blood pressure reading. I would cringe as the pressure tightened around my arm making my IV sting. It gave me a claustrophobic reminder that I was attached to multiple machines. Each time I would beg the monitor for good news, only for it to come back with another high reading.

Defeated, I rolled over on my side, watching the cypress trees sway in the coastal breeze through the hospital window. I thought about last night. Leftover pink and blue streamers hung from the blinds. The nurses had allowed a hospital version of a baby shower right at my bedside—only a few visitors allowed in at a time and for only a few minutes. If my blood pressure elevated at all, the shower was over. When I had asked if I could at least sit in a chair while they were there, she told me I was lucky they were allowing me to get up long enough to use the restroom. It had been great to see everyone and to open adorable gifts for the baby. But watching them leave had made me restless again.

I breathed in the scent of raspberries while enjoying some pampering. Mom had come to visit me and was massaging my puffy hands and arms with some raspberry lotion she had brought. My hands were as swollen as my feet! My teacher from hygiene school had also come to visit and check on me, as well as giving me updates on the State Board. I was ready. I just needed the doctor to release me so I could take the exam. However, if I was still assigned to my hospital prison, the next State Board wasn't until November. It would mean I would have to start all over in finding a suitable patient to work on.

The next morning, "Dr. Spock" came in wearing a white coat and holding a clipboard. He smiled, but I didn't smile back.

"What's wrong?" he asked. "If you're upset, you will raise your blood pressure."

Tears began to fall. "You won't let me out of this bed." I told him about the single exam standing in the way of my entire career.

The doctor listened as he nodded through my frustrated, pregnant tears, and took notes. "It seems keeping you here is causing more stress than if I sent you home. So, I'm going to release you, but you MUST remain on strict bedrest," he said, in a firm doctorly tone. "I do not recommend that you take your exam, but if you do... I don't want to know about it."

I beamed at him this time. Letting me go home brought me one step closer to becoming a Registered Dental Hygienist. The nurses came in to unhook me from all of the tubes and monitors. I called Nate for the dream-come-true ride home.

"Are you sure you're feeling well enough to do this?"

"Yes! I promise. I'll be lying down in the backseat all the way there, and all the way back. All I need is enough time to take the exam," I said, as I gathered my things. "You know, if you think about it, lying in the back of the car is really no different than lying in bed."

For the past few days, I had been following doctor's orders by staying in bed all day. Nate held the car door open for me so I could get in the back seat. He had lined it with blankets and pillows. My parents were already waiting in their car to follow us for extra support. They were very concerned about this decision. In my mind, if worse came to worse, and I either had complications or went into labor, I was in good hands. The State Board Exam was taking place at a well-renowned hospital—the University of California, San Francisco.

On our way to UCSF, we stopped in Gilroy to pick up my State Board patient. She rode in the front seat with Nate. She was everything I dreamed of when I was searching for a patient on which to take my exam. Not only did she meet all of the dental examiner's requirements for a State Board patient, but she was also super nice.

We arrived at UCSF. I sat up, taking in a deep breath, trying not to overthink my exam. I had everything I needed—Nate was right by my side, my parents were here for back-up support, I had a great patient, and my instruments were sterilized, sharpened, and ready to go. My parents gave me a big hug. After a good luck kiss from Nate, I walked through the doors.

Once the exam began, every move I made had to be checked. Each time I finished a given procedure, I would raise my hand for one of the examiners to come over. As the exam continued, I would look up to see Nate pacing the hallway through the square window in the door.

After a few hours, I raised my hand one last time. The examiner came over and escorted my patient into the back room for her final check behind closed doors. After fifteen very long minutes, my patient returned through the back doors, smiling at me with her freshly cleaned teeth. The examiner told me to pack up my things and that the results would be mailed to me in a few weeks. It was unsettling because the examiner's face didn't give me any indication of whether I had passed or failed.

I walked out smiling. The test was over and done!

Nate hurried over to me with a relieved look on his face, "How are you, Princess? How'd it go?"

"Everything went really well," I replied, "I feel great…but I'm ready to go home and lie down again," I smiled.

It felt amazing that the State Board was behind me! I opened the curtains and looked out at the park across the street from our house. It was a beautiful summer morning, the test was over, and I was feeling good. I started getting things ready to make breakfast and walked over to the Alhambra dispenser to pour a glass of water. As I was drinking, I noticed a black spot on the wall. I blinked, trying to clear my vision. When I opened my eyes, the black spot had multiplied, making my vision resemble how it looks after you've been looking at the sun. I blinked again, but instead of them going away, they kept multiplying.

This is *not* good. I immediately walked down the hall to wake up Nate. He reached for the phone to call the doctor who, instead of telling me to get more rest, told me to come straight to the hospital.

I didn't resist going to CHOMP this time—these spots definitely had me concerned! I just wanted to go in, get checked, and then come back home to rest. After all, the baby wasn't due for a few weeks. The last thing I wanted was to go back to the hospital and have them hook me up to all those machines again.

At the hospital, I was led into a private room. The nurse handed me a gown to change into. "How long am I going to be here this time?" I asked.

"That all depends on the baby," she answered, as I put the gown on.

Her response surprised me. She told me that because I had met the thirty-seven week goal, and my symptoms had gotten worse, they were going to induce labor.

My eyes widened. "Now? I'm having the baby now?!" I gasped.

The nurse gestured a friendly nod and began wheeling over a bag of clear liquid. "This is Pitocin—a medication that will induce labor and strengthen contractions. This is your first pregnancy, and you are still three weeks out from full term so this may take a while." I looked over at Nate whose stunned face mirrored mine. She tore open a fresh alcohol wipe to begin preparing my hand for an IV.

"Oh my gosh, I'm gonna have the baby today! We didn't even bring anything. You have work later today!" I blurted out to Nate. One after the other, my thoughts came racing out.

Nate, shaking off this unexpected news, started to assure me. "It's okay. Don't worry. I need to drop by work to let them know what's going on, and then I'll grab your things at home. I'll make it quick and be back as soon as possible!"

"Oh ... okay," my heart was racing. I was scared and excited and didn't want him to leave, but I knew he had to.

He lightly kissed my lips and then pressed his forehead against mine for a moment. "I love you," he whispered, "This is happening!"

"This is happening," I emotionally repeated Nate's words.

Even though Nate was fast, the round trip from Monterey to Salinas would take at least an hour. I watched him jet out the door, and then looked up at the clock on the wall already counting down the minutes until he would come back.

With a blur of activity, I was lying in a hospital bed hooked up to all the same beeping monitors in a short amount of time. Dr. Spock came in to check on me. He went into detail, explaining everything that was happening.

"You know ... if you wanted my blood pressure levels to stay low, telling me I'm having the baby *today* is not the way to do it," I joked.

He nodded with a smile. "I'll come back to check on you." The doctor left, and another nurse came in.

"Are we doing an epidural?" the nurse asked.

"No, I don't even want to risk the anesthetic affecting the baby. I'll just tough it out."

"Are you *sure*?" she asked, emphasizing her words. Her tone left no doubt she was in favor of the epidural.

"Yeah, I'm sure," I answered.

"What is your pain level," the other nurse asked, as she studied the Pitocin pack.

I looked at the pain scale on the wall. "Not even a one yet," I answered.

After things had calmed down a bit, I felt my first twinge of pain. As I sat there in the adjustable hospital bed with the back lifted up, I looked over at the monitor. I watched the line recording the frequency and length of contractions rise ever so slightly. All the childbirth classes came into my mind. Hopefully, I'll remember all of those breathing exercises.

One of the nurses entered the room, this time with a telephone, its wire stretched across the hallway from their front desk all the way to my bedside. "You have a phone call," she said, setting it on my lap.

"I have a phone call?" I asked, a little confused as to who would be calling me in the labor room.

"It's the police," the nurse informed me.

"The police?!" My head filled with sirens as adrenaline distracted me from the cramping I was starting to feel.

I picked up the receiver and held it to my ear, "Hello?"

"Is this Shelley Baker?" a man asked.

"Um, yes it is," I answered in a leery tone.

"I'm from the Monterey County Police Department. I pulled your husband over for speeding on Highway 68. He told me his wife was in labor at CHOMP. Are you in labor?"

"Yes, I'm in labor, I assured the officer. Is Nate okay?"

"Yes, he's fine. He's on his way to you right now." The officer explained, "I was just finishing my shift for the day when I pulled Nate over for speeding." His serious tone turned to humored guilt. "When I got home, I told my wife about the ticket. Oh man, I'm in the dog house now," he exclaimed. When Nate arrives at the hospital, tell him to rip up the speeding ticket. I just wanted to confirm that you are, in fact, in labor."

"Yes," I assured him with a bit of a groan, "I'm in labor."

"Congratulations," the officer added.

"Thank you!" I said as joyfully as possible, feeling the pressure of cramping as I talked. "And please thank your wife, too."

Within minutes, Nate rushed through the door with beads of sweat across his forehead. "I'm sorry that took so long. I'm here, Babe. How are you? How's the baby?" he stammered and grabbed for my hand. He was breathing faster than I was.

"Anything happen on the way to the hospital...?" I playfully questioned in an innocent tone.

Nate's head tilted to the side, confused.

"A police officer called," I refrained from chuckling.

"The police called you here?!" he asked, growing increasingly intrigued. "I told him you were in labor and he *still* gave me a ticket!"

I laughed, feeling the cramping slip away, "Well, that officer is in *big* trouble with his wife. He said to rip up the ticket," I smiled.

"Really, I can rip it up?" Nate asked, with a shocked look on his face. I nodded a yes. With enthusiasm, Nate instantly took the ticket out of his wallet and tore it into pieces.

"Your family's here. They are all telling you to hang in there!" a nurse said, poking her head in the room.

Contractions had arrived and were steadily intensifying as the sun set behind the Monterey hills. By 3:00 am, I had reached a level ten on the pain scale, where motherly groans had escalated into painful screams. The breathing exercises were completely useless at this point. Instead, I squeezed Nate's hand with all my might to get through each contraction. The nurse informed me I was having back labor in which the baby would be born face down instead of face up. Again, she said, "It may take awhile."

Too many numbers to be counted beyond the pain chart, I begged for the epidural. I had been so adamant about having a natural childbirth, but now I felt like I was going to die without it.

"Unfortunately, it's too late to give you an epidural now. You're too far into labor," the nurse explained with an empathetic tone.

"Then give me *SOMETHING!*" I demanded, longing for a broom stick to bite down on. With each contraction, I dug my nails into Nate's arm. My hospital gown was soaked with sweat. I was crying and shaking when they finally wheeled me into the delivery room.

After seventeen hours of labor, Dr. Spock met us dressed in scrubs instead of his usual white coat. The nurse placed a warm blanket on me to ease my shaking, but that was only a momentary ease. There was no ounce of comfort to offer now. All I could feel now was the baby pushing against my back in a seemingly desperate attempt to resist leaving the womb.

"Okay, Shelley, when I tell you to push, push really hard," the nurse coached. I was dying and she wanted me to push? "PUSH!" she yelled out, and my body listened.

At 9:19 am, there was a new life in the room.

"You did it, Babe!" Nate cheered. We were both sweating.

Out of breath, and instantly out of pain, I tried sitting up. "Is it a boy or a girl?" I asked.

"Congratulations!" the doctor replied as he handed our baby to the delivery team. "It's a girl!" Little Brittney Mae Baker let out her first wailing cry. She sounded like her mommy had sounded only moments ago! The delivery nurse gave Nate a pair of scissors to cut the umbilical cord, and then handed me our daughter to hold for the first time. Brittney's face nuzzled against my hospital gown as Nate and I gazed at her in complete awe. There were no words to describe the moment. We looked at the child our love had created. She was five pounds, eleven ounces, and nineteen inches of absolute beauty.

"What day is it?" I asked Nate, unable to take my eyes off our baby. With the explosion of events that had taken place these past couple of weeks, I had completely lost track of time.

He paused, contemplating what day it was. "It's July 24th!" Nate said enthusiastically. "You had Brittney on your birthday!" I gasped and smiled, knowing that our baby girl was the best birthday present ever.

Once we were ready, Nate followed as Brittney and I were wheeled into a room where our family whole-heartedly welcomed their newest addition. "Finally, a girl!" Mary cheered. Brittney was passed from one relative to the next, each one falling in love with her petite fingers and baby-soft skin. "Aw, look at her," one would say, noting her sleepy yawn. "Look at her toes," another would add, placing her foot against an adult-sized palm. There was so much to look at.

After a few days of making sure my blood pressure was back to normal and my toxemia was gone, Nate drove his ladies home. I sat in the back with my arms across the car seat like an extra safety belt. Brittney wore her white hospital cap, its pink pom pom bounced with every little bump in the road. Nate made a complete stop at every stop sign and checked every mirror before turning onto the highway. He drove at the exact speed limit, avoiding rushing cars, and of course any other cops waiting to give speeding tickets along the way.

Chapter 5

"Fire and Rain" by James Taylor

"WIPES," NATE REQUESTED, holding his hand out, palm up.

His assistant, Uncle Justin, handed him a wipe from the container he was holding. The boys were changing Brittney's diaper on the floor of her nursery, clearly ignoring her actual changing table that was right next to them. Their heads were wrapped in towels like surgeons in the middle of an operation. Justin followed Nate's commands.

"Powder," Nate continued in his serious tone.

All the necessary supplies circled Brittney's kicking feet. I wasn't sure if the Johnson's baby shampoo and the bottle of bubbles were added for effect, or if it was because both brothers lacked experience. They loved playing with Brittney. Their make-believe scenarios and baby-friendly games added new fun to their time together.

Powder in hand, Nate carefully aimed the bottle as Justin slowly lifted her little legs from the floor. The brothers looked at each other, giving a serious nod as Nate then meticulously tapped the base of the container for the correct amount of poofs. He wiped imaginary sweat from his brow and said, "Keep her steady." Justin nodded.

Brittney stared at their hovering heads. Once the new diaper was set, Nate pulled and stuck each tab to its precise spot. In full concentration, they adjusted their surgeon attire, shifting the towels to become makeshift hazmat suits. They safely transported the hazardous material, double wrapping the used diaper in a plastic bag, before carefully dropping it into the diaper pail.

"Phew!" that was a close one," Nate said, straightening his back. Justin's serious expression relaxed back into his teenage smile. Their procedure was complete. Little Brittney Mae, with her fisted hand in her mouth, looked up at her daddy and uncle completely oblivious to her *delicate procedure*.

The past couple of weeks felt like a crash course in parenting, and sleep had been next to nil. I wasn't sure which felt heavier, my eyes or my arms. As I walked back and forth from one end of the house to the other holding Brittney, I was dreaming of the moment that Nate would return home from work so I could have some back-up! Instead of Nate coming home with boxes of bruised fruit, now he would bring in decorated pink boxes filled with baby gifts from his co-workers. I thought it was so sweet that even though Nate would be leaving Star Market soon to start law school, they still shared in the excitement of our little bundle of joy—all seven pounds of her. Crazy how someone so little could keep us so busy. Busy and sleep-deprived!

Even when Brittney was sleeping, I couldn't. I was too busy worrying about little things like, will she be able to breathe in that position? Or, what if I fall asleep and she rolls over—she could need me and I wouldn't know. Or, is she too hot? Too cold? When will she be hungry again? Maybe I should check her diaper one more time? Being a first time parent was exhausting. After all the worrying, I would finally fall asleep…only to be awakened soon after by her crying.

Today had started about 3:30 am. After I had changed her diaper and fed her, she was wide awake and *stayed* wide awake. Although overall she was a good baby, today she just wouldn't sleep. As the day progressed, she had gotten more and more cranky and now that it was dark outside once again, she was non-stop fussy. She must be so tired, but now she was at the point where she was too worked up to sleep. All I could think to do was walk her around the house to calm her down. Somehow movement comforted Brittney, and the more I moved, the calmer she became. I paced back and forth trying to get her to sleep. I was losing my strength and every step became more difficult than the last.

As I paced back and forth from the hallway to the front door, I could feel my eyes stinging from my lack of sleep. I was a slave to her crying.

Brittney was the first baby I had ever known. No one in our family had a baby. None of our friends had babies. So of course, I had never witnessed or put much thought into how sleep-deprived parents of newborns could be—especially a slightly premature baby! All the classes, books, and doctor's visits…they were all to prepare for childbirth. But what about life *after* you bring the baby home? How are you *ever* supposed to sleep again?!

I followed my trail of matted down carpet where I had been walking back and forth for hours now. Brittney was finally quieting down…well, at least a little bit. My knees couldn't hold me up anymore. I had to stop. I had to, or I'd collapse.

The moment I sat down, the screaming began again. I looked down at our little baby swaddled in a pink blanket. Her eyes were shut tight and her bottom lip trembled as she cried and cried and cried. Trying to calm her down, I held her close to me and rocked her.

"Shhhhhhh ... shhhhhhh ..."

The crying remained constant.

"Why are you crying, Baby? Please ... just tell me what you need ... I'll fix it ... just tell me. Anything, ANYTHING, just please ... please stop crying ..."

I forced myself up and started my path again. She had gotten so worked up from my sitting down that now not even my walking seemed to work. I looked down at her crying and felt defeated. The lump in my throat turned into tears of my own.

By the time Nate got home from work, he had two crying and exhausted girls. I could hear him set his things down in the kitchen. He then walked over and stood in my path. I trudged right into his arms. He kissed the top of my head. "Hey, Princess," he whispered. I looked up at him. Even though he wasn't crying, I could see his tired, bloodshot eyes and I knew he was just as exhausted as I was.

I wearily shook my head, "I don't know what to do ... I've literally done everything I could think of, but she just won't stop crying." My extreme tiredness caused me to be overtaken by doubt and worry. "What are we going to do? Neither of us has slept for weeks. You're about to start law school and I don't have my exam results yet ... what if I didn't pass? If I don't start working before you quit Star, how are we going to pay our bills? And if I *do* start working, who's going to watch Brittney? Who's going to even want to watch her when she won't stop crying?"

Nate let out a long, deep sigh.

"Let's try taking her for a car ride. We'll pick up some food and we'll just drive around town for a while and see if she settles down."

"Okay," I sniffled.

Something about the moving car lulled Brittney right to sleep within minutes. Between the quiet, and a few chicken nuggets with fries and a grape slushy from Foster's Freeze, we both felt better. We finally got a moment of peace to talk about our day and things other than the baby. As we headed home, we drove around the block a few times to mentally prepare ourselves for Brittney to wake up again. I almost dreaded pulling into the garage. Nate and I looked at each other and held our breath as he turned the engine off.

To our pleasant surprise, Brittney remained sleeping. I thanked God the entire way from first scooping her up in the car to finally laying her in her crib. We tiptoed from the nursery to our bedroom. Without even changing clothes, we collapsed into bed.

A few weeks later, Brittney was lying on the couch next to the warm laundry I was folding. It was funny how doing housework with a baby was so different. Each task required a new place to set Brittney down.

As I folded another pair of jeans, I thought about the State Board and wondered if I had passed. I could be a Registered Dental Hygienist right now, but I wouldn't know until I finally got the letter in the mail. Being a dental assistant was great, but I couldn't wait to work as a dental hygienist. Also, I would be able to bring home a lot more income than I did as an assistant, which was something we really needed right now.

But, what if I *didn't* pass? Not passing this test would mean I would have to wait for months before I could even take the exam again. I'd have to leave the baby for a day while I retook the test—I'd also have to find a new patient—and then Nate would have to continue working extra hard to support our family of three. Nate had been working like crazy to help me get through Hygiene School.

Now *I* wanted to be the one to support us so he could focus on getting through law school. Mary suggested that Nate become a substitute teacher. Subbing would give him the freedom to choose whether he wanted to work or not, in case he got swamped with homework. Subbing would also allow him to work during the day since all of his classes were at night.

Lost in thought, I picked up more laundry out of the basket. I smiled at the significant size difference between Nate's socks and Brittney's little baby socks. As I continued folding, I saw the mail truck drive by the living room window and continue down the street to the mailbox. I jumped with excitement, my heart skipping a beat! After counting down the days for the past few weeks, I knew that my letter could definitely be here today. If not today, then maybe tomorrow — but hopefully today.

"Brittney! We're going on a walk," I smiled as I scooped her up from the couch and rushed to the nursery to grab her Snuggle from the dresser. I strapped it on myself first, and then placed her comfortably inside, leaving my hands free to check the mail for my long-awaited letter.

Our neighborhood had a common mailbox so it was just a short walk down the street. Before I put the key into our mailbox, I let out a deep breath. Brittney yawned, completely unaware of her mommy's big moment. I smiled down at her, "Okay, here we go," and I anxiously opened the small metal door to a stack of mail. Nestled in between the electric bill and a sandwich shop advertisement, I could make out a printed tooth on one of the envelopes. I saw the letterhead from the Department of Consumer Affairs: Dental Hygiene Committee of California.

It's here! My letter had finally arrived! I couldn't open it fast enough; I tore open the envelope and pulled the letter out skimming all the words until my eyes honed in on the word *Congratulations*.

Out on the street, I squealed as I carefully bounced Brittney in a motherly victory dance.

"We passed the exam!" I whispered to my sleepy baby, "We did it!!"

I joyfully hurried back to the house to call everyone—starting with Nate!

It took a few months, but by trial and error, we had started to get the hang of this parenting thing. Brittney finally began to understand that people are usually awake during the day, and sleep during the night. She was now sleeping longer at night. Through complete teamwork, Nate and I would actually manage to get some undisturbed sleep every night, too. Nate's nocturnal tendencies had come in handy with a baby in the house. He would take over when he would get home from his night classes, so I could go to bed. Then, when he was ready to get some sleep, I'd take over whenever Brittney would wake up.

My dental office welcomed me back after I graduated. I was happy to be back, and even more excited that I was returning as a hygienist. Working in the same office with Carrie—once again—made me love my job all the more. By now she had a year's worth of experience, giving me comfort that my *Big Sister* would be right there if I had any questions.

Nate and I had purposely scheduled our lives around Brittney. I was able to work a six-hour afternoon shift a few days a week. It worked out great—I got to spend every morning with Brittney. My afternoon hours gave Nate the freedom to accept subbing positions when the phone rang in the morning. He would work until mid-afternoon when the students were dismissed for the day. On the days that Nate and I both worked, there was a two-hour gap where we would both be gone. We arranged for Paul's younger sister, Christy, to babysit for us until Nate returned from subbing. He was then able to spend some time with Brittney before he would leave for night school. For those times in the evening when Nate had to leave for school and I wasn't home from work yet, the grandparents were more than happy to fill in the gaps. It was hectic, but we managed very well.

Once I was home again, and we waved goodbye to the grandparents, Brittney and I would have dinner and spend some time together until Daddy got home. I loved being a mommy. Our baby girl had completely turned our world upside-down, making it better and more fulfilling than I could ever have imagined. The days were long and tiring, but our growing family made it all worth it. Life was good, and we were happy. Before falling to sleep for the night, I would thank God for His many blessings. And then I would ask Him for just one thing—a few hours of undisturbed sleep, before doing it all over again the next day!

The sounds of a football game echoed through the house as I pulled an adorable pink onesie over Brittney's head. Although I had a few Barbie's growing up, they were never as much fun to dress up and play with as Brittney. Nate's shouting from the living room was the only thing louder than the game. I looked down at Brittney and smiled as I finished getting her dressed. "Daddy must be watching the Chargers," I said as I nuzzled her nose. Her little baby smile melted my heart.

I carried Brittney down the hallway. Nate was sitting on the couch, eyes glued to the TV. "Ohhhh, that's why you're getting all worked up," I chuckled, noticing all of the red and gold football players on the screen.

Nate loved football. His favorite games were either watching and cheering his beloved Chargers to win, or rooting for his least favorite team, the 49ers, to lose. Whenever the 49ers played, whoever was playing against them became Nate's favorite team for the day. Today, he was the world's biggest Seahawks fan. He was leaning so far forward, it was almost as if there was a magnetic force pulling him toward the TV. I handed Brittney over to Nate as he intently watched the game. It was hard for me to leave her; she was so cute all dressed up with a giant strawberry embroidered on her bottom.

"I just changed her," I told Nate. I had a few quick errands to run, but the most important thing I needed to get done was grocery shopping. Brittney needed more Gerber jars to get her through the week, and food, in general, was sparse. "Her bottle's in the fridge and she still has a half jar of applesauce to finish when she gets hungry..."

"Go, Go, GO!" Nate yelled out.

"Nate, are you listening to me?"

"IT'S GOOD!"

I turned around to see Nate holding Brittney's arms up like the field goal. I rolled my eyes and chuckled. "Nate, I need to leave."

"Yeah, Babe, I got it."

I smiled and kissed Nate and our baby girl goodbye.

I have to admit, it was nice to run a few errands by myself. As I checked things off my TO-DO list, I kept thinking about how much faster I was at getting things done without having to take Brittney with me. Although, after five months of being a mom, I was getting quite good at doing things with a baby in my arms. Things like holding a baby while picking up dry cleaning, or filling the car up with gas while finding lost pacifiers that had disappeared somewhere between the seats. It was, however, strangely lonesome walking the aisles of the grocery store without my little buddy. I usually had Brittney in her car seat, fastened to the grocery cart, so she could help me with the shopping.

I eagerly grabbed an entire case of Coke and added it to the cart. I needed caffeine! All those late nights of studying in college were like a mere introduction to the sleep deprivation of having a baby in the house. Although Brittney was finally sleeping longer, for months now, I had wondered if I would ever sleep through the night again.

With my errands complete, I walked in the door, grocery bags dangling from my arms. "Hey guys, I'm home," I said, setting the bags down on the kitchen floor.

"Hey, Princess," Nate called from the living room. He and Brittney were still watching football. I walked over to give Nate and my baby girl a kiss.

"Did she eat?" I asked, battling the commotion from the game, as I walked back to the kitchen and slid cereal boxes into our empty cupboard.

"Yeah, she ate," Nate answered.

I opened the fridge to put the milk in and noticed her bottle and jar of applesauce sitting on the top shelf, untouched. I paused. Confused for a moment, I called out, "What did she eat?"

"Nachos," he casually replied.

I almost dropped the milk from my hand. "Nachos!?" I stopped what I was doing and went over to check on Brittney. Nate had propped her up with pillows and blankets against the corner of the couch. "Please tell me you are not serious. She's just a baby!"

He shrugged, "What? She liked them."

It obviously didn't even cross my mind to tell Nate NOT to feed Brittney nachos. I wouldn't even think of bringing that up. Who would?! She didn't even have teeth yet; her lower front teeth weren't even due to erupt until next month. I was a super safe mom with no plans to feed her solid food until her pediatrician said it was time.

I stared at Nate with both hands on my hips. He looked at me with a guilty grin. I looked from him to the crumpled Taco Bell bag on the coffee table, and then over to Brittney. She was contently sitting there sucking on her pacifier as the football players ran across the screen in front of her. I let out a defeated sigh. I tried to be mad, but like always, he somehow ended up making me laugh instead.

"Nachos! Are you kidding me, Babe?" I shook my head. "I hope you at least mashed them up or something!"

I laughed and mumbled to myself as I returned to the kitchen to put away the groceries. "Just because I'm laughing doesn't mean I'm not mad at you," I called out.

Nate rushed into the kitchen, dramatically reenacting the football game with Brittney as the football safely tucked under his arm, and the crumpled Taco Bell bag proudly displayed in his other hand. He made all the sound effects, weaving through the grocery bags on the floor and imaginary football players coming at him. He threw the bag, with gusto, into the trash can and lifted the baby up, wiggling her around in the air. "Touchdown!" he cheered. I tried to maintain my mad face, but Nate's humor and Brittney's cooing at all her daddy's fun was too much for me to resist. I threw my hands up in exasperation, then laughed along with them.

I'll just need to remember to add *No Nachos* to my list of baby instructions next time I go grocery shopping.

"Okay birthday girls, smile!"

CLICK

Mom brought the camera down from her eye, and let out a laugh. "Awww... look at her ear!" my mom said smiling.

I turned Brittney toward me and laughed along with my mom. The pink headband on top of her light brown, wavy hair was a little too big, causing her left ear to bend down slightly as it slid toward the front of her head. I pulled the headband back in place again, and fixed the white collar of her matching pink polka dot dress as I set her back down on the dining room floor. As she walked off—in a Frankenstein kind of way—the headband began to slide right back to the front, pushing her ear forward again. Brittney was one-year-old now and head-to-toe adorable.

Our house was completely set up for the occasion. It seemed every room was full of decorations that stayed true to the themed colors of pink, blue, and yellow. Every balloon, streamer, napkin, and plate had matching patterns and colors. Presents wrapped in colorful paper were gathered together on a table in the living room. Some of the boxes were so big, I couldn't believe they were for a one year old. Family and friends were beginning to arrive as Mary—who went by *Gramma* to Brittney—placed a tray of cut veggies on the dining room table. "Do you think this is enough food for everyone?"

I nodded as I popped a few carrots in my mouth. "I'm pretty sure there's enough food here to feed the entire neighborhood."

Jon and Justin came up behind their mom for a few handfuls of *Fritos*, reminding me why preparing plenty of food was ingrained into Mary's head. With a mouthful of chips, Justin bent down to let Brittney toddle right into his arms. Brittney giggled as her uncles played with her.

"Hey, Shelley!" Paul smiled as he came through the door. The smokey smell of Santa Maria style tri-tip followed him in from the front yard where Nate and my dad were barbecuing.

I gave him a hug, "Hi, Paul! Wow, it's great to see you! Chris!" I smiled, seeing him walk in as I was hugging Paul. "I can't believe you guys came home from college for this," I said walking over to hug Chris.

"Are you kidding? We wouldn't miss it! Matt should be here soon." Paul looked over at Brittney and laughed, "Man, she's gotten big! She walks like a Baker, that's for sure."

Soon Nate and my dad came in with a big platter of tri-tip to set in the middle of all the trays and bowls of food our moms had been busy preparing. "Here's your hockey puck, Babe," Nate teased as he handed me a plate with an extra well-done piece of tri-tip with burnt ends. I smiled at Nate and took a bite. My dad laughed, shaking his head. "Shelley has always liked it that way… I just don't understand it."

"You guys don't know what you're missing!" I said, taking another bite. It was a nice change for me to actually get a moment to eat a warm plate of food instead of watching over a toddler who had just learned to walk.

Brittney was surrounded by love. If she wasn't playing with her aunt and uncles, she was being swooned over by Carrie (her godmother), or being followed around by grandparents trying to capture every single moment on film. She was the first grandchild for our parents, the first niece for our siblings, and the first baby in our group of friends.

After everyone was done eating, we gathered in the living room to watch the birthday girl open her presents. She balled the wrapping paper into her little fists as I untied the ribbons from each of her gifts. Justin walked over carrying a big box, a present he had gotten her with his own saved up money.

"Brittney, you got a horse!" I exclaimed, helping her tear off the paper. It was a plastic horse, low to the ground with big red wheels as its hooves. Brittney wasn't listening—her attention was on the shiny trimming in her hands. Nate helped Justin get it out of the box, while I assisted Brittney with opening the remaining gifts. Thanking everyone for the darling toddler outfits and toys galore, Brittney waved her ribbons as if she had won first place.

Although it was my birthday as well, and I had presents of my own to open, I was more excited to give Brittney her present from Mommy and Daddy. I had an artist paint a large wooden toy chest specifically to match her nursery. It was pink with little animals on it. Her name *Brittney Mae* was written across the top in big white painted letters. It would be a great new home for all the toys she had just been given.

The grandparents served everyone cake while Nate and I got Brittney ready in her highchair for her birthday cake surprise. Her whole face lit up as her dad brought in a small round cake and set it on the tray in front of her. Brittney took a moment to squish around in the frosting with her hands as she tried to figure out what it was. The moment she put her fingers in her mouth and tasted sugar for the first time, she was an explosion of excitement and energy.

Her first sugar rush caused her to start pounding the cake with her little fists. We stood back, giving her free reign over the cake and, boy, did she put on a show! Brittney slapped both hands into the frosting and screamed each time she took a bite. Everyone laughed, watching her dig to the bottom layer, scooping the cake into her mouth. She wiggled her frosted hands at us as if showing off her mess to everyone and the flashing camera. She was her own party's finale.

Once it got to the point where there was more frosting on Brittney than there was on the tray, I picked her up and carried her straight to the tub. Her sugar rush continued as I gave her a bath. I was laughing too much to mind that she had gotten my new birthday outfit all wet and sticky. I pulled a fresh shirt over Brittney's head and we went to join everyone in the front yard.

I held up Brittney's hand as we waved goodbye to a few friends who were leaving. Nate leaned against a truck in the street as we all stood there hanging out in the beautiful summer sunshine. Justin had brought out the horse he'd gotten Brittney and the two of them were playing in the driveway. It was so fun having everyone over and being able to catch up with our friends. Paul, Chris, and Matt laughed at the difference between this birthday party and the college parties they were used to.

All of a sudden, Brittney started crying out from the driveway. Our once cheerful birthday girl was seated on her new pony wailing dramatic sobs. Justin was holding her hands to the handlebars, completely frozen. He didn't know what to do with a crying baby.

"Oh, Honey," I said, coming to the rescue. I picked her up and rocked her in my arms as big tears ran down her cheeks.

"Sorry," Justin muttered, retreating into the house.

Just a few moments later, Brittney was grinning, showing off her four front teeth as she played with her dad in the grass. I went inside to grab more ice for the cooler outside when I heard a sniffle coming from down the hall. That sniffle didn't belong to my baby girl; I could see her smiling from the opened door. I followed the sniffles to our bedroom and found Justin sitting at the edge of the bed. It was very unlike him to be alone. He was usually hanging out with someone. As I walked into the room, the closer I got, I could see his dampened eyelashes.

"Justin, what's wrong?" I asked, sitting next to him. He hung his head looking down at the carpet.

"I didn't mean to hurt her," he confessed, eyes still on the floor.

"Hurt who?" I asked.

"Brittney. The wheels rolled over her toes."

"Oh, Brittney! Of course you didn't mean to. Babies get hurt and cry all the time," I said in a comforting tone. He shrugged off my words.

"But what if she thinks that I hurt her? What if she doesn't like me anymore?" He looked up at me, genuinely concerned that he had just ruined his relationship with his niece.

"Really," I assured him, "she's forgotten all about her toes and she's out playing in the yard right now, probably wondering where you went. She LOVES playing with you, especially when you and Nate dress her up and play Baby Knievel." That got him smiling. "How do you guys even come up with these games?" I chuckled as we got up. I changed the subject as we walked out to join everyone in the yard again. "Are you excited for our vacation?"

Justin smiled and nodded. He would be Brittney's backseat buddy on our trip to Southern California. When Brittney saw Uncle Justin return to the front yard, she held out her arms for him. I smiled watching him play with her, picking up right where they had left off.

Brittney was being fussy.

"Justin, could you check her diaper, please?" I asked from the passenger seat. Although we had an early start—we were only a couple of hours into our drive to San Diego—it seemed as though chaos was already brewing. "Nate, can you pull over soon? I need a bathroom break."

"We just left the house."

"We *did not* just leave the house," I scoffed.

Justin shook his head, "Nope, she's dry."

Ever since the birthday party, he finally understood that Brittney was a toddler, and toddlers cried ... a lot! I handed him a cracker to give to her. This was our first road trip with our little girl, so I had packed her diaper bag full of everything I could think of—including snacks for moments like this.

Nate was at the wheel playing air guitar along to Def Leppard's new album. If the road trip was up to him, Nate would skip all the rest stops and drive straight through to San Diego.

Brittney was screaming for a break. She squirmed in her car seat, the cracker being only a temporary distraction. It seemed she and the band's lead singer were screaming a duet. As if it wasn't loud enough, Nate joined in, mimicking Brittney's tearful pitch. For a brief moment, Brittney paused, her little eyebrows scrunched together as if she were disgruntled by her daddy's impersonation of her. Justin and I leaned forward into our seat belts, laughing at Brittney's apparent confusion and Nate's spot-on impersonation of a crying baby. Brittney took in a breath and let out a brand new scream, taking the noise to a whole new level.

Justin clapped his hands over his ears. "You're making it worse!" he yelled.

I held my stomach. "Nate ... stop making me laugh! ... I have to go to the bathroom!"

Nate let out his last impersonation, but Brittney continued to scream. Due to the fact that we were already in the car, our faithful backup plan of taking her for a drive was shot. I passed Justin her blanket and pacifier, which were basically useless at this point.

"Aren't you glad to be missing school for all this?" I joked with Justin.

He smiled, still holding his ears. "Anything's better than school."

"You're staying in school," Nate said.

"Justin, you have more friends than anyone I've ever met. You're so smart. Just pass all those classes and you'll be good," I added.

Justin let out a deep sigh and then instantly switched gears. "I'm hungry. Can we stop for some snacks?"

"We ate before we left!" Nate groaned.

"Nate, will you just pull over!"

He growled at me and then looked through the rearview mirror and growled at Justin in the backseat. Right up the road, Nate pulled the car to the side where there was no sign of a restroom, just dirt and weeds.

"You're all driving me nuts!" He picked up the map from the dashboard and rolled it into a pointer. "This one is being a big baby, you need to water the flowers… *again,* and Justin needs food. At this rate, we'll never make it to the game!" He sighed dramatically.

The cassette had finished a few miles back, so all that filled the car was Brittney's overdue demands for escape, and Justin's and my laughter. Bugging Nate was really fun.

Another ten minutes down the road we found a gas station where Brittney could toddle on a patch of grass, Justin could get a snack, and I could run into the ladies' room.

"Go now or forever hold your piss!" Nate said, as he looked at the map and checked the baseball game tickets.

Justin laughed as I rolled my eyes and smirked, "Very funny."

Once we returned to the car, Nate briefed us on the plan. "Okay, the game doesn't start until three. As long as we make NO MORE stops, we'll be able to make it on time." The break brought about a less chaotic drive and within hours we arrived at our destination.

Justin snapped a photo of Nate and me outside the stadium with Brittney strapped to my back. It was our first baseball park to mark off our list. Nate was extra fired up because Jack Murphy Stadium was also where the Chargers played during football season. Hundreds of fans, many dressed in the team colors of blue and orange, made their way toward the front gates.

"Are you really gonna see all the baseball parks?" Justin asked, as we showed our tickets at the gate.

"Yep!" Nate said.

"That's SO cool! I want to go on another trip with you guys, okay?"

"That'd be great," I smiled as we walked into the stadium.

We bought baseball park food for a late lunch and then carried it all to our orange seats. Sipping on sodas, we listened to the cheering fans. The announcers introduced each player as they stepped out onto home plate. San Diego was the perfect place for an outdoor stadium. The weather was beautiful, and just beyond the scoreboard was a panoramic view of the hillside. The boys watched the game while I took pictures of the players running around the perfectly manicured green grass of the baseball field.

Brittney didn't watch the game. She found the peanut shells crunching under her shoes to be way more exciting than baseball. I took a few more pictures as both brothers were leaning forward intently watching the game—their blonde hair peeking out from underneath the rim of their baseball caps. Throughout the game, Nate would point out different players that he had on baseball cards in his collection. Justin liked sports, but he was mostly enjoying every second of missing school to hang out with his brother. He wore his excitement all over his face. Brittney alternated from my lap, to Nate's, to Uncle Justin's, and then back to mine again—it was a challenge entertaining a toddler for the length of a baseball game. I bounced her on my knee, and we watched the wave travel around the stadium. When it got to us, I lifted Brittney's arms up in the air as it passed by.

After the game was over, we headed to our hotel. We had a full weekend ahead of us: Dodger Stadium in Los Angeles tomorrow, and the following day we would go to Anaheim Stadium to watch the Angels play. In between the baseball games, we had plans to go to Hollywood and Medieval Times. Even though we were down here for baseball games, we wanted to take advantage of being in Southern California and pack as much as we could into our trip.

We sat out on the balcony of our hotel room enjoying the view of the city lights. The light breeze of the Santa Ana winds felt refreshing as I leaned back in my chair and looked over at Nate and Justin who were talking about the game. Brittney was sitting on my lap, finally calming down after a long, exciting day. With my camera always nearby, I wanted to get one last picture for the night. Trying to get Nate and Justin to actually pose for a picture was sometimes an ordeal, but tonight it was easy. I snapped a picture of them from my chair as they leaned side by side against the wall of the balcony.

I smiled, "One ball park down, two to go! How many ball parks are there again?" I asked.

"Twenty-nine," Nate answered with a grin. I looked down at Brittney fast asleep in my arms. She was out cold. I think we might actually get some sleep tonight!

The dental office was operating like usual, but something about it being Veterans Day made the whole vibe of the day much more peaceful. Although our office was open, many people had the day off—including Nate and Mary. I had enjoyed every moment with him and Brittney before coming into work for the day. Nate had plans to use the rest of his day off to study for his upcoming midterms, either at the library or his mom's house.

I was almost done with my second patient of the day. All I had left to do was to update his periodontal measurements. At the beginning of the appointment, I had buzzed for the hygiene assistant to come in and chart for me, but I was still waiting for her. I looked at the clock; my next patient was due to arrive soon. As I waited for her, I double-checked my patient's now smooth teeth to make sure I hadn't missed anything. He was a long-time patient of the office, a very nice middle-aged gentleman that really needed to remember to floss every day rather than just before seeing me for his cleaning.

Where was she? I peeked out into the hallway to try and see where the assistant was. She was usually so good at popping in when one of us buzzed for her. I chatted with my patient a little more. Finally, it got to the point where I needed to start setting up for my next patient.

"Let's get you set up for your next appointment. I'll get your perio charting next time," I said as I led him to the front desk. As I said my goodbyes to him, the front door of the lobby burst open and the hygiene assistant came rushing in.

"I'm so sorry I'm late!" She hurried over to the time clock and punched in, "There was a huge accident. Both lanes on Highway 68 are basically at a complete stop." I watched her slip into her lab coat and walk through the door, making her way to the back office.

"This is the first time you are hearing about something that will affect the rest of your life."

I just stood there, absolutely riveted. I looked at the girls at the front desk; they carried on like normal. No one else seemed to have heard the voice I had just heard. My whole body was covered in goose bumps, and in that moment, I knew that I had heard the voice of God. My stomach tightened as I instantly thought of Nate. What if he hadn't gone to Mary's or the library? What if he went to his school in Monterey to study instead? He would've taken Highway 68 to get there.

I excused myself from the desk and hurried to the sterilization room to use the phone. I didn't want anyone to see how panicked

I was, especially from something so unexplainable. I dialed the number to our house.

"Hello?" Paul's sister answered. She was at our house babysitting, which meant that Nate had already left.

"Hi, uh, Christy?" I clutched the phone, "Do you know where Nate is? There's been an accident on Highway 68 and I, I just want to make sure he's okay."

"Yeah, I heard ... I'm watching it on the news right now. They haven't said anything other than it was a two-car collision or something like that."

As I held the phone to my ear, I caught a glimpse of the assistant seating my next patient. "I have a patient waiting for me ... could you please try to find out some more details of the accident?"

"Sure. Let me call the hospital. My mom should be working today. I'll see if she knows anything."

"Okay, thanks, Christy. I'll call you in a bit," I said and hung up.

My heart was pounding as I walked into my room. It took every ounce of self-control to hide my emotions from my patient as my mind started jumping to worst-case-scenarios. But if it wasn't bad, then why would God tell me that this would change my life? I said hello to my patient and started to review his health history. After taking his check-up X-rays, I reclined the chair. I opened a bag of sterilized instruments and pushed any thoughts of one of those cars in the accident being ours.

Oh God, please ... please, God ...

All I could think to do was beg God. I just kept reciting *Please, God* over and over again until I found a moment to excuse myself back to the sterilization room to call home.

"Christy? Any news yet?" I asked, trying to keep my voice steady.

"I … I'm so sorry … I heard one of Nate's brothers might've been in the accident … I'm not sure though … I'm still making some calls to try and figure it all out."

My heart stopped. *Oh, my God! Please God, let them be okay …* Just the possibility of one of them being in an accident made me sick. "Have you heard from Nate, is he okay? Which brother was it?"

"I-I don't know. It might not have been either of them. I don't recognize either of the cars from the news footage. I'm still trying to get all of the information I can. I'll keep calling around."

"You have my work number. Just call me as soon as you find anything else out!"

"Okay, I will."

"Thanks, Christy. Goodbye," and I hung up the phone.

The office seemed to be spinning. My mind raced. What do I do? I could hear the doctor drilling from one of the rooms down the hall … do I interrupt him in the middle of the procedure and tell him that I need to leave? Should I leave? I don't even know for sure if Jon or Justin were involved. They could be fine for all I know. If I did leave, who would see the rest of my patients?

I didn't want to draw any attention to myself. In a daze, I returned to my room and went into automatic as I tried figuring out what I was going to do. I bit my lip, resisting every urge to run out the door and rush home. As I started scaling my patient's teeth, I looked up and saw Nate standing in the doorway. I had never seen my husband so serious. His face was still, no smile lines and no gleam in his eyes. The assistant took over as I walked into the hallway with Nate. I was breathless, just incredibly thankful that Nate was here and not part of whatever had happened on the highway.

We went into an empty room across from the front desk and shut the door behind us. Nate stood in front of me, his skin looking pale. He hung his head slightly, his shoulders rising and falling as he tried to get out his words.

"...He's gone..." he choked out, his voice cracking as he gasped for a breath.

"Jon or Justin?" I asked, swallowing hard.

"...Justin..."

I closed my eyes tight and sank into Nate, my knees almost buckling. We held one another. My grip tightened, as if holding him tighter would keep us from completely dropping to the ground. Nothing was stable... nothing was quite real... but as long as I held Nate, I knew that he was there with me.

We stayed in that room for I don't even know how long. Long enough to catch our breath, I guess. My patients were rescheduled. We drove home to quickly pick up Brittney before going over to Mary's. I didn't change out of my scrubs. I can't say I even thought about it, or anything during those moments.

The car ride was silent. No radio. No talking. Just our still bodies in the unsettling silence. When we arrived, we had to park quite a few houses down from Mary's. The street was full of cars. A lot of people were over. Although Justin didn't care much for school, he was very popular. And Mary seemed to know everyone in town, so naturally when people found out, they started pouring into her house for support.

"The sheriff and coroner were here before I came to get you... they said it was quick—he didn't feel any pain..." Nate said, in almost a whisper, as we made our way to the front door.

Walking into the house was a surreal experience. The house was crowded with people... yet a silence filled the air. It made sense. I mean, what could anyone possibly say to a mother who just lost a child? I walked over to Mary and hugged her like I had never hugged her before—a long, unspoken *I'm so sorry*. She sobbed and trembled. Her heartbreaking tears made the moment even more unbearable. I turned and saw Jon and gave him the same kind of hug. It tore me apart to see everyone so devastated. Brittney, in her innocence, was happy to see Gramma and Uncle Jon, and hurried over to them. They immediately picked her up, bringing a slight smile to their faces even in the midst of utter tragedy.

We all started gathering in the living room as the local news station continued broadcasting the accident. Mary sat down on a chair directly in front of the television screen. Jon took a seat on the floor, dropping his head into the palms of his hands. He slightly rocked back and forth.

Nate and I sat next to each other on the couch as we watched the news footage of two completely totaled cars. The news anchor explained that a group of five teenagers was driving in a Camaro down the highway and most likely either got distracted or lost control of the wheel, causing a head-on collision with a Suburban in oncoming traffic. Each passenger in the Suburban, although severely injured, had survived and had been taken to the hospital for treatment, but all five teenagers in the Camaro were pronounced dead at the scene. I watched in horror as they showed a helicopter view of five blue body bags lying next to each other on the side of the highway.

Someone quickly got up and turned off the television. Mary hunched over in her chair in absolute agony as people surrounded her desperately trying to console her, all the while feeling so helpless and in shock themselves. The mixture of complete silence and wailing was absolutely soul crushing.

Nate took it upon himself to be the one to tell Jerry. We went into Justin's bedroom, which used to be Nate's old room, to make the call. I cried silently as Nate, with trembling hands, choked out the news to his dad that would devastate him. The conversation wasn't long…they didn't say many words to each other…it was mostly silence and muffled words as Nate explained what had happened. After Nate hung up the phone, we stayed together in the dark room for a while, just sitting on the bed together. We stayed at the house until late into the night. Eventually, we had to leave and get Brittney home and into bed.

The drive home had put Brittney right to sleep and I was thankful that she had been so good all day. Nate carried Brittney to her crib. I followed behind, watching him hold her so close, so tenderly…holding onto her as if reminding himself that he still had her. Brittney snuggled into her sleeping position, innocent and absolutely unaware of what had happened today. As I kissed her forehead, I wondered if she would remember Justin. He loved her so much and spent so much time with her…would she remember any of that at all?

We were both emotionally exhausted and restless. I could hear Nate building a fire in the living room. I got into some warm pajamas and pulled on a hoodie for extra warmth. I felt so cold. The chill wasn't from the autumn air—it was inside of me. It was like my blood had stopped circulating, leaving me chilled down to my bones.

I walked out into the living room, lit only by the fire. Nate sat on the couch staring into the pyramid of flames—orange flickers of light danced over his skin. His face was blank and his eyes were empty. The firelight that was reflecting in his pupils was the only source of movement. My active, full-speed-ahead husband was motionless for the first time since I'd known him. Even his knee refused its natural bounce. It deeply saddened me to see him this way and to know there was nothing I could do to take the pain away. I sat next to him, my head resting against his shoulder.

After a few moments, I softy spoke words that broke the silence, "I'm so sorry, Honey… I am so, so, sorry." My eyes filled with tears again.

Nate couldn't speak, so he reached for my hand instead. As we sat there in the dark, I thought about God. I felt so confused. I didn't understand how God could let this happen and I certainly didn't understand prayer anymore. I *thought* I had understood prayer… but now… now I wasn't sure I understood the purpose of prayer at all. Mary prayed for her boys every single day, specifically for their safety. Did God hear her? And if He did, what did her prayers matter if He was just going to take Justin anyway? God knew all along that Justin was going to die today. Why pray if God already has His plan for us? I sat there confused and cold.

Giving Nate his space, I moved to the floor, sitting with my legs pulled tight to my chest in front of the fire. I grabbed the poker and started adjusting the burning logs. There was nothing to say, nothing to break reality… Justin was fifteen, a sophomore, the youngest Baker brother… and gone. How could this be? We just took a trip together. He ate dinner with us, played games with Nate, and there were many times when I would pick him up from school so he could spend some time with Brittney.

I could feel the warmth on my skin, and as I stared into the fire, the flames began to hypnotize me into a deep state of thought. My mind began drifting back to a vivid childhood memory of me uncontrollably somersaulting in slow motion. As I rolled, I could see horse shoes and other objects, flying through the air in the back of our family car. There was no noise. No fear. But rather, a disembodied sensation of complete tranquility. Time didn't resume until our car had come to a complete stop. I remember my dad pulling me out of the car through the shattered window—with glass all over the asphalt. The sound of my mom screaming was the first thing I heard when the noise came funneling back. Our totaled Ford station wagon and twenty-four-foot trailer had jack-knifed across the highway — their wheels were still spinning in the air. My family and I had been in a major car accident. The First Responders were shocked that we all had survived with only a few small cuts from the broken glass. I was certain that Justin had not felt pain or been scared. I believed that, in some crazy way, it had been peaceful for him too. Nate and I sat for hours watching the fire burn down into embers.

The days that followed seemed to be nothing more than a melancholy blur. Time was different, the days all blended together, and grief was smothering. Nate dealt with his pain by keeping himself busy. He single-handedly organized and planned almost every aspect of the funeral arrangements. It was constant phone calls, gathering pictures, writing announcements, and choosing songs for the service. He also handled decisions for the viewing, the burial, and the gathering at Mary's house after the service. Although Mary was torn apart, she remained very strong and handled herself better than anyone could have expected. She showed her gratitude for all the people that came over for support by asking how they were doing and offering to feed them anything she had in the house. When Mary was alone, she journaled, cried, and prayed constantly. Jon dealt with his pain by leaving. Being around the house with sad people grieving Justin was more than he could bear, so he spent most of his time with friends doing things outside the home.

On the day of the funeral, family, friends, and countless students from Salinas High School packed the pews of St. Paul's Episcopal Church. My family, along with Paul, Chris, and Matt's families, sat close to the Bakers in the first few rows. Brittney was too active to sit through the service so Carrie offered to stand in the back of the church and hold her. If Brittney got noisy, she would take her for a walk so that she would not disturb the service. I knew she was in good hands as the service started.

I sat there listening to the Spring portion of Vivaldi's "Four Seasons." Mary chose that particular part of the symphony because it was Justin's favorite. Everything was a blur as I looked at the bronze casket in front of us near the alter, and then out into a sea of mourning faces. I had never seen so many people cry at the same time. It was completely heart breaking. I thought about what God had told me just days ago, and He was right — my life had changed forever.

It's interesting how one discovers more about a person after their death. As people gathered at Mary's house after the burial, stories of Justin began to fill the rooms.

Growing up, his interests had changed from Teenage Mutant Ninja Turtles to MacGyver. Because of his fascination with this Secret Agent's ability to use mundane materials to solve any problem, Justin and a few of his friends had made survival packages that held emergency water, canned food, matches, a whistle, and over-the-counter aspirin, and had hidden them all over the house. While one of Justin's friends was telling us the story, he led us around Mary's house pulling out small packages from random places like under Justin's bed and in the cupboard below the kitchen sink.

I also learned where some of the food from the Baker household went. Friends began sharing stories about watching Justin gather food from his house to donate to the local homeless shelter off Soledad Street. Grocery bags would hang from his handlebars as he rode his bike through the neighborhood and crossed busy roads to get to the shelter, Dorothy's Kitchen.

The stories were bittersweet. We all loved hearing them, but those happy memories would always revert back to despair once the realization of Justin being gone settled in again. When Mary sat down next to us, a classmate of Justin's pulled a chair up to her and sat down. He was quiet for a moment before he started to tell Mary a story about Justin he said he'd never forget.

"I was with Justin the morning of the accident," he said, pain reflecting in his eyes. "We had Driver's Ed together. When it was over, we still had time before school was going to start. I don't even remember really how it came up. Justin started talking about the french toast you made him for breakfast. I told him I hadn't eaten anything and I was hungry. He said he had five bucks for lunch and offered to get me some food before first period, so we walked across the street to Foster's Freeze. Justin was irritated that he had to go to school on Veterans Day and was talking about maybe ditching that day with a few of his friends. We sat at that big round booth in the back... I don't really know why I did it, but I started using my pocket knife to carve something on the table. It was one of those stars with a circle around it... I'd seen them on posters and stuff. Anyway, Justin saw what I was doing and told me that it was the sign of the devil. He told me to carve something else instead... it was some kind of fish symbol. I asked him what it meant, and he said 'Jesus.' "

We were all choked up by his story. Mary sat silently and wept, this time with a proud smile on her face. With all of this pain and anguish, it gave me comfort to know that Mary, or any of us, would never have to guess what happened to Justin when he died. He was in Heaven with Jesus Himself, waiting for her and the rest of us to get there.

Chapter 6

"Let's Hear It for the Boy" by Deniece Williams

"JERRY, DID WE GET a colander, I hope?" I asked my father-in-law, as I searched through the bags sitting on the kitchen floor.

"A what?" Jerry asked with a raised eyebrow. You'd think I had just spoken to him in a different language.

I chuckled, "You know, a colander. It's like a bowl with holes in it. I can't remember if we got one," I said, pulling things out of the last bag. "Nope, we must have forgotten. I guess I'll find *another* way to drain the potatoes," I smiled, shaking my head.

I was used to Jerry's bachelor lifestyle with the bare minimum of household items. Ever since our first trip to visit Jerry in Seattle, I knew not to expect anything more in the kitchen than non-fat milk, salt and pepper, and a cupboard packed with cereal. I had brought some things from home that I knew I would need for preparing a Thanksgiving dinner. However, space in our suitcases was limited as I had nestled utensils, a candle, and a turkey baster in-between our clothes, hairdryer, and Brittney's beloved pink blanket.

As usual, right after landing at the airport, Jerry had driven us straight to our favorite restaurant in Seattle, Thai Heaven. After dinner, grocery shopping at QFC was our next stop before making our way to Jerry's house. The store was packed and so was our grocery cart by the time we were finished. After unloading the car full of suitcases and brown paper bags, we all went out again to Target. This time we had to buy some kitchen essentials like a blender, mixer, cutting board, and a big aluminum pan to roast the turkey.

"I'll tell you, Shelley, if it wasn't for you, I wouldn't have half this stuff. But all the shopping is worth it to get a homemade Thanksgiving dinner. Are you going to make your gravy?"

"Yep," I said with a smile.

"Ooohooohooo" he jested, rubbing his hands together with enthusiastic anticipation. I laughed, noticing the similarities between how Nate and Jerry reacted to food.

Brittney's giggles traveled into the kitchen. Jerry and I both peeked our heads over the countertop where we could look straight into the living room. Nate and Brittney were playing on the carpet. It was so nice to hear some laughter and to see some smiles again. There hadn't been much of that over the past few weeks. The innocence of a toddler helped to lighten our first holiday without Justin.

Mary and Jon had stayed in Salinas for Thanksgiving. Mary needed some rest and for things to slow down giving her time to grieve. We took comfort in knowing that, although most of her family had returned home to Washington, her mom was still there and she had a constant flow of visitors checking in on her. Jon had plans to spend his time with friends. They were a big support to him getting through his first Thanksgiving without his younger brother. Nate and I, on the other hand, just needed to get away. A trip to one of our favorite places would be just what we needed to get a break from all the sorrow. Life since the accident had been like trying to walk around wearing a cold, heavy, wet blanket. Being here with Jerry made us feel relieved — or at least distracted. We were thankful for the plane tickets Jerry sent us so we could come visit. Jerry needed to be distracted, too.

It had been a busy morning with food preparation, but I was enjoying every minute of it... all except holding the raw turkey. I can't stand handling raw meat — and the disgusting bag of guts stuffed in the middle! My mom usually did that part, but she was at home in California, so today it was all up to me.

The house was filling with the aroma of the roasting turkey. After checking on the boiling pot of potatoes, I walked over to the living room. I laughed when I saw Brittney wearing big red boxing gloves. Nate had brought his old pair of boxing gloves with us, for really no particular reason. He and Brittney were having their own little boxing match. Nate, on his knees, bobbed and weaved around as our bright-eyed sixteen-month-old took a swing at her daddy. Heavy on the sound effects, Nate was pretending to be injured from her toddler punches. He wiped the sweat from his brow and took on the voice of Rocky Balboa. As he faced his contender in the ring, I grabbed my camera making sure to capture these moments. The match continued until Brittney's little swing turned into a dramatic knock out, and Nate flung himself backwards on the ground. Brittney squealed with laughter and went over to check if her daddy was okay. He popped up, grabbed her, and lifted her up in the air. Her heavy-gloved hands were dangling at her sides.

"When's that turkey going to be ready, Nice Lady?" Nate asked, setting Brittney back down on the floor.

"Soon," I replied as I smiled and walked back into the kitchen.

As I set the last bowl of food on the table, everyone pulled up white plastic lawn chairs brought in from the back yard.

"Dad, you need to get some REAL chairs," Nate laughed.

"What for? I usually eat in the living room on a TV tray," Jerry answered.

Before we took our first bite of the warm bounty of food on the table, we bowed our heads in a prayer. Nate thanked God for the great meal and time together. Brittney's highchair was pulled up next to Gramps—Jerry's chosen name when Brittney was born. With every dish of food that was passed around the table, I would put a small helping on her plate. No Thanksgiving dinner was ever complete without my mom's cranberry salad—a favorite Iowa recipe that had been passed down through the generations. I handed the bowl to Jerry. The recipe was like a taste of home for him. He, like my mom, had been born and raised in Iowa. Making sense as to why Jerry pronounced Washington with an R—*Warshington*—just like my mom did.

"If you guys keep this up, I'm not going to let you leave," Jerry said, "I always look forward to the company. It gets so quiet when you all leave."

Nate chuckled. "Well, I'm sure that you won't miss the mess." He gestured to all the food that had fallen from Brittney's highchair, as well as all of the toys scattered around the house.

Jerry laughed and grabbed for a biscuit. "You know... I've been thinking that it sure would be nice if you or Jon could learn my business. I know you're in law school and all, but *someday* maybe I could teach you some important things about running Marine Title. Sometimes I think about what if something were to happen to me? It would be nice if someone in the family would know what to do. No pressure though. I've always hoped that one of you boys would love the boat business as much as I do. I see now that both you and Jon have your own careers set in motion." Nate smiled. Boat registration had never been a passion for him like it was for his dad.

I sat there listening. I'm sure losing Justin had gotten Jerry—and all of us for that matter—thinking about how fragile life can be. Jerry took his last bite and leaned back in his chair rubbing his stomach. "That was delicious! I haven't eaten that much in a looong time," Jerry moaned with a smile. Nate nodded in agreement as he scrunched up his napkin and tossed it on his plate.

Brittney's short attention span was causing her to try and wiggle free from her chair. I took her straight to the tub, as Nate and Jerry began clearing the table. By the time I returned with Brittney all cleaned up, the table was all cleaned up, too. The guys had made themselves comfortable in the living room as they pushed Play on the worn out *Smokey and the Bandit* movie in the VCR. Even in their food comas, they belly laughed as Sheriff Buford T. Justice was in hot pursuit of the Bandit fleeing in his black Trans-Am. I swear, those two could say every line of that movie!

Brittney cuddled with me on the couch. I gazed out the big bay window that faced Lake Washington and watched occasional planes fly in and out of Sea-Tac Airport in the distance. Nate and Jerry laughing at their favorite movie, along with logs burning in the fireplace, added to the warm ambiance.

Their laughter became background noise as I started thinking about how much I loved Seattle. I had a lot of great memories here—my first taste of Thai food, first time on a kayak, first ferry boat ride, standing at the top of the Space Needle, and watching the amazing 4th of July fireworks reflect in the water from Gas Works Park.

A couple of summers ago, Jerry had rented a sailboat to take the boys and me out for a day on the water. I had never been on a sailboat, especially one so big! Jerry even let me take the wheel. I took pictures of the boys trying to jump on the ducks floating near the boat. Although they never landed on one, they had fun trying.

Now that Justin was gone, I would cherish that day even more than I already did.

Brittney made her way to the carpet. As she began to play with one of her toys, I thought about how much had changed since that summer. I smiled remembering that Nate and I had even picked out Brittney's name during one of our visits to Seattle.

Hmmm, maybe we should consider moving here someday. Nate could learn Jerry's business and I could get a job here. But we'd have to wait, at least until Nate graduated from law school. Nate still had two-and-a-half years of school before he would be finished, so we had plenty of time to think about it. The more I looked out the window and thought about the idea of moving to Seattle, the more I began to like it.

Over the next couple of years, Nate and I would often talk about a possible move to Seattle. We had gone through the dreadful anniversary of Justin's accident—twice now. Mary was understandably different to some extent, no longer wanting to listen to music or put up a Christmas tree. On the other hand, she was an incredible mom and grandma, a caring teacher to her fifth graders, active in church, and even played bridge with her friends.

Jon had taken up photography. Mary had helped out by having a dark room built in her garage. Nate and Jon had started up a small photography business called Access Studio, where the two of them would do weddings and other special occasions. Jon was the photographer, and Nate, in addition to helping Jon with their shoots, handled the business end. All those business classes he minored in at San Jose State had come in handy. Even though Access Studio was never meant to be a long-term commitment for Nate, at least he got to help Jon with his career goals and spend some time with his brother. Nate missed Justin terribly, but he was always strong about it. He had told me once that if he had to lose one of his brothers, he was glad it was Justin. He had been closer with Justin and had no regrets. Now he would have an opportunity to become closer with Jon, and that's exactly what he did.

By the spring semester of Nate's third year of law school, we had made our decision. Once Nate graduated next year, we were going to move to Seattle! Although it would be a temporary move, it was very exciting! With our young family, if we were ever going to do this, now would be the time. We had the flexibility to relocate for a while since Brittney was too young to start school, and our house was a rental. We'd come back to California once Nate passed the bar exam. For now, I would take a test to get a temporary Washington State Hygiene License. Nate already had a job lined up at his dad's successful business, Marine Title Company.

We were excited to call Jerry to let him know about our big decision. We felt really good, but it was far from a quick or spontaneous one. We had put years into thinking about it. There was a lot to consider — like where we would live, and how we could afford everything. The seemingly endless years of college were taking their toll on us financially, but we were almost there. All that was left was for Nate to finish law school and pass the California State Bar Exam.

Jerry was thrilled. He let us know that after Nate learned the ins and outs of the business, he, himself, would need to make a temporary move. There was a company in West Virginia that he needed to work with to research some vintage boat licenses that would benefit his company. He offered for us to house-sit for him, rent free, while he was gone. Even with me making good money as an RDH, what a blessing that would be for us in our attempt to pay college loans, let alone law school! Everything seemed to be coming together and the anticipation of our move only grew over time.

Even though Brittney was still a toddler, she was growing by the day. So was my baby fever. I had recently returned home from my first trip to North Carolina to visit my sister and her husband. The East Coast was their home now that her Military husband was stationed at Fort Bragg. The distance didn't stop me from being there to help bring my newborn niece home from the hospital. I couldn't put her down! By the time I flew back to California, baby fever had overtaken me completely. I wanted another baby, and this time, I wanted a boy.

I came across a magazine article that claimed to have the know-how on how to create a boy or a girl. According to the article, the chances of having a girl are higher. However, there were a few tips in upping the odds of having a boy. I found the article very interesting and had never really thought about the science behind getting pregnant with a specific gender. I guess I had always assumed that you just get what you get. We wanted another baby, and of course I would be thrilled with another girl, but if there were tips that would increase our chances of having a boy, I was excited to try it. The article stated that all there was to it was specific timing and watching the calendar for that window of opportunity. Nate wanted a boy as well, so he agreed to stay at arm's length until the specific time to test this theory—although that was easier said than done.

Even though we were following the plans to get pregnant with a boy, you can never really *plan* these things. One Saturday Nate and I were both getting ready for the day. Nate and my dad had tickets to a Giants game in San Francisco, while I had plans to go out to breakfast and spend the day with Brittney, Mom, and Mary. I was curling my hair at the mirror in the bathroom when I began to feel slight cramping. It dawned on me that the cramping matched up with the calendar. I knew if we were going to have a boy, *the* moment, at least for this month, was now. With my hair only half curled, I went out to the living room to get Nate. He wasn't even finished putting on his shoes before he was taking everything back off again.

Not wanting to say goodbye, we stayed right there in bed, my head resting on Nate's chest. The thumping of his heartbeat echoed in my ear. He hummed a melody while playing air guitar on my outstretched arm. I loved when he did that. The morning sunlight spilled in through the closed bedroom curtains—adding to the warmth that encompassed me. I closed my eyes and smiled, wanting to stay just like this forever. Creating life made this complete togetherness soar to another dimension. The love I felt for Nate radiated from the inside outward. It was the world now that stayed at arm's length, dimming the edges of reality...

I leaned against the door jam and inhaled deeply as I watched Nate putting his shoes back on. Our eyes met and we exchanged smiles. Nate walked over and took my hand. He kissed the top of my hand and then my lips. His old-fashioned charm made my heart melt.

"I love you," I said tenderly.

"I love you too, Princess," he replied with a grin as he grabbed his jacket and left for the baseball game.

At the restaurant that morning, I felt different. I just knew I was pregnant. I looked over at Brittney. My heart filled with happiness that our family was growing. As we sat there talking and eating, I smiled across the table at my mom and Mary, excited about the good news that I hoped to be sharing with them soon.

Mary was very loving and diligent about keeping fresh flowers at Justin's gravesite. Each time we went, I would go to the local florist and buy three Gerbera daisies—one from Nate, another one from me, and the third one from Brittney. We usually would all go together, but if we didn't, Mary would know we had been there when she saw the three Gerbera daisies. I looked down at the headstone marking Justin's gravesite. It was crazy how much things were changing—but this, this would never change. This is where we would visit Justin until Heaven.

Call it mother's intuition, but my feelings about being pregnant were eventually proven true by the pregnancy test, and later, the ultrasound. We couldn't endure over four more months of guessing the baby's gender or wondering if our experiment worked. We had to know. I smiled as the cold, gooey gel was spread across my tummy and the nurse moved the monitor, searching for the best view of our baby. Nate and I had our gazes fixed on the screen. At first, we couldn't tell what we were looking at. We began to make out a big black and white round blob and soon could see that it was our child's head. We watched in awe as the baby's legs kicked. The baby was active and it didn't take long for us to see exactly what we needed for the doctor to confidently declare, "You're having a boy!"

"Do you have a name picked out?" the nurse asked.

"Justin," Nate and I answered with tender smiles, "but we're going to call him by his middle name." There for the first time, in black and white on the ultrasound screen, we had just seen our son, Justin Ryan Baker.

Right after the appointment, we decided to go to breakfast and celebrate. Between bites, I would run out to the payphone outside the restaurant to let people know that we were having a boy! The waitress came over and noticed that I hadn't eaten much of my meal and asked if everything was okay with the food. I happily told her that I was just too excited to eat because we were having a boy. As we left the restaurant, Nate and I agreed that we had one more person to tell.

We walked on the grass with Mary toward the trees at the Garden of Memories Cemetery. She was unaware that we had already been there. As we stood at Justin's gravesite, Mary was greeted with four Gerbera daisies instead of our usual three. She cried happy tears, excited about a new baby, but sad that he would never meet his Uncle Justin. The pain would never go away, but at least now there would be someone to carry on his name.

It was a quiet morning, or maybe it was just me that was quiet. My mind was deep in thought about our baby boy. I loved him so much already, and I hadn't even met him yet. Brittney sat watching cartoons in her PJ's. Nestled in a mound of blankets and pillows on the floor, she watched with full attention as she munched on a bowl of crackers. Although I was in the room with her, the sounds from the movie seemed muffled, almost like the movie was being played from a mile away. I put my hands on my growing tummy. I wondered if Justin knew we are going to have another baby ... did he know it's going to be a boy who will be named after him? I thought about how the Bible says that God knits us together in our mother's womb. Lost in a daydream, I began to imagine Justin holding his nephew in Heaven and thought about what he would tell him. I began picturing a blue sky with big, white, puffy clouds. It was like a scene from a movie playing out in my head—Justin was rocking Ryan on a wooden rocking chair on one of those clouds. I grabbed a pen and began to write what my heart was seeing.

A Little Piece of My Heart
A rocking chair rocks upon a Heavenly cloud
In the future I see what you cannot,
A son will be born to Nate and Shelley.

He shall be named Justin Ryan, in memory of me.
How special he is to my heart,
I am with the one who will carry my name.
At this moment in time we are home together,
Ryan preparing for the experience of life.
Rocking upon this cloud, I hold him and cradle him
Oh, how I know the love this baby will have,
I have lived that love myself.
You will grow up with my family, Ryan.
I know the games, the fun, the things you will do.
I know the love, the attention, the guidance you will have.
How innocent this baby is that I hold in my arms.
Bless this child, Lord, who carries my name.
Let him always look home to You in Heaven for guidance.
Let him always follow the heart that You have given him.
It's time for Nate and Shelley to learn that they are expecting.
Embracing my nephew, the beautiful angels arrive.
As the angels take Ryan from my arms,
I give him a little piece of my heart and send him to you.

From my arms to yours,
Love, Justin

Nesting was something I had heard about but had never experienced due to Brittney's early delivery. I had taken on the traditional look of a mom expecting a boy—completely normal-looking from the back, but with a huge basketball tummy. My belly certainly got in the way, but it didn't stop me from spending the past few days cleaning everything in sight. It was odd cleaning my parents' home; it was almost like doing chores again. In our endless efforts to afford law school, we made the hard decision to move in with my parents—temporarily—before our big move to Seattle.

My due date was less than a week away and I was keeping my fingers crossed for either an early or late delivery. Of all the days for our baby to be due, it just *had* to be January 29th — Super Bowl Sunday. Not just any Super Bowl Sunday. This would be the game of all games for our family. The San Diego Chargers — Nate's favorite team — versus the San Francisco 49ers — Dad's favorite team!

The more I thought about my upcoming labor, the more I started to get both nervous and excited. Although I had already given birth once, it was by no means a normal labor because of the toxemia. For months now, I wondered what it would feel like to go into labor naturally.

Nate had already left for work and I was happy to stay in bed for as long as Brittney would let me. She was getting better about sleeping longer now that she was three-and-a-half. In just a few days though, we'd be back to sleepless nights with a newborn.

"Mommy?"

Well ... it was nice while it lasted.

I could feel the sheets tugging as Brittney climbed up onto the bed. I cracked my eye open to see a blur of pink as she laid next to me with her blanket.

"Can we watch *Lion King*?"

"No Sweetie, we need to eat breakfast first," I yawned.

"Oh ... okay, okay ... *then* can we watch *Lion King*?"

I rolled over to face her, "Yes, once this tummy is all full, we can watch *Lion King*," I said, tickling her tummy.

Brittney sat in her highchair wasting no time between bites so that she could get to Simba as soon as possible. I, however, was in no hurry to hear Hakunah Matata for the millionth time. When we were finished, I helped Brittney out of her highchair and she practically ran to the living room, plopping herself in front of the TV. I rewound the tape and pressed Play.

"Okay, you're all set. Mommy's going to go take a shower," I told Brittney, who was already mesmerized by the rising sun and loud music of the movie's intro.

Between the closed bathroom door and running water from the shower, it was like my own personal mute button. I let out a deep, relaxing sigh as I stepped into the hot water.

Under the faucet, I felt a slight pang in my lower stomach. I didn't think much of it, I had been cramping off and on for the past couple of days. This one was a little stronger, but within a minute or so, it was gone just like the ones before. I continued enjoying my hot, comforting shower. As I rinsed the conditioner from my hair, another pang began to cause tightening in my abdomen. I paused. They usually weren't so quick to come back. I held onto my stomach and waited for it to pass.

The cramping returned as I sat at my vanity set. I breathed through it as I set the curlers in my hair. *Was I in labor?* By the time I was done getting ready, the cramping had intensified.

I looked over at the phone that was sitting on the night stand. We had recently rented a pager just in case I went into labor while Nate was at work. I was so tempted to beep him, but he was trying to work as much as possible before the baby arrived. I certainly didn't want to bother him if this were just a false alarm, so I called my mom instead.

"Hey, Mom... I'm feeling a lot of cramping. It kinda hurts..."

"Have you called Nate yet?"

"No."

"Can you stand up?" she asked.

"I think so..." I began to answer. Then I caught a glimpse of myself hunched over the nightstand in the vanity mirror. I tried to stand. "Uh, actually, no... I can't."

"Call Nate right now. I'm on my way!"

I hung up the phone and without moving, I paged Nate at Fairview Middle School where he was subbing. The phone rang soon after.

"Princess ... What's going on? Are you okay?" Nate asked, slightly out of breath. Just the sound of his voice was comforting.

"Nate ... I think it's time to get me to the hospital ..."

"What?? Really?!"

"I don't know for sure if I'm in labor, but I'm having trouble standing up. My mom's on her way over right now."

"Okay, hang on. I was out with the kids at recess and ran in here to the office to call you. Let me see if I can find someone to cover for me ..." I could hear chatter in the background and the school secretary telling Nate to go and that she would get someone else to be with the kids.

"I'm on my way, Babe!" Nate assured me.

A little hunched over, I walked over to Brittney. "We're going to have to turn off the movie, Honey. Mommy and Daddy are going to go to the hospital," I said, pulling a warm sweater over her head. I played off the cramping and told her with a smile, "You might be able to hold your baby brother today!"

"I get to hold the baby today?" she asked, as I tied her shoe laces.

"Maybe," I answered, "The doctor is going to check me and see if it's time."

One by one, family began arriving at the house. Nate and I gave Brittney a reassuring hug as my mom picked her up.

"I'll take Brittney to daycare and meet you over at the hospital." Just as Brittney started to look bummed that she had to go to day-care, my mom comforted her. "It's okay, little one, you're not going to be there for long. Gramma Mary is going to pick you up soon and she'll bring you over to the hospital."

Once we arrived at CHOMP, Nate pulled right up to the door and helped me inside. A couple of nurses were standing at the front counter working on charts. They looked up at us and one of the nurses walked over toward me.

"I'm not sure, but I think I might be in labor," I told her. "I called my husband out of work and I'm going to feel SO bad if this is a false alarm."

Nate waited in the lobby as she led me into a room. After a quick check, the nurse put her hand on my shoulder. "Yes, you are definitely in labor, Honey. You're already dilated to six! You're going to have a baby today!" she said, with an encouraging smile.

As Nate entered the room, I felt instant relief that I hadn't made a big deal out of just cramps. The expression on Nate's face made it clear that the nurse had told him the news.

Soon after, my mom arrived which meant I had help on each side of the bed. During the escalating contractions, Nate was on one side holding my hand and saying "Aw, Honey, you're doing so good. I'm so proud of you," while my mom was on the other side saying, "Okay...you are almost done with this one, you can do it. Concentrate on your breathing," she would say each time I winced in pain. She began co-breathing, taking in deep breaths along with me.

With Nate and my mom coaching me through the contractions, we were getting through it well. Mom would go in and out of the room giving the family, who were gathered together in the lobby, updates along the way.

"Looks like you're about there," the nurse said with a smile. "We're moving you into the delivery room." Another nurse in matching blue scrubs came in and started wheeling the bed out of the room.

I was shocked! We hadn't been in there very long. With Brittney, I had been in labor forever it seemed, but with Ryan, I was in and out in just over an hour. Things were moving right along, and my mom left to give everyone another update. I was so excited that this pain was almost over and I would be holding Ryan soon!

HOURS later... I was once again screaming for an epidural. But just as before, it was too late for any pain relief. As the clock ticked away, the breathing techniques had become completely futile. The doctor would regularly come in to check on me. Seeing "Dr. Spock" enter the delivery room gave me high hopes that I was nearing the end of this all-encompassing pain. Both Nate and I were so thankful he was able to be here once again as we brought another baby into this world. But so far, each time he came in to check on me, he would then leave and I would get so discouraged. Why was he leaving? All this time in the delivery room trying to push the baby out, and still no baby yet?! It hurt so bad!

The nurse stepped out of the room and immediately both she and the doctor returned. This time the doctor stayed, which meant it was finally go time!!

"Okay, Shelley, we need you to give a long, strong push," the nurse coached, standing next to the doctor.

Once again, I thought I was going to die! I just couldn't continue with this unbearable pushing.

"PUSH!" the nurse continued her coaching.

I cried out in pain.

"You can do it, Honey. You're almost done," Nate squeezed my sweaty hand.

"Why is this taking so long?! It's like he's stuck!" I cried.

"I can see the baby's head," the nurse assured me.

"You're almost there," my mom encouraged.

With another push, I let out a loud wail.

And just like that, the pain was over and we heard our baby cry for the very first time. Exhausted and out of breath, my head fell back onto the bed.

"Congratulations," the doctor said, "It's a boy!"

The nurse placed Ryan on top of me, and my eyes gushed with love as I gazed at our handsome son for the very first time. "He looks just like his daddy," I said to Nate with a big smile. Ryan weighed in at 9 pounds, 3 ounces—almost twice the size of our five-pound baby girl! No wonder he took so long to deliver! Even so, the whole ordeal was considerably quicker than the first time with Brittney. Justin Ryan Baker was born on Monday, January 23, 1995, at exactly 3:00 pm—only six hours from start to finish!

Nate had already proudly nicknamed Ryan "The Boy" before we even left the delivery room. Our son was soon passed around the family that was circled around my hospital bed. We took our first picture as a family of four. Just as I had hoped this morning, Brittney got to hold her little brother, Justin Ryan, for the very first time.

Chapter 7

"Livin' On A Prayer" by Bon Jovi

"LADIES AND GENTLEMEN, as we start our final descent, please return to your seats and check to make sure that your seat belts are securely fastened."

With my seatbelt already buckled, I looked down at four-month-old Ryan, who was swaddled in his dinosaur blanket, snug in my arms. He wiggled a little bit and gave a sleepy yawn as the flight attendants collected all the remaining trash in preparation for landing. As I handed over my empty Coke can, she smiled. I'm sure that she, and probably some passengers, might have expected a very long and noisy flight, but Ryan had been sleeping in my arms the entire time.

Nate and Brittney had driven in one car and Mary followed behind them in my car. Since Ryan was too young for a long road trip, we flew. Jerry was going to meet us at the terminal, and I was so excited for him to meet his grandson.

Looking out the window, I smiled at the Kingdome, this dome-shaped stadium that was like a thumbtack pinned to a map marking our new hometown.

I gave Ryan a squeeze, "We're here, baby!" His green eyes widened as the pressure of gravity pulled the plane toward Sea-Tac Airport, wheels contacting the tarmac.

"Thank you for flying with us today," the Captain said over the speakers, "Welcome to Seattle."

I was certain we would never find another church like Cypress Community Church. This church on a hill, just outside of Salinas, had been our church home for years now. We got married there. We had made going to church every Sunday a priority in our lives ever since Brittney was born. We even had our favorite seats up in the balcony. Finding a church that we connected with, like we did with Cypress, was proving to be a lot harder than I thought it would be. We knew we had to keep trying though, because going to church on Sundays had become an essential part of our lives. Since the move, we had attended various services nearby, but nothing had felt like a fit to us quite yet. One morning we decided to try a church off Mercer Island.

It was a non-denominational Christian church that looked more like a college campus. With its multiple buildings, it took us a while to find where the child care was. We felt so bad checking in a pouting Brittney to the preschool class. Brittney wasn't comfortable with new people, but until we found a new church home, week after week, we had to check her into a new place with unknown faces. Brittney leaned into me, holding on to my skirt as I began filling out the forms. A volunteer extended her hand and welcomed Brittney to come and play with the other kids. Although Brittney didn't want to go, we had promised her a Slurpee from 7-11 after church. This gave her a solid reason to endure one whole hour of separation from Mom and Dad. Safe and content in Nate's arms,

Ryan watched what was going on with Brittney. He was too young to understand that our next stop was the nursery down the hall.

Ryan's vociferous protest to the volunteer who took him from our arms filled the air as we quickly waved goodbye and left the nursery. We could still hear him as we started walking down the hallway toward the service that was about to start. Leaving the kids with people that we didn't know never got any easier; it hurt me to see them so upset.

We found our way to the main building and sat up in the balcony just like we usually did at home. People began filling up the surrounding seats, talking and greeting each other as they got settled. I wasn't used to a church that didn't have pews. These padded chairs were more like what you would sit in at a movie theatre. In fact, the two large screens on each side of the pulpit made it *feel* more like a movie theatre than a church. I noticed there were Bibles on the backs of the chairs... but where were the hymnals?

The congregation silenced as a man in a dress shirt and tie came out to welcome everyone. I was used to a church where the pastor wore a black robe and would greet everyone while the choir, in their purple robes, walked up to the stage. The choir would then sing along as the organ played, but I didn't even see an organ here.

As this pastor welcomed the congregation, musicians began walking onto the stage holding microphones. Some even had guitars and one of the musicians took a seat at a large set of drums.

The worship leader energetically took a microphone, "Good morning, everyone! How's everybody doing this morning?" In reply, he got a collective "Woo" as everyone rose to their feet. Words then popped up on these giant screens as people started clapping along to the music.

Nate and I looked at each other with baffled expressions. I knew if I felt uncomfortable, then Nate definitely did too. As a teenager, he had gone to a private Catholic school that was so conservative that the boys had to have a ruler's width of space between the collar of their shirt and the back of their hair. I felt myself take a slight step backward. Is it even okay to worship this way? We had never seen anything like this. Even though Nate and I were always going to concerts, it was bizarre that a church could behave this way. It felt more like a rock concert than a church service. We felt totally uncomfortable and just couldn't bring ourselves to clap along with everyone else. My eyes searched for someone else who looked as uncomfortable as I was. Instead, everyone seemed to be enjoying the clapping and most people knew the words to the songs without looking at the screens. Some people even closed their eyes and raised a hand up in the air.

When worship was over, the pastor came up and told everyone to take a seat as he went over a few announcements. For the first time, I was relieved that worship was over. The pastor went on to introduce a guest speaker, Pastor Steve Walker.

Although I was a little disappointed that we'd come to try out this church on a weekend where they had a guest speaker planned, I was instantly captivated by this enthusiastic, young pastor. He spoke in a way that expressed how much he loved to teach about God. His evident love for The Lord was embedded so deeply that I rarely saw him look at his notes while giving his sermon—he spoke from his heart. He knew the Bible. As I sat there listening, I could feel God's Word penetrate my soul. By the time he finished his sermon, I wanted more. He had a lot to say, and we had a lot to learn. With one sermon, Pastor Steve had us over missing our old church. Before he left the stage, he gave an open invitation for anyone to join the sister church that he would soon be opening in Bothell called Canyon Hills Community Church. Bothell was a little further north, but for more sermons like that, the extra drive would be well worth it. He informed the congregation that until a church building was found, the services would be hosted in the gymnasium of a local junior high school. The church would have a humble beginning, but with God's help, he had hopes of it really being something amazing.

Nate and I knew that our search for a church home was over. Canyon Hills Community Church would be where we'd spend our Sunday mornings while we were living in Washington.

Finding our new church home made all of the drama this morning worthwhile. We picked up the kids and began to drive toward 7-11. I headed straight for a Big Gulp cup and filled it with Coke overflowing with ice. Nate and Brittney got creative at the Slurpee machine as they layered different flavors over each other creating the perfect blend. The Slurpee bribe had worked. We were all back in the car sipping on our drinks while Brittney proudly showed us her purple tongue.

Opening day at Canyon Hills arrived. Pastor Steve spoke from a podium set up between the basketball hoops in the center of the gymnasium. It was exciting to be part of a new church. Sunday after Sunday, more people were showing up. Each week we repeated the same things—driving to Bothell for church, Brittney being bribed with a Slurpee, Ryan screaming in protest at the nursery, and Nate and I deepening our walk with God. Over the weeks and months that followed, we soaked up God's Word through Pastor Steve. We took comfort in the fact that God was the leader of our family.

Worship, which at first was uncomfortable, started to become very enjoyable. The words and instruments were so powerful and moving that I often got goosebumps during the songs. After a while, I had even started joining in on the clapping and understood the physical expression in the joy of worshipping God.

Every week, Brittney would get in the car holding papers she'd colored or crafts she'd made. She would also tell us stories about what she learned in Sunday School. Ryan continued to display his dislike for us taking him to the nursery. We looked forward to the day when we could bribe him with Slurpees as well! All the while, Nate and I were growing in our Christian faith. We began to learn and understand the Bible on a deeper level. Nate and I would get into long discussions about what we were learning, and I loved how we were growing in our faith together. The sermons were so uplifting, giving us hope at a time when we were still in the climbing years of our lives. We had almost reached the top of the college mountain. It was so close, but the peak was still just out of reach until Nate passed the bar exam.

In the meantime, Nate was really enjoying working with his dad and learning the business of Marine Title Company. He had his own office, and as usual, learned everything quickly. Nate was an immediate fit in the office, and the co-workers all got a kick out of his witty demeanor. It was the perfect job for Nate until he passed the bar and we moved back to California.

As planned, the days of Nate working with his dad were short-lived. Jerry was leaving for West Virginia on the weekend. He would fly back for a visit at Christmas, but until then he really needed time on the east coast to expand his business. Jerry was so thankful to have us housesit for him, but truly the blessing was ours.

No need for cooking tonight because, after work, Nate and Jerry were bringing Thai Heaven home for dinner. I lit the greenish, coconut lime candle in the kitchen (I always had candles burning) and began setting the table as the kids played. I could hear the guys walking in from the garage and down the hall. They soon walked into the kitchen carrying multiple white plastic bags of take-out. By the looks of it, no one would go hungry tonight! Nate and I greeted each other with a kiss, as Jerry started pulling out styrofoam containers from the bags.

"Well, look at this! I've got a shrimp with your name on it," Gramps said to Brittney. He pulled it out of the container with a pair of chopsticks. She hurried her four-year-old self into the kitchen to check it out. Brittney loved shrimp, and excitedly reached for the reddish crustacean Gramps had found. Crazy how Gramps always seemed to find one with her name on it.

It didn't take long for the spicy aroma of our Thai food to mingle with the light, fruity smell of the candle burning in the kitchen. Family time and delicious food made for a cozy night as we all sat down to eat. I secured Ryan in his highchair and put little pieces of chicken and some sticky rice on the tray. He immediately began picking it up with his fingers and eating. He was sitting next to Gramps—aka *GoGo*. Our growing baby's babbling was progressing. He was still a little too young to talk, but babies have their own way of communicating. After days of our exaggerated pronunciation in repeating *Mama* and *Dada* and the *Buh Buh* sound to practice our names, Ryan had come to the conclusion that Brittney's name was *Bubba*. He would surely outgrow that when he got older, but for now it was really cute. Brittney seemed to like the nickname, and Nate and I even found ourselves calling her Bubba sometimes.

Our eclectic dinner setting looked like Thai Heaven's kitchen had exploded onto our table top. Jerry said he was really going to miss this favorite food of his and wanted to get his fill before he left. All the opened containers gave us a lot of choices for a scoop of this and a taste of that. And low and behold, Gramps found another shrimp with Brittney's—Bubba's—name on it!

As we ate, Ryan's jabbering made it clear that he was fully engaged in our mealtime together. The tray was empty and he held out both arms toward the food. We chuckled at all the white sticky rice adhering to his arms. Even at such a young age, we already knew that Ryan was a people person and thrived on attention. While I was putting small pieces of noodles on the tray, he saw us all looking at him and began squealing and kicking with excitement. From his vantage point in the highchair, he had a captive audience. His squeals crescendoed as he began waving his arms, causing pieces of food to fly through the air. "Okay Ry, that's enough," I said, as I tried calming him down a bit. He stopped kicking and took another bite, but when he saw us looking at him again, the show began again.

In an attempt to divert attention, Jerry advised, "Don't make eye contact. He'll stop once he notices we're not paying attention." On cue, we all looked away and within a matter of seconds Ryan was eating his dinner again—without all the noise and commotion. Nate and I looked at each other and smiled at this revelation. Our son had a healthy appetite for both food and attention, so not making eye contact would be our *go-to* when we needed to quiet him down at future meals.

We were all stuffed! I took Ryan out of his highchair and brought him over to the kitchen sink to clean him up. Jerry went in the living room and sat down in his recliner for the evening news. As I was washing Ryan's hands and face—and all the rice stuck to his arms—Nate walked into the kitchen with a handful of emptied styrofoam containers. I leaned to the side giving him room to grab the trashcan from underneath the sink, but instead, he stopped at the burning candle and scrunched his face. "What?" I questioned with a twisted smile, as I dried Ryan's hands and slipped his legs through the holes of his walker.

With an overemphasized sniff, Nate answered, "My dad said that he hates your candles."

I tilted my head at Nate, completely sure that he was just being facetious. "No, he *doesn't*!" I rebutted firmly. "Jerry?" I called out across the kitchen to the living room.

"Yeah?" Jerry asked, turning his head toward the kitchen from his favorite seat in the house.

"Nate said you hate my candles," I blurted out, getting right to the point with a chuckle.

After a short pause, Jerry said, "What? I don't hate your candles," he assured me. "I actually kind of like them. I mean, I wouldn't go out and buy one for *myself*, but I like when *you* have them burning." He looked at Nate, shaking his head laughing. "Geez Nate, I never said that."

"That's okay, Jerry, I believe you," I said confidently, looking right at Nate as I spoke. Jerry laughed at our marital dynamics, and Nate shrugged his shoulders at me, nodding with a scoff. "Yes he did," he whispered. There was nothing left to do but to playfully hit my bantering husband on his arm.

"In Jesus name we pray, Amen."

I lifted my head with a smile, "Thank you, Pastor Steve."

The pastor's heartwarming prayer asking God to be with Nate during his upcoming bar exam was just the encouragement we needed. His inspiring words set the tone like a coach amping up one of his athletes before a big game. With a grateful smile, Nate shook the pastor's hand. As we left the gymnasium to pick up the kids from Sunday school, I could see the look of determination in Nate's eyes.

The pastor's prayer, plus many of our own, kept Nate pumped up for the notoriously difficult exam that awaited him. After all of this time, this was the week that could change everything. It would be a grueling three-day exam, but Nate was ready. He had a passion for justice, his Juris Doctorate Degree, and he had even completed a California Bar Prep Course—just to make sure he had all his bases covered. I was excited that he would be flying back to California to take the test. We had been waiting for this moment for a long time. I would be just fine with the kids while he was gone, and some kidless days would be perfect for Nate so he didn't have to break his focus.

The morning of Nate's flight, I pulled up to the curb at the airport. He leaned over and gave me a kiss. I hugged him tight. "You're going to do great, Sweetheart. I love you."

"I love you, too," Nate said. He opened the back door, said goodbye to the kids, and grabbed his duffle bag to catch his flight to Oakland.

Nate returned from California a few days later looking relieved, like a huge weight had been lifted from his shoulders. It felt great to have the bar exam behind us. Now the only thing that was left to do was wait—the results of the exam would be posted in October. It would be hard to wait a few months before knowing the results, but keeping busy would help distract us. And keeping busy was never an issue for Nate and me—especially with two little ones. Nate was still learning his dad's business, I was temping with my Washington State Hygiene License, and we had every intention of making the absolute best of our extended stay on Mercer Island.

The Seattle sky took a break from the rainfall during the late summer months, making the weather perfect for showing our steady stream of company around this place we loved. Carrie and I talked for hours on the sandy shore of Lake Washington. My mom and I took the kids on carnival rides in Downtown Seattle. We took another friend and her family on a day trip to Tacoma where our kids got to see the dinosaur exhibit at the zoo. It was a packed summer and a lot of fun. I had even flown back home to California to visit my parents while Paul, Chris, and Matt were visiting, giving them time and space for a guys' golfing weekend with Nate. And Mary, well, I never considered her company, but rather a frequent part of our home.

What would we do without Gramma Mary—nicknamed Gramma Scary by guess who? Even though she lived almost nine hundred miles away, that didn't stop her from, well, anything we needed. Not only did she make frequent trips to get her *Gramma Fix*—as she called it—but she even flew up when Brittney broke out with chickenpox from head to toe. And, two weeks later, she flew back *again* when Ryan broke out with the same itchy red welts—courtesy of his big sister. Nate and I were so thankful for her support, due to the fact that I had already committed to sub some of those days in various dental offices. She was a complete lifesaver, but anytime we would thank her, she would always say things like, "I'm off for summer vacation anyway. I miss you guys, and it's just nice to be here to help." Mary was always very modest, but without a doubt, she would've been here in a flash no matter what time of year chickenpox showed up.

As the kids grew, Nate and I noticed the differences between our daughter and our son more and more. Brittney was a picky eater, whereas Ryan would eat anything—which I have to say, was really nice. On the other hand, Brittney was so good about playing by herself or watching a movie, and Ryan wanted to be held. All the time! He was such a fun baby who was also very cuddly and had a Prince Charming face. Not only did his amusing personality call for a lot of attention, over time he started to struggle with asthma which led to many doctor appointments.

The summer heat began transitioning into the crisp days of fall. Pumpkins, gourds, and cinnamon-scented pinecones decorated the store windows. The festive autumn decor brought with it added excitement this year—we were just days away from getting the bar results!

We took the kids to a pumpkin patch in the quaint, small town of Puyallup. Brittney picked out a small pumpkin that she proudly carried around all by herself, while Nate and I searched for an extra large one for Ryan. Back at home we dressed Ryan in a warm green onesie and set him inside the cleaned out pumpkin. His chunky arms and legs poked through the holes Nate had cut in just the right places—a perfect fit! We were all laughing. Ryan was having so much fun, he didn't even try to get out. He liked it there inside the pumpkin, giving me time to snap a few pictures of him with his chubby cheeks and big smile.

The kids were just the right age to be Pebbles and Bamm Bamm for Halloween. I bought an orange and black spotted Fred Flintstone costume and took it to a seamstress in town. I asked her to make a small dress with jagged edges for Brittney, and a loincloth with a torn hemline for Ryan. The kids fit the part very well and were adorable in their costumes. With Brittney's hair tied up with a bone, and Ryan holding a caveman club, we took the kids trick or treating to a few familiar houses nearby. They were having fun, but it was freezing outside! The Pacific Northwest's weather was a lot more seasonal! Even with some fuzzy jammies on underneath the kids' costumes, it was just too cold outside for these Bedrock characters. They were so cute, I was snapping pictures all night. We went back to the warm house and let Pebbles and her assistant Bamm Bamm hand out candy until bedtime.

Now we were just days away from getting Nate's Bar Exam results. I would often try to picture our lives back in California, and imagine in what town Nate might get hired. Just thinking about it got me exhilarated about our future. It's funny how a single test result would change everything.

I sat in the dark staring straight ahead without blinking. The rocking chair beneath me was still, but my thoughts were running wild. I cannot believe this, I just don't understand.

Instead of celebrating tonight, we were right back to square one. Square one! How? How was this possible?? We did everything we could think of. I knew God had heard our many prayers, but even Pastor Steve's moving prayer was answered with a "No." Why a No? Why would God let Nate fail? Nate was so intelligent and would undoubtedly be an amazing prosecutor. We had spent so much money on not only the exam, but the plane ticket, the hotel room, and a rental car. Oh, and not to mention the expensive bar prep course that obviously didn't help! All the money we had saved, money we could have used for other things...wasted. The culmination of tireless effort and preparation seemed all for naught. This huge milestone, the celebration we should be having right now...everything just fell right out of our hands, almost like a tease. Now we'd have to wait for the next test, which was months away, and do all of this testing and waiting *AGAIN*.

Nate was, of course, beating himself up for not passing. After a brief time of sharing our frustration and utter disappointment, this night had been a quiet night of thinking for both of us. We just needed time to sit and let it all soak in. Nate had gone into the living room where his quiet disappointment matched mine. He knew how I was feeling; he was feeling the same way...defeated.

After a while I got up from my rocking chair and walked into the living room. My heart ached for Nate. I sat myself on his lap and hugged his slouched shoulders.

"It's alright, Honey..." I said in a low voice through a weak smile. "You can take it again in a few months. You'll have more time to study and I know you'll pass next time."

We sat there for a few quiet moments, and then I put my forehead to his and sighed, "I'm tired. Will you tuck me in?"

Nate and I walked down the hall, passing the kids' room as we got into bed. The kids were asleep, oblivious to the disappointment Mom and Dad were dealing with. Nate didn't stay long, just long enough to warm me up and assure me that everything was going to be okay. With a kiss goodnight, he shut the door behind him and left. It took me a long time to fall asleep — my mind was too busy fighting off all the doubt and worry. The nonfulfillment of this long-term goal made my heart heavy. We had no choice but to carry on and try again when the test could be retaken in a few months.

Plan B went into motion. While waiting for Nate's second bar exam, we had decided that I would be the main provider, working Monday through Thursday, and Nate would work only on Fridays. With daycare costs pretty much cancelling out Nate's pay, it was more beneficial for him to stay home with the kids, and for me to increase my days at work. Nate was great with the kids and all of the household chores. I would come home tired from work to a home cooked meal, and Brittney would tell me all about how Daddy took them to watch the big planes. Nate had found an open field at Sea-Tac Airport where the airliners would fly right over their heads mere seconds before landing. The kids were super excited — it was their new favorite thing to do. And it was free!

We were under constant financial stress. Between Ryan's frequent ear infections and asthma attacks, the doctor bills were piling up. Not to mention, we had to save for the bar exam expenses all over again. It was a lot to handle, but we did what we needed to do.

My parents came to spend Thanksgiving with us. It was great to see them. We showed them around, and took them to Pike Place Market where we watched the fishmongers throw large fish through the air. We would have loved to take them out on a ferry boat ride, but Ryan's asthma only seemed to be getting worse and the doctor recommended that we stay within an hour of home, at least until the nebulizer, and our prayers, made a difference in Ryan's lungs.

My new patient was a middle-aged homosexual man. He had been diagnosed with AIDS, and was told by his doctor that he had approximately three months to live. However, he sat in the chair, and in an unwavering tone stated, "I'm gonna beat this." He was talkative and determined to convince me, or maybe himself, that he was not going to become a statistic in the global, and feared AIDS epidemic.

As I looked over the patient's health history, there indeed was an X marked in the "YES" column next to AIDS. This man's blood was contagious; one slip of my hand could result in me being cut, which would mean that I would be exposed to his blood or saliva and quite possibly get AIDS myself.

I took in a deep breath as I turned on the overhead light and reached for the mouth mirror. He was very thin with lips that held a bluish tint. As I instructed him to open, his chapped lips made it apparent that his mouth was dry. It took mere seconds to see rampant gum disease throughout. For years now, I regularly had my gloved hands in countless patients' mouths, but at the moment, I felt like I was in uncharted territory. The roof of his mouth looked bruised and his inflamed gums had isolated patches that looked almost purple. I stayed focused as I picked up the probe from the tray and began to measure his periodontal pockets. He needed root planing, a procedure that required needles, sharp instruments, and caused varying degrees of bleeding, depending on the health of the patient's gums. Even during today's initial cleaning, I expected him to bleed—a lot!

I didn't have time to think. This man was *my* patient, *my* responsibility. All I could think to do was to double glove and be very careful. No doubt, the doctor would diagnose root planing. For today, I worked mostly above the gum line, but even then, he bled with even the slightest touch. This poor man, his swollen gums must cause him such pain and discomfort. Even the topical anesthetic I had applied wasn't enough. I wanted to help him—it was my *job* to help him—but I didn't want to hurt him either. He sighed and I could feel his warm breath on my gloves. It took every ounce of self-control not to pull away from him.

Even though I had a mask over my face, I took in shallow breaths as if it would protect me. As I was doing the cleaning, I was trying to remember everything I had learned about AIDS. It was a fairly new topic, but I knew that it was transmitted by body fluids—and fatal. I kept my undivided attention on every move my hands made as I scaled the calculus. My green gloves were stained red at the finger tips. Anything further would need local anesthetic, so I sat the patient up and told him that I was going to call the doctor in for an exam.

The doctor came in and treated the patient with respect and kindness as well. I had finished the initial cleaning and the doctor confirmed the need for root planing. Before the patient left, the receptionist scheduled him for a two hour appointment with me, tomorrow.

I began the process of cleaning up the room for the day. Only this time, once I finished, I started again, followed by a third time—just to make sure it was completely disinfected. My mind began wrestling with the facts and emotions about this situation I was in. That patient was going to be back in my chair tomorrow, and he would need some serious work. The sharp instruments I was gathering served as a quick reminder of how easily I could poke myself. I had managed to get through his hour long cleaning appointment, but two hours of root planing, are you kidding me?! How can a man that is about to die of AIDS ask this of me? If I had what he had, I would never put someone else's life in danger like this! I have a family—a very young family—who depend on my salary while Nate is only one exam away from becoming an attorney. I am our main provider right now. We need the money, but is it worth the risk? I can't do it!

Before I left work, I knocked on my boss's office door. I took a seat facing the doctor who was sitting at his desk and told him what was on my mind.

"I cannot see this patient tomorrow, doctor. I have a husband…and a toddler…and a baby at home, and this man may die in the next few months anyway. What if I poke myself?"

I sat there looking at my boss, desperate for him to understand and excuse me from having to root plane that patient tomorrow. But instead, after listening to my concerns, he sighed.

"Shelley, we legally cannot refuse to treat this man. We need to treat him just like we treat any other patient. I'm just going to pretend that we never had this conversation and I'll see you tomorrow," he answered.

I was stunned. I felt trapped. It felt like the doctor wasn't even trying to understand. Giving the doctor a nod, I left his office burdened by the fact that tomorrow I would be required—by law—to treat this patient. Trying not to let fear get the best of me, I took the elevator down and then walked across the street to the parking garage. The entire drive home I talked to God.

God, I don't know what to do. What should I do? Should I quit?

I could feel the adrenaline pumping through my body as fear succeeded in taking over my thoughts.

At home, I discussed the issue with Nate as he sat in the recliner holding Ryan, who was fast asleep in his arms. Brittney was on the floor humming as she colored with markers, the ink bleeding through the pages. Still in my scrubs and jacket, I paced back and forth asking Nate the same questions that I had been asking God on the drive home.

"What should I do? Maybe I can call in sick…or maybe I should just quit. No, I can't quit…we have bills to pay…" I let out a deep sigh. "I don't know, Babe, maybe I should just risk it and see the patient. It's possible that nothing bad will happen. But what if I slip? I could double glove again, but that may make it worse if I can't hold the instruments as well."

I kept rambling—my mouth barely keeping up with my thoughts. I looked down at Ryan and just the look on his peacefully sleeping face calmed me down. I paused and then shook my head, "I just don't know what to do."

Nate sat in the chair listening to me and my distressed list of options. He scratched his chin in response. Although he didn't outwardly show his stress like I did, I could tell that it worried him, too.

"It'll be okay, Princess. We'll think of something," Nate assured me.

The humming stopped and Brittney popped her head up, an orange smudge on her chin. "Mommy?" she asked, getting my attention.

I rubbed the frustrated tears from my eyes. "Yes, Sweetie?"

"I thought you said Jesus could help with anything," she stated innocently.

I paused, taken aback by her unexpected input. "Yes, He can," I agreed.

"Then just ask Jesus to help you and everything will be okay."

Nate and I looked at each other and then at our wise little girl who had returned to her coloring. I walked over to her and gave her a grateful hug. God handed me the answer through our four-year-old child. Apparently all those Slurpees had paid off and our daughter could preach the truth.

After a night and early morning of continuous prayer, I found myself back in the doctor's office and he asked, "Are you going to see your patient today?" He looked right at me, expecting a relapse into our previous conversation.

"Yes, I am," I spoke in full confidence.

He leaned back in his chair, as if blown away by my answer. "May I ask what changed your mind?"

"My little girl," I replied. "She reminded me that Jesus is going to help me."

That day, I completed two quadrants of root planing on this patient. As expected, there was a lot of blood. I was nervous, of course, but my hands were steady as I smoothed each root surface. I didn't slip, and I could feel God cleansing the fear from me like curettes scrapping away the calculus.

Colorful lights and fresh snow decorated the town. It was Ryan's first Christmas, and he would be turning one next month already! Jerry was home for the holiday week, and Mary and Jon had flown in that morning. I was thankful for the upbeat energy of having our family together. Although Nate didn't really let it show, the lingering disappointment from the negative exam results had him in a funk. It hurt me to see him like this; he just couldn't seem to shake off the *fail*.

Jerry made a fire, and we all took a seat around the Christmas tree. One after the other, we exchanged and opened presents for hours. The kids were amped up from all the excitement of having our family together and the new toys that surrounded them. With the crackling logs keeping us warm, I set a couple of nicely wrapped presents in front of Nate hoping to cheer him up. I had recently taken his law school diplomas into a frame shop by my work to be matted and framed. Although he hadn't passed the bar yet, he *had* graduated law school, which was a huge achievement. He had earned these degrees. I figured that seeing how far he'd come would remind him of all that he had already accomplished. Someday, they would hang on the wall in his office.

"Merry Christmas, Honey," I said, as I watched him open them.

Nate pulled back the paper, and his reaction was completely underwhelming. His expression dropped, as if he didn't deserve the presents. He was thankful for the gesture, but didn't hang them up. Instead, he stored them away waiting for the day he felt worthy of displaying them.

With everything feeling so out of control, we found comfort in God and leaned on Him completely. The weekly Sunday sermons were like a breath of fresh air that gave us the strength we needed to reach this difficult goal. During the next few months our faith and knowledge of Christ grew. Through Pastor Steve's teachings, we learned new things like tithing, fasting, baptism, and mission trips. Tithing really pushed our faith because giving ten percent of our income was a lot for us. This was a time when we needed every cent we were making to pay our bills. But Nate and I decided to tithe our money no matter how challenging ten percent cut into our income. The decision felt right—a solid step toward trusting God to meet our needs.

Fasting was another spiritual discipline that was new to us. Nate and I wanted to fully engage, pulling all of these lessons together as an unquestionable action of our faith. We decided to fast twenty-four hours for each of the fourteen subjects on the bar exam. With the help of family and friends, each subject would be fasted and fervently prayed for by the time Nate would take the examination again.

As February arrived, our spirits were lifting. In just a few weeks, Nate would be able to re-take the bar, but first, we planned to take a little trip for our anniversary. We had been counting down the days to our get-away. Mary was going to fly up and watch the kids while Nate and I would spend the day skiing at the winter resort The Summit at Snoqualmie. We had two lift tickets and a box of snow chains all ready to go. I couldn't wait to break in my new teal ski suit, snow boots, and warm gloves that I was given for Christmas. Although Nate tried to plan a whole weekend stay at the Salish Lodge and Spa, we had decided to make it a day trip only. We just couldn't afford that kind of a trip yet. It would've been a dreamy weekend, but at this point in life, it was just that…a dream.

The kids were super excited to see Gramma Mary. She had everything she needed, right down to a signed doctor's note for the kids just in case of an emergency. We loved how we could just leave the kids with Gramma and not have to worry about anything at all.

Skiing the slopes of Snoqualmie was everything we had been looking forward to. It was fun, romantic, and the break we desperately needed from all of the stress. As the sun started to set, we packed up our things so that we could start the drive home to get ready for dinner. We had dinner reservations at the rotating SkyCity Restaurant on top of the Space Needle. Its panoramic view of the twinkling lights of downtown Seattle would be the perfect ending to our fun day together celebrating our eighth year of marriage.

Still in our ski clothes, we walked into the house. It was quiet. We found Mary sitting in the living room holding Ryan in the rocking chair next to the fireplace. She sighed in relief when she saw us walk in. "You came at just the right time—it's like an angel sent you home," Mary said emotionally. "I was so scared. Ryan's been wheezing for about a half hour now."

My stomach dropped, and I immediately picked Ryan up and sat down with him. I put my hand on his red cheeks and then on his chest, feeling the rapid rise and fall as he struggled for air. The whistling sound of Ryan's breathing continued as I handed him to Nate and went to call the doctor.

"She's going to meet us at the office," I said, as I hurried into the bedroom to change into some dry clothes. As I got Ryan into his car seat, Nate did a quick change and within minutes, we were pulling out of the driveway.

The doctor, who knew us well, started Ryan on a nebulizer immediately. "If this doesn't clear up soon, I'm going to admit him to the hospital," the doctor informed us as we sat there holding him during his treatment.

Within the hour, Ryan started to respond to the treatment and began breathing a little slower. I rested my head on Nate's shoulder as I held Ryan, thanking God for the air that was filling his lungs. After that night, we continued to stay within one hour of the pediatrician's office at all times and prayed for Ryan to outgrow his asthma.

Over the next week, Ryan's asthma was getting better, but he was still fussy. I also had noticed that lately he had been tugging on his ear. Nate threw his bag in the back of the car and shut the door. We started the drive to Sea-Tac Airport. All the subjects had been fasted for, Pastor Walker had prayed for us again, and Nate had spent countless hours studying.

"Call me when you get settled," I said, as we arrived at the airport.

"I will," Nate said with a nod. "Are you sure you're going to be okay?" he asked, looking back to Ryan in his car seat.

"We'll be fine. I'm going to call the doctor as soon as we get back home to set up an appointment. They always get us right in," I assured him. The last thing I wanted was for Nate to be distracted while he was taking the exam.

We kissed goodbye, and I drove away praying for God to be with Nate.

It was a good thing I had taken off the next four days while Nate would be in California because Ryan was tugging on his ear and crying a lot. Diagnosis...an ear infection. I drove from the doctor's office to the pharmacy to pick up Ryan's latest prescription. Brittney was being my big helper, holding Ryan's head steady as he cried and fought the medication that I was trying to give him. I thought the medication was going to help Ryan feel better, but instead, I gasped in alarm as his body began to break out in red welts from head to toe. I rushed him back to the doctor who told me he'd had an allergic reaction to Amoxicillin, and to never give it to him again. The welts he currently had prevented us from giving him a different antibiotic. There would be no way of telling if he were to have another allergic reaction. My poor baby would have to suffer through the ear infection with no medication to help.

Day after day, and night after night, I met Ryan's every need. Brittney was so helpful whenever her little brother needed anything. Every night I would talk to Nate on the phone trying to hide the chaos that was going on at home. I didn't want to give him any reason to be worried or distracted. I just wanted him to pass the exam! He seemed hopeful that he was doing well and he was even sleeping at night...unlike me. I felt like I had been hit by a train. I was literally begging God, desperately trying to make a deal with him. If he would make Ryan sleep, I would do *anything* He asked of me.

The next day, Jerry came home from West Virginia for the weekend. I was in the living room rocking Ryan after being up all night *again*. Ryan's welts had faded, but he was still suffering through his ear infection. With one look at me, Jerry immediately offered to watch Ryan so that I could get some sleep. I wholeheartedly thanked him, told Britt that Gramps was in charge, and went to bed.

When I opened my eyes, it was dark. Groggy, I looked at the clock—it was almost 4:00 am! I jumped out of bed and rushed out to check on Ryan. The lights were still on in the living room. On the carpet, and underneath the wooden coffee table, I found Ryan and Gramps sound asleep. The house was *finally* quiet. There were a few towels, and a pile of used washcloths on the floor. I looked at them with a tender smile and Jerry began to wake up.

"I'm so sorry, Jerry!" I whispered, "I was only going to sleep for a couple of hours, but I just crashed."

Jerry got up and shook his head. "That was one of the longest nights of my life! I've never seen anything like it. There were things coming out of every part of his body! I didn't know what to do, so I just grabbed a bunch of washcloths," Jerry explained. "Mary was always better at that kind of stuff than I was."

My prayer for rest had been answered, and I gave him a big grateful hug. He practically had a halo above his head for letting me get some much-needed sleep! "Thank you, Jerry. I'll take it from here."

The next day, the kids and I went to pick up Nate. I couldn't wait to see him and to ask how he did on his last day of the exam!

Right on schedule, I could see Nate walking out with the crowd of people who were also getting off the plane. I smiled, "It's Daddy! He's back!" Brittney went running up to him. He gave her a bear hug and picked her up.

"Hey, Princess," Nate said as we hugged with Brittney at his side.

"Hi, Baby! You're back! We missed you," I smiled at the sight of him. People bustled around our small party, rolling their luggage through the airport terminal. "How are you? Are you hungry?"

"Yes!" he exclaimed, pretending to eat Brittney's arm as he carried her. She giggled as her daddy told her she was tasty. Things were already back to normal.

"Did you eat before you flew out?" I asked.

"No," Nate replied.

"You must be hungry! I hope you had a big dinner last night," I said.

There was a pause.

"Babe ... when was the last time you ate?"

He set Brittney down and took Ryan from my arms and answered, "Breakfast ... before you dropped me off at the airport ..."

And then it hit me — Nate hadn't eaten the entire four days he was in California. He had literally survived on the *bread* of God, by fasting and praying, the entire time he was taking the California Bar Exam. I couldn't believe it! This man never stops amazing me. The human body needs food. How could Nate correctly answer the multitude of questions, and even essay questions, on an empty stomach? With God, I thought. The Lord helped him. I softly smiled as I stared at Nate in utter amazement. We drove straight home where I could feed my faithful, and very hungry, husband.

Waiting for the results was the worst part of the bar exam. All of the hard work put into reaching our goals somehow seemed to cause time to stand still instead. We were only halfway through our three months of waiting — for the second time. How is it that after everything we've done, our circumstances are still so temporary and uncertain? Nothing we could do would relieve us from this waiting. No amount of hard work or studying would make the results come any sooner. There was nothing to be done except wait.

Such a beautiful Saturday merely felt like another day as time's prisoner. What does it matter that we all are home today, and we live in Seattle where there are endless things to do? We can't do any of it because we can't afford it. Last Saturday, we had to get snacks from Chevron and charge them to our Chevron card just so we could take the kids out to the lake for the day. We never mentioned it to our parents, but we even had to take out a small loan just to host Thanksgiving for our families a few months ago.

Nate and I are both college graduates. How is it that we *still* don't have enough money? Time was really good at giving us our monthly bills, but it sure wasn't doing us any favors in bringing us closer to where we needed to be.

My whole body itched with an insatiable urge to move. I couldn't make time move faster, but I could certainly go on a power walk to relieve some of the stress. Brittney was still too young to keep up with me, and the walking stroller I had could only seat one, which meant today Ryan would be my walking buddy. Brittney was happily drawing in the living room anyway. I looked around for Nate, and found him standing out in the backyard looking out at the water off in the distance. The only thing worse than time going slowly was seeing Nate beat himself up because of it. He still wasn't over failing the first bar exam. He wanted so badly to provide for his family, but he also just had to wait.

I walked out to Nate and put my arm around his waist. "We're almost there, Honey. Two more months."

He gave me a silent nod.

"I'm going to take Ryan out for a walk. Will you watch Brittney? Then can you come and pick us up?"

"Yeah, sure, give me a call when you're ready."

I checked my pocket to make sure I had a quarter to call him from the payphone right outside the grocery store where I planned on ending my walk.

I gave Nate a long hug. I felt so helpless. Then Ryan and I left the house for some much needed exercise.

Even though Ryan had recently learned to walk, he was happy to be out with me as I pushed him in his stroller. I loved this stroller! It had three wheels: one in the front, and two in back, designed for walking fast, and that's exactly what I planned on doing. In a matter of minutes, we had arrived on the main road of Island Crest Way—a beautiful street lined with tall, green trees. The air was cold and fresh from frequent rainfall, and we were both bundled up for the walk into town.

As we walked down the hill, my eyes took in the beautiful scenery and the charm of the pristine homes that lined Island Crest Way. I was glad that Nate would be picking us up because the walk down hill was much easier than the walk back up the hill with the stroller. I admired a house with a stone, three-tiered water fountain gurgling in the courtyard that led up to the front door. Another residence had a lovely rose garden and pebbled pathway. As I passed by, I dreamed of owning our own home someday. The kids loved this street. Sometimes I would take them out for a walk to pick wild blackberries. Other times we would walk over to Dragon Park, which had a big purple dragon that kids loved to climb on. Mercer Island was a wealthy, safe town with a serene separation from the city. Each time I walked, I felt thankful and blessed to be housesitting here!

The road continued down the slope, where black and white caught my eye. I noticed a cop on a motorcycle hiding in between the trees just out of sight from all the cars coming down the hill. I watched as it took only seconds for the cop to rush out and pull over a car that sped past him. I couldn't help but feel sorry for the unsuspecting driver—I hate when that happens! As I passed by, the officer handed the man a ticket and returned to his hiding spot between the trees.

As I reached the bottom of the hill, I began thinking about the next two months. Nate's bar results would be in once again, and I felt both excited and anxious. I had such a strong faith in God, and in Nate, but what if he didn't pass again? We would have to do this wait a *third* time. We couldn't afford a second fail. We couldn't afford it financially, and we definitely couldn't afford it emotionally. My temporary hygiene license would expire before he had a chance to take it a third time.

Ryan began coughing and I halted.

Oh no, no, no, we cannot do an asthma attack right now.

I leaned over the stroller and took a moment to listen to his breathing. At this point, I was closer to his pediatrician's office than I was to the house. Both places had a nebulizer ready for Ryan's latest asthma attack. Poor baby. Between his asthma and ear infections, the pediatrician and I were well acquainted.

I continued watching him, with his chubby cheeks, as he began babbling again. I smiled, thankful for the air he was breathing today. And besides, we certainly didn't need another doctor bill. Our medical expenses, including the pediatrician, the ear, nose, and throat doctor, and well-baby check-ups along the way for both Brittney and Ryan, were climbing by the month. We were always good at making monthly payments, but between student loans and doctor bills, our budget was strapped.

We passed Mercer Dale Park where there were other moms walking with their kids on this clear, but chilly day. Ryan pointed to a dog being walked by its owner. The glamorous houses turned into tall apartments and condos as we got closer to town. Artsy stores and cafes lined the streets. People browsed through the shops while others stood in line at the many coffee shops. We traveled down the road to the grocery store where I took out my quarter and called Nate from the phone booth. With him getting Brittney ready, Ryan and I would have about a ten-minute wait. I hung up.

"Dang it!" I snapped as I hung up, quickly grabbing the phone in hopes that we were still connected. The dial tone met my ear and I began searching my pockets frantically for another quarter. I had forgotten to warn Nate about the cop hiding on his motorcycle. Once again, all I could do was wait and hope that the officer either had left his post, or that Nate was driving the speed limit!

Cars passed and so did the time. I just knew that the cop had pulled Nate over, rushing from his hiding place in a blaze of red and blue lights. Ryan and I waited until, at last, Nate finally pulled up to the curb and helped fold the stroller to put in the trunk.

"What happened?" I asked, placing Ryan in the car seat. Brittney was buckled in next to him with Meeko, her stuffed raccoon from Pocahontas.

Nate shut the back door and started the car. "I got a ticket," Nate said as he pulled out into the street.

I couldn't help but let out a disappointed, "Ugh, I knew it!" My stress began to bubble into anger at myself for only bringing one quarter. "I should have warned you! I saw that cop earlier."

"Babe, I was the one who was speeding," he said firmly, starting back up the hill.

"But none of this would have happened if I had just brought another quarter. One quarter could've saved us hundreds of dollars!" I sank back in my seat. "Why did you have to speed anyway? You were just picking us up from the grocery store."

Nate didn't say anything, and I didn't say anything more. All I could do was picture the latest bills coming in along with an added speeding ticket.

He put his hand on my knee. "I'll take care of it, Princess. Don't worry."

I put my hand on top of his. I knew he meant well, but the reality of it was that money was tight and I wasn't sure how we were going to pay the ticket. The touch of him calmed me as I tried to shake away the numbers and dollar signs.

Just like he said he would, Nate promptly took care of it. He sold some of his baseball cards and didn't tell me until after the fact so that I couldn't talk him out of it. I appreciated his sacrifice and was reminded that we would get through this time of waiting ... just like we always did.

In the still of the night, the only surrounding noise came from the muted hum of the tires beneath us and my heart pounding as we drove across the Floating Bridge. The darkened waters of Lake Washington reflected the moon and the lights of waterfront homes along the shore. Unlike the usual congestion of heavy traffic during commuting hours, the freeway was almost completely open. The clock on the dashboard glowed 11:33 pm

We merged left off the freeway and drove through a lit tunnel. The sound of our Jeep created an echo that bounced off the concrete walls. Back under the moonlit sky, we continued to make our way down to the harbor where docked yachts were gently rocking on the tranquil water of Lake Union. Nate turned off the engine in the empty parking lot in front of a high-rise business building with lake view windows and a surrounding restaurant that was currently closed.

With excitement and nervous energy, Nate and I walked hand in hand toward Jerry's business. The bar results were going to be released at 12:00 am, but we didn't have a home computer and couldn't wait until the morning. We wanted to know now! We had left the kids at home with Jerry so that we could use the computer in his office.

Nate took the keys out of his pocket and opened the front door. The building was dimly lit and deserted except for the night patrol officer in the lobby. We stepped into the elevator and Nate pressed the button for the seventh floor. We walked down the hallway and stopped in front of the glass doors that read Marine Title Company in gold lettering. Nate briefly paused before opening the door. I took in a deep breath to calm my thoughts and then stepped inside as Nate turned on the lights. We walked past the marble counters where receptionists would be transferring calls and helping clientele once the office opened in the morning. In the corner room, Nate sat at his dad's desk and booted up the computer. I looked at the clock, only seven minutes until we would know the news.

Oh God, *please* let it be good news this time!

As we waited, I wandered around the office. I had been in here many times over the years and always admired the clever decor of Jerry's office. He had it set up almost like a map of Washington. To the left, a large etching of the Olympic Mountain Range hung against the wall. Had there been a window rather than a wall, the actual mountain range would be seen. Another etching, one of the glacier-capped Mount Rainier, hung on the opposite wall that blocked its rugged peak. The big window, directly behind Nate, was like a frame for the spectacular view of the illuminated Space Needle.

"Okay, I'm on," Nate announced.

I hurried over next to him and watched the arrow drag through a list of names. As we searched for Nate's name to appear, I saw Mercer Island. My stomach tightened. It had to be Nate—probably the only law school graduate in Washington looking for California results. Nate scrolled up and there he was.

Nathan Andrew Baker: Pass

I squealed with delight, clapping and jumping as Nate shouted a "*YES!*" with a triumphant fist. He stood up with a beaming smile. We embraced. I cheered. We embraced again, breathing a tremendous sigh of relief at this wonderful news. Everything inside me was doing cartwheels. *He passed!! He passed!! Nate's an Attorney!*

Nate left a note for his co-workers, letting them know the good news when they would arrive in the morning. We shut down the office and walked out of the building feeling on top of the world. It took all my self-control not to scream the news and watch the lights flick on window by window as I'd wake up everyone surrounding Lake Union. Instead, I bounced in my seat on our drive back to the house while Nate turned up the radio. From the moon on this crystal clear night, to the city lights, everything seemed brighter.

Jerry was the first person we told. We were too excited to wait, so we woke him up in the middle of the night. He quietly congratulated us from under the covers. I held off yet another urge to scream the news, remembering our kids were sound asleep in the other room.

Although I had time to squeeze in a couple of hours sleep before my 7:00 am patient, I was just too wide awake to close my eyes. Nate and I were wired from this natural high. We were caught up in a powerful state of complete happiness—and relief—that outlasted the dawn. As I got ready for work, the news of Nate passing The Bar felt completely surreal—the thought kept repeating over and over in my head—*my husband is an Attorney! An Attorney! He passed The Bar!* I was so elated, I didn't even notice the traffic on my drive to work. When I arrived, I stepped into the elevator. As the floor beneath me began rising, I thought, *Nate is an Attorney!*

We left for California the following month. Jerry was back in Washington working again at his company, and my eighteen-month Dental Hygiene license would soon expire. We were moving back to Salinas temporarily while Nate would apply to all fifty-eight counties in California. We'd move and raise the kids wherever he got hired. The move itself happened fast and before we knew it, a moving truck was driving our things back to California.

Although we were thrilled that Nate could start his career, saying goodbye to Seattle tugged at my heart strings. I would miss Jerry, or *"Go Go"* as Ryan called him, the pitter patter of rain that lulled me to sleep at night, and I was really going to miss our church. A few days ago, I had made arrangements with a lady from Canyon Hills to send us Pastor Steve's sermon on a cassette tape every week. I couldn't wait to get the first one—it felt good to take a little bit of Seattle back home with us through these powerful sermons. As we drove south in our packed Jeep, I took one last glance at the Space Needle and watched it shrink away in the distance until it was completely out of sight.

If it were up to Nate, we would drive directly from Seattle to Salinas with no stops. However, with two small children, that was not an option—so we agreed to make it a two-day trip, stopping the first night in Oregon. Ready for a good night's sleep, we put Brittney between us and Ryan in an empty dresser drawer lined with blankets—the perfect fit for our one-year-old.

Nate and I were feeling good. It had taken almost ten years, but we had accomplished our goals—getting married, having children, finishing college, and passing our state exams. All that was left—at least for now—was for Nate to get sworn in, be hired as a prosecutor, and for us to find a home. Even though we were back at my parents' house, it would be a brief stay.

Nate's swearing in ceremony took place at the courthouse in Monterey. He didn't want to *make a big deal out of it*—even though it was—and only wanted to invite family and his three best friends. Everyone was dressed for the occasion as we sat in the courtroom and watched Nate and the Judge stand at the podium with the American Flag and the City of Monterey Seal behind them. Mary dabbed proud tears from her eyes as Nate held up his right hand and repeated the oath after the Judge. We took pictures after the ceremony. Then Mary took the kids home, while the rest of us went out to give Nate a toast, congratulating his accomplishments.

As days turned into weeks, and weeks turned into months, we began to feel disheartened. Nate sent out applications daily and we were just waiting for a response. It was as if we had stepped from one waiting room to the next, and now we were stuck. Eventually, we had no choice but to return to what we were doing before we'd left. Nate went back to substitute teaching at Fairview Middle School in Gonzales. And I, once again, returned to the dental office I had worked at for years. Besides the fact that Nate had passed the Bar, we were *exactly* where we were before we had moved to Seattle.

In our attempt to avoid getting settled in Salinas due to Nate potentially getting a job somewhere else in California, we went from living with my parents to moving in with Mary for a while. We thought Nate would get hired well before Brittney started kindergarten, but now here we were, filling out enrollment papers for her to start school. Nate and I were both working hard, but it was like we were on a treadmill, moving but not getting anywhere.

We came to a point of realization that this might take a while. We couldn't stay with parents forever—we had a family and needed our own space. We decided to look into renting a house, something that was inexpensive. We *hopefully* would not be living there long.

The only rental available was a neglected little two bedroom house that desperately needed cleaning. We were thankful to have our own place again, but... Ewww! I scrubbed down the entire bathroom with bleach just so the kids could take a bath. It wasn't just the bathroom, the kitchen also needed a lot of cleaning, and so did the light fixtures, the carpet... pretty much everything. Although it was a lot of work, cleaning gave me an outlet for all of my frustration. At least with cleaning, I could see immediate results—unlike this job-hunting process that was taking its sweet time.

We weren't going to move furniture in until the house was disinfected. I laid a blanket out on the floor in the living room for picnic style meals, which the kids thought was super fun, and that's when we discovered fleas!

It was all I could do not to just break down and start crying. Nate and I had just scrubbed the heck out of the house and now we had fleas jumping on our children and into our food. Nothing was working. I didn't know what to do anymore. I was so tired of this! I tried so hard to be hopeful and supportive. We both had worked so hard, yet we were getting nowhere. And now, we were in this house with not even a promise of anything getting any better. I was mad, discouraged, and just *done*. I was done striving for something that seemed like we were never going to get. I didn't understand what God was doing... or if He was doing anything at all.

After spending the evening performing chest compressions and mouth to mouth resuscitation on a mannequin, I pulled into the driveway of our awful—and temporary—rental house. The headlights illuminated the rickety garage door as it started to open. Irritated, I sat in the driver's seat listening to its rumbling.

"Man, I can't wait to leave this house," I grumbled, as I began slowly driving our Jeep in between all of the cardboard boxes stacked on each side of the garage.

When we moved in, we had agreed to only unpack the essentials due to this rental being transitional, kind of like an extended stay in a hotel. The walls were plain and the living room lacked its homey vibe with family albums and decorative couch pillows. Days and weeks had passed now, but Nate and I continued to pray and kept our focus on the goal: Nate being hired at a District Attorney's Office.

As I opened my car door, I saw Nate standing in the doorway. He had been watching the kids while I was gone. I maneuvered through the mounds of unpacked boxes and over to him.

"How was your class?" Nate asked, as I greeted him with a kiss.

"Good," I answered, not thinking much of it—the class was a routine course taken every two years in order to maintain an active RDH license.

"Did you learn CPR?"

"Yeah..." I replied, with a raised eyebrow.

"Good, because you're going to need it when I tell you this," he said, with an energetic grin.

I stopped and looked at Nate. "What is it?!" I asked.

"Stanislaus County just called and offered me a position as a Deputy District Attorney! They want to hire me!"

I felt a zing in my stomach and then gasped as my hands covered my mouth. "What? You got the job?!" I squealed.

Nate exhaled with a laugh at my excitement. "We're moving to Modesto!"

I bounced right into Nate's arms. Relishing the moment, we held each other for a very long and tight hug. The longer I held on to Nate, I could feel the emotion overtake me. This was our dream. It was really happening!

"Congratulations, Honey! You did it, you did it, you did it!!!" The moment we had been waiting for was *finally* here! Nate had been hired as a Prosecutor and he started in two weeks! I stood there absorbing this amazing news.

"Where's Modesto?" I asked.

Chapter 8

"Our House" by Madness

FROM A DISTANCE, I could see a tall, white water tower that read MODESTO in bold black letters. I looked out the window as we drove across an old historic bridge with railing and decorative pillars. On each side of the bridge sat a large sculpted cement lion, each resting with their front legs outstretched before them. With the car slowing due to an upcoming stop sign, I took a closer look at the lions. I noticed all of the cracks in their flowing manes, and the deterioration of their majestic faces. Although time seemed to have taken its toll, their eyes remained vigilant, almost as if they were giving their permission for us to enter town.

It had taken almost two hours to get from Salinas to Modesto. But as the water tower drew closer, I knew we were here—our new hometown. We continued northbound, driving parallel to railroad tracks. A few abandoned boxcars spray painted with graffiti sat off to the side in the dirt. My eyes took in every detail—a large factory off to the right, with workers wearing their yellow hard hats, and a taco truck parked in an empty lot. Then I caught sight of a homeless man holding up a cardboard sign asking for help. I was a little taken aback by my first views of Modesto, and wondered what living here would be like.

I looked over at Nate. "Are you nervous?" I asked.

"Nope," Nate said calmly. "Well ... maybe a little bit." He smiled.

I grinned back at him. I could feel butterflies in my stomach. "Well, I am," I said.

We spotted a pay phone outside a liquor store and pulled over to call the District Attorney's Office to let them know we were in town. They were expecting us. We wanted to double-check Nate's starting date and meet everyone before we looked for a place to live.

Nate parallel parked in a two-hour parking zone, and we looked over at the four story, beige building on the next block with STANISLAUS COUNTY COURTHOUSE engraved on the front of the building. My stomach tightened. I was used to being around dentists, but lawyers — I had no experience with legal professionals. What would they be like? Nate and I were both dressed nicely, but these people would be professionally dressed in suits and ties, and skirt suits. My nerves caused me to start overthinking. Should I shake their hands? Or, should I give them a hug? No, that might be a little too much. Maybe I should do that cheek kissing thing that I see in the movies where people greet each other by air kissing the sides of their cheeks. Do you kiss one cheek or both cheeks? Do attorneys do that? Oh God, please help me to make a good first impression. Being an attorney's wife was very new. Exciting, but unknown territory for sure.

Hand in hand, Nate and I climbed the steps leading up to the entrance of the courthouse. Nate held open the large door for me as we walked in. It all felt so official as we made our way through the metal detectors and the security bailiffs cleared us to enter. A statue of Lady Justice, in her long flowing white robe, stood tall in the lobby. She was holding the Scales of Justice in one hand, and a long double-edged sword in the other. I took in a deep breath and continued walking forward.

Within minutes, friendly people were wholeheartedly welcoming us to the District Attorney's Office. Immediately, I noticed their genuine smiles, and didn't really pay much attention to what they were wearing. It was wonderful meeting Nate's new co-workers, and I greeted them naturally—some with a handshake, others with a hug. No one welcomed us with an air kiss to the cheek. They were all friendly, down to earth, and I could tell I was really going to like these people.

We were soon in the Chief Deputy District Attorney's office. Nate and I sat down in the chairs that faced his desk. Nate thanked Jerry Begen for hiring him and taking a chance with a rookie who had no experience with courtroom trials. He then promised Mr. Begen that he would not regret hiring him. Mr. Begen looked at us and shared his own experience of when he was first hired at the DA's Office. He told us that he and his wife decided they would live here just long enough to get started, and then they would leave for a bigger and better place. "We decided to give it two years... that was ten years ago," he said. "Modesto is nothing fancy; it's the people that make this place great."

We walked back down the steps feeling a little lighter. As we pulled away from the District Attorney's Office, I looked out the window and smiled. Now that we had met everybody, my nervousness was swapped for excitement in anticipation of our new life here in Modesto.

We found a restaurant, and over lunch Nate told me about a neighborhood he had discovered when he had been here for his interview. When we finished, we drove over there and walked through a few of the homes that were for sale. We weren't sure if we could afford a house, yet when we saw the list prices of brand new houses, I began to blink back tears. Maybe this just might be possible. The reality of this dream was very emotional — everything we had worked for had come to fruition. We could afford to buy our first house! With Nate's salary, my salary, the very affordable prices in Modesto, and a little help from Mary towards a down payment, it was just a matter of choosing the house we wanted. So that's exactly what we did — we bought a house!

It was such a surreal moment, stepping onto the front porch of our newly purchased house. I looked up at Nate, who was holding the key in his hand. We shared a look of love, accomplishment, and humility. After almost ten years of striving to get to this moment, we were about to open the door, literally, to our new life in Modesto. Nate turned the key and opened the oversized maplewood front door. He swept me off my feet and carried me over the threshold into our new house. The kids and I giggled at his grand gesture. Brittney and Ryan rushed inside eager to explore all the empty rooms.

Our one story, four bedroom, two bathroom house was a new build. We even got to pick out the light fixtures, and the color of the carpet. I couldn't get over the L-shaped hallway — it made me feel like we had the biggest house in the world!

Jon walked in carrying a big box and set it down on the paver tiles in the kitchen. "Whoa," he said, as he took his first look around.

"Uncle Jon, Uncle Jon, look at this," Brittney squealed, as she tugged on him to follow her.

"I wanna get a picture of you out in front of the house." My mom said as she waved us over from the front door.

With a click of the camera, our milestone was captured on film. Nate was all smiles as he pulled out the FOR SALE sign from our front lawn. We posed next to the red sign reading SOLD in big white letters. A void in the grass was all that was left of where the sign used to stand.

We were at the end of a cul-de-sac, the house in the very middle. Our new neighborhood was right around the corner from the green fairways of Creekside Golf Course. There was another new community of houses being built around ours with freshly laid lawns and young trees. Empty lots awaited homes that hadn't been built yet. Our neighborhood was growing, the perfect place for our children to grow along with it.

While we were unloading the U-Haul, curious neighbors came out to introduce themselves and offer us some help. The families were young like ours, and one even had a baby on the way. Everyone was so friendly as they welcomed us to the neighborhood. While my mom and Jon were busy helping us unload boxes, Mary was back in Salinas helping us tie up a few loose ends. Once again our families were a huge help. It was so exciting to have them here with us.

The kids were feeding off all the excitement. Brittney was busy in her new bedroom figuring out where she would put all of her things, while Ryan was happy just to be following us around. I went out to my car to grab a few more things. When I turned around, I stopped as I saw Ryan standing in the driveway. It was like I was transported back in time to the afternoon when Nate sang me his song. I could hear Nate's electric guitar strum through my memory to the song he'd written for me ten years before. Ryan was the toddler he had penned in blue ink. When I saw him in the driveway standing next to the U-Haul waiting for me, it was as if the picture Nate had drawn next to his lyrics had come to life. With a lump in my throat, I smiled tenderly as I stood there looking at our son. That simple little doodle on a torn-out piece of notebook paper was now my life. I took a picture, quick to capture the moment before Ryan toddled out to meet me.

Everything was perfect. I couldn't wait to settle in, get a job, make some new friends, learn the town, and raise the kids in this house that already felt like home. It was amazing to have things permanent and not so temporary—like they had been for such a *long* time. And then it hit me... if Nate had passed the Bar the first time, our lives would be completely different right now. Modesto is where we were supposed to live and raise the kids. It's just two hours away from our family and friends in Salinas. We bought this great new house, Nate and I have our dream careers, and we couldn't ask for better neighbors. This was God's plan for us all along—we just had to trust and be patient.

One by one, the logistics of moving to a new town began falling into place. I had even found a job! After we bought our house, I needed to finish my last two weeks of work back in Salinas. I had brought a copy of the Modesto phone book back with me and just started calling dental offices in alphabetical order out of the yellow pages. A receptionist named Ern—short for Ernestine—had answered the phone the day I called to see if they needed a hygienist. We had somehow bonded before we even met, and I later heard the story of how Ern told the doctor's wife, Virginia, "You gotta take this call." I soon had an interview with Virginia, who was also the office manager. The interview went great and she invited Nate and me out to dinner at The Olive Gar*den* to meet the entire staff and their spouses. It was evident the staff at Dr. Bleakley's office was very close, and I looked forward to getting to know each of them.

After asking around, I was told about a lady named Molly Lamkin. I gave her a call and set up a time for us to meet. There's a feeling you get when you know something is right. You can feel it. And I felt that with Molly. I was greeted with a warm voice and a smile as I walked in and caught a glimpse of her. She was wearing a white Mickey Mouse T-shirt and sat rocking a baby by the fireplace. With nine adult children of her own, and countless other children she had watched over the last twenty-seven years, it was like she was born to be a mom. She loved each and every one of her daycare kids. Without a doubt, she was the one I wanted to watch Brittney and Ryan. The kids fit right in at the Lamkin home. Molly and her husband Bill had been married for thirty-nine years. They were an answer to prayer, and exactly who Nate and I wanted to be with the kids on the three days each week that I worked. Within a few weeks, I had both a job and the daycare provider of my dreams.

Monday, November 11, 1996—four years after losing Justin—just so happened to be the first day of work at my new job. Although this memory was always difficult, the holiday itself was good timing—the District Attorney's Office was closed for Veterans Day. It gave me comfort to know that Nate was home with the kids. Our time in Seattle, where Nate would watch the kids, was over. Now, I could work part time. Tomorrow, I would be home with the kids, and Nate would be returning to work after his three-day weekend.

I arrived at work ready to learn the ins and outs of my new office and get to know the staff and patients. Even though it was my first day, the faces of the office staff were familiar to me from our dinner together—now I just had to remember everybody's name. I remembered Ern's unique name though. Although she wasn't able to go to dinner with us due to a prior commitment, we had talked and it turns out Ern and I had a lot in common. We both were born in '68 and graduated high school in '86. She had already worked in the office for ten years, knew all the patients, and was like a daughter to the Bleakleys. And even though we had only recently met, I had a feeling we were going to be close friends.

By the time my last patient left, I was getting all settled into my new room. I really liked the unique decor. Dr. Bleakley had a passion for collecting old gasoline station memorabilia. In each room there was a shelf just below the ceiling upon which were lit gasoline globes. In my room, there were three big Shell Gasoline signs on the wall. I smiled. This room was a total fit for me—it literally had my name all over it! The north wall of my room was all window with a full view of the many inviting boutiques of McHenry Village. They were drawing me in, and I couldn't wait to spend some time looking through all of them. No doubt, I would find something I *needed* to start decorating our awesome house! All in due time. For now, making our first mortgage payment came before shopping.

Within weeks of starting my new job, I was handed an invitation for the Bleakley's Office Christmas Party which would be held at their home. With us being so new to town, Virginia had made arrangements for someone she trusted to watch Brittney and Ryan next door at their daughter's house. That way Nate and I could attend the party, and rest assured that the kids were close by and taken care of.

The Bleakley's home was elegantly decorated from floor to ceiling like an HGTV magazine cover. My eyes took in all of the Christmas trimmings that flowed from room to room—strings of glimmering lights, festive wreaths and garlands, ornaments, stockings, and the dinner table. A large rectangular dining table filled the entire living room. Every guest here tonight would be able to sit at the same table for dinner. When I saw the ice sculpture centerpiece, I couldn't help but wonder how in the world she managed to decorate the middle of the table with it being so big!

As we talked, I noticed the familiar aroma of tri-tip. My childhood town of Santa Maria was well known for the scores of Tri-Tip BBQs lining the streets every weekend. It smelled amazing, and I couldn't wait to take a bite. But for now, appetizers were being passed around as Nate and I were being introduced to longtime friends of the office. While chatting with co-workers and mingling with others we had just met, I took a sip of my Lemon Drop with Chambord and glanced off to the side. I watched as Nate meandered over to the dinner table. My head turned slightly sideways as I saw him reach for something. He turned around with a cheek full and a grin. Oh no, what did he get into?! As I walked over to Nate I soon figured out why he was grinning.

"Nate!" I somehow whispered a shout. He was eating the place card decorations! Looking around at the assigned seating, I saw each guest's name written in a beautiful font. Each card was embellished with an edible Christmas decoration next to the name. Although they were edible, they weren't meant to be eaten. Each little tree, snowman, and warm mitten was glued to the place card.

"Oh my gosh, Nate! We barely know these people," I started telling him as Virginia began walking over. Nate wiped his mouth with the back of his hand and smiled as he saw Virginia drawing near. I shook my head and put my head down chuckling. "I'm so sorry, Virginia. Your home is so beautiful and Nate... he..." By the look on her face, I knew that she discovered what I was trying to say. Instead of being upset, she began laughing, which only encouraged Nate to pull off another decoration from someone else's place card. By now, Ern had followed the commotion. Her outspoken, charismatic personality made people laugh. She seemed to feed off of the attention, and she got a lot of it. Without a doubt she could keep up with Nate's shenanigans, and before I knew it she had vivaciously told the entire office about Nate's choice of appetizers. I was glad that Virginia was humored by Nate's idiosyncrasies because he wasn't done. Nate spent the rest of the evening turning any *cute* Christmas decoration either upside down or backwards like he did every Christmas.

Monday arrived, and we were all back to work. Everyone was thanking Dr. Bleakley and Virginia for the fun Christmas party. Nate's name came up frequently throughout the reminiscing, and even some of the patients heard the stories of my one-of-a-kind husband *adjusting* many of the Christmas decorations. My new office had their first experience with Nate's sense of humor. Virginia had brought in the leftover tri-tip to the office, and had it heating up in a large crock pot all morning. The dental office smelled like a restaurant by lunch time, and patients would joke about staying around for lunch. It was awesome having an hour and a half for lunch break every day—an office perk that was easy to get used to.

One day we went to El Rosal for lunch. It was a delicious Mexican restaurant and love at first bite. It became my new favorite restaurant. The ladies from the office usually had lunch together, and as the days passed, it was usually El Rosal where we ate—at least one or two times a week. If there was ever a bit of extra time after lunch, I would run over to one of the shops in McHenry Village for a quick look at the home decor or clothing shops before returning to work for my afternoon patients.

As the days and weeks went by, it was nice getting to know the patients. One of my afternoon patients was a pastor. I told him we were new in town, and although we were trying, we hadn't found our home church quite yet. As we got to talking, we found out that our children were around the same ages. By the end of the appointment, he had given me his home phone number. He told me that his wife would be happy to show me around town and maybe we could take the kids to the park. By the time he left the office, he had written down a few churches to try, including his — CrossPoint Community Church — a non-denominational church in downtown Modesto.

Within a week, the kids and I had met the pastor's wife and their three young children. The kids played at the park while we talked. She was very helpful in filling me in on a lot of kids' activities both in and out of church. By the end of our time together, she had invited me to a scrapbook party she was hosting at her house. She encouraged me to call if we had questions or needed anything.

Modesto's small-town feel was turning into the perfect fit for us. We loved the open space of almond orchards that were starting to bloom with their pink flowering buds; the shops in McHenry Village that were always calling my name; the delicious food at El Rosal that I craved; but most of all, we loved the people. It was the people who made Modesto feel like home. Our co-workers, neighbors, daycare providers, and our new church were all so very welcoming. I already understood what Jerry Began had meant when we had talked with him in his office. It's the people who make Modesto a great place to live. Our family was very happy here.

"I can't believe they pay me for this," Nate said, coming in from work. He loosened his tie and leaned in to kiss me. "This is exactly what I want to be doing," he said with enthusiasm. Immediately, he noticed the potatoes that I had just finished mashing. He grabbed a spoon and took a bite. "Ow, ow, ow, hot, hot," he said, trying to cool the mouthful of potatoes by quickly blowing air in and out.

"Nate! Be careful, Honey, you're going to burn yourself!" I warned, as I had done many times before. Nate did this practically every time I was cooking or baking. No doubt, he would do this again — probably before we sat down for dinner.

"Congratulations on your guilty verdict!" I said, smiling. Nate had told me that I would always be the first person he would tell when the jury came back with a verdict. And since his very first case, that's exactly what he did. I thanked him for his phone call this morning letting me know the great news and gave him a big hug. He smiled.

"Oohhh Baby," he said with flirty eyes, his hands quickly feeling the sides of my body up and down with active, vivacious banter.

"Nate!" I giggled and playfully pushed his hands away.

The stress from his case was over, and Nate came home a bundle of energy. He took another spoonful of mashed potatoes. "Owww, ow, hot!"

I rolled my eyes and laughed.

He started to walk down the hallway to our bedroom to change his clothes. "When's dinner gonna to be ready, woman?!"

"Very funny, Nate," I yelled out from the kitchen. The kids could hear that Dad was home, and Ryan hurried down the hallway to see him.

"Boy!" Nate called out in one of his playful voices.

As I finished preparing dinner, I thought about Nate's amazing career. The DA's Office fit him like a well-tailored suit—he regularly came home smiling from a successful day of prosecuting misdemeanors. Nate looked forward to the day he would move up to prosecuting felonies. Although Nate always brought home a briefcase full of cases to prepare, he always put family before work, and he showed that every night. Long after the kids and I were fast asleep, Nate would stay up late working. He preferred to prepare his cases during the late night hours—the house was quiet, and it gave him time to concentrate on what he was doing without any interruptions. I admired how he cared for our family, even when work was busy and demanded a lot of prepping. He never complained or showed how tired he was; he would make it up by sleeping in late on Saturday morning.

"I don't like ribs!" Ryan cried out after I let him know it was time for a bath. The kids were having fun playing in Brittney's room, but the weekend was over and it was getting late. Even though it wasn't a school night for Ryan — he was still too young — Brittney needed to get up early. Her second-grade teachers were strict and had high expectations for their students. She needed to start the week with a good night's sleep to prepare her for all of the homework they gave each week. Even the spelling words were challenging — words like prestidigitation and mugwumpery. I often had to look up the definitions myself before quizzing her.

As the kids began picking up the toys, Ryan started in again, "I don't like ribs!" Tears began to flow. He knew playtime was over and the bathtub awaited. We were used to this — it was the weirdest thing — Ryan understood the word "no," but never said it. *I don't like ribs!* was his way of saying *no.* We had no idea where the phrase came from. We would hear about his distaste for ribs off and on throughout the week. *He didn't like ribs* when he — like tonight — had to take a bath, or when he had to get his haircut, or sleep in his own bed. And he defiantly *didn't like ribs* during his three-minute time-outs — one minute per year of his age. Ryan's longing for company made time-outs the absolute worst punishment imaginable for him.

Laughing on the inside, I corrected our toddler in a motherly tone. "Ryan, what you mean to say is 'No Mom, I don't want to take a bath,' " I explained to Ryan as I picked him up from the carpet where they were playing.

"IIII dooonnn't likkkeeee riiibbbsss!" Ryan carried on being overly dramatic. Did he not hear my explanation of the word *no*? Mental note, make sure Ryan understands the meaning of the word *no* by time he starts preschool.

Another summer had come and passed. We had learned a couple of years ago how to deal with Modesto's triple digit heat—by turning the AC on in April, and not turning it off until mid-October. The kids had their own way of cooling off—swimming in the neighbors' pools, and eating lots of Otter Pops.

Nate and I decided that this was the summer we would start going to baseball parks again. We took the kids on a road trip to see the *Colorado Rockies*. Ryan had a lot of fun playing Tee-ball—Nate was the coach—but this was his first MLB game. Brittney was only fifteen months old when we had taken her and Justin to the three ball parks in Southern California, so being at the venue of *Coors Field* felt like her first baseball game as well.

We covered a lot of miles and found that the kids were awesome travelers! They loved the open road, and we stopped to see many sites along the way—especially the natural beauty of the National Parks. While Nate and I were basking in wonder at the incredible scenery of the sandstone monuments of Arches National Park, the steep red cliffs of Zion, and the geological wonders of Bryce Canyon, the kids seemed to be more interested in finding lizards and chasing squirrels. The quarry at Dinosaur National Monument, however, had the kids' full attention. With countless fossils and relics of bones embedded in the rock, the kids were fascinated with exploring the same grounds where dinosaurs used to roam. They also liked the expansive Bonneville Salt Flats with white salt as far as the eye could see, but their favorite of all was racing down the Alpine Slides in Park City, Utah.

And then, during those long distant spans of driving when we wanted to put some miles behind us, I read Harry Potter out loud to the family. We finished the book by the time we returned home and looked forward to the second book in the series which was already out. Even though we didn't have another road trip planned for a while, our regular trips back and forth to Salinas would be enough time to continue the story.

It seemed unreal that Brittney was starting fourth grade already, and I was helping Ryan get ready for his first day of kindergarten. I was so emotional. It felt like I was saying goodbye to the baby and toddler years forever. And in reality, I was. Although we had always intended on having three kids, Nate and I had decided to stop at two. We had our daughter. We had our son. We were good. I wanted to freeze time though. Ryan had always been my little buddy. We would take Brittney to school, then do things like grocery shop and run errands. Even when I was cleaning the house or cooking, he was still there with me, and great company. He would watch cartoons or *help* me with whatever I was doing. But *now,* Ryan would be in school every day. My eyes had been tearing up off and on all morning. Change—one of the inevitable laws of nature—was always difficult for me. Ern had been razzing me at work all month about how hard I was taking this.

As I began putting Ryan's lunch in his Pokemon backpack, my mind began drifting back to a brief conversation I had had with a lady at Village Bakery when Ryan was a toddler. Occasionally, after Ryan and I dropped Brittney off at school, we would stop by McHenry Village to get a muffin and a hot chocolate for breakfast at the bakery. Ryan had fallen asleep in my arms as I stood in line to place my order. A lady came up to me with a tender look on her face. She smiled softly at Ryan, with his head resting on my shoulder. She told me that her kids were all grown up, but she sure missed precious moments like these. Fast forward a couple of years, and now I understood the lady at Village Bakery! While before I could only sympathize with her heartfelt words, now those prophetic words were my reality as well. Those transient moments pass, and all too soon become cherished memories that live on in a mother's heart forever.

After years of being married, I seemed to have developed a sixth sense about knowing when Nate was up to something. It was evening, and I was hanging up Ryan's laundry in his room. While I was in there, I noticed that the house was unusually quiet. Intuition told me to be on high alert. I stopped what I was doing and tried listening for Nate to see if I could figure out where he was without leaving the room. When I couldn't hear him, I just knew that he was going to try to jump out and scare me.

I poked my head out into the hallway. When I didn't see him, I stealthily slipped into Brittney's room and hid in her closet. Hiding from Nate was both fun and scary. And with it being night, the darkness gave me even more of a thrill. As I sat in Brittney's closet, the only thing I had to rely on was what I could hear. I held my breath and listened, trying to figure out where he was.

Nate's heavy footsteps thumped down the hall. As he got closer to Ryan's room, his footsteps lightened—which proved my intuition was right. He was totally trying to sneak up on me.

"Hey!" Nate shouted, as I heard him jump in the doorway of Ryan's room. He paused. I could almost picture him scratching his head in confusion. "What the ... ? Where's Mom?" he called out to the kids in the living room. I wasn't able to hear their responses, and although I couldn't see Nate, I just knew he was searching for me. His footsteps came closer as he stepped into Brittney's room. He flicked on the light. As he walked by, I could see the shadows of his feet underneath the closet doors. I squinted my eyes and took slow breaths. I struggled to keep myself from laughing or screaming — the only thing between him and me was the closet doors.

Although this scenario was somewhat typical, I had never outright hidden from Nate before. His scare tactics had spontaneously morphed into a game of Hide and Seek. Nate left the room picking up on the idea that I was hiding from him. He took the bait and seemed amused. He started playing up the suspense by humming the creepy theme song from the movie *Halloween*, "Dah, dah dah, dah, dah dah, dah dah daahhh!" He knew I didn't like that movie. Even the song gave me chills.

"I'm going to find you, Nice Lady," he taunted, as he headed back down the hallway.

The sound of him looking for me in closets and behind doors echoed in my ears. My heart pounded — I knew by process of elimination that it was only a matter of time before he'd find me. When I heard him go from the office to the dining room, I very quietly opened the closet door and hurried over to the small space between Brittney's bed and the wall. I quickly covered myself with pillows and blankets while trying to remain as hushed as possible.

I could hear Nate coming back toward the kids' rooms, determined to find me. He stopped. There was a moment of complete silence. With him not making noise, I had no idea where he was. Finally, I couldn't stand it anymore. I knew it was over. From the floor, I peeked my head up with a bonafide plea for mercy. When he saw me, he gave me a playful look that let me know that he was the predator and I was the prey.

He growled and pounced across the bed to get to me.

At my first scream, I heard the kids jump up from the living room and immediately rush down the hallway yelling out "23-19!!! 23-19!!!" These numbers, inspired by the movie *Monster's Inc.*, had become their code for helping Mom when Dad was on the prowl. The kids jumped on Nate's back to save me from his unyielding tickle torture. I laughed as Nate then turned his attention from me to the kids and began chasing them down the hall on his hands and knees. They both laughed and screamed, taking my place as his prey. Nate barked and growled, making ferocious sound effects as he devoured our kids. All was back to normal—our house was noisy again.

"Ryaaaaannnn!...Give it back!...Mom!...Dad!" Brittney yelled out from her room.

I looked across the countertop at Nate who was sitting on one of the barstools talking with me while I was cleaning up the dinner dishes in the kitchen. Discussing our plans for a weekend trip to Salinas ended abruptly—trouble was brewing with the kids.

"*You* can handle this one," I said with a smile, adding another plate to the dishwasher. Nate looked at me and he knew what I meant. I stayed in the kitchen happy to sit this one out. Just days ago, we had discussed situations like this. Nate was *always* the "good cop" and I was *always* the "bad cop." Nate got all the wrestling matches and amusing jokes, while I was stuck watching the clock on the microwave for time-outs and making sure that chores were completed. Nate was a bulldog in the courtroom, but when it came to the kids, he had trouble enforcing the law.

Nate got up as Ryan came running into the dining room gripping a Pokeball toy tight in his hands. Brittney was close behind him.

"Ryan took my Charmander!" she ranted.

"It's mine!" Ryan claimed, holding on tight to the red and white plastic ball.

"Nuh-uh! We traded. It's mine now!" Brittney reminded him trying to pull it from his resisting hands.

"Okay guys. Settle down," Nate said breaking up the argument.

Brittney marched back to her room with her reclaimed Pokeball. Brittney loved her room and was happy to spend time in there. Ryan had his own room, but he loved Brittney's room more. He was such a sweetheart, but as brothers often do, Nate and I knew that he would sometimes purposely do things that he knew would make his sister mad, just to get a reaction out of her. It seemed that it was sometimes a game for him just to push Brittney's buttons—and he knew right where they all were. The kids were best buddies, but sometimes—like tonight evidently—Brittney just wanted some time to herself.

"C'mon, Boy! Just give your sister some space tonight, okay?" Nate said, as he attempted to settle things down.

Ryan came over to sit on the other barstool next to Nate and we continued talking about the upcoming weekend. Within minutes, our names were being called once again. We looked over and the barstool was now empty.

"Mom! Dad! Ryan won't get out of my room!" Brittney hollered out.

Once again, Ryan hurried out to the kitchen. This time, however, he had a grin on his face, with the Pokeball back in his hand.

I gave Nate a look reminding him that the disciplining was all his tonight. I stood there with a grin watching how Nate was going to handle our unruly son.

"Boy!" Nate said in a gruff voice, and rose from his seat. Ryan hesitated mid-step as he was making his way back to Brittney's room. "If you don't stop that, I'm going to…" Nate cleared his throat. "Stay out of Brittney's room or I'll…"

We all paused.

In the momentary silence of waiting to hear the punishment to slip from the attorney's mouth, I shifted my weight from one foot to the other. "Stay out of Brittney's room or I'll…" he repeated.

Ryan looked up at his dad. Then Nate laughed, as if shaking the pressure off his shoulders. Every punishment had been adjourned in his mind. Ryan romped off down the hall with not a care in the world.

With my eyebrows lifted, I looked over at Nate. "Well… you really told him! I'm sure he is shaking in his shoes over *that* punishment."

Nate laughed, still shaking his head, and said, "I couldn't think of anything."

I wanted to be mad at Nate for not giving me a turn at being the "good cop," but it was really funny. We both laughed.

The dinner dishes were done, but apparently the feud of the Pokemon toy was not. Sounds from the quarrel continued down the hallway until I, the bad cop, took matters into my own hands.

"Bubba tricked me!" Ryan sobbed as I walked into Brittney's room.

"What do you mean?" I asked. The kids usually played so well together, but tonight they were arguing and I just wanted to resolve the conflict once and for all. "Didn't you guys both get a Pokeball in your Kids Meal?"

"Yeah," Brittney answered.

"Well then, why don't you both just play with your own?"

"Mine's better than Bubba's and I want it back!" Ryan claimed.

Brittney soon confessed that they traded their Pokeballs even though she was well aware that Ryan, by a stroke of luck, had opened the much better one. She knew that a Charmander Pokeball trumped a Geodude by far. It was apparent that Brittney had taken advantage of her four-year-old brother's lack of Pokemon knowledge to make the trade. She didn't care about Barbies, dressing up, or even shopping. For her, at least for now, it was all about the Pokemon.

They started arguing again and each tried claiming the Charmander. Although Ryan was only four, he was all boy—solid and strong—and his grabbing for the toy accidentally scratched Brittney.

"Owwaa!" Brittney called out, pulling back her scratched arm.

"Okay you two, give me both of the Pokeballs right now!" I ordered. One by one, the kids handed over their beloved treasure. "I know that you guys are really into these right now, but tricking Ryan? That is not okay. And Ryan, you need to stop bugging Bubs and give her some space sometimes. You scratched her arm. These toys are going to be thrown away, and you both have a four minute time-out to think about your behavior tonight."

"Wwwaaaaahhhhhh!" Ryan bawled, with tears running down his cheeks. I knew he wasn't upset about the toys, but rather the four minutes—which seemed like a lifetime—in his room alone. "Please, Mom! I'll never do it again! Give me another chance!"

Brittney walked over to quietly sit on her bed, while I escorted Ryan next door to his room. I knew she, unlike her brother, was more upset about losing the toys than the time-out.

"It's not fair! Please, Mom!" Ryan continued to plead.

"That's enough, Ryan. I'm going to set the microwave for four minutes. You can just listen for the microwave to beep and then you will know the time-out is over. You'll be fine," I said, trying to comfort him, yet keeping my stern tone. "Dad and I will be right down the hall, and Bubs is next door on her bed, and doing her time-out at the same time."

Ryan got up and began to inch his way down the hallway.

"No, no, no. If you get off your bed, I'm going to start the timer over at four minutes again," I warned, as I looked at him to make sure he understood. I could hear his blubbering as I walked down the hall to set the microwave for four minutes.

"Is it over yet, Mom? Ryan called out like a prisoner from his jail cell bedroom.

I looked over at the microwave. "You only have two minutes left, Ryan. You're almost done," I reassured him.

A minute, and a few seconds later, I saw Ryan's face peek around the wall of the hallway.

"What are you doing off of your bed?!" I asked Ryan, as I walked over to escort him back to his bed. Ryan was still sobbing and trying to convince me that he would never do it again. "You are making this worse than it really needs to be, RyRy. You could be done with your time-out, but now I have to start the microwave for four minutes all over again."

Ryan's sobbing turned to whimpering as he climbed back up on his bed. I walked out of his room to reset the microwave for this never-ending time-out. I looked over at Brittney, who was quietly sitting on her bed, listening to all of the commotion coming from Ryan's room.

"Uhhh," I grunted, as I plopped down on the couch next to Nate. "Well, a time-out is a very good punishment—for Ryan. He hates to be in his room alone. Brittney, on the other hand, is totally fine in there," I said. "Bubs seems to have her own inner rogue, just like her daddy," I said, with a smile, resting my head on Nate's shoulder. "In fact...I think she is actually *enjoying* the time-out!" I sat there thinking about it for a moment and then lifted my head right back up again. "She may need a different kind of punishment," I said, thinking out loud.

Before we knew it, the microwave started to beep. In a half second flat, Ryan was back snuggling his way right between Nate and me. This had taken a lot out of him and now he just wanted to cuddle and watch television with us. I smiled, getting cozy on the couch with the boys.

My eyes were getting sleepy, and I had to work the next day. So I got up from the couch to *degoop* and change into my pajamas. As I got to our bedroom, I looked down the hall and saw Brittney. She was still on her bed, content as could be, even though her time-out had long since passed.

We could hear the kids. They were in Brittney's room playing with Hedgehog—our new yellow cockatiel. Nate and I walked down the hallway to join them.

"Okay guys, put Hedge in his cage. It's time for prayers," I told the kids.

Soon after we got settled in our new house, we began praying as a family every night before bed. One by one, we would pray out loud to God. We expressed our thankfulness for our many blessings, asked for help with our concerns, and guidance in our decisions. We also prayed for our family and friends. Tonight we would continue to pray for people in other countries who didn't yet know the Lord. Last Sunday, our church had distributed a flyer encouraging families to pray each day for people in a different country. Ending each day with family prayers was a special time of sharing what was on our minds and in our hearts. It gave us the opportunity to understand each other on a deeper level and watch as God provided for our family and answered our prayers.

We used to say prayers in the living room. However, Hedgehog would chirp non-stop if he heard us all in the living room without him. So now, prayers were in Brittney's room, where Hedge could feel included.

Nate walked over to Brittney's bed and lay down on his stomach on the top of her comforter—his usual spot for prayers. Bubs put Hedge in his cage and fastened the wire door. She climbed up on her bed and got comfortable under the covers.

Squaaaawwwk! I looked up as I was taking a seat on the floor—*my* usual spot for prayers.

"Nate, you know he doesn't like that," I reminded him, as I leaned my back against the closet doors facing the bed.

"Whhaat? I barely touched his cage," Nate smirked, as he lay there with his knees bent, and his feet swaying back and forth in the air.

This had become a nightly occurrence. Nate's leg always seemed to *accidentally* drift toward Hedge's cage and touch it. Hedgehog did not like his cage being touched—especially at night. Nate knew this. We all did!

Squaaawwwk, squaawwwk!

Ryan, who had just sat down on my lap, laughed and jumped up on the bed with Nate and Bubs to get a closer look at all the ruckus. Nate *accidentally* tapped the cage again with his foot. Hedgehog pulled his ruffled feathers in tight and screeched, conveying a clear message of annoyance.

Nate took his leg away. "Are you a good for nothin' bird?" Nate asked Hedgehog, in a very soft and loving tone. Nate—always teasing—looked over at Hedge who gave him one last *squawk*. "Awww, are you a Dew?" Nate asked Hedgehog.

Ryan grabbed the end of Bub's comforter and used it as a pillow. "What does '*Are you a Dew*' mean?" he asked. Nate and I looked at each other and laughed at the sweet innocence of our four-year-old. Although the kids had heard this phrase their entire lives, it seemed Ryan was now old enough to know that those words didn't make any sense.

"Well, back when Daddy and I first got married, we used to have a bird named Bo," I explained. "He looked just like Hedgehog, except he was gray. Daddy would play with Bo, just like he does with Hedgehog." I gave Nate a look. "When Bo would get flustered, he made a noise that sounded like he was saying '*Dew*.' So…when someone gets upset or stressed, Dad calls them a Dew. Or, he says 'Ohhh, BoBo, it's okay,'" I said, in my best Nate impersonation.

We all laughed. Laughter was always a part of our time together. I loved that. Laughter. One of the many blessings I thanked God for.

"Go ahead, Bubbasaurus," Nate said.

Brittney was usually the one to start us in prayer. She began praying for a good day at school tomorrow, for there to be no spiders in her bedroom, and for God to help her teacher understand that it was all right to hold her pencil differently than the other kids. I smiled with my eyes still closed, and my head still bowed. "And God, please help…" Brittney put her prayer on pause, as she opened her eyes to look at today's date on the flyer our church had given us. After finding the date, she saw that tonight we were praying for Turkey. It was a good way for the kids to learn that not all people in the world were Christians. Last night we had prayed for Slovenia—a country where Christianity is a minority by far. "Lord," Brittney continued, "please be with Turkey and let them learn to love Jesus. Amen."

"Okay, Boy," Nate said.

Ryan bowed his head, and asked God to keep us all safe in the night, to be with Mommy and Daddy at work tomorrow, and to please help Hedgehog not to be so grumpy at night. "And God," Ryan continued, "please be with all of the turkeys."

I opened one eye and peeked over at Nate—who was the first to respond, soon followed by Brittney and me. Everyone's eyes were open now as laughter, once again, filled the room. Ryan looked up from his prayer with a confused expression. Nate was smiling and shaking his head as he belly laughed.

"What?" Ryan asked. "Tell me," he said, not having a clue as to what was so funny.

"It's okay, Boy," Nate said, as he sat up and put Ryan on his lap. "We're not laughing with you, we're laughing at you."

"Naaate," I said, understanding my husband's sense of humor. Ryan was too young to understand the teasing.

After Nate and I had said our prayers, and we all said The Lord's Prayer together—our usual ending to prayer time, we explained to Ryan that Turkey is the name of a country, as well as a bird. Nate gobble gobbled at Ryan as he tickled him. He reached over to touch Hedgehog's cage one last time before tucking in the kids for the night.

I grabbed a towel, turned out the lights behind me, and opened the french doors from our bedroom to the backyard.

Ahhh, the inviting sound of bubbling water. I closed my eyes for a few seconds and took in a deep breath with a smile—I could almost feel the powerful air jets massaging away my busy day.

Squealing and hugging the towel close to me for warmth, I hurried over to the hot tub. "It's freezing!" I called out to Nate, as I made my way over to join him. I threw the towel on the bench and rushed over to the spa steps. The steam from the heated water was slowly rising into the chilly winter air.

"Nate!!!" I yelled out.

He was standing in the hot tub, blocking my entry with his arms folded in front of him, a big grin on his face.

I wrapped my arms around myself, wiggling around to keep warm. "It's not funny, Nate. I'm not even kidding! Let me in!"

He stood there—like a wall I couldn't move—smiling at my duress. I don't know how he does this, but I started laughing even though I was so mad at him. "Move out of the waaay, I'm freezing!" I began tussling with him, making every effort to move my robust husband out of the way. After a few seconds of grappling with each other, Nate backed up and let me in. Quickly submerging myself into the hot water, I instantly felt relief from the cold. Nate leaned his head back against the side of the hot tub smirking.

"How is it that you are such a gentleman and open doors for me, but you block my way into the hot tub? You *never* do that in the summer," I added. "Only when it's freezing cold outside," I said, in an annoyed tone.

"It's just because I love you so much," Nate teased, as he came over and took hold of my feet. He began massaging my feet—kind of a nonverbal apology. It worked. It was a beautiful clear night lit only by the stars and the street lamps out in the cul-de-sac. The hot tub had lights, but we rarely used them. Taking a soak in the starlight was one of our favorite things to do at the end of the day.

I leaned my head back and looked up into the night sky. I caught sight of the full moon and chuckled. Well... *that* explains a few things. I fixed my eyes on the moon's surface and studied its features—it was so vivid tonight. "The man in the moon is watching us," I said. Nate looked up at the sky with me. "I can see he's mad at you for not letting me get in the hot tub tonight," I joked. "You better watch out," I warned, raising my eyebrows.

Nate laughed.

The vastness of space was so hard to wrap my head around. I sat there in the bubbling hot water, admiring the star-studded sky—a chain of lights with no beginning or end. "I wonder how far Heaven is up there? Forget the man in the moon, *GOD* saw what you did to me tonight, too," I smiled.

Nate smiled, and released my feet. We sat there gazing up at the sky.

"You know, I was doing my Bible study homework for class tomorrow night. All kidding aside, God can be really strict." I took my eyes off the sky and looked at Nate. "I was studying the part where Moses struck the rock with his staff a couple of times and then water started flowing out of it." I paused. "God got really upset. Because of that one thing, Moses wasn't allowed into the Promised Land," I said, feeling bad for Moses. "After all of those years of wandering around the desert, Moses couldn't go in! Why do you think God got so mad at him?"

"Yeah, the Israelites roamed for forty years," Nate said.

"Forty years?!" I sat up. "I knew it was many years, but forty?! That's more than my whole life!"

"I think maybe God got upset because Moses struck the rock out of anger. Or, maybe because he was taking the credit away from God. I need to read that part again. But yeah, it seems really strict," Nate agreed.

"This whole study has been fascinating. I didn't know a lot about the Ark of the Covenant before this class. Now I know what the Holy of Holies is. Oh yeah, and the Levites. God struck a man down dead for reaching out to catch the Ark before it fell. That seems kind of harsh. The man was just trying to help, but he wasn't a Levite."

"You know that's what *Raiders of the Lost Ark* is all about," Nate looked over at me.

"It is?! I guess I never really thought about that. Well, I *was* in junior high when that movie came out. Hmmm, I'm going to ask everyone in class if they know that."

"Well, it's Hollywood's version anyway," Nate clarified.

"I'm about half way through this Bible Study. I haven't seen that movie in years. Let's watch it when I get done with this class. Then I can see how much of it is real, and how much of it is Hollywood," I smiled.

"Okay," Nate agreed.

"You know a lot about God and the Bible," I told him.

He looked back up into the sky. "Many years of religion classes," Nate said.

I leaned my head back again and looked up into the sky with Nate. "God is kind of hard to understand sometimes," I said. "I remember when my dad was so sick in the hospital. One of the nights I spent in the hospital with him, I heard a lady moaning and crying out in pain. ALL night. It was hard to hear her in so much pain. I remember feeling upset with God for not helping her. I just imagined God up there in Heaven with His streets of gold, while this poor lady was in agony. Do you ever wonder how God can be enjoying Himself in Heaven when there is so much pain down here on earth?" I turned my head to the side and looked over at Nate.

Nate nodded. "Yeah, I wonder about that sometimes," he said in a somber tone. "You should hear the details of this case I'm working on." Nate shook his head. "No child should ever have to go through what this little girl has endured. I met her at the hospital," Nate continued. "I wanted to adopt her right then and there."

"I don't think I want to know what happened to her," I replied. "It's so hard for me to get those thoughts out of my head ... I'll think about it too much. I'm still thinking about that lady moaning in the hospital a few years ago."

"Yeah...you don't want to know," Nate looked over at me. He took in a deep breath. "We better get out. I have *a lot* of work to do tonight," Nate said, as he stood up.

"Nooo. I don't want to get out. It's so cold out there!"

Nate got out of the hot tub—seemingly unaffected by the cold—and walked over to grab my towel off the bench for me. I quickly wrapped it around myself and ran into the house. From inside, I could hear Nate pulling the cover over the hot tub and locking it up for the night.

As I changed into some dry clothes, I thought about our talk tonight. Nate and I have had so many great talks while soaking in the hot tub. We talked about God a lot. I loved that. We were still learning, but when I think back over the years, we have grown so much in our walk with God. I can't say we understand God's ways entirely, but the trust is there. The faith is there. The relationship is there. It has been amazing watching the kids grow in their faith as well.

That thought reminded me. "Time for bed, kids," I called out. I walked down the hallway in my PJ's. "Come on guys. Go brush your teeth and meet in Bub's room for prayers."

It all started with Girl Scout Troop 703—scrapbooking that is. Brittney was a tween now, and no longer had an interest in earning badges and selling cookies. But back when she was in elementary school, I had scrapbooked each of the girls a "yearbook" of all their girl scout events, and I was hooked. I had been the troop's leader, and one by one, as the girls earned badges for learning things like *Saying No To Drugs*, horseback riding, experiencing Tea Party etiquette, and attending an American flag ceremony, I was right there capturing those fleeting moments with a camera.

After a few years of Girl Scouts, I moved on to scrapbooking our own pictures. And now years later, here I was sitting down at my scrapbook desk in the study. I glanced at this year's manifold of pictures. There were so many, I didn't even know where to start! 2003 had been an awesome year with an extra dose of fun! Every one of these photos captured a memory that I wanted to hold onto forever—and scrapbooking was the perfect way to make that happen!

I smiled. The kids were back in Brittney's room playing video games. Their GameCube would keep them busy all night. Nate was showering after all the yard work he had just finished. My plan for this December Saturday night was nothing more than scrapbooking and basketball—the NBA's Sacramento Kings game was just about to start! We were big-time fans, and for sure there would be a lot of hooting and hollering around here tonight as we cheered on our team. But for now, I needed to decide which pictures I was going to scrapbook. Sitting on my chair in the study, I leaned to the side to watch the tip off of the basketball game. The game had officially started. I picked up a stack of photos taken in the Caribbean and started looking through them while I waited for Nate to join me for the basketball game.

Over the years, my perpetual trips to purchase scrapbook supplies from *Oh For The Memories* resulted in me having practically everything I needed for my own in-home store. Scrapbooking—or *Crapbooking*, as Nate called it—had become somewhat of an addiction, and one of my most favorite hobbies ever. Dr. Bleakley's wife, Virginia, and I would feed off of each other's mutual enthusiasm for embellishing our photos and turning them into works of art. By now I had a trunk full of finished scrapbooks in the living room. My dream was for the kids to be able to look back at these books someday when they were grown and remember all the fun days of their childhood.

Virginia and I had been to a number of scrapbook conventions in California over the years, but *this* year we got to fly to Seattle for the Creating Keepsakes Scrapbook Convention at the Meydenbauer Center in Bellevue. It was a packed three-day weekend spent taking lots of classes and shopping our way through a multitude of vendors with the latest and greatest products and tools. We stayed with Jerry while we were there. He let us borrow his car while he was at work, and he even treated us to a cruise around Lake Union on his new yacht. It was so cool of Nate to take care of the kids while I was gone—they had a great time together eating seafood and watching sci-fi movies all weekend. Nate would always tease, but I knew he fully supported my fervor of scrapbooking our memories.

Every year we would take the kids on a big summer vacation. Approximately a month after getting home from our trip, we would take them out to lunch and reveal next summer's travel destination. It was a really fun tradition that gave them an entire year to look forward to our next family vacation. In the meantime, it gave Nate and me time to save, and for me to scrapbook our latest photographs.

We had gone on two unforgettable trips this year. The first one was a Caribbean cruise with our Salinas friends. The eleven of us met up in New Orleans' French Quarter for a formal dinner at Brennan's. After enjoying our Creole cuisine, and trying Banana's Foster for the first time, we made our way to the neon lights of Bourbon Street. Our effervescent night ended in the early morning hours at Cafe Du Monde for another first time treat of warm beignets sprinkled with powdered sugar.

We made memories all over the Caribbean by snorkeling with stingrays at Grand Cayman; Nate and Paul golfing in Jamaica while Chris' sister Joanna and I rode on a bamboo raft down the river; and all of us driving our different colored dune buggies around Cozumel. Every day was a new adventure, but our nights of dancing with the cruise ship's rock band was my favorite of all. Our week of being young and childfree was an absolute blast! We felt—and acted—like teens again, but with all the benefits of adulthood.

I set down the Caribbean pictures on my desk, and reached for the photos of our family trip to Washington, D.C. Nate had a three-day conference at the National Center for Missing and Exploited Children in Alexandria, Virginia. We had decided to turn Nate's conference into a family vacation. While the kids and I waited for Nate to get done with his lectures and meetings each day, we would sleep in and do things like swim and watch movies until he got back. When he returned, we spent the rest of the day taking in all the must-see monuments and sites of our nation's capital.

At the end of Nate's conference, we extended our stay for another week. There was so much to see, including another MLB stadium not too far away. The nostalgic, old fashioned feel of Camden Yards was remarkable considering how recently it had been built. We watched the Baltimore Oriels' 8-4 victory over the Anaheim Angels, and then made our way to Little Italy for a legit Italian lunch, and finished our day on a big purple Chessie Dragon paddle boat in the harbor.

It was such a fun family trip. Bubs and I even celebrated our birthdays while we were there. Brittney turned twelve—she was almost a teen!—and I turned thirty-five. I loved my age and wanted to stay thirty-five forever. Even more, I wanted Bubs to stay twelve forever! We made so many great memories while we were in Washington, D.C., but my very favorite was when we visited the open-air Jefferson Memorial one evening. After seeing the nineteen-foot bronze statue of Thomas Jefferson, we walked down the marble steps of the circular rotunda and sat down. It felt so good to sit. We had walked so much this week!

As we took in the spectacular twilight view of the Potomac River, tiny, intermittent flashes of golden light caught our attention. The kids saw fireflies for the first time that night and were fascinated by them. Nate and I sat on the circular white steps of the memorial and chuckled as we watched the kids trying to catch the blinking lights. The fireflies' luminous colors of yellow and orange flashed all around us. Ryan walked up the stairs to Nate and me with his hands cupped. Apparently he had captured one and was about to show us. "Did you catch one, Boy?" Nate asked as Ryan began slowly opening his hands. He wanted to show us, but didn't want it to fly away. "Be *really* careful, Boy, fireflies bite!" Nate warned convincingly. Fully alarmed with this new information, Ryan flung his hands open before he got bit. He was only eight, but it didn't take long for him to realize that his dad was joking, and fireflies were harmless. Sometimes it's the simple things you hold the most dear, and after all the walking and touring of countless attractions, what my mind cherished most was that night under the cherry trees of Potomac Park.

As I scrapbooked, I caught sight of the Mountain Mike's delivery guy walking into our courtyard lit with white icicle lights. I set my scissors down on the desk and got up to go answer the door. The *ding dong* of the doorbell must have sounded like a dinner bell ringing for the family to come and get it. Nate walked into the living room all showered and ready to eat, soon followed by Brittney and Ryan—*Super Smash Bros* on a brief hold for dinner. Sounds of the Kings taking on the Phoenix Suns and our family talking and cheering the Kings on filled the air as we ate our pepperoni pizza at the coffee table in front of the television. Life was so good. Although there were stockings that hung from the mantle of the lit fireplace, and many enticing presents under the decorated Christmas tree, I had everything I ever wanted right here in this living room. I imagined Nate and me many years from now reminiscing about the *Good Old Days.* Those days that we would remember and miss would be the days we were living right now.

Chapter 9

"After All These Years" by Journey

"LOOK HOW CUTE HE IS!" Brittney said, holding on tight to the glass terrarium. I looked in close to see a small, reddish-orange salamander with black spots sitting on a piece of bark. Brittney was the lucky seventh grader chosen to take care of the class pet over spring break. The little guy had no fur to make me start sneezing and wheezing, so how could we say "no" when she asked if she could bring him home? Unlike her dad, Bubs had a fondness for animals. I didn't share her excitement for the salamander either; I would have preferred a dog. My allergies wouldn't allow that though, so we just enjoyed our bird and our visiting amphibian.

A few days passed with the salamander being a salamander, lazily lying on the twigs and moss while Brittney played her Gameboy. She was completely enjoying the break from school and homework. The only thing she needed to do for the next week was to watch over the salamander and make sure he had food and water. Unlike Hedgehog, salamanders don't need much attention, so it would be easy...

"What's wrong?" I asked, when I saw the look on Brittney's face as she walked in from the garage early one morning.

"I looked everywhere, Mom. The salamander got out. I—I don't know how he got out; the lid's still on, but I can't find him anywhere! Where could he be?" Brittney asked in despair.

I walked with her over to the counter and leaned forward as I looked through the mesh lid into the terrarium. The salamander was in fact gone. We began looking under, over, and in-between everything in the house, garage, and yard, trying to uncover any possible hiding places.

"My teacher is going to be so upset! And everyone's going to hate me!" Brittney thought out loud, anticipating the kids' reactions when she returned to school on Monday morning without the class pet.

"It'll be okay, Honey. There are still a lot of places we haven't checked yet," I said, trying to make Brittney feel better. As we continued the search, I could hear the shower running. Nate was up getting ready for work.

"Good morning, Princess," Nate said, as he walked into the living room with a towel wrapped around his waist, and a toothbrush in his mouth. "What are you guys doing?" he asked as he brushed his teeth.

"I can't find the salamander, Dad!" Bubs answered in tears.

"Awww, Bubba," Nate said, with a mouth full of toothpaste, as he put his arm around her.

I filled Nate in on the missing salamander as I followed him back to the bathroom. After he rinsed, he went out to tell Bubs that he would help her look for him as soon as he finished getting ready. In his suit and tie, Nate moved the heavy things around the house. They looked under the couch and her mattress, and even behind the fridge, washer, and dryer. The red spotted salamander was nowhere to be found.

That night Bubs was the first to speak as we said our family prayers. She bowed her head with hopeful, clasped hands, "Dear Jesus, please…please help me find him. Let him not be hurt, or be hungry. Please help me not get in trouble for losing him, and for everyone to not be mad at me."

Brittney checked the salamander's terrarium daily, hoping by some miracle and answered prayer that the class pet would find his way back. And as each disappointing day passed, Brittney knew she would have some explaining to do to the class.

Our family continued to pray for the missing salamander until spring break ended. School would be back in session the following morning. Sometimes prayers just don't get answered the way that we hope for. That evening we simply prayed for Brittney's teacher to be understanding, and for the kids not to be upset with her.

I was usually the one to drop Brittney and a few of the neighbor kids off at school, but this morning one of the neighborhood moms offered to drive. She had a conference with her son's teacher. Under normal conditions that would be great, but this morning was different. Brittney was so worried about returning to school that she didn't sleep well last night. I told her that I could still drop her off.

"Maybe I should talk to your teacher?"

"It's okay, Mom. I'll ride to school with everyone."

"Are you sure, Honey?" I asked, wishing there was something I could do to help.

She nodded in defeat, "Yeah, I'm sure." I hugged our downcast daughter goodbye and wished her well for the day ahead. "Thanks, Mom," she said, and began walking down the sidewalk to our neighbor's house. I sighed, watching her walk slowly with her backpack slumped over her shoulder, the empty terrarium in her arms. She climbed in the backseat of the van filled with middle schoolers.

Oh God, please be with Brittney today, I prayed, as I walked back up the driveway to finish getting ready for work. Bubs was on my mind all day as I wondered how her teacher had responded to the disappointing news. I thought about the students too, and how they reacted. Hopefully they were understanding and didn't drill Brittney with a lot of questions. Throughout the day, I even told a couple of patients about the runaway salamander.

Mid-afternoon, Ern peeked her head into my room with a wince to let me know Brittney was on the phone. I excused myself from my patient and walked over with her to the phone. Ern stood next to me eager to hear what had happened at school today. I picked up the phone in anticipation of my daughter needing to be comforted.

"Hi Bubs," I said warmly, ready to tell her that I was so sorry that her day was so difficult, and that I was really proud of her for being so brave.

"Mom! You're not going to believe what happened this morning!" Brittney exclaimed. "I couldn't wait to get home to call you!"

Taken aback by Bub's excited tone, I asked her what happened.

"Okay, so I was in the van with everyone this morning, and Aaron's mom came out to the car. She was excited about something and wanted to show us, so we all followed her into the backyard. When we got out there, she pointed to the pool's vacuum. It was the salamander, Mom! He was sitting right there on the hose! I couldn't believe it, and hurried over and scooped him up! I went back to the van and put him in his cage!"

"What?! Are you serious?!" I asked Brittney, shocked by what she was telling me. This is unbelievable! Never did I imagine today turning out this amazing!

Bubs said the teacher and students welcomed her and the class pet back when she got to school. She never shared with them the details of the past week. Partly because she didn't know how she could ever explain how that little five-inch salamander walked halfway down the cul-de-sac and found his way safely into the neighbor's backyard pool!

God, the real teacher, had answered all our prayers mere minutes before the school bell rang. What a lesson He was teaching our family. Sometimes all we can do is pray and wait in faith for His appropriate timing. The little salamander was delivered back to the classroom, unharmed, and no one ever knew he was missing.

Nate opened the car door and handed the basketball to Ryan in the backseat full of tweens and teens. "Okay Boy, it's you and me against the *Girl-illas* today." From the passenger's seat, I glanced over to see Nate snickering like Muttley from his all in good fun jesting. The girls from next door were joining us today, and even though there would be four of us girls playing against only two boys, it somehow seemed *even*. I turned around to check if everyone had their seatbelts on and a water bottle for this sunny spring day. Summer was still a few weeks away, but the recent rise in temperature, and the roadside strawberry stands with freshly picked sweet berries, made it clear that the cold days of winter were long gone.

Within a few minutes, we were pulling into the back parking lot of Johansen High School. None of the kids went to school here yet, but Brittney — the oldest of the four — was getting close. She would be starting high school in the fall. The kids were all familiar with the basketball courts though, and by the looks of it, as we parked the car, they were all open!

It didn't take long before we were all running up and down the full court. We knew the rules of basketball—we'd watched the Kings play all the time—but for us, we kept it simple. The first team to score ten points wins the game. And any player who gets a violation must pay his or her penalty by handing the ball over to the opposing team member for a shot at the free throw line. The best of three games wins.

Both teams were playing well, and I fed off the competition of a hard game of basketball. Brittney's habitual slow dribbling to the hoop made her a sitting duck to the opposing team. All anyone had to do was charge at her and the ball was easy to get. Ryan, on the other hand, was more like me—fast on his feet, and zealous to make the next point by either making a basket himself or passing it to Dad to dunk it from under the rim.

"Traveling!" Ryan called out as Bubs bumbled the basketball trying to keep Ryan from stealing it. Everyone momentarily stopped running, and I wiped the sweat from my forehead. None of us were star athletes by any means, but our huffing and puffing showed that we were all getting a good workout.

Referee Dad made the call with beads of sweat running down his face. "Okay, ball goes to the boy," Nate said, catching his breath. "He gets a foul shot."

"But, Dad," Bubs grumbled. "I couldn't even move! Ryan wasn't giving me any space!"

"It's okay, Bubbasaurus, you just need to keep dribbling. Or pass it to someone else," Nate said, as he walked over and put his arm around Bubs neck. We all made our way to the hoop and lined up by the white sidelines painted on the asphalt. From behind the free throw line, Ryan stood ready to shoot. We all watched the basketball hit the backboard and fall into the net. "Good job, Boy!" Nate said, as they high-fived each other.

"Just because you guys are up a few points does not mean you're going to win," I teased the boys, as I passed the ball to one of the girls. Our game continued as the six of us raced up and down the court. Basket after basket, our boys vs. girls match was anyone's game. Ryan made a steal and searched for his teammate. But Nate had stopped and was calling for a time out.

"Hold on, I just gotta catch my breath," Nate said, holding his arms behind his head.

I walked over to Nate. "Are you okay, Honey?" I asked him. It wasn't like him to stop a game for himself.

"Yeah, I'm fine," he assured me. "I just need some water," he said, blowing it off.

"Okay, let's take a water break," I called out. We were all thirsty anyway, and happy to take a breather. I looked over at Nate drinking from his water bottle with his head leaned back. Hmm, I thought as I took a long drink of water myself. I was getting worried—and really regretted not bringing my cell phone—as I watched him take deep shaky breaths.

After a small break, we were back in the game. That was until Nate called for another time out. An instant red flag went up in my mind. This was so unlike him.

The kids all walked off the court and over to the grass to get their water bottles. I didn't want to make a big deal out of this, but I was definitely concerned. Yes, we were running a lot, *and* it was a hot day, but two time-outs? I gave Nate a couple of minutes to take another drink and catch his breath again.

"How are you feeling?" I asked Nate as I walked over and leaned into him. "I think we're done for the day," he answered back. I nodded agreeing, and told him I would let the kids know.

"Why are we leaving?" Ryan asked, confused as to why we weren't finishing the game. We had never left in the middle of a game before.

"Dad's tired...and we all need more water, right?!" I answered, playing it down. But as Nate and I walked side by side to the car, I told him that he should see a doctor. I could hear Ryan bouncing the basketball on the sidewalk up ahead of us as the kids made their way back to the Durango. I was ready for Nate to say, "No"—which he did—but I had more to say.

"You know, if we take the kids back home, and then go to the emergency room, they can check you today. It'll actually save you time," I reasoned with Nate. "That way if you need further testing, they can do it right there. Then you won't need to take time off work."

I was amazed when he answered, "Yeah, that makes sense." Nate saw a doctor next to never, and when he did, it was because I set the appointment up myself. I was so thankful that he didn't put up a fuss about going to get this checked.

After many hours in the emergency room, we left the hospital with a prescription and a referral to see the cardiologist. Nate's breathing had returned to normal, but the echocardiogram they had done on him showed some kind of a heart murmur and arrhythmia. Nate saw the cardiologist soon after, who put him on a couple of cardiovascular medications to be taken daily until his next appointment in three months.

In retrospect, I thought about our ten-day Florida vacation we had just returned from a few weeks ago. It is not much of an exaggeration to say we had gone on just about every rollercoaster, ride, and waterslide—in every theme park—in the entire state—at least twice! Bubs got over her fear of rollercoasters on our trip and would go on virtually anything now. We had an absolute blast, and when we waited for our flight back home at the airport in Orlando, I told

Nate, "You know, we are *never* going to be able to top this trip." He nodded with a smile, wholly agreeing. We had swum with dolphins, splashed on twisting and turning inner tubes, and had done 360s on air-boats through the everglades with alligators swimming around us. *But, oh my gosh!* I thought. So many of those high speed roller coasters with intense drops and inversions had posted warning signs that actually prohibited people with heart conditions from riding them. We had no idea Nate had a heart condition. *Oh God,* I thought. *Thank you for keeping him safe.*

Nate didn't seem bothered by the heart murmur. He assured me he felt totally fine, and that he had no intention of slowing down, neither at home nor at work. He continued to play on the DA's softball team every week. The players wore navy blue T-shirts with white lettering that read "D.A. Softball — Where 3-Strikes has a Whole New Meaning!!" Nate came up with the slogan. Although I always brought a phone with us now every time we exercised — just in case of an emergency — Nate continued with life as usual. And life as usual with Nate was always a lot of fun!

I reached over Nate and hit the snooze button to stop the alarm's beeping. With my eyes still closed, I rested my head on Nate's chest. His deep inhaling breath made it clear that he hadn't even heard the alarm. My head moved slightly up and down with Nate's breathing as he continued his sound sleep. Although morning was dawning, our room was holding on to the last of the night's sleepy darkness. I loved that our bedroom was on the west side of the house — giving us a bit more time before the rays of the sunrise inevitably illuminated our room. I nestled into Nate, enjoying every second of snoozing. In nine minutes the alarm would go off once again, and the day would begin.

The beeping alarm jarred me out of my peaceful rest for the second time, making it clear that my time was up. *Snoozes should definitely be longer than nine minutes*, I thought as I hit the off button and rolled back into Nate.

"Two more minutes," I groaned, too comfortable to move. Maybe the shower would wake me up. Nate needed to start waking up too—eighteen holes of golf awaited him.

As I started to get out of bed, Nate placed his hand on my hip. "Do you know what day it is?" he asked, in a raspy morning voice.

I turned back around to Nate who was lying there with his eyes partially open. "It's Wednesday, Honey," I answered, in the fading darkness.

"No. The date. Today's a special day. Do you know what it is?" he asked.

I began trying to think of what day it was as calendar dates flipped through my mind. I thought about birthdays, anniversaries, and even special dates of family and friends. It was September 5, 2007—a day that had no special meaning as far as I knew. I shrugged my shoulders. "Uhh… it's special because you guys are golfing today?" I answered, guessing. Maybe I just wasn't awake enough yet—I had no idea what he was talking about. What was I forgetting?

"Nope. It's not golfing. You give up?" Nate asked, sitting up in bed.

Growing increasingly intrigued, I nodded, "Yeah, I can't think of *anything* that happens on September 5th. What is it?" I questioned.

"*Today* you have officially been a Baker longer than you were a Palato," Nate said, with a sleepy grin.

With a pause, I tilted my head to the side. "Really?!" I asked, smiling back at him. I knew our twentieth anniversary was coming up in February, but I hadn't really thought about it quite like that. Genuinely humbled with this unexpected news, I sat there for a moment contemplating how nineteen years of marriage could have possibly gone by so fast. I happily gave Nate a big hug. He growled—just to make sure the moment didn't get too mushy.

Energized by this awesome—and very precise—information, I got out of bed and walked over to Nate. "I love my name. And I *love* being your Mrs." I said to Nate, and kissed him as I heard a door shut out in the hallway.

No doubt, it was Jerry who was up and getting ready for the day—these days, we practically had to pull the kids out of bed in the mornings. He had flown in from Seattle yesterday, and rented a car for the drive to Modesto. By the time Jerry had arrived in town, the kids were home from school, Nate and I were off work, and dinner was almost ready. The house smelled like an old-time Iowa favorite, beef and gravy over biscuits—requested by Nate, knowing his dad would love it. It was a treat for us all to be together for dinner. Only seeing each other a couple of times a year due to the distance and our busy lives, we had a lot to catch up on.

Jon was driving up from Southern California this morning to meet Nate and Jerry at the golf course. With a late morning tee time, Jon would have no way of avoiding the peak time of congested LA freeways. He was probably in it at this very moment, wending his way through the early morning rush of people trying to get to work on time.

The Baker boys looked forward to their annual golf trip—affectionately called a *JM*. They traveled all over for their *Justin Memorials*—Hawaii, Arizona, Palm Springs, Monterey, Idaho, and then other times, like today, it was Central California. Work was busy for Jerry, so they were keeping it simple this year. I completely supported their male bonding time, sending cigars and homemade chocolate chip cookies along with them. One year I even sent a

Saturday Night Live: Best of Chris Farley video for them to watch in their hotel room—which I heard got watched many times.

I got ready for the day in no time, feeling high on life by the way the day had started. The kids, however, needed to speed it up. I had to get them to school, and me to work. "Ten more minutes, guys, and then we have to leave," I called out to the kids as I went out to check on Jerry. I found him outside at his rental car, taking his golf bag out of the trunk. I walked out to his car and wished him a great day out on the greens with his boys. I told him about how today was a special day, and filled him in on the details of Nate's unique news for me this morning. Jerry was surprised and a little taken aback. "Where does Nate come up with this stuff?"

Nate walked down the driveway with his blue golf bag slung over his shoulder. "You ready, Dad?" he asked, as he dropped his clubs in the back of his truck and came over to join us.

"I'm ready," Jerry answered. "It was nice sleeping past 4:30 today," he grinned. "No working out for me this morning. I figured we'd get enough exercise golfing today." I smiled, remembering the year we lived on Mercer Island. Like clockwork, Jerry would start each day lifting weights in the garage before he left for the office. "It'll be great to see Jon, too. I've been looking forward to this trip for weeks!" Jerry smiled.

"Tell Jon 'Hi' from me," I said. "We'll see him tonight when you guys get back. The kids can't wait to see him, either," I smiled. "Uncle Jon's like a big toy for them!"

"Yeah, we're gonna meet Jon at the club house for a big breakfast before our tee time," Jerry said, rubbing his stomach. Food and golf always went together for the Baker boys—in that order, too! Nate kissed me goodbye and told me not to wait up for them. They had a full day planned.

After seeing them off, I drove the kids to school and headed to work. As I drove, I got to thinking that I needed to start looking into a plane ticket to North Carolina. Every year or so, I flew back to spend some time with my parents. Nate and I would take turns and alternate a few of our vacation days—Nate golfing, and me to North Carolina—so we could each spend some time with our families.

Long after the sun had gone down for the night, I heard laughter and commotion coming from the garage as the guys walked into the kitchen. The guys looked a tad drained—and red—from the sun. By their moans and groans, I would guess they were full from dinner. Very full!

"Hi, Honey," I said, as I walked over to give Nate a kiss. "Hi, Jon!" I said, giving him a big hug and helping him in with his things.

"Uncle Jon!" the kids immediately shouted, and they scurried over to see him. Starting now, they would be velcroed to *UJ* for the rest of his visit.

The men continued to groan. "How was your day?" I asked Nate.

"NOYDB," Nate answered, in a teasing tone with a grin. Jerry squinted his eyes, not really sure what that meant as he got comfortable in a recliner. By the looks of it, Jon was too busy being distracted by his niece and nephew to hear Nate's answer to me.

"Naate," I said, tilting my head, and resisting a smile. This is Nate—lovingly waking me up this morning with the news of how long I have been a Baker—right down to the day—and then answering me with "*None of your dang business!*" come sundown.

"Okay then, I'm gonna ask your dad," I said, teasing back. I knew Jon didn't stand a chance of answering, due to the kids making up for lost time with him. Just like Gramps, they only got to see Jon a couple of times a year as well.

Jerry sighed happily as he leaned back in the recliner. "Aw, what a day we had!" He filled me in on how Jon arrived late due to the

LA traffic, and how they had to forgo breakfast in order to make their tee time. They had agreed to abstain from eating for the entire day in order to pique their appetites for dinner. He told me that all they could talk about, after playing each hole, was the feast that awaited them at The Farmer's Catfish House—their most favorite eatery in the whole state of California. I laughed as Jerry continued, knowing exactly where he was talking about. It was an obscure, old, refurbished gas station several miles outside of Modesto. Hidden away in the corner of an orchard, it was one of those quirky little family owned restaurants that the guys loved!

I sat there listening, enjoying hearing about their day. After golf, Jerry said that they headed out for their ultimate *post game reward*. "I was riding with Nate, and Jon followed in his own car," Jerry laughed. "Nate was driving like a bat out of…," Gramps paused, not wanting to cuss in front of his grandkids. I smiled as Gramps cleared his throat and continued. "So, after a while, poor Jon calls Nate to see how much further we had to go. Nate told him that we were getting close, and to just be patient. A half an hour later"—Jerry made sure to emphasize the timeline—"Jon calls again to ask Nate if he knew where he was going?" Jerry chuckled, shaking his head. "We were all tired, sunburned, and on the verge of starving. Oh yeah," he remembered, "and almost out of water!"

"Add almost out of gas to that list!" Jon said from the couch, with the kids sitting right there next to him. The guys were *all* chuckling now.

"So Nate fires back, '*Dang it, Jon, stop yapping… I know exactly where I'm going!!*'" We all looked at Nate as he shrugged with a guilty smile.

Jerry continued, "Of course, all this time I'm prodding Nate like a drunken cowboy with a wicked set of spurs." He carried on with his story about how Nate, in his inimitable good-natured manner, didn't talk back to him, but instead drove even faster in a desperate attempt to get him off his back. "We wandered down every dusty and bumpy old back road imaginable for close to another hour. Nate was determined to find this place no matter what. I'm absolutely convinced we would have continued running in circles for another three days if that's what it took! But, there again, that's just Nate being Nate," Jerry laughed as he looked at his eldest son.

"Oh, but it doesn't stop there! Out of sheer chance, we *finally* found the restaurant. And a parking spot. Once we got out of our cars and caught a whiff of dinner coming from the kitchen, Jon and I instantly forgave Nate for getting lost," Jerry teased.

"I wasn't lost," Nate emphasized with an amused smile.

"That all changed, though, when we walked through the door and we were told it would be at least another twenty to thirty minutes to get a table. We were driving around so long and the place was packed. The tables were all filled up with *other* people enjoying *their* dinner!"

"Oh no!" I said laughing. We were all laughing at this point. I could picture this so well—the scenario was playing out in my head like a comedy movie.

"So," Jerry went on, "we were finally seated, and immediately began to freak out the waitress. When she handed us the menus, we simply shot back by saying, '*Never mind, we'll each have one of everything, make it fast, and whatever you do, keep those mason jars filled with water!*'" They all laughed, and held their aching stomachs. "I've never been this stuffed in my life!" Jerry moaned. "We devoured every last bite off those old beat up tin plates."

"Yeah," Nate said, "Jon called me from his car on the way home, and I couldn't even make out what he was saying. Something about eating the whole thing," Nate belly laughed, followed by a groan. Nate and Jon had made their way over to their dad now, all sitting back with their feet up. Somehow, I knew the guys wouldn't be moving from the recliners for a long time tonight.

"You know I'm never going to let you forget how lost we were tonight, Nate," Jerry told him.

"We weren't lost," Nate insisted. "I knew where we were the whole time."

Nate walked in the front door and set his briefcase down next to the hall tree. As always, we reunited with a kiss. It was great to see him at the end of this busy day, but tonight he had unexpected news that put a knot in my stomach. He was home late due to a routine cardiology appointment after work. Nate began telling me that the cardiologist noticed some changes and wanted him to have a Transesophageal Echocardiogram—a TEE—at the hospital next week.

I sat down on one of the kitchen bar stools, listening to every word of this unsettling news. Nate went on to tell me that this type of EKG was more comprehensive than the one he had a couple of years ago. Although Nate said the TEE was a simple out-patient procedure, he would need sedation. The doctor would be guiding an ultrasonic type of flexible tubing that would pass through his mouth, throat, and into the esophagus. Due to the esophagus being closer to the heart, they would be able to obtain more detailed images of the heart and arteries.

The next week we were at the hospital. Nate remained fully composed when they called him back for his procedure—he was always like that. I waited in the lobby and prayed to God for them to figure out what was going on with his heart. After a few hours of waiting, a nurse called me to the door. As we walked down the hallway, she told me the procedure went well and that Nate would soon be ready to be released. I saw Nate right behind the curtain and gave him a hug. The nurse urged no eating—Nate's throat would be numb for a while—and went over some paperwork. She left us, saying the doctor would be right in.

Within minutes, the cardiologist came in to say we had a diagnosis. He found a fairly rare condition called Hypertrophic Cardiomyopathy—HCM. He went on to give us an in-depth explanation, and then summarized it by saying there was an abnormal thickening of the walls of the ventricles in his heart. He made it clear that this was not Coronary Artery Disease and had nothing to do with cholesterol or fatty deposits limiting blood flow. HCM is genetic, and often goes undiagnosed. He encouraged us as we listened to this disturbing information by saying most people with this condition can lead a normal life without any issues.

I asked the cardiologist about what could be done to treat HCM. He told us there was no treatment. However, he did increase Nate's prescribed medications, and advised him to keep up with his regular cardiology appointments. I took a deep sigh. It was very difficult to learn about this heart condition that neither one of us had ever heard of. Nate lived such an active, normal life. Until that basketball game a couple of years ago, we had no idea there was a problem with his heart at all.

Our family was at such a fun time in life, it was very upsetting for us to learn about this diagnosis. The downs in life are to be expected, but I was having a hard time dealing with *this* one. I would do anything for Nate, and I just felt so helpless. But I took comfort in the fact that Nate was really good about taking his medication every day. I know he was because I picked up his prescription refills every month. He was also good at going to his cardiology appointments. And above all, our family prayers each night would always include a prayer for Nate's heart. Kind of ironic... nobody had a bigger heart than Nate!

Carrie and I both had summer birthdays. To celebrate, we would make plans each year for a weekend of fun together. Last year, we had driven to the Sierra Foothills to stay in the charming little gold rush town of Murphys. We did a little shopping, toured the vineyards, and did some wine tasting. But the highlight of our trip was the Carrie Underwood concert at the Ironstone Amphitheater. We had so much fun last summer that we decided to do it again this summer!

This year, the American Idol winner was playing at the Dixon May Fair, so I was spending the weekend with Carrie and her family in Folsom. As Carrie and I were driving to the concert, we were talking about Carrie Underwood's latest album—*Carnival Ride*—that would be released in a few months. And then we started talking about the concert last summer in Murphys.

"Hey, that reminds me," Carrie said. "Bryan Adams is going to be at Ironstone in a few months. Danny and I just got tickets!"

"Really?!" I asked, excited for this valuable information.

Nate was a *huge* Bryan Adams fan, and with his fortieth birthday approaching, I had been thinking about what I wanted to do for him. A *happy* birthday for Nate was a forgettable day. One without balloons, a cake with his name on it, or candles to blow out. I had learned that the hard way when I threw Nate a surprise twenty-first birthday party! He *does not* like the attention! To him, people singing *Happy Birthday* was a form of drawn out torture. Nate made me promise that I would never throw him another birthday party—especially a surprise party! But in a few months, he would be forty and I wanted to do something very special for him!

"When is it?" I asked Carrie.

"Umm, I can't remember," Carrie said, picking up her phone to check the date. "It's Friday, October 5th," Carrie answered, after looking it up.

"That's peerrfect!," I said, enthusiastically. "*That's* what I'll do for Nate's birthday! I've been racking my brain trying to figure out how to make his fortieth a big deal, without making it a big deal," I tried explaining.

Carrie chuckled. "That'll be fun! It's the last concert of the season so they are having a sit-down dinner inside if you really want to do it up. Without doing it up *too* much of course," she smiled. Carrie knew Nate and his need for not getting a lot of attention. "I can't believe he didn't even go to his college graduation," Carrie said.

"Or his law school graduation either!" I added. "He *thinks* he is making it easy for me by telling me not to bother doing anything. But it actually makes it *more* difficult!" I started thinking, "You know, Paul is really into Bryan Adams, too. I'll give Traci a call and see if they want to join us. That would be so fun for the six of us to go together. I really don't think Nate would fuss about going to a concert with our best friends for his birthday—especially if it's Bryan Adams!"

As Nate's fortieth drew closer, I couldn't help but give him a hard time. When I would leave the house, I would say things like, "I'll be really busy today. I have a lot of things to do for the huge surprise party I'm throwing you." I would smile and Nate would growl. And, just in case I had forgotten, he would remind me that it was "just another day" every time his birthday even vaguely came up.

After almost twenty years of being married, I knew how to make Nate's birthday special. Thursday, October 4th—his actual birthday—Nate went to work in hopes that nobody knew it was his birthday. Then Mary, without him knowing, drove over from Salinas and joined us for a tasty family dinner at Bella Italia. After ordering, I surprised Nate with the Bryan Adams tickets—third row, center stage! He was happily surprised. I knew it was a legitimate surprise too, because if he knew about the concert, I guarantee we would've had tickets already. After dinner, Mary took the kids home while Nate and I spent the night at the Double Tree. Although we needed to stay in town due to Nate working the next day, it was so nice to have some time for just the two of us.

Paul and Traci had already arrived from Salinas by the time Nate got off work Friday night. After he did a quick change from a suit and tie to a pair of blue jeans and a baseball jersey, we headed out to the foothills of Murphys for the concert! When we arrived at the outdoor amphitheater at Ironstone Vineyards, we bundled up in our jackets and walked across the parking lot to find where we would be eating dinner.

Once inside, and warmed up from the brisk fall air, we made our way to our reserved table for four. The room was filled with round tables lined with white table cloths and matching white place settings. Chatter of other concert goers filled the room as we took our seats. The server asked us what we would like to drink, as he poured water into our goblets.

Paul reached for a warm artisan roll. "On our drive over to Modesto, we listened to that *Chronicles* three pack you got me," he told Nate. "He'll probably sing a lot of those greatest hits tonight."

Nate nodded, "Yeah, when that came out a couple of years ago, I wanted to get one for you, too. I knew you'd get good use out of it," he said, dipping his bread in olive oil and taking a bite.

Paul laughed. "I *still* can't believe our parents let us drive by ourselves to his concert back in high school!" Paul looked at Traci and me, and continued. "Nate hadn't had his license very long. That was back when you just got your EXP," Paul said to Nate. "You had to learn how to drive a stick shift!"

I smiled at the mention of Nate's blue car with the IMKRAZE license plate. That car had broken down for good when Nate was getting close to graduating from San Jose State. I remember being pregnant with Brittney when Nate called me from San Jose saying he needed a ride home, and a new car.

As dinner was being served, the guys continued reminiscing. "After school, we drove *all* the way to Cal Expo in Sacramento and went to the concert. We got back late that night," Paul laughed, remembering. "And we still had to go to school the next day. "Man," Paul shook his head. "I'd never let our kids do that!" Traci completely agreed. So did Nate and I.

"Yeah, that was back on his Reckless Tour," Nate said, remembering that night. "He was climbing the charts fast back then with *Run to You* and *Summer of '69*. Man, he's been doing this a long time now. And he still sounds as good as he did twenty-five years ago."

"How many times have you guys seen him now?" I asked. Nate and I had seen him a number of times over the years. Paul had even joined us for one or two of those concerts before he met Traci.

Nate thought about it for a few seconds. "I'm not sure. I've lost count over the years."

"Well, tonight's my first time," Traci said.

"He puts on a great show," I told Traci, and then looked over at Nate. "And now…all these years later…we're celebrating your fortieth birthday!" I smiled at him without making it too big of a deal. Paul led us in a toast to Nate, and to the concert that awaited us.

The usher, shining his flashlight on our tickets, started showing us to our seats. As we continued walking closer and closer to the stage, I eagerly looked at Nate, knowing he was very much enjoying his fortieth birthday. Nate and Paul left to go get a beer while Traci and I stayed and kept our eyes peeled for Carrie and Danny.

Ever since we got the concert tickets, an idea had been budding in the back of my mind. I needed to try to make my idea happen. I checked the time. I'd have to make this fast!

I looked over at Traci, bundled up next to me in her black winter coat. “I’m gonna try to find a way to get Nate backstage to meet Bryan Adams,” I said, scooting out from the reserved section. “They’ll probably say *no,* but I’m gonna give it a shot.”

“Uh, oh ... kay,” Traci slowly responded.

Determination to make this happen had taken over my every thought, as I walked up to a lady guarding the front section where we were sitting. She shook her head at my request, and I moved on. I rushed over to another employee and asked him. It was nearly a full lap around the amphitheater, and a lot of *no’s*, until I made a connection with two young men guarding a roped off area on the far side of the venue. I told them how it was my husband’s fortieth birthday, and what a huge Bryan Adams fan he was. “How can I get him backstage to meet Bryan Adams?” I asked.

They looked at each other. “I don’t know,” one of the young men said, looking as if he really wanted to help.

“I think you have to have tickets to get backstage,” the other guy said.

“Where can I get a ticket?” I asked, in a hurry with the time running out.

“I don’t think you can now.”

“You know,” the first guy said, as if thinking out loud, “if anyone can help you, a guy named Mike can.” The other guy nodded and seemed to agree.

“What does Mike look like, and where can I find him?” I asked, feeling a spark of hope.

“I don’t know where he is right now, but he’s wearing a Boston Red Sox jacket.”

“Thank you sooo much!” I told the guys with a big smile. Immediately, I started running through the crowds of people in search of a red jacket.

Adding a few more *no's* to my collection, I ran up to a lady guarding a gated section. "Hi," I said, as I ran up. "I'm looking for a man named Mike. Do you know him?" I asked. Right when she was about to answer me, I saw red! "There he is!" I blurted out as I jumped up and down with excitement and pointed to a man in a Red Sox jacket coming out of a back door. I immediately caught his attention as he noticed me eagerly waving and pointing to him. He started walking over!

"Are you Mike?" I asked him, as he reached the gate.

"Yeah," he answered, looking at me. "Who are you?" he asked, unsure of what was going on and how I knew his name.

Winded from running, I said, "Hi Mike! I was told if anyone could get me backstage to meet Bryan Adams, it would be you!" I explained. "It's my husband's fortieth birthday! He's the biggest fan," I told him, crossing my fingers and hoping I wouldn't hear another "*no*."

It took a bit of convincing, but after a minute or two, he nodded his head and said, "Alright, go get him. Make if fast and meet me back here at the gate," he instructed. "I'm not promising *anything!*" he warned me as he left to go back inside.

I raced toward our section and started waving for Nate. I knew he would be looking for me.

I caught Nate's attention down the aisle. "Carrie and Danny are already here," Nate called out, trying to get the message through all the people and noise.

I nodded and continued to wave him over. When he had made his way through the row of people, I clasped Nate's arm in urgency and led him straight toward Mike.

He was waiting for us at the gate and leaned forward saying, "Just letting you know, this *never* happens. Tonight's your lucky night."

"What's going on?" Nate asked me. Mike handed us each a red back stage pass and led us up the steps to the back door. Everything was happening so fast! I could feel my heart thumping under my jacket!

I thought he was leading us to a line or waiting room of some sort. However, when Mike opened the door, Bryan Adams was standing right there in his blue jeans and plain white T-shirt! He looked just like his CD cover. The singer was signing autographs and taking pictures with other fans. My eyes grew wide as I looked at Nate, whose eyes were even wider. At least *I* had a heads up about what *might* happen. But Nate was utterly shocked! *Was* this actually happening?!

Mike took us to a small line which was down to its last handful of fans. Within a few minutes, we were shaking Bryan Adams' outstretched hand. Star struck and still in shock, Nate went on to tell Bryan Adams about how he'd been a longtime fan, and how he'd been to his concerts many times over the years. "So many, he's lost count," I said to the rock star. Bryan Adams seemed to appreciate Nate's sincerity, judging by the smile on his face as they continued to talk for a few minutes. The photographer came over and asked us to pose for a picture. Bryan Adams stood in the middle of Nate and me, wrapping his arms around our waists. *I can't believe it! I can't believe it!* My mind screamed! *The side of my body is pressed up against Bryan Adams. Bryan Adams!* The camera flashed.

We were his last fans of the night's *Meet and Greet*. Nate shook his hand again, thanking him for letting us in, and I gave him a hug. Mike wrote down our email address and told us the photo would be sent to us in a week or so. We were escorted to the side door. We walked down the stairs and out toward our seats. Nate and I were both pumped with adrenaline and in a bit of a daze, all at the same time. Nate gave me a hug so tight it hurt! He really doesn't know his own strength, but I didn't care. I was on happiness overload and in shock at what had just happened.

"How?!"... Nate started to ask as we walked back. He smiled and hugged me tight for a second time. "You're awesome! How in the world did that happen?"

"Happy Birthday, Sweetheart!" I beamed, thrilled that Nate was having a fortieth birthday he would always remember!

"*You* are my Princess!" Nate reached for my hand and squeezed it. Within minutes we were back with our friends, and Bryan Adams was rocking the stage.

"Five minutes, people!" Nate called out, as we were all getting ready for church. This fortieth birthday weekend had been awesome! I was still all smiles from our Friday night out with our friends and Bryan Adams! Paul and Traci were back home now, but Mary was going to stay until late afternoon today. The Seattle Seahawks were playing, and Mary—being born and raised in Washington—wanted to root them on. Nate's Chargers were playing later today, too. Sunday afternoons were all about football, and everything we needed for a BBQ was ready to go when we got home.

Some traditions never change. The kids were no longer children being encouraged to go to church with a Slurpee, but that didn't stop us from driving straight to 7-11 after church every Sunday. Mary stayed in the car when we pulled up. Her Parkinson's was making it a little more difficult for her to get around these days, so the kids concocted a one of a kind Slurpee for Gramma and brought it to her. As soon as we got home with our slushy drinks, the big screen was turned on and Nate was checking his players.

All throughout the week, Nate would diligently tally the points of his Fantasy Football team, *The Prosecutors.* At the beginning of every football season, the Salinas men would gather in Paul and Traci's basement for Draft Night. Nate looked forward to it every year and would drive the two hours to Salinas right after work. It was always a big night with the friends sitting at a long table facing the wall of team charts. The guys would sit there, strategically picking out their players, while puffing on cigars at a table covered with boxes of pizza and cans of beers.

The delicious smell of the burgers wafting in from the backyard was making me hungry! While Nate was outside BBQing, Mary and I finished up in the kitchen. "Save some room for lunch," I told the kids who were filling up on all the snacks we had out on the kitchen counter.

Mary and I walked over to the couch in the living room and sat down talking. With football on the big screen in the entertainment room and burgers on the grill, Nate was walking in and out of the backyard checking on both the game and the burgers.

We looked over to see Nate walking into the living room where we were sitting. I smiled when I saw him—he still appeared to be riding high from the concert Friday night. And now, with an afternoon filled with football and great food, life was good. Nate bluntly looked at Mary on the left side of the couch and pointed... "YOU! The woman who bugged me for the first twenty years of my life." He then turned to me on the right... "And YOU! The woman who has bugged me the last twenty years of my life!" Mary and I looked at each other and had a good laugh. Nate's so funny. He just randomly comes up with these crazy things. But both of us women who bugged Nate for the past forty years knew that was his way of saying thank you for a great birthday weekend.

"Have you told the kids yet?" my mom asked. With the phone pressed to my ear as I walked, I paused briefly before responding.

"No. Not yet. We thought we'd wait until after the holidays to tell them," I answered, feeling almost guilty for the news that awaited Bubs and Ryan.

"How do you think they're going to take it?" my mom questioned.

"Not good." I shook my head envisioning Nate and me telling the kids we were going on a mission trip to Mexico in the spring—a trip they both did not want to go on.

A couple of months back, Dr. Acree and his wife Bonnie—also a dental hygienist—had asked me if my family and I would be interested in going on a mission trip to Mexico with them. I hadn't worked at the office for very long, but I knew that their family, and even some of the staff, went there once a year—photographs of past mission trips lined the office hallway. They told me we would be providing dental care for special needs and at-risk children at the 450-acre Rancho Santa Marta. While some of these children were orphaned, others were rescued from abuse, abandonment, and even sex trafficking. Our church was involved with this upcoming mission trip, as well. In fact, one of the pastors was planning on joining us. I asked them for some time to think about it, and we'd let them know.

"Man, Mom. This has been one of the most difficult decisions we have ever made!" I expressed, as I continued walking.

"Yeah, I know it has," my mom agreed in a serious tone. For a while now, she had been a sounding board and a vital part of discussing the pros and cons of this possible trip. There were a lot of things to consider—time off work for Nate and me, the kids missing a week of school, the cost. All of that could be worked out fairly easily though. The *thing* that had made this decision so very difficult was the issue of safety! Agreeing to this trip would mean deliberately taking our family into Mexico—a place where the U.S. State Department had issued a *DO NOT TRAVEL advisory* for American citizens. It was a volatile time of drug cartels, kidnappings, and gang violence in Mexico. And the assurance of military checkpoints with soldiers armed with rifles was of no consolation to us. Mary vehemently did not want us to go and was making herself sick thinking of us crossing the border. Jon didn't want us to go either, and had asked us what he could do or say to keep us from going. And the kids, once they heard of even some of the cons, wanted to opt out.

I continued my laps around the block and switched my cell to the other ear as my mom and I carried on our conversation. "Nate and I talked about this over and over for months, Mom. *And*, after *all* of those long discussions, we decided to say *NO*," I said, with a nervous laugh. "Our family will *not* be going on this mission trip. Right now, it would just be too risky!" I said, justifying our final answer—or so I thought.

"Yeah, I know," my mom said. "Last time we talked, you were going to call the Acrees and let them know that you weren't going." So Dad and I were surprised to get your message that you *are* going now," she said, in a confused tone.

"I *did* call them, Mom," I explained. "But they weren't home, so I left a message for them to call me when they returned. And before they returned my call, I got the mail." I paused. "You're not going to believe what was sitting in the mailbox," I said, shaking my head.

"What was it?" my mom asked. I could tell, even though she was across the country in North Carolina, that she was on the edge of her seat.

"There in our mailbox was our weekly sermon CD from Canyon Hills Church entitled *Advice From A Runaway Missionary Jonah*. Can you believe it?!" I asked.

My mom gasped.

"For months now, Nate and I have been asking the Lord for His guidance in our decision. And then, right before I could say "*NO*" to the Acrees, God's answer was right in my hands. When Nate got home, I told him about the sermon that had arrived. We listened to it together, and both agreed God was telling us not to fearfully run away from this mission trip, just like Jonah did," I explained.

"Oh, Shelley. That's God talking to you," my mom said, assuredly. "You guys need to go." I nodded in agreement as I continued walking.

"I know this has been a very difficult decision for you guys to make, but I think you made the right one." There was silence on the line for a few seconds as I soaked in my mom's words. They were comforting for me to hear. "I feel like God wants you to go." Her tone made it clear to me that she understood our initial dilemma, but now God had stepped in.

I stopped talking for a few seconds and drew in a long breath. "When God calls you to do something, He sure has a way of making it happen, doesn't He?"

"Yeah, He sure does," my mom concurred.

Life gets so busy, it was nice to have time to fill my mom in on the details of why we had changed our minds.

A lot had happened in a short amount of time, and by the time the Acrees returned my call, our answer had changed, and I simply told them "We're in!" Our mission trip as a family to Mexico was life changing, and one of the most significant experiences of my life. Nate and the kids felt the same way, and we agreed that we wanted to do this again someday. By the time we returned home, all four of us appreciated everything — water, toilets, English, etc. — more than we ever had before. But above all, our relationship with God and each other had expanded in a way that cannot be achieved from the comforts of home. I believe that God answers prayer in many ways. This time His answer arrived by mail.

We sat under the trees watching Ryan's football practice, *very* thankful for the shade. I felt bad for the winded players in the scorching heat. Late afternoon was always the hottest part of these summer days, but that didn't stop the coach from having his team *warm up* by running laps before the hours of football drills began. Although we had watched the team's every practice, I still couldn't help but wince at the impact noises as the players repeatedly pummeled each other. Even though they were protected by helmets and pads, the sound effects always made me cringe.

Mary was here for a visit. As a football lover and mother of three boys, she proudly watched her grandson rush and maneuver his way through teammates for the day's drills. Nate had driven to Ryan's football practice straight from work, as he usually did, and was the only dad on the sidelines in a suit.

"Good job, Boy!" He cheered number fifty-two, as he loosened his tie.

Brittney relaxed on a blanket next to us with her sketchbook. We were all going out to dinner tonight with Gramma after practice. I looked over at Brittney as she was drawing, lost in her own world of imagination. Art had been her *thing* since she was old enough to hold a pencil. She was growing up so fast. Tomorrow she would turn seventeen! It was bittersweet to think about Brittney starting her senior year of high school next month.

Off to my left, the golden hues of the lowering sun caught my attention. A profound feeling of nostalgia started to fill my heart. I sat there taking in the warm colors of the evanescent sun and sighed. Metaphorically speaking, the sun was setting on my thirties, like the fading daylight was reflecting the passage of time. I continued my gaze, wanting to hold on to these moments and not let go. Nightfall would soon blanket my thirties into memories of days gone by. Tomorrow I would turn forty. I quietly sat there thinking. A loud whistling noise snapped me out of my trance, and I looked out onto the field.

The coach was giving the panting football players a much-needed water break. Hydration was essential in July's triple digit heat in the Central Valley. Ryan, in his black jersey, came over for a quick break. He guzzled from a thermos full of water, and then poured the rest over his head before running back out onto the field.

Nate sat down with us under the trees. We continued watching the team practice, but my eyes inevitably returned to the golden sun nearing the horizon. It felt like I was watching the ball drop in slow motion.

Nate noticed my distraction. "You alright, Honey?" he asked.

"Yeah," I'm fine, I answered with a half smile. There was nothing to be sad about, really. The kids were growing up; our careers were in full swing; we were able to travel and see baseball parks all over the country; our friends were getting married and starting their families. My thirties had been the pinnacle of all things good. Resisting change, I wanted life to stay just like this forever. I took in a slow, deep breath.

"Do you want to know where we're going for your birthday?" Nate asked from his chair, distracting me from my thoughts.

My eyes widened as I turned my head toward him. "Yes!" I said, excited to finally hear about my surprise. Nate had something planned and I'd been waiting for weeks to find out what it was!

"Too bad. You have to wait until tomorrow to find out," Nate said with a smirk.

"Nooo Nate! C'mon, tell me!" I playfully pushed his arm. I could tell he wasn't going to tell me; he was having way too much fun making me wait.

Mary smiled at her son's teasing. While we were gone, she was going to watch the kids, and drive Ryan to his football practices and game. Maybe she would even have time to take Brittney out to practice her driving—which was still a work in progress!

The players were kneeling, signaling the end of practice and the coach's final words. As we packed up our chairs and belongings, Ryan walked over to us for more water, and wanted to know where we were going for dinner. Even drenched in sweat, he looked just like his dad with his dark blonde hair and green eyes. Nate put his arm around Ryan's neck and told him he did a good job out there.

"I think you should tell me where we're going!" I smiled at Nate as we headed to the cars.

"I'll tell you at lunch tomorrow," Nate said calmly.

"But I need to know what to pack," I reasoned with him.

"You'll have plenty of time to pack. We're leaving the day *after* your birthday. And that's all you get to know for now."

I was so excited to find out where we were going, and yet my heart felt conflicted. One moment I wanted to capture the sun and beg it not to set on my thirties. The next moment I couldn't wait for tomorrow to hurry up and get here! I looked over to take one last look at the fleeting sun before we drove away. It was gone. All that was left was the lingering afterglow of a beautiful sunset and the glory days of a decade that was hard to say goodbye to.

Sunrise the next morning brought with it a new year for Brittney, and a new *decade* for me. Our anticipated birthday lunch had arrived. Brittney began opening her first gift. She was a huge Maroon 5 fan and was thrilled to pull out two concert tickets from the envelope—one for her and one for her best friend. The kids were just getting to the age where we would let them go to concerts on their own—as long as one or both of us drove them there *and* was in the parking lot waiting for them when the concert was over.

Nate handed me three cards. "Open this one first," Nate said, sliding the top card toward me. I set the other two cards down on the table and looked across at Mary and the kids with a big smile. I opened the card and found a piece of folded white paper inside. As I read the card with a big 40 on it, I tenderly smiled at what Nate had written.

Nate made a low growling noise, and we laughed as I began unfolding the paper. My hands felt kind of shaky from all of the excitement. The first words I saw were Newark, NJ! It was a plane ticket!

"*What*?! We're going to New Jersey?!" I gasped, completely shocked, and a little puzzled. I turned to look at Nate sitting next to me.

"I'm taking you to see *Grease* on Broadway in New York," he answered with a smile.

My jaw dropped open. "Are you serious?! Really?!" I gave Nate a big hug. "I can't believe this!" I said, as I squeezed him tight.

"Open ours now!" Brittney said. As I opened it, two twenty dollar bills fell out of the card.

"Whoa," I said, surprised by the falling money. I smiled as I picked up the twenties from my lap and began reading their card and what they each had written inside.

They began to fill me in. "Those are for you and Dad to get a Philly Cheesesteak Sandwich at *The Swan*!" Ryan said, excited to explain what the twenties were for.

"What?!" I asked. "No ... way!"

"Dad's taking you to Philadelphia so you can get your favorite sandwich!" Ryan explained. I looked at them trying to believe this was happening.

My heart was racing with excitement. “I can *not* believe this!” I thought back to a couple of years ago when we had taken the kids to Philadelphia to watch the Phillies play. We had eaten lunch at *The Swan* before the game. Each sandwich cost twenty dollars and took fifteen minutes each to prepare.

“Remember, you said that the Philly Cheesesteak Sandwich was the most delicious thing you had ever eaten in your whole life, and that you’d go all the way back just for another sandwich?” Brittney reminded me.

I chuckled and smiled. “Yeah, you’re right. I did say that, didn’t I?” I answered, nodding my head.

Ryan laughed. “Remember, you said if you were ever on Death Row, you’d order a Philly Cheesesteak Sandwich from there for your last meal!” The whole table was laughing. *Man,* I love my family! I got up to give the kids a big hug.

“Well ... it’s a good thing Dad’s gonna take me there to get one. I don’t plan on being on Death Row anytime soon!” I laughed as I walked back to my seat and sat down.

“Yeah, Nate’s work might have a problem with that,” Mary laughed.

“And there’s one more,” Nate said, handing me a birthday card from Mary. She had typed me an affectionate letter about turning forty, and enclosed two tickets to see *Mamma Mia!*. The surprises just kept coming! “I can’t believe this! Bubs and I just went to the movies to see *Mamma Mia!* last weekend. And now I’m going to get to see it live on Broadway!” I reached over to give Mary a big thank you hug.

“It was all Nate’s idea,” she said with a grin.

“Yeah, well, I know how much you love that lame movie,” Nate rolled his eyes. I threw my head back laughing, imagining Nate sitting through all those girly songs. Watching Nate's expressions during the show was going to be entertainment in itself!

"Thank you, guys, sooo much!" I said, feeling the love that went into all of these very thoughtful surprises. "I would have *never* guessed *any* of these awesome birthday presents," I told my family, holding the cards tight to my heart. I looked at my lunch still sitting on my plate untouched. I was just way too overwhelmed to eat. Our server wished me a happy birthday and wrapped up my lunch to go.

I gazed out the window as the plane started its descent into Newark. The sparkling view of the city's skyline at night reminded me of a poem Nate had written many years ago. I thought back to when Nate and I would write poems to each other when we were dating. In a momentary flashback in time, it was like I could hear Nate reading his poem to me...

I can see the lights of the city from here,
A cluster brightening the darkness.

What a sensational view of life,
Thousands of people like glowing candles.

The rising heat of the ground,
Making the scene sparkle.

Up here it seems so calm,
A beauty unnoticed when down there.

We were just teenagers back then. I sighed with a smile. Leaning into Nate, I thanked God for this one-of-a-kind man, and for this very special time we had together for just the two of us. I also thanked Him for the precious memories that live in my heart of our life together. I was so very thankful for this love-story life that God had blessed me with.

Our plane came down for a landing in Newark, and after collecting our luggage and hailing a taxi, we were dropped off at our Jersey City hotel—a birthday present from my mom—she was in on it, too! By the time we took our luggage up to our room, we were really hungry—we had passed on the airplane's *dinner menu* and wanted to wait to eat until we landed. Sometimes it's the simple things that make a trip great. And right now, all we wanted was pancakes! On a late-night quest for food, we strolled hand in hand down the street until we found a twenty-four-hour diner with the world's best coffee, and no wait.

Nate had every detail of our trip planned. First thing in the morning, he led me to the subway station across the street from our hotel. Standing on the platform in the mezzanine, I could feel the rumbling of the subway approaching on the tracks. From the moment we stepped into the subway car, I felt like I was caught up in a dreamlike whirlwind of NYC birthday bliss of flashing lights, honking horns, and billboards that rolled down the sides of towering buildings like giant wallpaper. One minute we were in a taxi cab, and the next minute we were in Times Square being led to our reserved table for lunch at Sardi's. As we enjoyed our meal at this legendary restaurant, I looked around at all the walls that were lined with caricature pictures of celebrities.

Before I knew it, we were sitting in a theatre on Broadway with a *Grease* Playbill in our hands. The lights dimmed, and I got goosebumps when I heard the first notes of the film's intro song, "Grease is the Word." With a sentimental smile, I thought of the Salinas ladies when the musical got to the part where Danny and Sandy sang "Summer Nights." Back home, no wedding reception was ever without *Grease* songs—at least for the girls anyway. "Summer Nights" was when the guys left the dance floor and got a *beverage*.

Carrying a bag with a newly purchased *Grease* hoodie, we left the theatre to spend the rest of the afternoon exploring the borough of Manhattan—the heart of NYC. We had been here once before. A couple of summers back, we took the kids on a road trip from Boston down to Philadelphia. We had packed in everything we possibly could do on that very fun family vacation, but there was so much more to see! So we set out to see all we could before *Mamma Mia!* this evening!

There is nothing like walking around bustling Manhattan—and I wanted to see everything! We stood in awe of the *spectacular* 360 degree view seventy stories high atop Radio City Music Hall. After that, we headed off to Grand Central Station, and then made our way to Madison Square Garden.

Our whirlwind continued with a yellow taxi dropping us off at another Broadway theatre with lights and posters lining the venue—our second show of the day! *Mamma Mia!* was a fun and energetic show. I *loved* every bit of it—especially when Nate would flair his lip and growl at the glitz and glam of disco balls and dancing queens in spandex jumpsuits.

I was laughing out loud at how eager Nate was to leave the show as we exited the grandeur of the brick theatre. We made our way down the street for a slice of pizza and continued walking to Central Park. We arrived at a horse-drawn carriage seemingly waiting for us at the curb. I stood still and looked at Nate in wonder. He nodded with smiling eyes. Nate's old fashioned charm had me feeling like the luckiest girl in the entire world as the coachman helped me up into the carriage. I felt caught up in a dream as the carriage began to move, and I could hear the majestic white horse's metal shoes begin clopping down the road. Nate and I held hands as we took in the beauty of our midnight carriage ride through Central Park. We were enveloped by the lush greenery of giant trees, and gardens of countless flowers reflecting their color by the dazzling city lights, and stars in the midnight sky. Stone arches enhanced the ambiance, while bridges in the distance made for a perfect backdrop for the ponds and fountains flowing with water. At the end of our horse-drawn fairy-tale ride, the coachman took a photo of Nate kissing me.

As we walked back to the subway station, I leaned my head into Nate's arm. "Thank you, Baby," I said with a tender smile. "Today has been one of the best days of my entire life. I don't want it to end."

"It's not over yet," Nate smiled. "One more stop."

Once again, I was surprised but all in for wherever Nate was taking me. We walked down the stairs, swiped our MetroCards, and walked through the turnstile. The subway station was considerably less congested at half past 1:00 am The subway arrived right on time, and we boarded a train for Brooklyn.

When we exited and took the stairs back up to the surface, I expected more noise, lights, and crowded streets of people walking in every direction. But we were in a residential area with not a single person in sight. Nate grabbed my hand and led me into a dark alleyway.

"Uh, *you know,* if someone were up to no good, we would *never* be found out here," I whispered. "Do you know where you're going?" I asked, trepidatiously.

"No," Nate said with a grin, turning into another alley and avoiding a line of trashcans.

We eventually arrived at a metal fence half covered in shrubs. Nate pulled the creaky gate open and took my hand again. We walked into the unknown together, lowering our heads as we followed a dirt path under a thicket of trees. As we entered a clearing, I gasped. Before us was a parkland that spread to the water's edge with a panoramic view of the glittering lights of the city, and of the Manhattan and Brooklyn Bridges. I looked over at downtown

Manhattan in the distance and the reflection of the lights in the water and smiled. We had never been here before, but I recognized it. I knew exactly where we were!

I turned toward Nate, both excited to be here, *and* excited that I had figured out where we were. "*Now* I know why you brought me here," I giggled happily. "This is the park from *Thirteen going on Thirty*!—where Jennifer Garner and Mark Ruffalo chewed Razzles and jumped from swings." Nate knew I was a sucker for *chick flicks,* and this park was from one of my favorite scenes in the movie.

We walked in the grass toward the water, marveling at the bridges and the multitude of far-off buildings. We passed by the empty benches on the wooden walkway and stopped at the iron railing. Due to it being well past 2:00 am, we had the whole park all to ourselves. At a loss for words, my kiss told Nate how much I loved this, while a myriad of lights illuminated our embrace. These moments felt like a romantic dream. Nate wrapped his arms around my waist, and I looked at him with a warm smile.

"You really thought of everything, didn't you?" I said, slightly shaking my head. "This trip, Baby… this has been the *best* birthday I have…," I suddenly stopped in mid-sentence. For a moment, I began thinking of my nineteenth birthday when Nate asked me to marry him at the top of Jack's Peak! And then, I thought, Brittney was born on my twenty-third birthday! He waited patiently for me to continue. "I, I was just…" Nate smiled and nodded. He knew what I was thinking even without me finishing. Our unspoken words became magical moments of a full conversation between our hearts as we looked into each other's eyes. Nate pulled my hands up to his lips and kissed them. "Happy Birthday, Princess."

We left NYC with great memories of the best of times. We checked out of our hotel and headed south in our rental car for the short drive to Philadelphia. In less than two hours, we would arrive at *The Swan* for my edible birthday present from the kids! I had the two twenties in my purse, and I was ready to spend them!

"I'm gonna take a picture of my Philly Cheesesteak sandwich and send it to the kids before I take a bite," I told Nate. "I can't believe we get to eat there today!" We had skipped breakfast that morning to save room for the delicious meal that awaited us. We had to make it a fairly quick lunch though, as our plane was due to fly out of Philadelphia that afternoon.

As we drove over a bridge leaving town, I looked out at the New York Harbor. There she was!—Lady Liberty raising her torch of golden flames into the blue summer sky. I sat there in awe of this iconic national monument towering over the tour boats coming in and out of Liberty Island. That was us a couple of years ago. We had taken the kids there on one of the harbor's Circle Line Tour Boats. Due to 9-11, we had not been able to climb up to her crown, but just being there and standing next to her was amazing. And now, it was still hard for me to take my eyes off of her, but when I heard the familiar tune of a piano beginning to play, I tilted my head to the side, and looked at Nate.

"Is this song really on the radio right now?! I asked, as Billy Joel began singing… *"Some folks like to get away, take a holiday from the neighborhood."* Maybe Nate had put the CD in while my eyes were fixed on Lady Liberty? It would be just like Nate to do that, too. Back when we were dating—and CDs hadn't been invented yet—Nate would set up specific songs on his cassette tapes to play when he would pick me up, and I'd get in the car. I was always so touched by the thought he put into our dates.

"Yeah," Nate nodded. He looked pleasantly surprised by the DJ's choice of music as we continued our drive.

"What perfect timing!" I smiled. "It makes me like this song even more." Nate turned up the radio and we listened to "New York

State of Mind" as we continued our drive. The Statue of Liberty was no longer in sight.

I could feel the warmth of the sun shining through the car window as we drove, and I started to think about everything we had done this weekend. "I wish we could start our time in NYC all over again. That was so fun!" I looked at Nate, so striking in his black Ray-Ban sunglasses.

"Just so you know, that was the *one* and *only* time you will ever get me to watch *Mamma Mia!*" I could see him resisting a smile.

"Aw, c'mon. You know it was so good! I think you liked it."

Nate shook his head and shoulders, almost as if he were shaking off an infection.

I started cracking up. "Yeah, well *I* loved it!" I paused, smiling, relishing the memory of Nate watching it live with me last night. "You must *really* love me a lot to sit through the whole thing," I teased. Nate started growling. I happily looked out the window—everything seemed right in the world.

Halfway through our drive, I noticed a distinct end to the blue sky—almost as if a straight line had been drawn where the blue sky ended and a black sky started. I took my sunglasses off and squinted my eyes trying to figure out what we were heading into.

"What is that up there?" I asked Nate. "It doesn't look like rain clouds. It's like a solid black sky... in the middle of the day!"

"Looks like we're going to hit some weather," Nate answered, looking up at the sky.

This was so unlike California weather. In California, when it is going to rain, we would have dark clouds, or even a dark sky. But this... this was a completely black sky, and we were driving seventy miles per hour in that direction.

Within a short time, we were in torrential rain so heavy that cars were pulling over from the blackout conditions. The windshield wipers couldn't keep up. We pulled over to a gas station, waiting out the downpour.

"You better try calling the airport," Nate said. "Our plane might have a weather delay."

I reached for my purse to find my phone and our plane tickets. Nate didn't have a personal cell phone—he never wanted one. Everyone at work was given a BlackBerry a few years back. He had initially declined the offer, but later accepted his first cell phone. Co-workers had since moved on to an updated smartphone, but Nate didn't see the point. The old one still worked fine.

I called the airline from the gas station and smiled as I listened to the recording. Due to the black clouds and heavy downpour of rain, our flight had been cancelled. The storm itself was our ticket to a full day in Philadelphia!

With the gift of extra time, we no longer had to rush to get to the airport—we were able to leisurely enjoy our Philly Cheesesteak sandwiches from the kids. Although the flights remained cancelled until early morning, the rain had stopped, giving us a chance to drive over to the Philadelphia Museum of Art and run up the *Rocky Steps*. Nate loves that movie! He was just like Rocky on those seventy-two stone steps, racing me to the top and punching the air. Nate knows every line of that movie *and* can say them in a legit Rocky voice. So basically, I spent the rest of the day with Rocky Balboa. The heavyweight champion and I even had time to drive over to Penn's Landing for an evening walk, and for him to air punch a few things along the Delaware River Waterfront.

We arrived at the Philadelphia Airport in the middle of the night for our 6:00 am flight back home. With only a few hours' sleep at a nearby hotel, we rolled our luggage up to the check-in counter. The airport was packed with delayed travelers napping on the floor, or sipping their 4:00 am coffees. Announcements informed passengers of rescheduled flights and gate changes. We found our way to a small row of vacant chairs lining an old, sloped, narrow hallway. It seemed as though no one wanted to sit in these eccentric chairs, but I didn't mind. I was just thrilled we got extra time in Philly! We shared this narrow hallway with a small food and beverage cart sitting directly in front of us. I sat with the luggage, while Nate took a mere few steps forward to get a cup of coffee, a hot chocolate, and something for us to eat before our flight home.

I closed my eyes for a few moments. We had fit *so much* into these last few days. It had been a trip of very little sleep. With my eyes still closed, I could hear Nate approaching. He was saying something about Father Carmine throwing him down a blessing. Oh, Nate. Chuckling, I opened my eyes, and Nate handed me a breakfast burrito.

"Thanks, Rocky," I said, unwrapping breakfast.

We sat there, side by side, in our slightly tilted chairs. I could see the big windows down the narrow hallway as we ate and watched the planes taxi in and out of the terminal as the workers waved their orange batons. Our wait was almost over, and soon we would be boarding our plane for home. I nuzzled into Nate, and took in a deep breath—*he* was always my favorite place to be. New York, Philadelphia, or even our home town Modesto, nowhere could compete. My paradise, at that moment, was the two of us sitting in these peculiar old chairs, in the slanted hallway of a noisy airport.

My thoughts began to slow as I turned off the light and got into bed. I pulled the comforter over me, and reached for *Conquer,* embracing my pillow's cozy serenity. With my sleepy eyes closed, I lay there in the fluffiness of the warm blankets and waited for Nate to tuck me in for the night.

"Steamroller!!!" I instantly opened my eyes and began bracing myself for the inevitable flattening. My protest was nothing more than background noise to all of Nate's pulverizing sound effects while rolling over the top of me with his two hundred plus pound body.

"Ughh! Nate!" I groaned in a playful, yet irritated tone.

Having misjudged the distance to the edge of the bed, Nate rolled off onto my vanity chair ... again!

"Nate!, I *just* had that repaired from the last time you steam-rolled me."

"Son of a ...," Nate lightheartedly chuckled under his breath as he got back up to his feet and collected the pieces of my broken chair. Nate had his own twist to this saying by leaving the last word — the cuss word — out. It was always just *son of a ...*, and that's it.

The hallway light spilled into our dark bedroom, enough for me to make out his satisfied smile very clearly. "Aw, c'mon Baby. You know I love you," he teased. Somehow, he had managed to accomplish both waking me up *and* breaking something with a single steamroll. Impressive, but I could see in his eyes that he wasn't done yet as he walked over to lock the door.

Nate walked around to the other side of the bed, pulled back the covers and got into bed with me. My eyes were no longer sleepy. Knowing he had my undivided attention, Nate smirked, and drew an imaginary line down the center of our mattress with his index finger.

"This is your side. This is my side," he said with confidence, looking ready to enforce his rules. Nate knew exactly what was going to happen. Although I was well aware that his provoking was reverse psychology, that was beside the point. I wanted to be on Nate's side of the bed now — my side simply wouldn't do. Just minutes ago, I was ready to peacefully fall asleep for the night, but not anymore. I energetically rolled over to *his side*, and the wrestling match began.

Although Nate had the size and strength advantage, my vigorous determination at least caused him to work up a sweat. Whether it be in play or passion, rolling around in bed with Nate was always a good time.

Once again, we heard the "times up" sound — Ryan was knocking on the door. It was always Ryan.

"What do you want, Boy?" Nate answered, with a pseudo sleepy voice. I giggled from under the covers on Nate's side of the bed.

"Dad?" Ryan said from the other side of the door. "It's time to read our Bibles. When are you coming out?"

"... Okay ... just give me a few minutes to say good night to Mom." We could hear Ryan go back down the hallway into Bub's room.

Nate gave me a big kiss and got up to grab his clothes and his Bible. "Nooo, don't go," I whispered, wrapping myself around Nate in every way possible. Nate chuckled and started tickling me, knowing I would loosen my grip — I'm so ticklish!

I stayed in bed and rolled back over onto my side with a smile. Nate always made me feel so loved. I could hear Nate and Ryan getting settled in his bedroom. Awhile back, they had decided to read the entire Bible in a year and were currently making their way through the Old Testament. As I lay there in bed, I looked at the thin line of light shining from under the closed bedroom doors and thought about Nate.

Okay, what's the catch? I sincerely asked God. Nate's such a great dad. He is strikingly handsome. He is fun and makes me laugh every day. He is so smart — an attorney for crying out loud! He sends me flowers and makes me handmade cards. He is reading the Bible with Ryan. Out on the table sits a stack of files which will keep him up into the early hours of morning. But he never complains. Files of criminals that have committed crimes here in Stanislaus County — the county he is passionate about protecting.

He loves to dance, travel, and even used to help change diapers! Thank you, God, for this amazing man. I love him *so* much. After being married almost twenty years, I still haven't figured out what the catch is…

Photos

Daddy's Little Girl, 1991

Bath Time with Uncle Justin

Precious Moments, 1995

Our Little Pumpkin

Birthday Girls, 1996

Nate's Swearing-In Ceremony, 1996

Nate's Drawing is now our Current Life!

Arches National Park, 2000

Nate and Paul Golfing in the Caribbean, 2003

St. Louis Cardinals Baseball Game 2004

Discovery Cove in Florida, 2005

Ironstone Vineyards with Carrie, 2007

Happy 60th Gramma! We're Going on a Cruise!

Germaine's Luau in Hawaii, 2009

Chapter 10

"Broken" by Lifehouse

AT A ROUTINE CARDIOLOGY appointment in the spring of 2010, Nate was told about a procedure called Alcohol Septal Ablation — ethanol being injected into a small artery that supplies blood to the thickened area of the heart. The alcohol kills the tissue and shrinks it to more normal size. His cardiologist had given him a referral for a consultation with a highly regarded cardiothoracic surgeon at UCSF.

We drove to San Francisco to meet with the heart specialist a number of times over the next few months. We were told he was one of the best in the country. After reviewing Nate's medical records, various testing, and exams, the cardiologist agreed that ablation would be very beneficial. He told us that he had performed this non-surgical procedure hundreds of times over the years and found it to be quite successful in helping patients with HCM. He and another cardiologist answered all of our questions, one being how soon we should do this. We had an upcoming mission trip to Mexico, a family reunion in Iowa, and a vacation to Chicago all within the next few months. The doctor told us to enjoy our plans, and to schedule the ablation for after we returned.

It was getting late and Mary's toy poodle Chloe needed a walk. A walk would be good for Nate and me as well—a healthy way to relieve some of our anxiety. Although never dramatic, I'm always more outspoken about my concerns. Nate, on the other hand, invariably keeps a calm and collected demeanor when it comes to stressful matters. No doubt though, down deep he was feeling the same way I was. Tomorrow was a big day, but we were ready—as ready as you can be anyway for a procedure that involves both a cardiologist and the ICU.

I fastened Chloe's leash to her collar, and Nate and I left the house headed for the canal. A leisurely walk alongside the canal at night would give Chloe a bathroom break. More importantly, it would give Nate and me some last-minute time together to mentally prepare for tomorrow.

Chloe—a one-year-old puppy bursting with energy—was always ready for a walk, and I was thankful for her bright pink leash. Her black fur camouflaged her so she blended right into the darkness. We walked past the golf course, lit only by the lights from the surrounding neighborhood houses and the summer stars. I looked over to the shadowed weeping willows that decorated the landscape of the fairways that were closed until sunrise.

"I'm glad we have a chance to walk off all of those chips and salsa we were devouring before dinner," I said to Nate, as we reached the canal. "I almost didn't have room for dinner!" I joked.

"Yeah, that was really good," Nate agreed.

The croaking frogs in the canal sounded like a concert of God's nature as we walked. "It was great to have your mom and Jon with us for dinner too." I held on tight to Chloe's leash as she walked ahead of us, pulling a bit. "So nothing to eat for you after midnight, right?" I asked.

Nate growled as he nodded. We walked in silence for a couple of minutes. "Thanks for fasting for me today," he said, looking over toward me. "You and the kids really didn't need to do that. Everything's going to be fine. It's not even a surgery."

"I know, Baby," I said softly. "I was praying all day that everything goes perfectly tomorrow. And I was dreaming of El Rosal all day too," I smiled.

As we continued our walk, an ominous feeling began creeping into my being. I looked at Chloe to make sure she was okay. She was totally fine doing what dogs do, sniffing and exploring everything around her. I brushed off the feeling and kept walking. Nate and I talked about our day at work, but I just couldn't shake this foreboding feeling. What if there were a wild animal up ahead that was going to attack us? Or, maybe there was a homeless or drunk person up to no good. The further we walked, the more uneasy I became.

I reached for Nate's arm and stopped walking. He stopped walking as well and looked at me. "What's up, Nice Lady?" he asked, unsure of why we had stopped. "Are you okay?"

I shook my head as I answered, "I don't know why, but I have a really bad feeling inside." I told him my thoughts about possible danger out there in the dark. We had walked this canal countless times over the years in both the day and night, and I had never felt like this before. "I think we should turn around," I told Nate in an earnest tone. Holding onto Nate, I looked around in the darkness.

"Okay. That's fine. I don't like walking anyway," he teased. The two of us led Chloe across a cement walkway over the canal and headed back home.

The next morning arrived, and I could hear Mary—an early riser—in the kitchen making coffee. Nate and I were just getting up for the day, but the kids were still in their rooms sleeping. With both of them being on summer vacation, they probably stayed up until all hours of the night with Uncle Jon, who was crashed on the living room couch.

Before leaving town, Nate and I prayed together. When we were done, he said goodbye to the kids and told them he'd see them later in the day.

As I locked up the house, Mary got in the back seat of the jeep while Nate was putting his things in the trunk. We all buckled up and headed west for San Francisco. Today was going to be a very long day. I was so thankful that Jon was at home with the kids. The three of them would meet us at UCSF when the procedure was over.

As we got closer to the hospital, I closed my eyes. I wasn't sleepy, but rather needed a few moments to face the reality of the procedure that was soon to take place. I opened my eyes to the sound of my phone. It was Ern sending her humorous well wishes to Nate. I chuckled when I read her text.

"Ern says when you wake up in the hospital, your nails are going to be painted." I looked over at Nate behind the wheel. He smirked knowing that was Ern's way of sending her love. Mary chuckled from the back seat. Nate's nickname for Ern was E.T.—her initials. His wedding gift to her was a large bag of Reese's Pieces and a card that read *Phone Home*.

After making our way through the morning traffic, we pulled into the covered garage at UCSF Medical Center and parked. Nate grabbed his overnight bag and his briefcase. I looked at him. "I don't think you are going to need your briefcase while you're here, Honey."

"I have some things I need to do. I'll be in bed for a day or two with nothing to do so I might as well get some work done," Nate said. "I'll be going back to work as soon as they let me out of here. Hopefully tomorrow," he added.

I completely disagreed about him returning to work tomorrow, but simply shook my head knowing it was useless to talk him out of bringing his briefcase inside. I will definitely talk in person with the cardiologist about Nate's recovery, and see to it that he follows doctor's orders.

After checking in and filling out many forms, a nurse led us behind closed doors. She showed Mary and me to a waiting room down the hallway, and then took Nate with her to get him prepared for the procedure. It all happened so fast, but the nurse said she would come back for us so we could see Nate before they started.

We patiently waited until the nurse returned and then led us to a room down the hall. We walked into the room and right away saw Nate sitting up in a hospital bed with a blanket over his legs, and an IV in his arm. Mary and I walked toward Nate. I heard voices and looked over to see two doctors sitting by the far wall talking amongst themselves. One was the cardiologist we had met last month — the one who would be performing the ablation. Mary hugged Nate, and then gave us a moment together. I could feel the tears in my eyes as I sat down on the bed next to him in his blue and white hospital gown. Part of me wanted to take his hand and run from this place. The other part of me wanted him to have this procedure. This ablation would help him to breathe better. It would help him be able to exercise without getting winded. I leaned forward with a hug. "I love you," I said, feeling a couple of tears run down my cheeks.

"I love you too, Princess," Nate said warmly. "Don't worry. Everything's going to be alright." I reached for his hands and squeezed them tight. Holding my emotions inside as best as I could, I lovingly smiled at him, and then walked out of the room with Mary by my side.

"I need to use the restroom," I told Mary as we walked down the hall. She waited for me in the hallway as I walked into the one-person bathroom. Once I stepped inside and locked the door behind me, I stood in the middle of the bathroom and cried for a couple of moments. I had stayed strong in front of Nate for the most part. Now I just needed to let it out, and trust that God would watch over the man that I loved.

After wiping my eyes, I met Mary in the hallway. We walked to the cafeteria for something to eat. Neither one of us was hungry, but we had a long wait ahead of us so it would be a good place for us to sit for a while.

"Thank you for being here," I said to Mary as I reached for her hand from across the table.

Her eyes were watery too as she looked at me with a slight nod. "I wouldn't miss being here. I'll help however I can," she stated. Mary sipped her cup of coffee as we talked. I had taken a few bites of a blueberry muffin, but left it on the plate when we walked back to the waiting room.

It seemed to take forever, but eventually the cardiologist walked through the doorway of the waiting room. We both stood up at the sight of him. "Everything went well," he informed us in a doctorly tone as we walked toward each other. Still in his scrubs, he led us to another room across the hallway. In a dimly lit room, the cardiologist sat down with us and began showing us on a computer screen some before and after images of Nate's heart. He pointed to the left ventricle and said it was a difficult procedure and took longer than anticipated, but he was able to successfully accomplish the ablation of the thickened wall. Mary and I took a sigh of relief at the doctor's great news. God had answered our many prayers.

The cardiologist smiled, knowing we were thrilled with the fantastic news he had for us. "They have already wheeled Nate into a room. In fact, I just talked with him," the doctor said with a chuckle. He's doing fine and listening to *Tesla* on his iPod. Nate said he's hungry so we're going to let him eat a little something."

I couldn't wait to see him! *Thank you, God!* I said over and over and over in my head as we followed the cardiologist to the Intensive Care Unit. There was a full-on jamboree going on in my heart!

We arrived at the alabaster colored room to see Nate wide awake. His eyes smiled when he saw us walk in. I walked over to the window side of the bed and reached for his hand. I pulled his outstretched arm in close to my heart and held on tight. It was *so* great to see him! "You did it, Babe," I said with a big smile. "How do you feel?" I asked.

"I feel fine," Nate replied. "I'm hungry though."

"Yeah," I smiled. "The Doctor said he's going to let you eat something."

While Mary was talking with Nate, I walked around the room looking at all the hospital equipment — the rhythmic beeps from the heart monitor sounding as background noise to our conversation. I'd never been in an ICU room before. I walked to the other side of the bed and saw a wire, secured with dressing, inserted into the side of Nate's neck. My eyes followed the wire to a pacemaker attached to his hospital gown. It hurt to see all that, but I was thankful for it. The doctors had told us during the consultation that he would have both a pacemaker and a defibrillator as a backup. I sat down on a chair, and a nurse came in and asked me to fill out some more paperwork. As I began filling out the papers, I could hear the kids' voices as they approached.

"Hi Dad," Brittney said, as she walked a little cautiously over to the hospital bed. She was looking at the wire in Nate's neck, but didn't say anything about it.

"Bubbasaurus," Nate responded, giving her a reassuring hug that everything was okay.

"It's The Boy," Nate said, seeing Ryan walk in the room with Uncle Jon. Ryan smiled, and walked over to sit with him on his bed. "Hey, Juanathan," Nate greeted his brother. Jon grinned and walked over to Nate. "Brothers gotta hug," Nate said in a Chris Farley voice. Everybody laughed, and although we were in the hospital, everything seemed back to normal.

Nate's food arrived, and his eyes smiled again. We decided to leave Nate to his dinner while we all went out to get something to eat ourselves. I had lost my appetite until I knew Nate was okay, and now I was hungry. "We'll be back," I told Nate cheerfully. I was so elated and beyond thankful that this procedure was over and everything went so well. Mary, Jon, the kids, and I all walked across the street in search of a place to eat.

The restaurant's food was nothing special, but our joy at the table made everything feel like a celebration. We were all so happy and relieved that Nate was doing well, and even having dinner himself back in his room.

It was getting late. We all walked back to the ICU wing. Nate was still in bed and pulled the headset wires from his ears as he saw us walking in. I looked down at the remnants of food on the tray. It wasn't much, but at least Nate got a little something to eat. I sat down on the chair next to his bed. "Are you in any pain, Honey?" I asked, looking at all the monitors and wires surrounding him.

"Nope," Nate shook his head like it was nothing. It felt good to know he wasn't in any pain, but I didn't quite understand how that was possible. I felt sure they had him on pain meds, but knowing Nate, he probably declined them. After visiting for a while, we thought it best to give him some time to rest. It had been an intense day like nothing we had ever experienced. The kids said goodbye to their dad, followed by Mary and Jon. I lingered a few minutes in the room after everyone had left, delaying my goodbye as long as possible. I stood up and reached for his hand as I smiled at him. “You did so great today, Honey.” Nate smiled back at me. I snuggly held his arm up close to my heart again, just like I had earlier except from the other side of the bed. I took a deep breath. “I’m gonna go,” I said, still holding his arm to me.

“Yeah, I’ll get some rest and see you tomorrow,” Nate said, chuckling that I wasn’t letting go.

“I love you, Sweetheart,” I said warmly.

“I love you too, Princess,” Nate replied, getting me with those green eyes of his.

I leaned into the hospital bed and gave Nate a kiss. After one final squeeze, I released his arm and walked out of the room. When I stepped into the hallway, I paused. I turned back around to look at Nate one more time before I left. He smiled at me from his bed. I smiled back, and then walked away.

Everyone was waiting for me by the elevators, and we began making our way to the parking garage. San Francisco’s city lights faded in the rearview mirror as we caravanned back to Modesto. We were only home a few minutes when the phone rang. Ryan picked it up, and I could tell by the way he was talking that it was Nate. Ryan finished talking and said, “Okay, here’s Mom,” and handed me the phone.

“Hey, Honey,” I smiled, putting the phone up to my ear.

“I was just calling to make sure you guys made it back home alright,” Nate said.

“Ah, yeah, we just got back. We made it home safe and sound,” I assured him, happy to hear Nate’s voice again before I went to bed. “How are you feeling?” I asked.

“I feel fine. Hopefully they’ll let me go tomorrow,” he answered.

"Well, you just get some good sleep tonight," I responded to his optimism, "and we'll be back to see you tomorrow."

"Okay, will do. I love you, Princess."

"I love you too, Baby," I said with a smile, and hung up the phone.

Although I was tired from this stressful day, I climbed into bed happy. I closed my eyes, feeling refreshed by the cool air streaming out of the AC vents above my head. These hot August nights are brutal. I rolled over on my side, thanking God over and over again for helping Nate with his procedure today, and fell asleep.

I was awakened a few hours later by the sound of Ryan opening the bedroom doors and walking toward me in bed. "Mom," he said in a distraught tone, as he handed me the phone. "It's the hospital! They need to talk to you!" A surge of anxious energy bolted through me as I instantly got to my feet and hurried into the living room. Ryan and Jon were still up and attentively stood right there with me. "Hello," I said into the receiver with urgency.

"Is this Mrs. Baker?" a lady asked.

"Yes, is Nate alright?" I quickly responded.

"...No..., No he's not..."

My heart stopped. "I'm very sorry, Mrs. Baker..." she continued. With an outburst of tears, I listened to her words in a paradoxical fog. It seemed impossible for me to wrap my mind around what she was saying. "What??!!!" I wailed, shaking my head back and forth. "No, no, no! This cannot be happening!" I heard a crashing sound and looked over to see Ryan punching the wooden bar stools. Brittney and Gramma came out to the living room in their pajamas, awakened from all of the commotion. I could see Jon telling them. The whole family was shattered in a million pieces. Jon slid against the wall to the floor with his hands covering his face.

I can't even remember what else the lady on the phone said other than we needed to get to San Francisco.

During the middle of the night, when most people were fast asleep, the kids and I, along with Mary and Jon, fell into a vast calamity. The news was so utterly devastating that the five of us would be forever impacted and bonded by that single moment.

We were all in *major* shock. The very first call I made was to Pastor Cliff who immediately came over to the house. I could feel my body trembling as he talked with us in the living room. Being the Minister of Pastoral Care at our church, he compassionately guided us, helping to mitigate our swirling minds. After answering our many questions, he began informing us about the necessary first steps to take, and the heart-rending decisions that soon awaited us. It was all so overwhelming that I felt like I was going to throw up. We had so much to do, starting with the many phone calls to let people know the devastating news.

Before Pastor Cliff left, he prayed for us...

Our Father,

We come to you because we do not understand how this could happen. We are crushed and undone. We were all so happy and confident with the successful procedure, and the hopeful future it brought to Nate and Shelley and family.

God, this is not at all what we expected. Help us to understand and believe that You are in control and can somehow bring good out of this unexpected tragedy.

We know that Nate is home safe with You. Help Shelley and the kids to be able to understand in time how to live with this news. We know you love Nate and his family, and ask that you will help them find a way to fill the void created by his going Home. Help us all to entrust him into your loving care.

Thank you for the hope in the resurrection of Jesus, and that someday they will be reunited with Nate. And when that reunion happens, they will never be parted again.

In Jesus' name, Amen

We were all inconsolable. Even so, his prayer felt like oxygen to me. After a grateful hug for his direction and vital prayer, I walked Pastor Cliff to the front door and opened it to the darkness of the night sky.

"I'll be back again later today, after you all return from San Francisco," he said, with his Bible in his hand. "If you have any questions, just give me a call."

"Okay," I said with a nod, and slowly shut the door to the reality of what I had to do next.

I sat at the breakfast nook table with the phone in my hand. "Once I make this first call, the news is going to spread like wildfire," I said to my family.

It did.

I was in a trancelike state, not moving a muscle. My heartbeat felt weak, almost like my heart was too despondent to pump blood while this phone call was happening. The fragile nuance of this conversation evoked painful memories. I was instantly caught up in a flashback of sitting next to Nate when he called Jerry with the tragic news of Justin being in a fatal car accident. And now, 18 years later, here I was with Mary on the phone with Jerry, telling him that although the procedure went well, Nate had suddenly died. Twice now I had been present for Jerry getting a parent's worst nightmare phone call.

Clearly, the bit of false security I had when Nate went in for his procedure was all for naught. Evidently, it was wishful thinking, but I truly didn't think that God would allow Mary and Jerry to lose another child. It had given me comfort to believe that Nate was in an allegorical safety net due to Justin already being taken at such a young age.

Mary wept as she hung up the phone. "Jerry is going to get an airline ticket," she said with her voice cracking. "He'll be here as soon as possible."

I sat on the edge of the bed and called Paul and Traci's home phone. With each ring, my heart ached at the devastating news I had to break to them.

"Hello," Traci answered in an apprehensive voice. Getting an unexpected call that early in the morning was never good.

"Traci," I cried. "It's Shelley." It was a crushing and poignant moment where few words were needed. I was having trouble articulating the words my mind couldn't grasp. She intuitively knew.

"Oh, my God! No, no!" Traci called out. I closed my eyes for a few seconds hearing her sorrow.

"Is Paul there?" I managed to ask.

"No, he's still at the gym," she answered.

Choking back the tears, I asked, "Can you let everyone in Salinas know?" Traci wholeheartedly agreed to do what I had asked of her and said they would help in any way possible.

"I'm so sorry, Shelley." Traci expressed emotionally.

As we said goodbye, I bowed my head and closed my eyes. Paul, Chris, and Matt's lives were about to change forever. Their *best friends four-pack* had just gone down to three. I sat there and cried imagining this heartbreaking news spreading around Salinas.

We had already been up for hours, but at daybreak Jon drove the five of us to San Francisco. After walking into the hospital, we stopped at an empty waiting room next to the ICU. Mary and Jon stayed in the hallway as I walked into the small room with the kids. They sat down on the chairs next to each other in silence.

"Gramma, Uncle Jon, and I are going to meet with the cardiologist now," I said softly to them. My heart ached beyond words. I paused. "Dad is here," I said, trying my best to keep it together. "After we talk with the doctor, you can see Dad if you want to... but if you don't want to, that is completely okay," I assured them.

Brittney answered saying, "I don't want to see Dad like this."

"Me neither," Ryan immediately agreed, "Not like this."

"Okay, that's totally fine," I reiterated. "But just so you know, if you don't see him now while we are here, you will never have this chance again." Taking a deep breath, I continued. "I'm going to see him," my voice cracking as I spoke. "I *need* to see him to believe he is really gone."

The kids completely supported my decision, and mutually agreed that they did not want to see him. They wanted to remember their fun-loving dad how he was.

Mary, Jon, and I met with the cardiac surgeon who told us that Nate had had a heart attack. He was the only one of his patients who had ever died after having this procedure. The cardiologist could offer no medical reason, and told us everything was fine when he left the hospital that night. He hopelessly tried to explain something for which he had no real answers. He told us that they desperately tried resuscitating Nate for a very long time with no response. Evidently, he went into Code Blue—cardiac arrest—a couple of hours after his phone call home to check on us. The last thing Nate and I ever said to each other was *I love you.*

Both Mary and Jon decided to see Nate as well. As the three of us silently walked down the hallway toward the room Nate was in—the same one he was in yesterday—we noticed a curtain pulled across the door to the room. In a motherly manner, Mary told Jon and me to wait outside. She wanted to check things out first before we went in. We nodded our consent and watched as she stood there for a moment before she stoically pulled back the curtain and walked into the room.

Wrapped in dreaded anticipation, Jon and I stood there side by side intently holding hands. The only thing we could see was the curtain draped right in front of us.

Jon and I were clenching each other's hands so tightly I could feel a throbbing pulse as our blood coursed through them. We stood there motionlessly as we waited for Mary to return.

In time, Mary came out of the room crying. Grief-stricken, she told us she didn't think we should go in. I appreciated her protectiveness, but it was essential for me to see Nate. Jon wanted to go in, too.

I was deliberately vague about my one-on-one time with Nate once I met up with my family by the elevator. Although they were all waiting for me, no one asked questions. It was mutually understood that words wouldn't suffice in this circumstance. The five of us left UCSF and didn't look back. As Jon drove us home, I looked down at Nate's wedding ring loosely encircling my finger. I held it up to my heart as we drove, and asked Jon to stop by McHenry

Village once we got back to Modesto. I wanted to get a chain to wear Nate's wedding band around my neck.

We were back from San Francisco, and quite literally in shock mode. It was the afternoon, roughly 12 hours since the devastating phone call, but in that short amount of time, the entire trajectory of our lives was changing right before our eyes. Many family and friends, who lived both locally and out of town, had arrived at our house. I glanced at the kids in the midst of people gathered in the dining room. The overwhelming devastation in their eyes took me right to the depths of their souls. As a mom, all I wanted to do was protect them and take away their pain. But I couldn't. I felt completely helpless. How could the kids—both teenagers—possibly know what to do with these intense feelings?!

"Bubs, Ryan," I said, to get their attention. They both looked over at me. "Come here," I said, gesturing for them to follow me to Ryan's room. I shut the bedroom door. "Sit down. I want to talk with you guys for a few minutes." They both sat down on Ryan's bed. I stood facing them with all of the love in the world, along with some very hard truths that I needed to talk with them about.

"I've lived long enough to know how things like this can go. Something tragic happens, and people find ways to make themselves feel better," I said, looking at both of them as they sat there listening. "Traumatic events like this often pave the way to drugs, alcohol, and the list goes on and on. People find ways to cope with the pain, and can make some really bad decisions." I took a deep breath and continued. "We are in a time like that *right now*," I said in a parental tone. "This is a time where we can either go *this way*," my hand motioned to the right, "or, we can go *that way*," my other hand motioned to the left. "A lot of people go off in the wrong direction at a time like this, but I want us to go in the right direction. God will help us," I said, nodding my head. "*I* am going to go in the right direction. Both of you are going to have to make your own decision about which way *you* will go. This is not a decision I can make for you." Both kids sat still on the bed, seemingly immersed in thought. Although they didn't announce a decision while sitting there, it was evident they understood my point. I know my kids and didn't worry about the route they would choose; I just wanted them to be aware of how bad decisions can have a domino effect. I felt secure that they, like me, would hold on to God with all of their might.

The vortex of grief hit us in overdrive. The devastating news was out via many avenues—phone calls, social media, a statewide APB, and various cable stations were broadcasting the news of Nate's passing on the television. Immeasurable acts of love began pouring in on us. Family and friends began filling our house. Beautiful bouquets of fresh flowers were delivered daily, one after the other. Hands were being held, and prayers were being said. Boxes of tissue were in every room. More floral arrangements and plants were arriving. Meals, fresh fruit, snacks, and drinks were delivered. The doorbell was ringing. Helping hands were everywhere.

In a medical context, doctors and patients understand a pain scale—a numerical measurement designed to communicate its intensity. This quantitative number—sometimes referred to as the 5th vital sign—is also a triage to determine the degree of urgency. Bereavement has its own type of pain scale. When grief strikes the heart in such catastrophic proportions, the human body and soul cannot survive. And for those fatal numbers that extend beyond the pain chart, God Himself steps in.

I'm well acquainted with both. Not only had I used the medical version of a pain scale during two natural childbirths, but God granted me a large dose of *Spiritual Novocain* to deal with the loss of Nate. The kids felt it too. It's an unexplainable, supernatural calmness at a time when calm is not humanly possible. Pastor Cliff explained it Biblically by reading Philippians 4:7 (NASB) "And the peace of God, which surpasses all comprehension, will guard your hearts and your minds through Christ Jesus."

These days we were undoubtedly living out this Bible verse. There were moments when I was able to talk with people—almost like Nate just wasn't home from work yet. The Spiritual Novocaine and complete shock got us through many important decisions and events. But then there were other times when I was grieving so deeply that I couldn't even stand up. My knees felt like they were going to buckle right under me. Night after night, I would walk into the entertainment room where Carrie was trying to get some sleep on the couch. It's almost as if she were expecting me as I would collapse into her arms and heave out emotions to the point of exhaustion.

It was Saturday night. Sunday morning was only a sunrise away. Going to church on Sunday mornings had been our normal for a very long time, but I really needed to think about going *this* week—*nothing* was normal anymore. Just three days ago, life as we knew it came crashing down. Just *the thought* of going to church for the first time without Nate pained me to the core. Even so, I felt we should go. Not only did we need God more than ever now, but I also wanted to keep some sort of normalcy in our lives.

The kids were good with the decision, and we would have a lot of support. Mary, Jon, and Carrie were going with us, Jerry was there, and my parents had just flown in from North Carolina a couple of hours ago. They would be going too.

It took a few cars to get us all there, but we drove to the late service at CrossPoint Church. We walked up the stairs to the balcony and made our way to the section we sat in every week. From a distance, I felt a stabbing pain at the first sight of our usual seats. As we neared, I noticed friends sitting there in the pews. It was so heartening to see them there waiting for us, and then more friends began emerging. We even noticed friends who didn't go to our church sitting on the surrounding pews. I could feel the love. They were all here to help temper the sting of our first church service without Nate.

Worship music began playing, and my tears began flowing. As I stood there trying to endure the song, Ryan took my hand from one side, and Bobbi—a co-worker, and dear friend—took my hand from the other side. I also felt a hand on my shoulder from the back of me. Although the music intensified the raw emotions of my grieving heart, the tangible comfort helped me to survive each worship song. It would be a long time before I would be ready to sing again, but I was here.

When the service was over and the congregants began leaving the sanctuary, our friends stayed, and even more joined us up on the balcony. Pastor Cliff came up to see us as well, and I introduced him to some family and friends he hadn't met yet.

Facing the pain of walking through CrossPoint's doors without Nate this morning felt both exhausting and somewhat empowering. It was the right decision for the kids and me. Although it was extremely difficult, there were no regrets. Nate would want us to be here. The love and hugs coming from everyone here made it very clear we were all in this together.

I shut the front door behind me and began walking down the cul-de-sac toward the neighborhood mailbox. Nate had been gone for over a week now, and this was the first time I had collected the mail myself. I felt lethargic as I unlocked the gray square door and grabbed the pile of mail from inside the box. As I began walking back to the house, I flipped through the bills and envelopes of different colors. Multiple sympathy cards and letters were arriving daily. A yellow padded envelope from Canyon Hills Church in Washington caught my attention. In the last nearly 15 years of living in Modesto, we hadn't missed a single sermon from Pastor Steve. Like clockwork, one arrived every week. Nate would always write an N on the CD with a Sharpie pen when he was done listening to it. I would do the same and write an S. For those times we listened to the CD together, Nate would write NS, and for those sermons with an exceptional message, Nate would put a + sign next to our initials. My heart ached as I realized this would be the first sermon CD that wouldn't have an N on the cover.

I tore open the yellow envelope and reached inside for the CD. I read the title and stopped walking. *Why Does God Allow Bad Things To Happen?* The sermon was dated August 1, 2010—four days before Nate met God in Heaven. With a lump in my throat and tears in my eyes, I walked back to the house. These timely sermon subjects never ceased to amaze me, yet my heart felt conflicted. On one hand, I wanted to rush home and listen to the pastor's Bible-based reasoning on why God would allow this to happen! But on the other hand, when I was done listening to the message, my Sharpie written S would stand alone.

Amongst the innumerable decisions to be made, I specifically chose to have Nate's Celebration of Life Ceremony on Friday, August 13, 2010. He would like that. We were expecting a full church with packed pews. Family and friends worked diligently for an unforgettable memorial service to commemorate Nate's life. Mary and Jon were in the study writing a eulogy. The kids and I were searching for specific favorite pictures to give to Jon's girlfriend Lisa, who was tirelessly working on a video that would be played at the service. Our next-door neighbors, the Tomainos, moved their RV into our driveway to help sleep some of the many loved ones staying at our house. Jerry was dealing with the funeral home arrangements and paperwork. My parents were making calls to reserve necessities such as white tents, canopies, and coolers for the get-together at our house after the reception. The Krauts, our next-door neighbors on the other side, were frequently bringing over gifts and bags of frozen yogurt from the Yogurt Mill. Carrie, Paul, and I were going to the funeral home to pick out an urn. Chris was cooking in the kitchen. Matt was trimming and watering plants in the yard to keep them alive in the sweltering heat. Carrie kept organized lists of people, phone calls, and contact info I needed. Cars lined the streets. Flowers, plants, and food continued to be delivered. All the while, prayer filled our home. God's Word and the power of prayer kept me in survival mode.

It was like a scene right out of a movie. I looked out of the limousine's window. The motorcade of police officers—dressed in their Class A uniforms—surrounded the vehicle and proceeded to escort us from Melones Court to Nate's Celebration of Life Ceremony. I was having trouble wrapping my mind around all that was happening. These moments in time felt like some kind of grand illusion as we watched multiple uniformed officers on their motorcycles both leading and following us through our neighborhood. Paul's brother-in-law, Brian—a detective—had even been given permission to drive a Salinas patrol vehicle to Modesto to join in on the motorcade representing Nate's hometown. Our family sat there in silent awe observing this vigilant formality of honor.

As the procession continued down the familiar streets of our town, we watched the formations of motorcycle officers blocking traffic at each intersection making way for us to coast right through stop signs and red lights. It was utterly surreal as our convoy continued to downtown Modesto without stopping. In route to our church, the motorcade intentionally drove by the District Attorney's Office. The streets were lined with a multitude of people. The magnitude of this sight overtook my entire being. Law enforcement, other employees, and citizens were all waiting for us to drive by in loving reverence of Nate. Countless people were saluting, crying, and waving as we drove down 12th Street and circled the block of the Court House.

As we approached CrossPoint, I saw an additional crowd of people waiting for us in front of the church. The limo pulled up to the curb and I saw one of my favorite patients, Glenn. And then I saw Matt, and many of our Salinas friends alongside of him, watching us arrive. Every aspect of life felt unreal as our family was immediately taken into a back room.

Pastor Claude Terry met us there to go over some last-minute details of the service while people continued taking their seats. I had asked him to officiate the service due to him getting to know Nate on our Mexico mission trip a couple of years back. Dr. Acree and Bonnie were in the room as well. Dr. Acree would be reading

Nate's eulogy, and Bonnie would be reading a letter I had written to Nate — I was advised by many people not to read it myself.

The love from countless people filling the sanctuary was palpable as we made our way to the front row of Nate's Celebration of Life and sat down. My brain knew why we were here, but my heart just couldn't let go. This had to be some sort of terrible misunderstanding. I swallowed hard at the framed picture of Nate in a suit and tie displayed on the stage next to a large floral arrangement. Although his face usually lit up a room, today the room was filled with heartbreak and despair. I could hear people sniffling amid the stillness.

Pastor Terry welcomed everyone and started the ceremony with some personal remembrances of Nate. He read aloud Nate's favorite Bible verse, *"You are the light of the world. A city set on a hill cannot be hidden; nor does anyone light a lamp and put it under a basket, but on the lampstand, and it gives light to all who are in the house. Let your light shine before men in such a way that they may see your good works, and glorify your Father who is in heaven."* (Matthew 5:14-16, NASB). He also read the *Prosecutor's Bible Verse* — as Nate called it. *"Whoever says to the guilty, 'You are innocent,' will be cursed by peoples and denounced by nations. But it will go well with those who convict the guilty, and rich blessing will come on them."* (Proverbs 24:24-25). He stepped away from the podium in respectful silence.

Dr. Acree came up the steps with Bonnie beside him. He introduced himself and began reading Nate's eulogy, getting choked up as he read. When I had asked him to be the one to read Nate's eulogy, he accepted and said it would be an honor. After Dr. Acree was done, Bonnie read my letter to Nate. I sat there listening to *my own* words of endless love to Nate and a promise to take care of our children until we were together again in Heaven. It meant so much to me to have them take part in the ceremony. Not only were they my employers, they also were my friends.

Everyone watched as Ryan walked up to the stage. He said good afternoon to everyone sitting in the rows of pews. In high reverence, he proceeded to give a very loving and humorous tribute to his dad. He spoke about Nate's honorable character, and then everyone chuckled as Ryan talked about some of Nate's endearing quirks. Filled with awe, I listened to my son's faithful heart as he spoke about God's plan, and although he didn't understand the timing, whatever was right in the eyes of God was right with us. He ended the tribute to his dad by saying that when we got to Heaven, Nate would be waiting for us and would give us one of those big bear hugs that we all love.

It was a beautiful ceremony, splashed with amusing idioms—*Nate-isms*—and anecdotes from friends and family. Jon gave a heartfelt brotherly tribute to Nate, saying, "He was born with the light of joy in his soul...and the touch of a mischievous prankster." Leave it to Nate to get people smiling and laughing at a time like this. Paul spoke, with Chris and Matt standing beside him, paying homage to the eldest of their best friends four-pack. In virtually synchronized births, the boys were born one after the other, close in time, resulting in them being a *second generation* of best friends. It seemed foreign to see only three standing there now.

The District Attorney, Birgit Fladager, walked up to the microphone followed by an assembly of co-workers from the office. They all stood behind her as she spoke about Nate, calling him a gem. With sincerity in her words, she said Nate was happy. Relentlessly hardworking. He was funny. Ethical. Fun to be around. She called Nate the nicest man she had ever met. And at the end of her touching tribute, she read a list of some of the many nicknames Nate had for his co-workers. Briefly pausing between sobriquets, she gave each person mentioned a chance to gesture or wave, acknowledging their nickname with a bittersweet smile. When she was done reciting a list of nicknames, she closed with, "This is the *Blue Falcon* saying, 'It's time to go home, Nate.' We will always love you."

The lights dimmed, and the first notes of "Heaven" began to play. I could feel the tears pooling up in my eyes to this song of a million memories. Bryan Adam's voice filled the sanctuary, while pictures of Nate's 42 years of life began playing out on the screens. Images of Nate as a child, his teenage years, our wedding, Nate holding our newborn children, and cherished pictures of vacations with family and friends were set in motion to the corresponding lyrics. This loving video would be treasured forever, and I was so grateful to Lisa for her professional efforts in putting this timeless video together.

The touching ceremony in remembrance of Nate continued as the Color Guard waved their flags. Our neighbor Whitney—who was just starting 1st grade when we moved in and was now in college—and Lisa's daughter Holly, sang "Temporary Home" by Carrie Underwood. Their beautiful voices reminded all that our time here on earth is just that, temporary. After a moving message by Pastor Terry, Nate's Celebration of Life ended with Whitney and Holly singing "Amazing Grace."

Our family was escorted across the street, while the attendees began exiting the service. We walked into the banquet room with many caterers and volunteers getting ready to serve hundreds of people. The law team took it upon themselves to completely provide the food, set up, and service. The room was filled with tables, many large floral arrangements, and a big screen for a video Marlisa and Carol—co-workers of Nate—had made to play at the reception while people were eating. On each table were numerous photo cards of Nate arranged around the floral centerpieces with pens for people to write notes or memories on.

Within mere minutes, people were starting to walk through the doors of the reception. Before I knew it, there was a literal line out the door of people waiting to hug me, shake my hand, or introduce themselves. With warmest regards, countless people told me stories of how Nate influenced their lives. It was a whirlwind of emotions as I talked with people I hadn't seen in years, to people I saw often, and even people I have never met. Even in Nate's absence, people gravitated toward him. His legendary positive force will keep his memory alive forever.

Hours later, while tables were being cleared and floral arrangements were being loaded up to take to retirement homes, I took one last look around the room. The reception was more than I could have ever asked for. The behind-the-scenes work that people put in to making that day so memorable was a debt I could never repay. My thankful heart was overflowing with gratitude for the people in our lives. I felt blessed beyond words.

My eyebrows furrowed. This was *so* weird. I could hear the low humming sound of the refrigerator in the kitchen. Nate was notorious for *Disturbing the Peace*—the house was so quiet without him. It was such a stark contrast to how full of life our home used to be. I grabbed a pillow off the couch and lay down on the carpet next to my pen and paper. I began writing a prayer to God, my first sentence noting the fact that I had never noticed the white noise of the appliances so audibly before.

As my thoughts made their way onto the paper, I concisely wrote down ten things I needed God to help me with. The only way I could possibly survive this nightmare was with His sovereign help! When

I finished my prayer, I folded the paper and walked to the bedroom and put it in the drawer of the nightstand. As I walked back to the living room, I began to think about how Nate and Ryan weren't able to finish their aspiration of reading their Bibles—from Genesis to Revelation—together. I wondered how far they had gotten and began looking around the house for Nate's Bible. I found it on the desk in the study and sat down on the chair as I opened its ragged burgundy cover. Carrie had given him this Bible as a present when he graduated from law school back in 1995. Fifteen years of Nate learning God's Word had worn the leather right off of the binding!

As I flipped through the thin pages of the Bible, I noticed Nate had various verses underlined on most every page. All of this blue ink would lead me right to the place where they had stopped reading—for their unknowingly final time. The pages crinkled as I continued my search. Approximately half way through Nate's Bible, I noticed that the blue underlining stopped. *Hmm, they made it to Psalms,* I thought. A blue star next to Psalm 139:16 caught my attention. I had flipped through a lot of pages and had not seen a star next to any scripture until now. "Your eyes saw my unformed body. All the days ordained for me were written in your book before one of them came to be." I stared at the verse without moving. How was this possible?! Did Nate leave this for us to discover? Could it be possible that he knew he was going to die?! Nooo, I thought, shaking my head. There's no way he knew. Or did he? Maybe it was God relaying this message to me. But why then would Nate have a star next to it?

One day closer to Heaven! I thought to myself as I reached in my purse. I pulled out my pocket calendar and, with a lifeless stare, I looked at all the big red X's—starting with Thursday, August 5th.

I took off the lid of my felt pen and crossed off today's date with another big red X. I found pure pleasure in crossing off days of my life—it had become my favorite thing to do. I *earned* that big red X. It was my reward for surviving another day, but more importantly, crossing off another day brought me one day closer to Heaven. My heart already lived there, I just had to wait for my body to catch up.

"It's like my mind has become a DVD replaying these same visions over and over in my head," I tried explaining to Pastor Cliff. He was such a Godsend and always allocated time in his busy schedule for us. Sometimes he would just stop by to check on us, but the majority of the times he was at our house, it was from me calling for CPR—Pastor Cliff Resuscitation—on my broken heart. I felt like I was going to die, or at the very least, I was going crazy. "I see Nate in the hospital bed," I cried. "I see Ryan handing me the phone in bed. I see my kids hurting. How do I get myself out of this black hole of unrelenting perpetual visions?!"

"Shelley," Pastor Cliff said—he always started with my name when I asked him questions. "God tells us in His Word what to do with these kinds of thoughts." Both relieved and intrigued, I looked at him as he opened his Bible to Philippines 4:8-9 (NASB) and read a verse that I had never heard. *"Finally, brethren, whatever is true, whatever is honorable, whatever is right, whatever is pure, whatever is lovely, whatever is of good repute, if there is any excellence and if anything worthy of praise, dwell on these things. The things you have learned and received and heard and seen in me, practice these things, and the God of peace will be with you."* He closed his Bible.

"Intentionally think about these kinds of things. God is with you, and He will give you peace," Pastor Cliff said assuredly. Neither one of us spoke for a moment, and then he said, "Losing a loved one is hell." I nodded, wiping my eyes with a tissue. "But as a believer, this deep grieving is the closest you will ever get to hell. For a non-believer, earth, and its many blessings, is the closest one will ever get to Heaven."

I meditated that night on both God's Word that Pastor Cliff had read, and also the thought he had shared about grief being hell. That thought becoming a catalyst for me taking it a step further and thinking about people who were actually in hell at the present time. Even though I was practically crippled from the pain of grief, I had loved ones around me, I had water, food, and a soft place to lay my head. I took in a deep breath. Albeit harrowing, I was thankful that I was here, and not there. My home is with God in Heaven, giving me an eternal perspective of hope. I *will be* reunited with Nate someday, I reminded myself. This grief has an expiration date!

Long were the nights of grieving. I was unequivocally emotionally exhausted. My eyes were stinging, and they felt puffy. As the morning began to dawn, I *finally* fell asleep.

A couple of hours later, my eyes opened to a fully dubious sensation—life was an enigma. Did I just have the worst nightmare of my life? Or, did I just wake up from a 24-year romantic dream where I was a princess? Was Nate real?

Chapter 11

"Rainbow" by Kacey Musgraves

"I FEEL SO USELESS," I told Carrie, as I looked down at my feet and noticed my pace was slower than normal. A lot slower. My usual power walking speed had dwindled down to just putting one foot in front of the other. The gravel crunched underneath our tennis shoes as we made our way to the Dry Creek Trail, just a short walk from home. The familiar scent of the tall eucalyptus trees filled the morning air, and I could hear the sound of trickling water in the stream at the bottom of the hill.

"Yeah," Carrie agreed, as we followed the pathway to the paved trails. "You *are* kind of useless right now." Carrie quickly corrected herself, as we both chuckled a bit. "What I *mean* is that it's okay. All you need to do is focus on yourself and the kids right now."

"Well, I feel like all I'm doing is crying. Even when I'm not crying on the outside ... it never stops on the inside." Just saying those words made me start tearing up again. I grabbed for a tissue in my pocket.

"Shelley, I can't even imagine what you are going through. You have been so strong. You absolutely amaze me. Look at all the decisions you've had to make day after day. Nate's Celebration of Life was such a beautiful ceremony. You and the kids are so loved. We are all here for you guys. Let us do everything," Carrie said, as she stopped for a moment and looked at me. If all you do today is just breathe and make it through another day, then that's enough."

I took in her words, and stared ahead as we continued our walk. Carrie was here for the weekend, and I was so glad she was back. She had missed a lot of work over the past few weeks to be here for us. My best friend was doing everything from answering calls, organizing food, keeping an ongoing list of the multitude of cards, food, flowers, and gifts coming in, praying over us, and repeatedly giving me a shoulder to cry on. She helped me to think clearly and helped remind me of things I needed to do. I felt like I needed a babysitter. Although I was usually quite independent and active, I just didn't want to be alone right now. I felt strength and comfort from having loved ones close by. Each day, it took all of my strength to just survive another day. Grieving the loss of Nate was an all-consuming misery and completely exhausting. In addition to that, all of those days and weeks without sleeping was taking a toll on my mind. It was taking a toll on my body, too. Maybe this walk would help to loosen up these stiff muscles of mine.

Our walk down on the trails was more like a stroll, but it gave Carrie and me time to talk—just the two of us with no distractions. We talked about a lot of things, but as usual, we talked about God a lot. And right now I needed God's Word more than ever! His Word was like a lifeguard, saving me from going under.

"How in the world do people survive this kind of pain without God?" I asked, shaking my head.

Pausing, Carrie answered, "I don't know. I guess that's why a lot of people turn to drugs, alcohol, work...whatever helps them deal with the pain."

"Well, there's not a drug in the world strong enough to take this kind of pain away!"

Carrie and I made it back home and we sat down on the couch. It was only morning, but the heaviness of my eyes made me feel like it was night already. Ryan started stirring on the air mattress at the sound of our voices. Ever since Nate had passed, he didn't want to sleep in his room. We set up an air mattress on the living room floor where Ryan could get some rest, and not be alone in his room. Ryan had always been a people person, preferring the company of family and friends over time to himself.

"Morning, Mom. Hey, Carrie," Brittney said softly as she walked into the living room to join us. She sat down on the air mattress next to Ryan who was just starting to wake up.

"Good morning Bubs," I said, and then realized that was a stupid thing to say. It wasn't a good morning at all. No need to correct myself though; we were all well aware that life was *not* good right now.

"Do you want some coffee, Brittney?" Carrie asked. "I made a pot when I got up this morning. Tell me what you like in your coffee, and I'll get it for you," Carrie said as she started to get up.

"Aw, coffee sounds great, thanks. I can get it though," Brittney answered. She got up and walked toward the kitchen.

"Bubs," Ryan called out in a deep, sleepy voice from the air mattress. Brittney stood at the counter fixing her coffee just the way she liked it. "Bubba," Ryan tried again to get her attention.

"What?" Brittney answered.

"Can you get me a cup too?" Ryan asked. I looked over at Ryan. His eyes told the story of what we had all been through these past few weeks.

"Hey, Mom," Brittney said, as she walked back into the living room with a mug of coffee in each hand. "I have to go to the mall today. I need to get a few pairs of black pants," she said, as she handed Ryan his coffee—just like his dad, he liked his coffee black too. Do you guys want to go with me?"

I paused for a moment. "Work pants?" I asked her.

"Yeah, I start back up again next week," Brittney answered, sipping her morning coffee. She was a hostess at Red Lobster and had taken off a couple of weeks from work. Her boss had been very understanding, telling her to take all the time she needed. But now it had been a few weeks, and she just wanted to do *something* that felt normal again.

"Sure, Honey. We can do that." Although I really didn't want to go to the mall, I didn't want Bubs to go by herself. "Let's all get ready, and then maybe we can grab a bite to eat while we're out," I answered.

Before we left the house, I looked through a stack of gift cards to find one for a restaurant right by the mall. All of the gift cards sitting on the desk looked like a pile of love to me. So many people had enclosed a gift card inside their sympathy cards to us. We appreciated every single one of them—it was so helpful to not have to think about grocery shopping and cooking at a time like this.

Lunch was good, but an effort. Everything, including eating, took all my strength to just get through. There were triggers all over town. When the hostess led us to our table, I felt a stabbing pain in my heart. We walked by a table where the four of us had eaten lunch just last month. Now people sat around that table chatting and seemed to be enjoying their lunch break. All I could do was look away. I didn't look back at that table the entire time we were eating.

We finished lunch and walked across the parking lot to the mall. The kids went off to find Brittney's work pants while Carrie and I made our way to Macy's. Brittney said she would call me when she got what she needed. Although shopping was usually one of my favorite things to do, I really didn't care to shop right now. I couldn't wait for Bubs to call so we could all go home.

My conflicted heart felt like it was battling an impossible combination of wanting to be around people and wanting to be by myself—all at the same time, which made no sense. During the day, I longed for nightfall, and for the day to just be done. Then when it was night, I ached for the darkness to go away and for the sun to rise. I felt like I constantly had a million thoughts going through my mind—so many thoughts that I couldn't quite catch a single one. Yet at the same time, there was an aching emptiness inside, like there was nothing there. My soul was crushed to the point of feeling dead. How then could a dead spirit be overloaded by countless emotions? Confusion, anguish, loneliness, disappointment, fear, loss, distraction, and sorrow all raced through my mind and in my heart. The list went on and on like a tangled web of emotions. And the anxiety! It was the worst, like nothing I had ever experienced. All of those intense emotions made me feel like I was going crazy!

Being a little short of breath, I headed toward the back doors of Macy's. "I'm going to step outside for some fresh air," I told Carrie.

"Oh, okay," Carrie said as we walked right past the racks of clothes and customers shopping and exited the store. I just needed to be still for a moment so I could think straight.

"While we're out here, I'm going to call home to see how Danny and Ethan are doing," Carrie told me.

"Okay," I nodded. As she began talking, I took a few steps over to the side of the cement bridge we were standing on and leaned into it. Gazing down at all the cars in the parking lot below us, I took in a deep breath. Thoughts of the reality of losing Nate were taking over my mind. He would never eat at that restaurant with us again. Never. Never ever, ever again! I had been on the brink of tears ever since I saw the table at the restaurant, but now there was no holding them back. The flood gates opened and tears began running down my cheeks. I wiped my nose with a tissue. *God, I miss Nate so much*

I can't even breathe! I could feel the bridge pressing deeper into my stomach as I gripped the cement to hold me steady. I gasped as I tried to calm down all of the thoughts and emotions that were spinning in my head so fast they were making me dizzy. Again, I took in another quick breath as heartbreak and panic overtook my every thought. I gasped for air. There was nothing. It was like the hot summer air had no oxygen in it! My heart began pounding so much so that I could feel its beating in my neck. The more I cried, the harder it was to breathe. I felt like I was suffocating as I continued gasping.

"Shelley?" Carrie called from behind me. "Are you okay?" she asked, as I felt her hand on my shoulder. I let go of the bridge and turned toward her. Carrie stood before me, her face studying mine.

"I—I can't breathe," I cried out. My lungs felt as if they were collapsing under the weight of the world.

"Hey," Carrie gripped my arms and pulled me toward her. "Look at me. Do what I'm doing." She slowly breathed in through her nose and exhaled through her mouth. I tried to do what she was telling me, but I couldn't stop crying, and I still couldn't catch my breath. "Look at me, Shelley!" Through the tears, I looked at Carrie and desperately tried mimicking everything she was doing. Shadowy figures began to fill my peripheral vision, but I didn't look at them. I put my head down, embarrassed by all the attention.

"Do you need some help?" I vaguely heard a voice asking.

"No, no thank you," Carrie said to the crowd who had started gathering around us. "Please, just give us some space." Her eyes returned to me. "Do what I'm doing," Carrie repeated. I kept my focus on Carrie and followed her lead. "Good. Now do it again, Shelley. C'mon, breathe in slowly through your nose." I attentively watched her as we breathed in and out together, over and over and over again. Carrie stood right there in front of me, coaching me back to normal breathing. It felt so good to get some air! When

I finally began to breathe normally again, all I could do was hug Carrie until I got myself together.

"Thank you," I whispered to her as we let go of each other. Carrie had been so brave. She had completely taken charge and did everything right to get me breathing again. I felt at a complete loss of words for how thankful I was to have her here with me.

I reached into my purse and pulled my phone out to check if there were any messages from the kids. They should be done by now, but after what just happened, I had completely lost track of time. We began to make our way back to the inner court of the mall. Holding the phone up to my ear, I listened to a message from Ryan. In a troubled tone, he said that he couldn't find Bubs. I immediately called him back to find out what was going on.

"We were supposed to meet," Ryan tried explaining, "but she never showed up. I tried calling her a bunch of times. Why isn't she answering her phone?" he asked, frustrated.

In an effort to ease him, I calmly responded, "Maybe she ran into one of her friends, and is just running late. Or, maybe she lost her phone, and she's looking for it... Ya know, Carrie and I are right outside Macy's where we split up. Just come over and meet us here, and we'll figure it out."

While we waited for Ryan, I tried calling Bubs, but it went straight to voicemail. I tried again with the same result.

When we saw Ryan walking toward us, he looked as anxious as he had sounded on the phone. He tried calling Bub's phone again, but, just like with me, it went straight to voicemail.

"Let's just wait a little longer. I'm sure she's on her way," Carrie tried assuring us both.

Ryan didn't even make it a few minutes before he said, "I'm going to go look for her." He just couldn't wait; his mind was set on finding Bubs. "You guys wait here in case she shows up."

He left in the direction of where he had last seen her, and soon disappeared behind the escalators carrying people up and down between the floors. My heart sank. It's like I had stepped out of complete chaos, only to fall right back in. The immense grief and stress the kids and I were going through was making simple things like eating lunch and finding a pair of work pants next to impossible. My thoughts looped back to the conversation about feeling useless I had with Carrie this morning on our walk. Just surviving another day was tremendous work and would be all I could accomplish today—just like Carrie had said.

Although Carrie and I were concerned about Bubs, we weren't in panic mode, at least not yet. We stayed right there and waited to hear from the kids.

"Carrie, can you call Pastor Cliff for me? Tell him I need to talk to him when we get home."

I could hear Carrie explaining to Pastor Cliff the very short version of what was going on as I stepped forward, my eyes searching for the kids. *C'mon Bubs. Where are you?*

"Pastor Cliff said he'd come over, and to call him when we get home," Carrie said, walking over to me.

I sighed, "Thanks, Carrie." Just knowing Pastor Cliff was coming over helped to soothe this ongoing train wreck of a day.

Time passed and Ryan returned without Brittney. His flushed cheeks showed how much ground he had covered in his search. "She wasn't there. I couldn't find her anywhere," Ryan said, winded, shaking his head.

"I'm sorry, guys!" Brittney called out as she hurried over to us. We all sighed in relief at the sight of her. I closed my eyes for a few seconds, *Thank you, God!*

"Bubs!," Ryan said. "Where were you! I've been looking all over for you! We were supposed to meet. And why weren't you answering your phone?"

Bubs started explaining, something about her phone dying, and the line, and…I don't even know. All I knew was that we were all here, all safe, and I wanted to go home!

As planned, Pastor Cliff was knocking on the door soon after we got home. I asked Carrie to take the kids out for frozen yogurt at The Yogurt Mill, and to drive slowly. I didn't want the kids to hear what I was going to tell Pastor Cliff.

Like countless times before, he sat on the couch with me. He always wore a suit and tie, and held his very worn black Bible. I looked over at him and paused, my face blank. That momentary pause quickly turned into grief-stricken emotion blurting out of my soul. "I want to die!" I began sobbing. "I feel like I'm going crazy….I can't do this!" I shook my head. "I really can't. And even if I could, I don't want to. *I just want to die!"* I said, very slowly. "I actually think I'm already dead anyway." Again, I was crying so hard it was hard to breathe. It seemed impossible for me to cry *and* breathe at the same time today. I blew my nose and tried slowing my breathing down like I had done with Carrie at Macy's just a few hours ago.

"Shelley," Pastor Cliff said, looking right at me. I grabbed another tissue and looked down at the carpet trying my best to keep it together. "What about your kids? They need you," he said.

Pastor Cliff was right, but there was an inward war going on inside my heart. "I want to be with the kids *AND Nate*. *All* at the same time!" I added, trying to explain this relentless battle of emotions.

"I know you do, Shelley," the Pastor said with empathy. "But, you can't. Nate's time here on earth is done." His words were the truth.

"But why? Why can't our family be together?" I cried, begging for an answer. "I just want life to go back to normal. I want the four of us to be together," I cried out in frustration. It seemed impossible for my brain to comprehend that Nate was gone.

I was thankful the kids were with Carrie, and they weren't here to see me like this. The Yogurt Mill—even though the lines were long, and Carrie was intentionally driving slowly—wasn't that far away. They were due to be returning any minute now, so I had to somewhat pull myself together.

Pastor Cliff and I sat there talking for a while, and once again, I thanked him for coming right over. "I sure have been keeping you busy, haven't I?" I asked redundantly, with an ever so slight chuckle. I didn't need an answer. Since Nate had passed away, I was well aware that Pastor Cliff had had his hands full with me. My thankful heart didn't know what I would do without him.

Before leaving, Pastor Cliff once again prayed from Philippians 4:7—a verse I had gotten to know very well these past few weeks. He prayed for *God to give me a peace which surpasses all understanding, and to guard my heart and my mind in Christ Jesus.*

"Amen," I said. I hugged Pastor Cliff goodbye. The kids walked up to the house with Carrie. She thanked him for coming over and handed me a small white bag. Although my leaden heart still felt too heavy to continue living, it felt a smidgen lighter from a hard cry. I pulled out the styrofoam container and saw my favorite—chocolate and vanilla swirl, always topped with a double shot of roasted almonds. I smiled at Carrie and the kids, grabbed a spoon and took a bite.

I could hear the phone ringing inside the house as I got out of the car. *Oh no!* I thought. Fumbling to find the house key, I rushed over to unlock the door. But it was too late. Nate's voicemail greeting began playing on the phone's answering machine. My heart ached at the sound of Nate's voice. It was like he was right there. However, when I opened the door, the kitchen was empty. My brain knew that Nate was gone, but my heart always held on to the hope that all of this was just a terrible nightmare from which I would awake.

This same scenario had been playing out for days, actually weeks now, but I just couldn't bear the thought of removing Nate's recording. It gave me comfort in knowing his voice was still on the phone. Yet hearing him talk was not only very deceptive, it was deeply painful as well. Every time the phone rang, I would either run to pick up the receiver or urgently call out for someone to answer it—desperately trying to intercede Nate's recorded message before it started. Carrie knew the drill, and would rush to the phone to take a message before Nate's voice came on. But she wasn't here today. It was the end of August—24 days, to be exact, since Nate's passing. Some of the initial company and visitors had lightened up a bit, but we still had family and friends frequently stopping by.

No words were needed, as Mary, Jon, the kids, and I all silently walked into the house. Vibes of disconsolation from hearing Nate's voice filled the room. I set my things down on the hall-tree and slipped off my shoes.

"Jon, can you change the answering machine to one of those generic *Please leave a message after the beep* recordings?" I asked solemnly. Jon, who because of his profession and his recreational interests, could do *anything* tech related, said he'd take care of it.

I went to change out of my church clothes. When I returned to the kitchen, Jon was already working on the phone. "Is there any way to save Nate's message so I can keep it?" I asked Jon. He nodded, "Yeah, I'll see what I can do."

With a slight, but thankful smile, I washed my hands and began taking some food out of the fridge for lunch. Mary came over to help. The exceedingly generous amounts of food, snacks, and desserts that had poured into our home for weeks had been more than enough to feed not only us, but also the steady flow of people we had coming in and out of our house every day.

A co-worker friend of mine had recently taken it upon herself to organize meal deliveries with the three dental offices I currently worked for. Each of the three offices had begun taking a week of delivering daily meals to us. Sometimes it was homemade, other times it was take-out from favorite restaurants like El Rosal, The Olive Garden, or Mountain Mike's Pizza. The constant bountiful blessing of food was so very appreciated by our family. And the cases of bottled water people would bring over for those hot August days were very appreciated as well.

We gathered in the kitchen, each of us putting together a plate of food from all of the choices sitting on the counter in front of us. It was a nice break for it to be just the five of us, if only for a meal. We found comfort in each other. Bubs ate quickly; she needed to get off to work. Mary would be leaving soon as well. Although she hadn't returned to work yet, she needed to get some things done back in Salinas. I began loading up the dishwasher after Bubs and Gramma left. Dishes were minimal without having to cook, reducing the cleanup time to mere minutes.

Jon was finishing up with the phone when the doorbell rang. "I'll get it," I said. I opened the front door to a warm smile from my friend CJ. Her long blonde hair rested on a present she was holding in her hands. We were bonded by our working together as hygienists the past few years, and by our deep love for Jesus. It was great to see her. She had already helped so much. I gave CJ a hug and invited her in.

As we walked into the kitchen, I recalled the last time I had seen her. Brittney found me inconsolable one evening and had called CJ to please come over right away. Lost and confused, I was sitting on the closet floor sobbing when my puffy eyes caught a glimpse of her walking into the dimly lit bedroom. She sat down with me on the floor and held me tight as we both cried. "CJ...what am I supposed to do? Where do I start?" I asked, as I looked up at Nate's suits hanging above my head. With tear-filled eyes, she told me she could not fathom what I was going through and said she would always be there for me. She really helped me that night, and now my dear friend was back—again.

We walked over to the kitchen table and sat down. Jon looked over from the phone and said "hi" to CJ. He had been staying at our house a lot and had grown used to our revolving door of friends.

"We all miss you at work," CJ said. "Some patients have been asking about you, and they send you their love." With a soft smile, I told her that I missed them, too. "Here, I have something for you," CJ said, as she handed me the wrapped present. "You have no idea how much you have been on my mind...and in my heart...and in my prayers. So, I wrote you a letter," she said, taking it out of an envelope. "It's the only way I could express everything I have been feeling inside. If it's okay, I want to read it to you before you open the present."

"Okay," I nodded. She unfolded her letter, and paused briefly before speaking... "To my dear friend Shelley," she said with emotion, and then began to read her letter. I sat there listening to CJ's every word as she talked about love, and how Nate and I brought Romans 12:9-12 to life for her. She included God in every part of her letter, and went on to talk about Mark 6. As she continued reading, she related my current circumstances to the story of Jesus walking on water. His disciples were struggling because the wind was against them. Jesus walked on the water to His disciples, and when He got into the boat with them, the wind ceased.

"Shelley, this is a terrible, disastrous, stormy time for you. Jesus sees and knows you are struggling through this tragic time. But just like Jesus stepped in to help when His disciples were struggling, He will calm this time for you, too. I know that Jesus is reaching His arms out to you and your family and holding you tight." I smiled through the pain as she concluded her letter talking about Nate and me. "Your relationship will always be so special, so magical. After being married over twenty years, you two still acted like newlyweds. You and Nate had that unique relationship that few ever acquire." Her words of solace touched my heart, momentarily tempering the relentless sting of heartbreak. "I love you. Your friend, and sister-in-Christ, CJ." She folded her handwritten letter and put it back in the envelope.

I looked at her from across the table and mouthed a sincere "Thank you." With a heart filled with gratitude for her friendship and uplifting letter, I walked over and gave her a hug. We stopped hugging, and then the only thing left to do was hug again.

"Open your present!" she said with a smile. I walked over to the table and opened the box. I pulled out a framed golden cross with Numbers 6:24-26 written next to it. "The Lord bless you and keep you; The Lord make His face shine upon you, And be gracious to you; The Lord lift up His Countenance upon you, And give you Peace."

"Thanks, CJ," I said warmly. "My heart could sure use some peace."

"Oh, that reminds me. I have something else for you." She handed me a small stack of fluorescent colored index cards. I looked down at the bright green, pink, orange, and yellow cards to see a handwritten Bible verse on each of the colorful cards. "I thought you could place these around the house, so you and the kids are surrounded by God's Word," CJ said. After a big thankful hug, we said our goodbyes and she left.

"Uncle Jon," Ryan said, as he walked into the room. "Are you ready to take those pictures now?" Jon had brought his professional camera with him to help Ryan with his photography homework. The assignment was to take pictures showing motion. *Everyone* should have an uncle like Jon! Ryan had missed the first two weeks of his sophomore year. I had talked to his principal, teachers, and football coach, explaining what had happened, keeping them updated along the way. Ryan recently started back to school and had a lot of homework to catch up on. As Ryan gathered the photography equipment, he asked if I wanted to go with them.

"Yeah, sure," I answered. It would be nice to get out in the fresh air. I grabbed my sunglasses and a hat for the heat, and the three of us started heading out for the Dry Creek Trail.

Past the white metal gate, we walked down the steep hill and within minutes had reached the curvy trail lined with oak trees. This trail, frequented by runners, bikers, and people walking their dogs, was one of my favorite places in Modesto.

A plethora of photo opportunities awaited the guys. From squirrels (*Peskies,* as Nate would call them) climbing the trees for shade, to turtles sitting on logs in the creek, and leaves swaying in the delta breeze, the guys would have no problem capturing motion in a picture. Ryan and Uncle Jon began talking about the project and stepped off the pavement and into a field. They began meandering around nearby tree trunks and through the variety of vegetation that surrounded the path. From the trail, I watched the two of them with their photography equipment pointing out different things to each other.

Although it was typical to see others along the trail, it was quiet down here today. For as far as I could see in either direction, there was nobody in sight. My walking came to a standstill, and I began to think about Nate. I could hear Ryan and Jon talking nearby. Leaning my head way back, I looked straight up into the sky past the tops of the towering oak trees. My eyes looked up to Heaven. I thought about Nate being with God at this very moment. *Hi Jesus, Hi Nate,* I said in my head, as I gazed up thinking about them being together. From slightly behind me, color caught my attention. I immediately turned around to see a vivid rainbow shining above me in the clear blue sky. Never in my entire life had I seen a rainbow like this—they were usually an arch that touched the horizon on both sides. This rainbow was upside down, in the shape of a smile!

A surge of energy permeated through my soul as I stared up in the sky. I marveled at this phenomenal smile above me and thought about the fact that it wasn't raining—or even sprinkling for that matter. How *could* this be? I wondered. The right side of the radiant rainbow began to fade, and then I remembered where I was. I turned around to Ryan and Jon.

"Hey, guys! Look!" I pointed up to the sky so they could see the brilliant inverted arch of colors. They both stopped what they were doing and looked up to see what I was pointing to. "Hurry, Ryan! Try to get a picture of it!" I called out to him. I watched as he focused the camera up to the sky and took a picture. "Did you get it?" I asked, looking back and forth between Ryan and the rainbow up in the sky.

Ryan checked the camera and nodded. "I got it, Mom!" he assured me with a thumbs up. I walked toward him to see the picture on the screen. There it was! I was incredibly thankful Ryan was able to capture this unforgettable rainbow in a picture before it faded away. I stood there in reverent wonder and admiration for this kaleidoscopic smile from God and Nate.

I woke up the next morning thankful for the few hours of sleep I got. The last full night of sleep I had was with Nate. I wondered how I would ever sleep through the night again, but seeing the rainbow smiling from Heaven yesterday was a powerful reminder that God was right there with me. I reached for my phone. Carrie faithfully sent me a Bible verse every morning to help me get through one day at a time. I started reading her text...

Aug. 30, 2010

Shelley—I was praying and looking up verses about rainbows last night because of the amazing one He showed all of you yesterday. This verse I found is God talking about sending a rainbow as a promise (covenant) and this is the verse... Genesis 9:15 "I will remember my covenant between me and you and all living creatures of every kind. Never again will the waters become a flood to destroy all life." I thought what do floods have to do with Shelley and her family, and I felt like God was telling me your tears are like the flood, and He won't let your tears (sadness) destroy you and your family's life. There is hope. God sent you all a rainbow yesterday as a promise of life to you and your family.

Love you, Carrie

I smiled. Once again, Carrie's text—she *always* gave God all the credit—gave my completely drained soul the energy to get up and face another day. And I was thankful for the energy due to the mountain of decisions I needed to make, people I needed to meet with, paperwork I needed to fill out, and forms I needed to sign. The *To Do List* was long and intense, but Jon was here for another week to help me handle one thing at a time. Every one of the tasks would be difficult, but cleaning out Nate's office at the District Attorney's Office was going to be the most crushing of all.

Jon and I pulled into the brick DA's Office parking garage across the street from the Court House. The attendant was expecting us and waved us in. Kristy, the Administration Assistant and a dear friend, would always call down to the parking garage for them to let us in. We got out of Jon's silver metallic truck and saw Kristy waiting at the door. She greeted us with a hug, and we followed her inside to the elevators. As we waited for the elevator doors to open, Kristy looked at me with empathetic eyes. She knew what we were here to do. We stepped into the elevator and Kristy pressed 5. The button for the fifth floor illuminated, and the elevator began to lift. "There are a lot of people who want to see you while you are here," Kristy said. "Aw, I want to see them all too," I replied, with a tender smile.

As we walked through the office, many people stopped us along the way to talk and get an update on how we were doing. Everyone here had such a special place in my heart. Kristy walked with us to Nate's office. "I'm going to give you guys some time," she said. "There are some people that wanted me to let them know when you got here. I'll be back."

"Okay," I said. My throat tightened at the sight of Nate's empty desk chair. My eyes then traveled to a big stuffed teddy bear sitting on the desk. It was wearing a white polo shirt embossed with the DA's Office logo. I walked over to the bear and picked it up. Nate had a shirt just like this at home. Feeling comforted by holding this brown bear wearing office attire, I looked up to the ceiling above Nate's empty chair. With a soft smile, I stood there gazing at the handful of yellow wooden pencils stuck in the white panels of the ceiling.

"Nate sure had a knack for that." I looked over to see Rob, in his suit and tie, coming into the office.

"Hey, Rob," I said with a smile, and went over to give him a hug. Nate called Rob *"Zip Code Boy"* because he had been born and raised in Motown—another name for Modesto. The usual banter between Nate and Rob was very entertaining for all. Kristy returned to the office to join us.

"Yeah, I was sitting right here talking with Nate when he did a lot of these," Rob said, looking up at all the pencils hanging above us. "I don't know how he did it. He would do a quick flick of his wrist and they would somehow stick," Rob said, as he flicked his wrist upward demonstrating Nate's technique. "And he always did it while he was sitting down," Rob added.

That sounds just like Nate," I said, with a soft chuckle.

"Did he use glue?" Jon asked.

Rob shook his head, "No glue. All those pencils are held there by the sheer force of Nate's flick."

I looked over to see Nate's law school diplomas hanging on the wall. My mind flashed back to our Christmas in Seattle when I gave those to him. He had been so upset with himself for not passing the bar exam the first time, and now 15 years later, there were convicted criminals behind bars all over California because of Nate's thirst for justice.

Jon picked up the address card file with alphabetical dividers that was sitting on Nate's desk. He flipped through the addresses, each card showing his brother's very legible all caps letters in blue ink. "Oh, Nate," Jon said with a shake of his head. "I can't believe he *still* had one of these things. He could've had all of these numbers on his cell phone. They don't need to be handwritten anymore."

I chuckled momentarily and walked over to the window. I picked up a family picture we had taken in Boston and looked at it. That was such a fun trip. And then I saw an orangutan Beanie Baby sitting on the windowsill. I knew exactly why that was there. I smiled at the inside joke Nate and I had about an orangutan from his 21st birthday in Vegas many years ago. I picked it up and held it, too.

With a palpable sense of loss, Jon and I began boxing up Nate's belongings to take home. One by one, people began gathering in the office. With everyone standing in a big circle in Nate's office, I told them about the rainbow I had seen yesterday—how God and Nate had smiled at me from Heaven. This heartwarming story seemed to ease the mutual sadness in the room. None of us wanted Nate's belongings to be removed from the office.

As the days went by, I could not stop crying. Deep in the throes of anguish, I called Carrie once again. Although I didn't hide my grieving from the kids, sometimes—like tonight—I would cry in my room with the door shut. I sat on the closet floor, weeping as I dialed Carrie's number. As soon as she answered the phone, I blurted out, "I can't do this, Carrie! It hurts *so* bad I think I'm gonna die," I sobbed. Every word I said, I meant. Literally.

"I know it doesn't seem like it now, but you can get through this," Carrie assured me. With an incredulous sigh, I just sat there on the floor in the dark, listening. "God is going to help you every step of the way." I could hear Carrie's voice cracking as she talked.

There was a brief moment of silence on the line. The magnitude of this pain was so intense, it was not even possible for me to explain to Carrie how badly it hurt. "The pain I feel in my heart is not even describable with words," I cried. "There's *nothing* to even compare it to," I tried explaining. "Nothing."

After a long talk, and even longer cry, I began to calm down a little bit. Or, maybe I had just plain exhausted myself instead. Carrie ended our emotional conversation with a prayer as she usually did. I was very thankful for her prayer; I was having a terribly rough night. Before we said goodbye, she told me to choose a Bible verse and say it over and over in my head to help me get through the night.

After I set the phone back down, I opened the bedroom doors and walked over to the kitchen table. Until that night, I hadn't yet read the verses that CJ had given me—grieving was a full-time job.

Following Carrie's advice, I randomly grabbed an index card from CJ's pile. To my surprise, this one was not a Bible verse, it was a prayer. I began reading the card, *Lord, help my friend to glimpse the rainbow through the tears, to see your light shining in the darkest night. Amen.*

This prayer almost brought me to my knees. *Oh my God!*, I thought, as I sat down and looked at the neon green flashcard. CJ had given me this prayer right before we started out for our walk on the trail that Sunday afternoon. That very day, I had seen a rainbow! Her prayer to God for me had been answered. I *had* glimpsed a rainbow through my tears, and it was God's light that was going to help me through this very dark night. I read CJ's card over and over again throughout the night, just like Carrie had told me to do, until I fell asleep.

I pulled a lightweight jacket over my head and zipped it up. The days were still hot, but sitting on the bleachers tonight at Johansen's Football Stadium might be a little chilly. I picked up the lapel pin Shawn Bessey had designed and attached it to my jacket. Hundreds of these cherished pins were worn in memory of Nate, showing all the things that were important to him in his lifetime. Brittney and I got in my jeep and drove the couple of minutes over to the high school.

It didn't take long after walking into the stadium to see a bunch of friends who came to support Ryan. I almost cried at the sight of everybody there. All those people — neighbors, co-workers, friends, were amazing and I was so thankful for them in our lives. A few of the guys from the DA's Office had even taken Ryan out shopping for his football gear and were here to cheer him on. I was so thankful for their helping hands. They definitely knew more about football gear than I did.

Nate would have loved to be here tonight watching Ryan play football, I thought, as I sat down after saying hi to everyone. Even though we were surrounded by love and support all over the bleachers, there was an enormous void next to me. A void so deep that, even if the entire town of Modesto sat right by my side, it would still not be filled. Here we were trying our best to do normal things again, but half of me was gone and nothing was fun anymore. Losing Nate was like a life sentence of heartache. Was this our new normal?

I woke up and rubbed my eyes. The morning light was shining around the edges of the closed curtains. The best part of my day was now—the transient first few seconds when I was not awake enough for reality to pummel me. The succeeding few seconds were the worst part of my day—the part when I became more fully awake and remembered Nate was gone.

The mere seconds of the best part of my day were gone in a flash this morning. Real life hit me when I saw the black teddy bear from the DA's office, instead of Nate, lying next to me in bed. With teary eyes, and a heavy heart, I reached over and pulled it in close to me. Even though it was only a stuffed animal, it felt good to hold something.

I want a dog, I thought as I sat up. With my arms still wrapped around the bear, I sat there thinking. *A boy dog, and his name'll be Dewey. Nate would like that—never in my life have I been a bigger Dew than I am right now.*

I got up to grab my robe and walked into Bub's room. "Morning, Mom," Brittney said, glancing my way from her dresser mirror.

I walked over and sat on the floor against the wall.

"Are you okay," she asked as I sat there a moment.

"I want a dog, Bubs."

Brittney stopped straightening her hair and turned toward me. "A dog?" she asked. "But you're allergic to dogs..."

"Well, I'm not allergic to Chloe. There's gotta be a dog out there that I'm not allergic to, and I need your help to find it. "I want a puppy. A boy puppy, and I want to name him Dewey," I said, looking right at her as I spoke.

"Wow, Mom! I never thought I'd hear you say that," she said with a look of surprise as she put her brush down on the dresser. "Aw, I love the name Dewey," she said, in a sentimental tone with a slight chuckle. Without explanation, she understood the name. We were a house full of *Dews,* so he would fit right in.

Bubs knew a lot about animals—especially dogs—and had even thought about becoming a vet back when she was in high school. She began informing me about dogs and telling me some important facts. "Puppies are great, Mom. But just so you know, they're like toddlers and get into *everything*. They go under beds, into closets, and they put everything in their mouths. They chew things up. Dogs really do eat homework."

I smiled, and was thankful for her helpful input, but my mind was set. "All that's fine. I want a dog, Bubs. I'll take such good care of him and give him so much love and attention. It'll be good for me. And right now I have time to bond with him and train him. I've decided not to go back to work until the beginning of the new year," I informed her. She looked at me agreeing I was nowhere near going back to my normal schedule yet. It had been almost two months since Nate had passed now, and I still cried frequently every single day.

"So we're really getting one?" she asked.

"Yes. Yes, we are," I nodded. "I'm going to need your help finding him. Let's go wake Ryan up and tell him," I said, as I got up from the floor. We both walked into the living room. The weight from both of us sitting on the air mattress Ryan was sleeping on caused him to roll a bit toward us, waking him up.

We told Ryan the news. It was so uplifting to see a bit of excitement on the kids' faces. Dewey was already bringing joy into our home, and we hadn't even begun the search. The three of us went right to the study and sat down at the computer.

"I'll show you some hypoallergenic dogs, Mom," Brittney said, scrolling through pictures and videos of puppies. There were a lot of different types to choose from, but the second I saw a picture of a little white dog with his front paws up on the steering wheel of a car, I knew that was *the one*. "I want one like that!" I said, with my eyes fixed on the screen.

Within a couple of weeks, we had found a breeder in Sunnyvale that had a fresh litter of Maltipoos. They would be ready to adopt the first week of October, giving us a bit of time to prepare for our new family member.

The day had arrived for us to drive over to Sunnyvale. Carrie had called earlier in the week. She had Fridays off and said she wanted to join us. Jon was on his way to Modesto as well and would arrive sometime in the evening. They both continued to make frequent trips to spend time with the kids and me. Today would be just a day trip for Carrie, but Jon would be staying for the weekend, and would get here about the same time we returned home with Dewey.

We all loaded up in Nate's truck for the trip. Being in his big white Chevy Avalanche made me feel comforted. I still needed to figure out what I was going to do with his truck, but it was nice to take a break from all these poignant decisions. *Today* we were picking up Dewey.

As we made our way over the golden hills of the Altamont Pass, I looked over at the gigantic white wind turbines that dotted the landscape. Their mighty blades spinning around at such high velocity gave the appearance of effortless gliding. But the tranquility of these massive blades in motion would soon end. The Bay Area's stop and go traffic awaited us just past these rolling hills.

With the kids' help directing me from the printed MapQuest directions as I drove, we found the breeder's house without a problem. She met us at the door, and we followed her into the living room. Right in front of us were two litters of puppies in a large pen. They were all so adorable. Some were nuzzled up together napping, while others were romping around their wired enclosure.

The breeder, with her wavy blonde hair tied back in a ponytail, walked over to the pen and began telling us about the puppies. By the way she talked, I could tell she had been doing this for many years. She picked up a little black and tan Yorkie, saying "This one is a friend to everyone. Energetic too," the breeder added, as she set the puppy down with the others. "But you're looking for a male dog, right?" she asked.

"Yeah," I nodded. "I want a boy Maltipoo."

Carrie and the kids stood beside me as she picked up a little white puppy that looked just like the picture. "This one is very chill, and just likes to be held. If it were up to him, he would sit on my lap all day, and I wouldn't get a thing done." She held the puppy up for a couple of minutes for us to look at him, and then walked around the pen to show us another Maltipoo. "And *this* one's his brother," she said, as she exchanged puppies in her arms. The two pups looked alike, but different at the same time. The first one's hair was more wavy. This puppy more closely resembled a Maltese than a poodle. "He is very affectionate and cuddly too," she said as she looked at him resting in her arms. "But don't let this sweet face fool you," she jokingly warned, placing her fingers on the sides of his cheeks. "This little guy's got a spunky side to him." We all thought that was funny, and I smiled at her candid description. I found it so interesting how in just a few months of life, the pups seemed to already have their own individual personalities.

After observing the puppies interacting with each other, and asking some questions, we told the breeder we were going to go get some lunch and talk it over. We'd be back in an hour or so to buy one of the puppies. We left her house and drove over to a nearby restaurant.

"Which one do you like Mom," Ryan asked.

"I want to get the spunky one. His personality reminds me of how Dad was—a good man, *and* a bad boy." I chuckled at the bad boy part. Then I began tearing up because I had to use the word *was* when I talked about Nate. "The spunky one is Dewey," I said, wiping my eyes with a bittersweet smile.

After lunch, we drove back to the breeder's home and I showed her which one I wanted. She leaned over and picked him up out of the pen and handed him over to me. I looked down at sweet little Dewey. How soft and warm he was as I held him in my arms for the very first time.

After an hour or so of signing papers and receiving both verbal and written instructions on how to care for a puppy, we left Sunnyvale with a care package and the breeder's last words of advice, "Don't spoil him."

Carrie offered to drive us back home, so I could hold Dewey on my lap. I already never wanted to put him down. I wrapped him up in a blanket as she started the truck, and I couldn't take my eyes off of this little white puppy with black lips and a pink freckled belly. He was so good and stayed right there cuddled on my lap all the way home.

We turned onto our cul-de-sac and saw Jon's truck parked in front of the house. "Uncle Jon's here," Ryan said cheerfully. Jon and Ryan had been texting each other back and forth as we drove home so we knew he was getting close.

"We're home," I said to Dewey, as we pulled into the driveway. The kids got out of the truck to go see Uncle Jon who was walking up the driveway. "Hey, Jon," I said, carefully holding on to Dewey as I gave Jon a big hug with one arm. I pulled the blanket to the side so Jon could take a peek at our puppy.

"Hey, little guy," he said with a tender smile, and began petting the top of his head. I watched Dewey's little black nose wiggling as he sniffed Jon's fingers. The entire rest of the evening was spent in the living room playing with Dewey. We all sat in a circle on the carpet so he could walk around and get familiar with his new surroundings. He was so cute and seemed to bounce more than walk as he explored everything in the room. Ryan had his new flip phone out taking pictures of Dewey and capturing those sweet moments of his first night in his new home.

"Oh...it's getting late," Carrie said, noticing the time on the big clock in the dining room. "I'm going to need to get going." She began getting up from our circle on the carpet. We all stood up and let Dewey roam around as I helped Carrie collect her things. Before leaving for her drive back home to Folsom, Carrie said a prayer. She thanked God for this day, and for bringing Dewey into our lives. Even though the pain was still intense for us all, our playful little puppy brought a much-needed uplifting vibe into our home.

"Is he going to sleep with you tonight?" Jon asked after Carrie left, as we began settling down for the night.

"No," I answered, lightly shaking my head. I felt very protective of our marriage bed, and although I adored this little guy, he was not potty trained. I was not emotionally ready for the high possibility of an accident. "I got a doggy bed for him," I told Jon. "But the breeder actually said to put him in a crate at night. So we stopped to get one on the way home. It's still in the back of the truck. There's so much to learn about having a dog." I picked up Dewey and cuddled him in his blanket. "It's gonna be hard to put him in the crate tonight. I've been holding him all day. But the breeder said it's good for him to sleep in a crate. She said the small space is comforting, and it will help him get into a routine. She also said it will show him who's boss," I chuckled with empathy as I looked down at an innocent Dewey in my arms.

Before I put Dewey down for the night, I turned off the lights and rocked him back and forth in my arms for a long time. It seemed to be as comforting for him as it was for me. He was like medicine for my aching soul. I kissed the top of his little head and put him inside the crate with a blanket and a chew toy. After checking the latch, I left him in the washroom and walked to my room to get ready for bed.

I hadn't even reached my bedroom when the whimpering began. I stopped right there in the hallway and listened to Dewey. His whining soon escalated into clamorous yelps and howling—making it very clear that he was not happy about being sequestered in the laundry room by himself for the night. The kids and Jon walked over and gathered in the hallway with me as we listened to Dewey.

Ryan put his hands over his ears. "Is he going to do this all night?" he asked.

My overactive immune system had prevented me from ever having a dog, so I had zero experience with raising a puppy. This was like having a baby in the house again! "I sure hope not," I answered with a wince.

I walked over to the laundry room and picked up a disturbed little Dewey out of the crate to comfort him. He immediately calmed down once I held him close to me. I began rocking him back and forth, back and forth, over and over again until his eyes closed. I could feel my eyes growing heavy. The rocking was putting *me* to sleep. I just hoped it was enough for Dewey to stay asleep. I knelt down and carefully placed him back in the crate. He stood up and began wailing again before I had even left the room.

The next day, after no sleep for any of us, we drove to the store to buy ear plugs—one set for each of us. Jon and the kids were joking that Dewey sounded like a Velociraptor. He was as cute as could be all day. But when nightfall arrived, and he was put in his crate, he whined and cried all night. Again! The ear plugs were useless, and by the third night Dewey was in bed with me.

Dewey was like an angel sent down to me from Heaven. He was my sidekick and we were together every day. I had the time off to bond with him, and as each day passed, I learned more and more about this little guy's personality. He hadn't responded to his name yet when I called him, but he was still a puppy and there was so much for him to learn.

My full speed ahead life had literally done a 180. These days my life was one step at a time on a good day. Other days I was stuck in the miry clay of grief and couldn't move at all. The highlight of my life though was my kids and my puppy. I loved it best when we were all together at home. The independent soul that I was born with had also done a 180. It was like I needed a babysitter—I didn't like being alone in the house. The kids had figured that out without me saying a word. Brittney had even called in sick last week just to stay home with me, and Ryan would text me Bible verses when he was away. My kids were the best and I adored them.

Ryan was over at Johansen for Mock Trail practice one night, but Brittney was home watching *Cloverfield* in the entertainment room with the lights out. The kids were just like their Dad and somehow enjoyed these frightening sci-fi movies. I wasn't watching it with her, but the surround sound was making the walls shake with noises of some kind of cryptic monster wreaking havoc on people who seemed to be screaming and running for their lives.

I watched Dewey walk past his pen and into the entertainment room as I cleaned up the kitchen. We had set up a pen for him with everything a puppy could possibly need. He had a fluffy bed with a blanket, food and water dishes, toys, and, of course, puppy pads—housebreaking was still a work in progress!

Eventually when all of the ruckus came to an end, Bubs came out of the entertainment room with her empty popcorn bowl. "How was the movie?" I asked.

"Oh, it was great. I love that movie. You wouldn't like it though," she added.

"Yeah, I can tell by the sound effects that it's not my kind of movie," I agreed with a wince.

"Ya know, Mom, Dewey was right there in the room with me while I was watching the movie. That movie's loud!" she said. "And he didn't react to any of it. Not even when he walked right past the speaker."

I tilted my head, wondering what she was getting at. "Dewey might be deaf," Brittney reasoned.

Hmmm, I thought. My mind straightaway drifted back to the past couple of weeks with him not responding to his name, but I shook it off. "No, Honey, he's just a baby," I responded, to this unexpected notion.

"I doonn'tt knnoow," Bubs said at a slow pace. There's a chance he could be. Plus he's white. White dogs are more likely to be deaf." I looked at Bubs in wonder as she enlightened me with all of these unforeseen facts and observances. Nate used to call her Cliff Clavin due to her knack of "little known facts." If Nate was here right now, no doubt he'd be imitating that character from *Cheers*, and we'd all be laughing.

"I need to go pick up Ryan," I said, happy to change the subject. "Do you want to drive over with me?" I asked Bubs, holding on to the hope that my puppy was just a late bloomer.

"We think Dewey might be deaf," Bubs divulged to Ryan as soon as he got in the car after practice.

"Nooo, Bubs. I do *not* think that," I said remaining hopeful, as Ryan simultaneously blurted out, "What? Dewey's deaf?!" Our conversation continued while Dewey, completely oblivious to the topic, sat there on my lap as I drove us back home.

"The Maroon Five concert's this Friday," Brittney reminded us when we got home.

"Ooh, that's right," I said, glancing off to the side, watching Dewey jump up on the couch. Under the circumstances, I had forgotten about this concert. Brittney was still a big fan, but nothing was as fun without Nate. Last month we had gone to the Green Day concert at the Shoreline Amphitheater. The timing was inopportune, but we already had four tickets, so Jon went with us. We all tried to enjoy ourselves, but it was the first concert without Nate. Then a few weeks ago—inopportune timing as well—Carrie and I had gone to Stockton to see Carrie Underwood. Nate and Carrie's husband Danny had surprised us with tickets for Mother's Day. Both concerts were another rip to my heart, and I couldn't wait to go home.

Friday night arrived, and we were just about ready to leave for the concert in Sacramento. But first, I needed to finish getting Dewey settled. We would be gone until late at night, so I took him outside to "be good"—as Mary called it—right before we left. He was already attached to me and was, at the moment, the epitome of a *Dew* as I sat him down on his puppy bed and fastened the pen's latch. I reached down to pet him from outside the pen. "It's okay, Dewey" I reassured him. "We'll be back."

We could hear the opening band playing as we walked into Arco — yet another place of memories. Not only had we seen many concerts here over the years, but Arco was home to the Sacramento Kings. Within these arena walls, we had stomped the floor, rooting for our team on several occasions.

The kids and I actually had a really good time at the concert. Not great, but at least I wasn't crying, making this third concert without Nate a veritable success. We walked out to our car alongside thousands of other concert-goers, and joined the long line of stop and go traffic. Brittney reached from the backseat to turn the band's music back on. It was Ryan's turn to ride up front for the drive home. While being stuck in this gridlock of vehicles trying to leave the arena, my mind began drifting back to Nate and me — with our abundant teenage energy — running like the wind after our first concert. We had stayed until Van Halen finished their encore, and as the band formed a line onstage and bowed to their screaming 5150 fans, Nate and I rushed out the doors. We ran without stopping until we reached Nate's blue EXP that he had parked right next to the exit gate. We laughed as we caught our breath, and with no wait, pulled right out of the Cow Palace.

As I drove, I smiled at this cherished memory instead of tearing up. From that first concert on, we ran as fast as we could to the car after every concert, and had even taught the kids *the way* to leave a concert. But tonight we had walked to the car, and that was okay. Although I hadn't felt like running, I was really enjoying this time with my kids. They were growing up so fast, and I wondered how many years I had left with them before they moved out on their own. I shook that harrowing thought off, not allowing my mind to even go there at the moment. In a very short time, my thoughts had gone from flashbacks of Nate and me running wild and free, to a glimpse of the kids inevitably packing up their belongings and moving out. Straightaway, I consciously brought my thoughts back to present time.

"Maroon Five was really good," I said to the kids, as the traffic's pace began picking up. I knew it was the first time Ryan and I had seen them, but with Brittney, I had lost track. "How many times have you seen them now, Bubs?" I asked.

"Three times," she answered, "and I can't wait to see them again." I smiled. It was so good to see the kids doing normal things. And besides, the kids were raised on music. Concerts were a way of life for us. But now there were no more unused concert tickets, and I wondered if I would ever be up to going to another one without Nate.

It was good to see the backed up concert traffic behind us now as I took the southbound on-ramp and merged onto Interstate 5. "Well, let's get back to our deaf dog," Bubs said from the backseat.

"Bubs!" I negated in a motherly tone, as Ryan snickered next to me. "He's not deaf. He's a little angel from Heaven."

"A *deaf* little angel," Bubs belabored her point.

Ryan laughed out loud at his sister's cavalier statement. "Hey, Hey, Hey! That's enough out of you two," I called out half-jokingly. But this recurring discussion over the last few days had me wondering if it could be true.

"I'll bet Dewey *really* needs to go outside," I said, as we pulled into the garage. As soon as I opened the door to the house, the noisy house alarm sounded. I walked down the hallway to the control panel and pressed the combination to disarm the alarm system. When I turned around, I saw the kids looking at Dewey. Despite the commotion of our arrival home and the alarm, he was fast asleep in his puppy bed that was pressed up against the wired pen.

"See, Mom, the alarm should've woken him up," Ryan said. Having said that, he intentionally walked into the kitchen and returned with a big pan and a wooden spoon. As Dewey continued sleeping, Ryan walked over to the pen, kneeled down right by Dewey's head, and began banging the bottom of the pan with the wooden spoon. Bubs and I stood there intently watching as the loud drumming sound reverberated around us.

Ryan stopped the banging, and the three of us stood there watching Dewey. His eyes were still closed, and I could see the rise and fall of his furry little body as he breathed. I took in a deep breath. "You're right. He's deaf," I said to the kids with a sulky pout. I reached down to pet my sleeping puppy, and he startled at my touch. "Aw, Dewey," I said, as I unfastened the latch. He immediately walked out of his pen wagging his tail, excited to see us. I picked him up and held him extra close. No wonder he sounded like a Velociraptor those first couple of nights in his crate—he had never heard a dog bark!

The next day I had Dewey at the veterinarian's office. He was tested, and minutes later we had a confirmation. Dewey was deaf. Actually, "profoundly deaf." The vet said he can have a completely normal life with one imperative exception—to never let Dewey outside without being on a leash.

Secured in his blue harness, I left the office with Dewey on his leash. He wagged his tail and sniffed everything along the way as we walked. He was born deaf and didn't know life any other way. I picked him up and put him in the car with me. His diagnosis somehow made me feel an even deeper connection with Dewey. He needed me as much as I needed him.

I gave Dr. Bains a big hug and thanked her. "Just think about it, and let me know. It might be good for you and the kids to get away," she said warmly. With a soft smile, I nodded and then shut the front door as she left our house. I walked over to the couch and sat down. I needed to think about this before I told the kids. The Periodontal Dental Convention in Honolulu, Hawaii, was approaching. Months ago, Dr. Bains had made plans for our office staff to attend. During her visit, I had told her there was no way I could go then. I couldn't leave the kids. She understood. In fact, she was expecting that, and in turn, offered to send the kids along with me for an all-expenses paid trip.

I sat on the couch thinking about our conversation. Dr. Bains told me that Nate's Memorial Service was one of the most beautiful she had ever attended. She had gotten to know Nate and the kids while we went on our last office trip—a cruise to Alaska. She told me how she had watched the four of us in the pool one afternoon, laughing and having fun together. I smiled, remembering. On that day, the ocean's turbulence had the cruise ship rocking back and forth—and so was the water in the swimming pool. When the ship would lean onto its side from the strong ocean waves, the four of us would gather in the corner of the pool where the water was receding. We would squeal in anticipation of the water returning with full force. Seconds later, the powerful pool water would inundate us, knocking us all around. We would laugh and laugh and then do it again. We did that over and over. I sighed. That was only two summers ago. But now, everything in life had drastically changed forever. How could we possibly go to Hawaii? We had just been there last summer celebrating Brittney's high school graduation—back when life was normal and fun. Now, nothing was normal. Or fun. I shook my head. I didn't see fun being a possibility without Nate—not even in Hawaii.

Nate and I had been to Oahu twice. The first time was just the two of us. The second time was with the kids. Gramma, Jon, and Lisa joined us that time as well. We all went to a luau, swam in the ocean with the giant turtles, went snorkeling, touring, and hiking. Even Hawaii had memories. If we went, this would be our first family trip without Nate. As thoughts continued to run through my mind, I looked down at the floor, and let my body slowly slide down off the couch and onto the carpet. As I sat there, I began thinking about school for the kids. Brittney was taking classes at Modesto Junior College, and Ryan was just starting his sophomore year of high school. They had already missed many days of school due to everything we were dealing with. How could I possibly take them out of school again for a week in Hawaii? And Dewey—sweet little Dewey. Where would he stay while we were gone? He was so little...and deaf! I loved him so much already. Every night he cuddled up with me, and I rested my head next to his soft and furry little body. He was so warm—like Nate was. It was like he was born to help me survive this nightmare.

I could hear the kids opening the refrigerator door. They were probably ready for something to eat. I got up and walked into the kitchen and began unpacking the dinner that Dr. Bains had brought over. I hadn't cooked for weeks now, yet meals were delivered day after day, week after week. The love we continued to receive blew me away. It just kept coming. As we ate, I talked with the kids about Hawaii.

I got into my jeep, set my purse down on the seat, and backed out of the garage. Looking behind me, as the car drove in reverse, was painful. My neck was so stiff. This overwhelming sadness and stress felt like it was turning my body into concrete. Good thing I was on my way to an appointment with my therapist. What would I do without Carrie? She had made phone calls, done research, and practically interviewed a number of counselors searching for the perfect Christian counselor for me to see. She knew I was going to need professional help to survive losing Nate. Someone trained to help people, like me, who find themselves walking through the valley of the shadow of death.

Today was my third visit with the counselor. Before meeting her for the first time, Carrie had already told her all about me, and what had happened. I was so thankful for Carrie paving the way for me. I felt a connection with the therapist right away. She was authentic, and fully engaged in my feelings, yet she challenged me to look past my deep pain. She was encouraging, and talked about God a lot. I liked that. In my 42 years of life, I had never felt the need to see a therapist, so this was all new to me. But now, I was flat out in survival mode. Emotionally worn out, I focused on just surviving the next hour. Thinking about an entire day was just too much at this point. I desperately needed grief counseling, and was thankful to be there.

I was crying so hard, it was difficult to talk. "How?" I asked, as I looked at the therapist. "How in the world are the kids and I suppose to have fun on a trip to Hawaii?!" I reached for another tissue to blow my nose. Again. "We have memories all over the place in Hawaii. My heart hurts enough without pouring salt all over these raw emotions," I cried out.

The counselor took a few seconds before responding. "I can't even imagine what you are going through. But I do know that, in addition to all of the cherished memories you have of Nate in your heart, you have God. The hard truth is, Nate can't go to Hawaii with you and the kids this time. But God can. He was with you on your first trip, He was there on your family trip celebrating your daughter's graduation." She paused, "God will be going on this trip to Hawaii with you also." I knew she was right and believed everything she had said. But it hurt. It hurt so much. Her words were so hard to hear—they replayed in my head—*Nate can't go with you to Hawaii this time*. I started crying again and reached for another tissue and added it to the growing pile of tissues on my lap.

"There are a lot of things to do in Hawaii," the therapist encouraged. "Maybe you and the kids can do something that you never did with Nate. You can make new memories. Shelley, you will always hold your memories with Nate close in your heart. You get to keep those forever. But I would like for you to try to make some new memories without Nate. Hawaii sounds like a good place to try this out. I think you should accept this very generous offer. Go to Hawaii. Make some new memories," she said, with compassion in her eyes.

Kristy from the District Attorney's Office once again was at our house. She was such a great friend and liaison between us and the DA's Office. She came by regularly delivering cards, notes and messages, gifts, and food.

"The office put a little something together for your flight to Hawaii," she said with a smile. She handed me a gift bag, and I called the kids over. They started pulling out snacks, gum, magazines, games, and candy. The law team of Modesto thought of everything. Dog care for Dewey was even covered. Richard Balentine, a Criminal Investigator from the SVU whom Nate highly respected, and his wife, Cheryl, promised Dew would be well taken care of while we were gone.

The plane began picking up speed down the runway and lifting up into the air. I looked out the window and couldn't help but dream about the plane crashing. Dying in a plane crash would definitely be less painful than how I felt. It would be a lot faster, too. Certainly faster than the last three months of intense grieving. It was the worst. Although I was not suicidal, I had no desire to live anymore. None. But, I didn't want to leave the kids. So, if the plane crashed, the kids and I would be together, and we would instantly be in Heaven. We would meet God who would, as promised, wipe every tear from our eyes. There would be no more death. There would be no more pain. We would be back together with Nate, and our family would be complete once again. I continued looking out the window and into the sky. I couldn't wait to die.

Mid-flight, I began thinking about the first time Nate and I flew to Oahu. It was our fifth wedding anniversary trip. Nate had handed me a card during our flight. I opened it up, and inside was a handmade card—Nate made me an anniversary card every year. They were the best cards ever! That year, it was a handmade crossword puzzle with questions like Our First Movie Together. I read and answered each question, determined to fill in each of the blank squares on the card with letters and words. I started to tear up once again, remembering sitting next to Nate as we flew over this same ocean.

By the time our plane landed and we had collected our luggage and checked into our beautiful beachside hotel, the kids and I were hungry. We drove our rental car to a restaurant and walked in the front door. A crowd of people waited to be seated as I made my way to the hostess stand to check us in.

"Hi. How long of a wait is there?" I asked the hostess, holding my breath it wouldn't be too long.

"Hi there. How many people in your party?" she asked.

Without thinking it through, I had just set myself up for a question that almost brought me to my knees. I paused, feeling the pain in my heart. She held her pen against the waitlist, listening for my answer.

" ... Three," I said breathlessly, as if she had just kicked me in the stomach. I closed my eyes briefly, having a difficult time accepting the reality of that one word. My eyes opened to see the kids being blindsided with the same reality of the word *three*. We looked at each other, and without words, we realized the hard truth that we were no longer a family of four.

"It'll be about ten, fifteen minutes," the hostess said, oblivious to what had just happened. She continued to greet people and jot their names down as we walked back with a pang of sorrow.

We sat down on a cushioned bench as we waited to be called. I hadn't thought about it, but apparently, just the three of us hadn't gone out to a restaurant since losing Nate. With so much food in the house from family and friends, we hadn't eaten out much. When we did, there was always someone with us. Jon came for a number of long stays, as did Carrie, and Mary was with us a lot. We also had friends visiting all the time—work friends, the Salinas gang, and Pastor Cliff daily. My thoughts were interrupted by the hostess calling my name and leading us to a table of four, for three. The kids sat on one side, and I sat next to an empty chair to the left of me.

The next day at the Perio Convention, I sat and listened to the speaker, but didn't retain a word. I learned nothing. Instead, I wrote Nate a letter. It reminded me of when Nate and I used to write letters to each other in junior college when we were apart. But back then, Nate was merely across campus in another classroom. Now, Nate and I were in different worlds. Literally. Nate couldn't come meet me after class anymore. And for me to meet him, I'd have to die.

Hawaii and its serene beauty began to lighten our load as the days went by. I found comfort in knowing that friends from work were close by, but most important of all, I was with my kids. Besides having a few classes to attend, our days for the most part were open to enjoy Hawaii. Although the pain was still all-consuming, the kids and I were together and enjoying our vacation. I was very thankful for the distraction.

We started each day with an amazing breakfast buffet at our hotel. While we were eating, we gazed at the outdoor ocean view of paradise, and it was comforting. I took one last bite of the fresh pineapple before the kids and I walked back to our room. The Perio Convention classes were finished, and the entire day was free to do whatever we wanted. The kids got comfortable in our room—flipping through the channels on TV—while I walked down to the lobby to collect some tourist brochures.

I had spent part of last night out on the balcony crying on the phone with Carrie. It sure was nice to get away, but the pain came with us. I could hear the ding of the elevator going up and down as I took the stairs instead. Activity helped me. I'd rather be descending a few flights of stairs than standing in an elevator. Hmmm, I thought as I looked through the rack of brochures. The lobby was in constant motion with people coming in and going out to the beach. The advice from my grief counselor echoed in my head, "Do something different in Hawaii. Something you never did with Nate. Make new memories."

I rushed back up the stairs with a brochure in my hand—I couldn't wait to talk the kids into this one! Actually, I wouldn't have to talk Ryan into anything. I knew without asking he would be on board. But Bubs, she would be the one I needed to talk into this! As I climbed the stairs, I began chuckling, imagining what her response would be when I told her what I wanted to do.

"Hey, kids!" I said, as I walked back into the room. "Guess what I found?!" I held out the brochure with a smile.

"Let me guess, Mom. You went down to find brochures on the most dangerous and life-threatening things to do in Hawaii," Bubs said with a humorous, yet sarcastic tone.

"Haha, ha, very funny, Bubs!" I laughed as I spoke. My daughter's sarcasm always got me laughing. "How about we go shark cage diving!?" Just saying those words to Bubs made me laugh even more.

"I'm in!" Ryan sprung up immediately. "Can we go today?"

"See, your brother's in. And I'm in. We just need you now, Bubs," I pleaded, with my hands shaped like a prayer.

"Nooo waaay! I am NOT getting in the water with sharks!" She sat up from her comfortable spot on the bed where they were watching TV. "Are you kidding, Mom?!" she asked, with hopes that I was.

Ryan and I spontaneously teamed up and began enthusiastically informing Bubs about all of the many reasons she should say yes. I tried reassuring her about how safe we would be inside of the cage. Ryan talked about the awesome underwater shark pictures he could take. He continued on with how cool it would be to swim with sharks, and then I offered to buy her a T-shirt with a big shark on it. I would buy us all a T-shirt!

Brittney's "Nooo Waaay!" soon acquiesced into us driving to North Shore for our shark adventure. I've always been a bit of a thrill seeker, but when we pulled into the parking lot, my stomach tightened and zinged! There in front of us was a big cage with metal bars.

After a safety briefing, and signing a number of consent forms, the boat disembarked from Haleiwa Harbor. The kids and I looked at each other with eyes full of excitement, laced with fear, as we anticipated what awaited us out in the open water. Anything—sharks included—would be easier than what we had lived through these past three months.

Miles away from shore, the boat stopped. As we looked out and saw shark fins cutting the water's surface, I could practically hear the Jaws theme song playing in the background of my thoughts. It was almost like they were expecting us. In awe, we watched the sharks' full bodies gliding through the water.

The captain and his crew began lowering the cage into the water, and then waved us over. With our snorkel gear hanging around our necks, we walked over to the edge of the boat. One by one, we used the attached ladder to ease ourselves safely into the submerged metal cage. As we bobbed up and down in the ocean, the cage began floating away. A long yellow rope was our only connection to the safety of the boat.

I secured my goggles, and then lowered my head to be face down in the ocean. As I breathed in and out of the snorkel, I took in the thrilling view of sharks swimming all around us! The metal bars of the cage brought about a visual sense of protection, but there was one wall made of plexiglas. Before us, we were swimming with an illusion of open water—an arm's length away from all of those teeth! My mind began playing tricks on me as I came face to face with a shark. I put my hands out to feel the clear plexiglass, just to be sure it was really there.

The kids were pointing out sharks and other fish that were swimming by. Our muffled talking to each other was somewhat understandable. They pointed out a little orange fish. Before we knew it, that little orange fish was in the cage with us. Ryan snapped a picture. We resurfaced and spit out our snorkels. "Aww, that fish is going to get eaten alive!" Bubs said, as we bobbed up and down. We caught our breath for a couple of minutes, and then returned to the sea below us. This time we just held our breath so we could go down deeper inside of the cage. Submerged, we caught sight of what we had feared—the little orange fish getting swallowed by one of the sharks. With wide eyes, the kids and I looked at each other through our goggles. We started swimming back up for more air.

"Did you see that, Mom?!" I could hear Ryan asking as I resurfaced.

Bubs came up and spit out some salty water, "That poor little fish! I *knew* that was going to happen."

We went back under the water. But this time, instead of watching the sharks, I watched the kids. The three of us were making new memories, and what a way to start. This was amazing!

Dr. Bains had made arrangements for the staff and their families to spend our final day in Hawaii sailing the tropical waters on a chartered catamaran. With the ship tied to the dock, a crew member held out his hand to help us all climb aboard the rocking vessel.

It was a beautiful sunny day, the perfect weather to top off this memorable trip I was so thankful for. The large catamaran set sail, and CJ joined the kids and me as we explored the deck and cabin. What a treat this was! At full throttle out in the ocean, we saw a pod of dolphins swimming alongside the watercraft as if they wanted to join our party. We all gathered around watching them jump and splash.

After a while of mingling with friends and enjoying the drinks and appetizers, the kids and I made our way to an inviting netted area between the paralleling hulls. It was like an oversized hammock, with just enough room for the three of us to fit. We began crawling out over the netting, but with the ship's rocking we kept losing our balance. We repeatedly rolled into each other and laughed out loud as we crawled to the center of the open mesh. We lay face down and looked into the turquoise salty water—it was refreshing to see such vivid color. Since Nate had passed, it was like all the colors in life had faded to black and white.

As the skipper plowed ahead into the waves, the kids and I bounced and rolled all over the smooth netting. With nothing to hold onto, we just laughed and laughed at our spirited buoyancy. The sound of our laughter was like being reunited with an old friend. The kids and I were genuinely laughing. It felt so good. A wonderful reminder of how much I missed this forgotten basic aspect of human nature in our lives—laughter!

February 13th had arrived once again. But instead of our anniversary being my absolute favorite time of the year, it was now the day I was dreading the most. I knew today would be thoroughly depressing, so I had planned ahead just to survive this day. I wanted—no, I *needed*—something to look forward to.

Last month I called Paul and asked him for a favor. I asked him to write down everything he remembered about the night Nate and I met. Every detail of that summer night was a golden memory in my heart and soul. That night was the first page of our love story. But those memories were from *my* perspective. I was interested to hear about that night from Nate's perspective, and Paul was the perfect person to make that happen. He had been with Nate that night. In fact, they had spent most of that day together because they had both worked the late shift at Star Market. I asked Paul to fold up whatever he wrote, and then seal it in an envelope and mail it to me. I would save it for February 13th—today—to read.

This special day landed on a Sunday, and I was so thankful to God for that. There would be no better way to begin this very difficult day than in church. Although the worship songs still made me tear up, I could feel the Lord's presence as I sat there with family and friends. I thought about how only God Himself could have arranged this first anniversary without Nate to land on a Sunday, giving me that extra love and support from Heaven that I very much needed.

My mind drifted as the pastor spoke. I began to think about how many of these *special* days were landing on a Sunday. The day I saw the smiling rainbow was a Sunday. Ryan's 16th birthday—the first one without his Dad—had landed on a Sunday last month. Bub's and my birthdays coming up this summer—our first one since losing Nate—would land on a Sunday as well. Sweet little Dewey was even born on a Sunday. No doubt God was with me every day of the week, but special occasion days, like our anniversary, were the most painful of all. For them to land on a Sunday, time and time again, gave me comfort in knowing God was extra close.

The kids were concerned about me and took it upon themselves to do everything they could to help me get through the day. They had a dozen red roses sitting on the table when I woke up that morning with a card that read, *"They that love beyond the world cannot be separated by it. Death cannot kill what never dies,"* by William Penn. They had grown up seeing a vibrant bouquet of a dozen long stem red roses in the house every year for our anniversary. Every year Nate would send them to me at work. Flowers had not been delivered to me at work this year, but the kids made sure that I had red roses.

Although the kids had offered to take me wherever I wanted to go, or do anything I wanted to do to get through the day, what I really wanted was to spend some time alone. I could feel their love, and also the love from the many prayers that I knew were going out for me today. Paul's letter had arrived in the mail a week or so ago, and I really wanted to read it. I had also saved a gift bag from I'm not sure who, and a card from the DA's office that was hand delivered this week.

After we got home from church, we walked over to check on Dewey. He was such a little baby, sleeping on his comfy dog bed waiting for us to get back home. We had something to eat, and I thanked Bubs and Ryan. I told them how proud I was of them for their love and courage. They both had lost their dad at such a young age. The teenage years can be hard enough without something as devastating as the loss of a parent. We were learning together how to endure these *firsts.* Holidays, birthdays, and now anniversaries, as they arrived one by one.

I grabbed a blanket from the couch and walked down the hallway to our bedroom—I could hear the tag on Dewey's collar jingling behind me. He was awake, and my best little buddy. *Is this still our bedroom?* I pondered as I entered the room. *Nate hasn't been in here for months now.* I tried making sense of that thought as I spread the blanket on the floor next to our bed. I looked at the bed. *Is this still our bed?* My mind understood that *our* bed was now *my* bed, but my heart…my heart said that this would always be *our* bed. I went back down the hall to collect the cards and a gift bag I had been purposely saving for today. When I got back to the bedroom, I set them each to the side of the blanket. The kids came in to remind me that they would be here if I needed anything. I hugged them both and then shut the bedroom door behind me.

I sat down on the blanket, and Dewey immediately sat down on my lap. Leaning my back against the dresser, I sat there in silence slowly petting his soft white fur and fully understanding the unconditional love of a dog. I began talking to Nate in my head and told him how much I missed him, *especially* today. I cried as I thought about where Nate and I would have been at this very moment if he were still here. On President's weekend every year, Nate and I would take the kids to Mary's house in Salinas. They would be in great hands while we were away celebrating our anniversary weekend.

After we got the kids settled, Nate and I would have big grins on our faces as we backed out of Mary's driveway waving goodbye to her and the kids.

Our first stop would always be dinner at the Chart House—the same restaurant we ate at the night Nate proposed to me. And even though we were no longer two teenagers searching for the prom, that same young love had always lived inside of us. We ate there every anniversary for 22 years—with the exception of the year we lived in Seattle. Our evening in Monterey, with dinner, shopping, and a movie, was just the start of our weekend away. Seascape Resort had a suite reserved for us! Aptos, just south of Santa Cruz, was where we would spend the rest of our weekend every year. Our time at Seascape, in our beachside suite overlooking the Monterey Bay, was as good as life gets. Our weekend abode with an ocean view of crashing waves, a gas burning fireplace, and *always* a bottle of *Asti Spumante Sparkling Wine*, was our paradise on earth. Locking ourselves away from the world was romance at its finest and I felt like the luckiest girl in the world being there with Nate.

I sat on the blanket in somber silence. That's where Nate and I would be at this very moment if he were still here. The pain of missing him made me slowly fall to my side and lie down on the blanket. Dewey readjusted and cuddled up next to me. I pulled my bent knees in close, almost as if I were holding myself through the pain. My grieving was so deep, all I could do was rock back and forth as I longed for the day to end. My God, I thought. I'm going to have to live through this day again next year. And the next year. And the next year. I stared ahead at the carpet and then closed my eyes. In the darkness of my mourning heart, I dozed off.

When I opened my eyes, I noticed that the room was a little darker. Thankful for February's early sunsets, I looked over at Dewey. His eyes were closed. I sat up and reached for the closet light switch on the wall, and noticed the cards and gifts sitting to the side of me. I reached for Paul's letter, looked at it, and then set it back down. I wanted to save this one for last.

I picked up a card from the District Attorney's Office and smiled. Right away, I recognized the gift certificate. It was for Salon Salon—also a favorite place of mine in Modesto. Nate used to call it, "The place so nice, they named it twice." With a slight smile, I opened the card and read everyone's thoughts about how much they were thinking of me today. They gave me a generous gift card to spoil myself with some much-needed relaxation. I couldn't believe they would all send me an anniversary card. How would I ever be able to express to them how much this meant to me?

I reached for the gift bag and pulled out a card. It was a sympathy card that read, *In Loving Memory of Nathan Baker*, and was dated January 17, 2011. The card was signed by a group of operating engineers that I was not familiar with. I hope to meet them some day. They gave me a *Comfort Edition* Bible inside a fragrant cedar box. I was thankful that I had opened it today, and even more thankful for the hope of comfort.

Once again, I picked up Paul's letter, and this time I opened it. Even with a broken heart, I felt a bit of excitement as I pulled out the handwritten letter. I could feel my heart beating as I began to read...

"Most people know that Nate and I are best of friends. Our friendship started when we were in diapers. We have a bond that two friends growing up is hard to duplicate." With my full attention, I continued reading as Paul talked about them growing up, goofing off as kids, going to high school together, their first concert to see Bryan Adams, and being inseparable. And then he talked about one weekend in late July of 1986, after working the late shift, when Nate's life changed. I smiled, as I continued reading about Chris inviting the guys to the party of a friend whose parents were out of

town. Paul went on to talk about them driving over to the party in Nate's blue EXP, license plate IMKRAZE. I smiled again. This letter had my full attention as I kept reading.

He talked about people sitting at the table playing Thumper or Mexicali. I chuckled because it wasn't either; we were playing Poker. I continued reading. Paul was talking about the party. *"I didn't think anything of it when Nate said, 'Let's get out of here.' He wasn't into the party scene."* That sounds just like Nate, I thought. *"After we were in Nate's car, we crossed W. Alisal Street on Acacia heading toward Mission Park when Nate asked who the brunette was sitting at the table."* I eagerly read every word. I had never heard this before, and was so glad Paul agreed to write this letter. Paul went on to say he didn't know who Nate was talking about, so Nate decided to turn around and show him. I smiled warmly and kept reading. Nate had never mentioned this. *"The plan was to park two to three houses down from the party, sneak up to the window by the table, look in, and Nate would show me. We pulled it off. Nate pointed out Shelley to me through the window that night. For the first and only time, I saw Nate determined about meeting and dating a girl. He said he was going to date her. I don't really know how he pulled it off after that, but he focused on Shelley from that point on. Nate's life changed that night."* I held Paul's card up to my heart and took a deep breath as I soaked in the words from his letter. I brought the letter down and kept reading. *"Sometimes we never fully understand the things that happen in our lives. However, I do understand and know this: you meant everything to Nate. That will never end. God bless, Paul."*

Paul's heartening letter was more than I could have ever asked for to get me through the first anniversary without Nate. I cherished it and read it again. Twice. I cried myself to sleep that night, holding tight onto Paul's letter—and Dewey.

Chapter 12

"Vertigo" by U2

AFTER HOURS OF TOSSING AND TURNING, my attempts at getting some sleep were futile. I was in too much physical pain to sleep. *What is wrong with my body?!* I thought, as I picked up little Dewey and got out of bed. As I slowly walked down the hall toward the living room, I noticed the illumination of the television screen in the darkness, and then saw Brittney resting on the couch.

"Hey, Mom," Brittney said, in a soft raspy voice.

"Ah, Bubs," I said with solicitude as I sat down on the couch with her. Dewey went over to lie down on the blanket she had covering her lap. "How are you feeling?"

"Same," she answered. I could see the glassiness in her eyes as she spoke. Brittney had been diagnosed with mononucleosis a few days before, and had been told not to go to school or work for a couple of weeks. Between her grief, college courses, and work, she was beyond fatigued. "How 'bout you?" she asked.

" ... I hurt everywhere," I quietly answered. "It's like my body has turned into concrete," I tried explaining. "Walking is even difficult.

This stiffness has been intensifying for months now." I looked over at Dewey on Bub's lap with his eyes closed. He looked so innocent and comfortable. I smiled faintly at him. "You know, I was having trouble at work today putting my gloves on," I shook my head. "I've been wearing them for years, but it's like they didn't fit anymore. A few gloves even ripped when I was trying to put them on. My hands are so swollen," I said, as I rubbed them together, almost as if I were putting lotion on.

"You need to go to the doctor, Mom," Brittney said, unsettled by these details.

"...Well...you and I are just a *mess,* aren't we?!" I jested with a rueful smile.

It was April now, but these past eight months of intense chronic grief had seemingly battered our immune systems. At first the pain was all emotional, but now the pain had overlapped into the physical realm as well. The shock and adrenaline had faded. And all that God-given Novocaine—my dental way of paraphrasing Philippians 4:7—had faded as well.

I looked over at the TV that Bubs had put on mute when I sat down. "What're you watching?" I asked, and then answered my own question when I saw Rapunzel's long blonde hair. Bubs and I watched Disney's *Tangled* and ended up falling asleep on the couch.

I walked down the hallway with Dewey into the living room again the next night, and the next night, and the next. Bubs and I were getting used to falling asleep on the couch together. This pain was not going away, so I made an appointment with my doctor. He ordered a full panel of blood work and put me on a corticosteroid medication for extreme inflammation. The doctor felt it was a result of long-term stress, the nurse swore it was a Vitamin D deficiency, but it was all the same to me. I just wanted this physical pain to go away, and it eventually did! I wish there was a magic pill for the emotional pain as well, but there is no pill in existence that could take away *this kind* of pain. The only prescription for grief is God.

In time, Brittney got over her mono, and I got over the inflammation and swelling. We were back to life, but nothing was normal anymore. Memories of Nate were everywhere throughout the entire town, evoking cherished remembrances of happy times. Those memories were nothing but painful reminders of all that we had lost.

After months of contemplation, prayer, and long discussions with family and friends, the kids and I decided to move to Long Beach. Not only would we be close to family, but Southern California is also where the kids wanted to go to college. Ryan still had two years of high school left, but he agreed to make the short-term sacrifice for the long-term benefits. Mary decided to retire and leave Salinas so she could join us in Long Beach. Jerry even left Seattle and moved to Palm Desert just a couple of hours away. We all agreed that we wanted to stay together.

After weeks of Jon and Lisa going to Open Houses in search of a house for us to live in, one became available right across the street from them. The real estate market in SoCal was ridiculous compared to the Central Valley, but I bought the three bedroom, one bathroom, fixer upper before it even officially went on the market. It was only half the size of what we were used to, but I needed to think ahead. The kids were getting to the age where they would be on their own within the next few years. I wanted to lock them in their rooms and never let them leave, but at least, for now, we would be together.

I have a strong animosity toward change, and even more so, I down-right hate goodbyes. Although I certainly felt moving was the right thing to do, I dreaded all of the goodbyes that were soon to happen. We would definitely come back to visit and keep in touch, but we were going to hugely miss all the people we very much loved and cared about in Modesto.

The time had come; we needed to start packing. Ryan was only one year old when we moved in, and Brittney was just starting kindergarten. Now, one was in high school, and the other in college! I stoically looked around this home we loved and resisted removing a single thing. I wanted to forever remember everything just as it was. Once we started packing things up, it would *never* look like this again.

"Ryan," I said, approaching his room.

"Yeah, Mom?" Ryan answered, as he picked up Dewey who had just walked into his room alongside me.

"We need to start packing." He looked at me. Ryan was always so strong, but the deep sadness in his eyes was like a window into his hurting soul. "I want you to video tape every single room. I always want to remember our home this way." I felt my stomach flutter, and I paused. "And then we'll start packing."

Our home was indelible on my heart and in my soul, but it gave me comfort to know we would have our house on tape if we ever wanted to see it again. Brittney and I watched Ryan start filming, and then we went out to the backyard and waited until he was done. It was too hard to watch. Ryan came out back and nodded, signaling it was done. The three of us walked back into the house and began disassembling our home piece by piece.

There came a point where I was so utterly inundated with decisions, phone calls, tasks, responsibilities, paperwork, and heartache that everything turned into a God given blur. Somehow I was both fully functional and spiritually paralyzed all at the same time. Family and friends surrounded the kids and me with helpful hands—from organizing an estate sale, packing everything we owned in boxes, filling a couple of U-Hauls and a trailer, to just being there for a needed hug. Yesterday the DA's Office had even hosted a very touching lunch for the kids and me so everyone could say goodbye. Their loving gesture meant so much. They were more than Nate's past co-workers to us; they were family friends that I planned to always keep in touch with.

Moving day arrived. The plan was for Paul, Chris, and Matt to drive the loaded U-Hauls and Paul's jam-packed truck and trailer to our new house in Long Beach. A neighbor family was going with us to help us transport our belongings as well. Their daughter Whitney—who sang at Nate's Celebration of Life—would ride with Brittney in her car, and Ryan would be with me and Dewey in my car. From the driveway, I watched as the guys began backing up the vehicles, and one by one, made their way down Melones Court for the five plus hour southbound drive.

Before we left, the kids and I slowly walked around the completely vacant house one last time—it was all so surreal. These walls that once echoed with laughter were now nothing but empty space. There was no need for words as the three of us went from room to room to say our unspoken goodbyes. As we walked out the front door, I stopped and looked back. I blew our beloved home a kiss, and locked the front door.

Dear Shelley,

Looking back... although very painful... it is amazing to see how far you have come. If Nate could tell you, he would probably say how incredibly proud he is of you! Also what a wonderful mother you continue to be to the kids, despite your circumstances, and that he is so happy you all have continued to stay close during very difficult decisions that are changing the course of your life... all the while holding each other up.

It's so hard to see you leave Modesto and the close proximity we have had... but I know it is for the best. I can clearly see over these past few months God's plan for you unfold before my eyes. Long Beach will be your new home.

I pray that you continue to feel God close to you and find a good church home. I will miss you all terribly but am only a phone call away.

I look forward to our visits together and will really lift you and your family up in prayer as you begin a new journey.

I love you very much! Carrie

It took a few months to get unpacked and relatively settled, but summer was winding down and we were no longer living out of boxes. We were learning our way around town, and already had a few favorite places to eat—including Jon and Lisa's house across the street. Brittney was starting Long Beach City College, and Ryan was starting his junior year at a high school fairly close to the ocean. He had never been the new kid in town, and I completely understood. I also had moved to a new town the summer before my junior year of high school. It was difficult, but I held out hope that, in time, he would find his way like I had. And Dewey was adapting well. Our new house had a big bay window that he sat in, keenly watching the cars, people, and dogs that passed by. Dewey was our new home's doorbell.

Right away, we found a nondenominational Christian church called SeaCoast Grace that we liked a lot. It was a big church with multiple services and a lot of Bible Study classes throughout the week. The sermons were Biblical, and the worship music was incredible. The singers could have easily made a career out of their voices that often gave me goosebumps! Carrie was encouraging me to go to GriefShare there, and had even been in touch with the class's leader who had called me and introduced herself. I was resistant to go, but I was glad I did. Turns out, there were four of us in class—all in our 40's—who were recently widowed. Through sharing in our homogeneous sorrow, special friendships were blossoming.

I felt very blessed with both new and longtime relationships in my life—providentially, one of my best childhood friends, Flo, lived nearby in Anaheim! We had met as 7th graders in junior high and had become fast friends. She camped a lot with me and my family at the lake every summer, and she had even been a bridesmaid in our wedding. Flo—or *Monthly*, as Nate endearingly referred to her—had stayed with me at our apartment the night before Nate and I got married. It was so great to reconnect with her. We started going on very long walks to different restaurants across town—or even the next town!—justifying an edible reward for all of our steps. I was a bigger fan of lengthy walks than she was—God love her—but she was always willing to endure my request with an authentic smile entwined with a tad of humorous sarcasm. Flo's a Christian as well, and I absolutely loved the talks we got into as we walked. She became a big part of holding me up with God's Word and was a prayer warrior for my healing heart.

I have recently started back to work at a new dental office that involves a commute. The only way to learn all of these highways is to jump right in—that, and GPS! Back home I knew so many patients, and now, every name on my schedule was another patient to introduce myself to. There are a lot of things I miss about Modesto, but I really like it here in SoCal. Living here is both a fresh start and a welcomed distraction.

For the most part, sites around town don't trigger constant memories. Even so, our street *did* have memories of Nate. One Thanksgiving a few years ago, Jon and Lisa had rented an RV for Nate and me to sleep in during our visit. It gave me comfort to look right across the street to where Nate and I had slept. We had visited Jon and Lisa as a family many times over the years and it was comforting to me that Nate had been here.

The kids and I made a lot of trips to Modesto. It helped with the home sickness to go back and visit friends often. Spending time together with familiar faces was always so uplifting for us. We are there so regularly I actually still run errands at my favorite places when we are in town. And when Ryan was ready to take the DMV's behind-the-wheel test to get his driver's license, I set up the appointment in Modesto instead of Long Beach. He passed! And just like Brittney a few years earlier, Ryan had no choice where to drive—both kids' first solo drive was to church. Their freedom of driving was contingent on a prayer with the pastor before they drove anywhere else!

I wished Nate could be a part of these exciting milestones in life, like Ryan getting his driver's license. We missed him terribly. But all things considered, life was going as well as can be expected. In addition to going to GriefShare class at church, I was also seeing a grief counselor in Fountain Valley. I no longer cried every day; however, every time I sat down on the counselor's couch, my pain came gushing out. I saw my grief counselor many times, but I will *always* remember one particular session. The grief counselor had commended me on how productive I was, yet she wasn't convinced that I was healing. To sum it all up, she thought I was on autopilot. She asked me when I was going to start living again? She believed I was going through the motions of life, but not *really* living. I understood what she was saying, but I was very active in life. Yes, I was still grieving, but how much can you really enjoy life with a broken heart? My lungs were still breathing and my heart was still beating, but inside, I was dead.

I thought about her words the entire drive home. I exited the highway and was stopped at a red light when I noticed the license plate in front of me that read LIVAGAN. *You've gotta be kidding me,* I thought, and reached for my phone hoping to snap a picture before the light turned green. These unique things that happened to me are so extraordinary that it made me feel good to have a picture. I have an enlarged and framed picture of the smiling rainbow above my bed, and was able to get a picture of this license plate as well. Serendipity, or maybe just plain coincidences, are how unbelievers would explain happenstances such as these. But the exact subject of my counseling session just happened to be written on a random license plate right in front of me! Believers, however, know that is God speaking.

I love God so much, and was so thankful for Him reiterating through a license plate the concept of me living again, but He knew I was still really struggling...

Feeling the pressure of grief welling up inside of me once again, I was in no mood for traffic congestion on Highway 105. *THE* 105, I thought—Southern California *lingo* was still fairly new to me. As I was driving down East Imperial, I noticed the Embassy Suites Hotel up ahead. I sighed. That's where we had all stayed the night we returned from our last mission trip to Mexico. That was only a year ago. And now my life had changed forever. A stabbing pang hit my heart at the sight of the hotel lined with palm trees, drawing closer as I continued to drive. Every day on my drive to and from work, I would intentionally look the other way, toward LAX, to avoid seeing this hotel. Today, however, I deliberately fixed my eyes right on it as I approached, using only my peripheral vision to drive. I looked over at the arched portico of the hotel, all the while trying to keep my eyes on the road. I could almost see Nate standing there.

Just months before Nate had passed away, this very spot had been a happy place. I continued driving, remembering that night as it played out in my head...After enduring many hours of caravanning from Mexico, and being caught up in the abundance of traffic and interconnecting freeways of Southern California, the mission team was excited for a fun last night together before returning home to Modesto the next morning. All the ladies went to Taylor Swift's *Fearless* concert at Staples Center, while the guys went to a Dodgers game. That night, the guys made it back to the hotel first, and many had already gone to bed. The ladies returned later because we stopped for a late-night breakfast on the way back. By then, we were all pretty exhausted after driving all day, and then attending the concert, not to mention the awesome week we had just spent in Mexico. After parking the car, we walked up the sloped sidewalk and saw Nate standing in front of the hotel waiting for us. He wanted to make sure we got back safely. I remembered his warm grin as he saw us walking toward him. He hugged me, asked about the concert, and escorted us back into the hotel almost like a bodyguard. That was Nate.

As I merged onto the 105, the flood gates of my lamenting heart and soul began to burst wide open. I started bawling so hard that all I could do was let out an utterly bloodcurdling scream. I screamed out at the top of my lungs until I completely lost my breath. Over a year of accumulated grief came pouring out in anger now, and I let it!

I screamed out a long piercing wail again! And again! And again! I could feel the soreness of my throat from the force of these repeated fiery screams, but I didn't care!

Breathing hard, I could feel the mascara stinging my eyes as the tears ran down my cheeks. My nose began running and I lifted my arm to briefly dry my face with my sleeve. This would *not* be over anytime soon. It had taken more than a year for me to reach this point. A year! Up until now I had felt too dead to scream — but now that was over.

"AAAAAHHHHH!," pausing only long enough for more air. "AAAAAHHHHH!" I thought about Pastor Cliff and how he had assured me time and time again that it was okay to be mad. "God has broad shoulders," he would always say. "He knows how you feel and wants you to get it out." It had always been hard for me to be mad at God. I love Him. I trust Him. I respect Him. It made me feel uneasy being mad at God — almost like it was a lack of faith, or a step back in my love for Him. Even my grief counselor had encouraged being angry as a part of grieving. I had never really liked that idea, but now... now it was GO TIME with God! One on one, just me and Him. Was this me coming back to life, so to speak? God's spiritual anesthetic was *definitely* gone now. Anger consumed me to the core of my being for the unendurable pain I felt inside from the reality of losing my husband and best friend.

"HOW could You let this happen, God?!!!" I raged. "42, really???! Are You kidding me?!!! That's all I get?! We got cheated out of growing old together! Robbed!!!" I screamed for as long as my lungs would let me. "I want to see Nate!" I wailed in fury. Tears of frustration streamed down my cheeks. "I want to see him RIGHT NOW!" I demanded. "You know I love You more than *anything* in life," I yelled at God as if He were sitting in the car with me. "You *promise* to be close to the brokenhearted, so *here I am!*" I caught my breath for a moment, but I wasn't finished. This heart-to-heart with God was not over yet!

"You say You can do anything, but You *can't* be my husband. You say that I have everything as long as I have You! Well, you know what?" I yelled out, "I can't hold You, God. You don't take my communion cup and put it with Yours like Nate did. You're not the one who tucks me in, and strums my arm like a guitar as I fall asleep. You don't steamroll me, and chase me around the house. I can't dance with You, God!" Images of Nate with a tie wrapped around his head began filling my thoughts, along with flashbacks of parties and celebrations where Nate would *own* the dance floor! Those many nights were a blast, and the reality of that never happening again only fueled my fire all the more!

"You don't steal cookies off the cookie sheet. I can't soak in the hot tub with You." My thoughts were overflowing, and as soon as I thought of something else to add, I passionately yelled it out. "Jesus, You came into this world to experience *everything* that a human feels... but You never lost a spouse so You actually *don't* know how I feel right now! I miss Nate so much, God! I want him back!!!"

Taking in a deep breath, I continued to drive. The overload of emotions I was feeling began to somewhat settle down as I sat there quietly in my seat. Never in my entire life had I felt such out-right raw emotion exploding from within. My throat felt so abraded, I wondered if I'd have a voice the next day. I can only imagine what people might have thought if they had seen me through the window, but I didn't care. I really didn't care.

I noticed I was almost home. I paused and shook my head. That drive usually takes 45 minutes to an hour, and I don't even remember it. I couldn't tell you one way or the other if I had inched my way forward through the traffic, or if I had made good time. All I know is that, by the grace of God, I made it home safely. And in some strange way, I felt reinvigorated as I pulled into the driveway and turned off the engine.

I turned the hair dryer off and picked up my cell phone. There was a text message from Bonnie letting me know that another mission trip was planned for Thanksgiving week next month, and wanted to know if I would be interested in going. Her text read that they wanted me to go but would completely understand if I wasn't ready for taking this first mission trip without Nate. As I went back to drying my hair, I thought about the trip, and wondered if the kids would like to go. Maybe it would be too soon for them. Would it be too soon for me?

Am I ready for this? I asked God, as I dabbed a bit of make up on. I began reflecting on all of the things that used to scare me about going to Mexico. My mind instantly drifted back to a talk I had had with Nate one afternoon at the Raley's Deli. I called him that morning from work, in between patients, asking him if we could meet for lunch. I was kind of freaking out about the upcoming second mission trip, and needed Nate to help calm my nerves. He sat down with me at a booth next to the window. I had already ordered us our favorite turkey paninis. While we waited for them to be grilled, I began telling him about all my concerns. "You know there are travel warnings *again* not to go to Mexico! What if we get arrested at the border for bringing in all of the dental supplies? What if the kids poke themselves with a contaminated instrument? What if I go to jail for working on patients without a license to practice in Mexico? What if one of us gets kidnapped and held for ransom?"

I found myself just sitting at my vanity recollecting Nate's calm demeanor, and how he let me vent for a few minutes before he spoke. He told me that he understood and had also thought about some of those same possibilities. Nate informed me that he had already let one of the detectives know where we were going, and when we would be back—just to play it safe. After assuring me we were doing the right thing, he told me he felt we would return home safely, just like we did last time. He went on to say that, of course, there was always the possibility of something bad happening to us on the trip. I'll always remember what he added after that. He told me that *if* something were to happen to us on the mission trip, there was no better way to enter the Gates of Heaven than by doing the Lord's work. I smiled recalling Nate's wise words. *Well ANYTHING is easier than grieving!* I thought, as I rolled my eyes and got dressed for the day. Needless to say, I no longer feared going to Mexico! My only concern was the emotional aspect, and if I was ready to go to another place filled with memories.

Due to school, the kids were unable to travel to Mexico, but they fully supported my decision to go. I was packed and ready. I hugged the kids and Dewey goodbye, and wished them a Happy Thanksgiving—they would be with nearby family for the holiday. As my luggage and sleeping bag were loaded into the utility trailer we were hauling, I climbed in the back seat of Dr. Acree's blue Hummer. At the break of dawn Saturday morning, our two-car caravan set out for Mexico once again.

After hours of catching up with each other while driving south, we stopped for lunch just minutes from the border—close enough to see the giant arch in Tijuana. We soon joined the line of cars waiting to cross into Mexico. After another wait for Border Patrol to search the trailer, we continued our journey. As I looked out the window, I immediately became engrossed in the view—everything from the country's red, white, and green flag waving in the breeze to poverty-stricken slums. The border's vicinity was packed with young and old selling tourist trinkets and food items to make a living. Each time I was here, it never took me long to appreciate living in the United States of America.

Well past Ensenada, on the dusty hillside highway, I ended up dozing off. As the car began slowing down, I opened my eyes to see the big wooden Rancho Santa Marta sign. We were here. The Hummer turned to the right and I could feel the bumpiness of the dirt road as we approached our destination. It was a warm late afternoon with blue skies. As I looked out the window, I could see the children busy with their school activities, but at the first sight of the dental clinic and dorm rooms, memories instantly ambushed me.

Car doors began to open, and I could hear everyone from our group talking outside as they started to remove cases of water, coolers of food, and personal belongings from the attached trailer. My eyes were filled with tears. I sat in the car alone—almost as if I were trying to hide from all of the memories that surrounded me. I felt like a hostage to the acrimonious triggers of grief that repeatedly attacked me no matter where I went. I hadn't even gotten out of the car yet and I knew my decision to go on this trip was a big mistake!

Within a few minutes, Bobbi and Bonnie came to check on me, and saw that I was overtaken by emotion. With one on each side, they showed me to a small dorm up on the hill where the three of us would be staying for the week. It wasn't the usual dorm room we stayed in with a row of bunk beds on each side. This one was more private, and would only fit a few people. We had the whole place to ourselves, and I was comforted to learn that I even had my own room with a door.

They helped me get settled with my belongings and said that I could do anything I wanted. If I wanted company, they would stay. If I needed time to myself, they would leave, and then come back to check on me. They even told me if I wanted to stay in the dorm all week and never leave, that was okay too. And, if at some point I wanted to come out and slowly join in, they would all be there for support. I was so thankful for my great friends.

At the moment, I felt like I just needed some time to myself, so Bonnie and Bobbi gave me a hug, prayed with me, and then left to help everyone unpack the vehicles. In the empty room, I sat on the couch and cried. It had been a little over a year now, and I still couldn't believe Nate was gone. Never again would he be here at Rancho Santa Marta.

After a while, I walked over to the window and pulled the curtain aside. The sun had set, but surrounding lights, along with the stars and moon, made it bright enough for me to see everything fairly well. As I looked around, all I could think about was how much I wanted to go home! What was I thinking?! *I never want to be here again! How can I possibly treat anyone in the dental room when I am this upset?* I asked God for a blessing—for *something, anything* good that could come out of this trip that I did not want to be on.

Bonnie came back to check on me along with Bobbi who thought I must be hungry and asked if I wanted something to eat. I was getting hungry so Bobbi left to make me a sandwich. While she was gone, Bonnie and I sat there talking for a while. Soon, Bobbi came back with some food and we all sat down to eat together. Bobbi told me that she had bought me a book to read while we were here, and walked over to get it out of her suitcase. She quickly returned and handed it to me. I held the book in my hands and read the title, *Heaven is for Real: A Little Boy's Astounding Story of his Trip to Heaven and Back*. The title actually brought a smile to my face—I loved hearing more about Heaven. I opened the cover to Bobbi's handwritten words, *"For to me, to live is Christ and to die is gain. Philippians 1:21. Because of our eternal hope of glory, with love, Bobbi.* I gave Bobbi a big hug for this thoughtful gift and couldn't wait to start reading it.

This trip certainly wasn't what I had envisioned. The next two days I did nothing but lie on the bed in my room. The air was crisp, and I felt safe and secure wrapped up in my sleeping bag, almost like a swaddled baby. I talked with God a lot, and somehow found solace in staring at the wall for hours. And in between staring at the wall and crying, I began to read the book that Bobbi had given me. My three days of being closed up in the room with the door shut were both exhausting and very cathartic.

I began to think about the dental team, and about the steady flow of patients that came in and out of the clinic doors each day. There was a lot to do. Tomorrow would be Wednesday—our fourth day here—and I hadn't treated a single patient yet. I began to gear my mind up toward stepping out of this room, and maybe seeing a patient or two tomorrow.

I faced the pain of heartache head on as I walked into the dental clinic. With God's help, and great friends, I was able to finish the week seeing numerous patients. Memories of Nate blowing up gloves and squawking like a chicken to make the kids laugh, and the x-ray room that Nate helped to build only a year-and-a-half earlier filled the clinic. I missed Brittney and Ryan too. Bub's large hand-painted portrait of Dr. Acree was still there on the wall. I smiled at my daughter's artwork. Paintings of squeezed tubes of flowing toothpaste and dancing teeth decorated the walls around the lobby.

When I sat down on a clinic chair, I saw the makeshift suction collector. I shook my head and smiled, remembering Nate and Ryan digging holes out back every evening after closing down for the night. They would remove the accumulated waste that had been suctioned out of the mouths of the day's many patients. It was a job that no one wanted, but Nate and Ryan took on the challenge, and seemed to be somewhat amused by the grossness of it all. I could almost hear Nate saying, "C'mon, Boy, let's go take care of this." Ryan was right by his dad's side as they dug the hole and took care of business.

We would be leaving the next day after the church service. No doubt the traffic would be heavy due to it being the Sunday after Thanksgiving. It felt good knowing I had survived my first mission trip without Nate. I couldn't wait to see the kids the next night when I got home! Dewey had probably been waiting for me in the window at Mary's house since I left, and I couldn't wait to see him either! I had finished the uplifting book Bobbi had given me. Before going to bed, I strolled around the grounds by myself and found the house that Nate and Ryan had helped to build. The work they had put in a few years ago was now somebody's home. I walked away with a warm smile and walked over to the fire pit. Incandescent smoldering ashes were all that was left from the bonfire earlier in the evening. I sat down next to its fading heat. Being alone under a canopy of stars gave me special time to talk with God. I thanked Him for this time here at Rancho Santa Marta and also thanked Him for giving me the strength to see patients. With a peaceful heart, I walked back to the dorm and fell asleep for the night...

I found myself standing alone in the shadowy darkness of a room with no walls. A nebulous glow of light coming from beyond a cracked door ahead of me caught my attention. As I gazed at the light radiating around the edges of the door, I became intimately aware of Nate's presence in the room with me and began to spiritually feel him holding me close. He wasn't tangible, but I could see and even feel him. It was like he never left. Yet, there was an unspoken mutual understanding of everything that had happened. Nate's arms were my safe haven, and I melted into his loving embrace. "Don't ever let me go," I said softly to Nate. I felt embodied by a supernatural calmness as he held me in his arms.

My eyes opened, and I caught sight of the wall I was so familiar with. I knew right where I was. Lying still in my sleeping bag, visions of Nate holding me played out in my mind. I took in a deep breath and briefly closed my eyes. With a soft smile, I lay there thinking about my incredible dream. I thought about the glowing light on the other side of the door. That's where Nate lives now. And then I thought about the fact that the door was only cracked open — certainly not wide enough for Nate to fit through. I never saw Nate enter the room, he was just there. He met me in my darkness and held me. I remembered telling Nate to never let me go. And then I realized he never did let go of me. Nate was still holding me when I woke up.

Still in bed, I remembered asking God for a blessing here in Mexico. On the last night of this Thanksgiving week, God answered my heartfelt prayer with a vivid dream of Nate. In my dream, our time of holding each other was as close as I could possibly get to being in Nate's arms on this side of Heaven. I had thought Nate would never again be here at Rancho Santa Marta. But he was. Somewhere in that great chasm between Heaven and Earth, Nate held me in his arms.

The car radio played as I drove down Lakewood Boulevard on this typical 72 degree, sunny Southern California day. I began making a mental list of all the errands I had to run that afternoon. I had so much to do and was thankful for the day off work to give me the time I needed to catch up. *Oh yeah, Dewey needs dog food,* I thought, as I began braking for the red light up ahead. As I waited at the light, I instantly recognized the repetitious beats of the song that was just starting to play on the radio. It had been many years since I had heard this heavy metal classic, but the familiar tune felt like a punch to my stomach. My hand reflexively hit the button to make it stop before Autograph started singing "Turn up the Radio." Nate loved this song.

Even though the music was no longer playing, my thoughts had stepped back in time to a memory of Nate and me on a road trip. I saw the light turn green through tear-filled eyes. Although it was bittersweet to remember, I thought about that road trip and how I had surprised Nate with this song on a CD. We had stopped at Chevron, and while Nate was filling up the tank, I went into the Food Mart to get us a cold drink and some snacks. As I waited for the cashier to ring me up, I picked up one of the CD's displayed on the glass counter. It was a compilation of 80's hits from various artists. I smiled when I saw "Turn up the Radio," and handed the CD to the lady to ring it up, too.

Nate was done filling up the car by the time I returned with a bag of snacks. He reached over for his unsweetened iced tea. "Look what I found for you!" I told him, and handed him the CD from the passenger seat, pointing to the song.

"Aw yeah!" Nate said with his mouth already full of Gobstoppers—another treat in the bag. He kissed me with multi-flavored lips and began unwrapping the CD. Nate had the song playing before we had even pulled out of the gas station.

Although my mind knew I was driving around Long Beach running errands, my heart was in the car with Nate listening to "Turn up the Radio" over and over again. I could almost see Nate playing his air guitar on the steering wheel as we drove.

At the next red light, I looked in the rearview mirror and dabbed my eyes with a tissue. *That's it,* I thought. *I can't listen to music anymore.* There was always something there to remind me of Nate—especially with music. I finished my errands with the radio off.

The radio stayed off for weeks until one day Bubs was in my car. We were backing out of the driveway on our way to get lunch when she turned the radio back on.

"My car doesn't play music anymore," I said, in a melancholy tone. "Too many memories." She looked over at me and began searching for The Fish—a Christian radio station that was well known in Southern California. Nate and I raised the kids on rock music—and sometimes even took them to concerts with us—but we were also very familiar with Christian music from worship in church.

As we drove to the restaurant, Bubs and I talked and listened to The Fish. Some of the songs I recognized, but a lot of the songs and artists were new to me. From that day on, the radio station never changed. Every time I was in my car, I listened with a thirsty heart. The interactive radio personalities shared Bible verses, testimonies of hope, and uplifting music. Christian music deepened my faith, and as the artists sang, I listened.

One afternoon when I was driving, a new song began playing on The Fish. I was taken aback—the lyrics seemed to reflect *everything* I was feeling inside. Whoever was singing this song gave words to my feelings. A couple of weeks ago, I had somehow survived *what would have been* our 24th wedding anniversary. The kids tried comforting me with red roses again to help fill the void, but February's intense sorrow kept me longing for March to arrive. I pulled into a nearby parking lot, and sat in the car intently listening to this song about hurt colliding with the healer. I felt such a connection with not only the lyrics, but also the sincere emotion of the singer—no doubt, he *gets* grief.

I sat in the car thinking about that very collision—that exact moment, in the early morning hours of August 5, 2010, when the Lord collided with our tragedy. That split second when everything we knew was about to change forever.

As the days and weeks went by, I clung onto this song—"The Hurt & The Healer," from the Christian band MercyMe. I would wait for it to come on the radio every time I was in the car. The singer seemed to understand my deep suffering. Since it was a new release, the station would air this MercyMe song often. The song would make my chest tighten as my heart soaked up the message. Every time I listened, it was a reminder of God's promise to breathe life back into what was left of me.

"C'mon Mom!" Ryan said, looking at me. He was waiting for an answer as the three of us walked across a parking lot in Washington, D.C., to get some lunch, but I was *not* ready to commit.

I took in a long deep breath as I continued walking, my lips fluttering as I exhaled. "I don't know, Ry," I shook my head. "I heard once you step on the plane, you have to jump or they'll *push* you out!" I emphasized, trying to talk some sense into my fearless son.

"They won't need to push us out, Mom. We're going to jump!" he assured me, determined to get me to concur with this insanity. Just the thought of skydiving gave me the jitters as I squealed out loud! Nevertheless, the adrenaline junkie inside of me knew there was a huge probability that Ryan would actually succeed at talking me into this.

"Count me out of this one! Don't even think you will *ever* talk *me* into skydiving!" Bubs said matter of factly. Ryan and I smiled at each other. "My whole life you guys have been talking me into things! The Tower of Terror, and all of those other scary roller-coasters you guys made me go on." I watched her as she thought of more things to include. "Swimming with sharks!" she carried on. "Climbing all those stairs in Hawaii, and swimming in the ocean when there were those *big* yellow warning signs of jellyfish! Oh, and remember when you guys talked me into hiking to the top of that mountain in Mexico? There were scorpions!" She wasn't done. "Taking crazy long walks with Mom. You know I could have died doing those things!"

"You *can't* die from walking, Bubs!" I laughed, as we reached the restaurant and Ryan opened the door for us.

"Ahhh," I said, feeling an instant cool down from the air conditioner inside of the restaurant on this hot and humid summer day.

"Well, it *felt* like I was gonna die," Brittney stressed, trying to make her point as she walked inside. "My feet were killing me! Ohhh my gosh, it feels so good in here!" she said, closing her eyes for a second. Ryan and I chuckled at Bub's sarcastic temperament, but neither one of us tried talking her into it. Poor Bubs. She was born into a family who enjoyed heart pounding adventures. We regularly pushed her out of her comfort zone. As a child, she had no choice but to join in; however, now she was an adult. She could make her own decisions, and I would never pressure her into agreeing to *this* one. This one was big!

"As I recall," I said assuredly, "you enjoyed every single one of those events *and* have done most of those things again because you had so much fun."

"Yeah, I did," Bubs agreed. "But I am *not* going skydiving with you guys," she reiterated. "And I still don't like walking," she added.

"That's okay," I responded. "I'm probably not going either," I said, looking over at Ryan with a smirk.

The hostess walked up to us. "Table for three?" she asked, as she grabbed a few menus. It had been almost two years now of a table for three. Although it always hurt, at least by now, we were somewhat used to this dismal scenario.

We nodded, and followed her to our seats. Once we ordered our food and drinks, Ryan picked back up where we had left off. "At least it'll be a distraction to help us get through the day," Ryan said. Our table of three was a painful reminder of the fact that August 5th was approaching—for a second time. And to make things worse, this year's August 5th just happened to be the exact day I would have to leave Ryan in Modesto. It had been an incredibly tough decision, but I agreed to let Ryan live in Modesto his senior year with dear friends I trusted. He really wanted to graduate from Johansen High School with his friends. Even though I felt it was the right decision, that didn't help my heart from feeling the pain of that dreaded day approaching. The distraction of skydiving might just be the perfect remedy for helping me survive that day.

After lunch, we walked back to our hotel. As we walked, we passed a TGIF Restaurant, and it reminded me that Brittney was just days away from turning 21. She would turn 21 in Washington, D.C.—her/our second time of having a birthday here. I told her I would buy her her *first drink* at midnight on her birthday. We were here in D.C. for 10 days due to Ryan being asked to attend a leadership conference for a week. The trip prompted us to attempt to go to a baseball game. Awhile back, the kids and I had decided to finish Dad's goal of seeing all the ballparks in the U.S. So when this conference came up, we decided Nationals Park would be our first ballpark without Nate—when the four of us were here in 2003, Nationals Park didn't yet exist.

The kids and I made the best of our time in Washington, D.C., but grieving is a very long journey of ups and downs. One minute we were having fun gliding through the city on Segways, and the next minute I was outside crying on the phone to Carrie about how miserable it was to go to our first ballpark without Nate. Other moments we were cooling off in the pool, and walking to Georgetown for some delicious Italian food, only to be triggered by another familiar site reminding us of years back when we were all here together. Memories were everywhere, and Washington, D.C., was no exception. However, the three of us made some good new memories before returning home to SoCal. We returned with a Washington Nationals pennant to add to our collection, and a decision — I agreed to skydive with Ryan.

Family surrounded Ryan's car that was packed to the brim with everything he would need for the next nine months. His college plans were here in SoCal, but this temporary move back to Modesto would allow him to graduate high school in his hometown with friends he had grown up with. Ryan's senior year would be starting on Monday, so we were leaving a little early to give him a few days to get settled. We both hugged everyone goodbye in the driveway. Emotions were running high. Not only was Sunday the second anniversary of losing Nate, but it was also the day I would be leaving Ryan in Modesto and flying back home, alone. Even so, we had found a way to help us deal with this twofold emotional wallop — Ryan and I were going skydiving tomorrow!

I sat in the passenger seat as Ryan drove, and turned around to look at all of his belongings stuffed in the back of his car. The front wheel of his mountain bike was hanging out of the back window. "I can always bring anything you need with me when I come to visit you. And, you know... I'll be there *all* the time," I said, in a *missing you already* tone. "I don't want to miss *anything* of your senior year.

But, by the looks of it, you brought *everything* you own," I said, looking at all the boxes of clothes, his laptop, camera gear, and his snowboard. *Ahh,* I thought, catching a glimpse of his blue Bible, and a family picture on top of his skateboard.

Ryan chuckled, "Yeah, I'll let you know if I need anything, Mom."

"Oh my gosh, it's almost tomorrow!" I expressed, sounding both excited and terrified. "Are you ready?!"

"Yeah, I am." Unlike my high-pitched squeal, Ryan's answer was solid. "Are you?" he asked, looking over at me. I could see so much of Nate in his familiar green eyes.

"Well ... *anything* is easier than what we've been through, right?!" I responded.

I could feel the palpitations of my thumping heart as we pulled into Lodi's Parachute Center the next morning. Nonetheless, we were both determined to go through with this! To get us amped up and mentally psyched, we had just finished the 45-minute drive with rock music up at a loud volume. Ryan and I ended up belting out lyrics to the songs shuffling on the playlist as we approached Lodi—and the closer we got, the louder we sang. They were feel-good moments of singing along, and we saved the best for last as we joined in with Tom Petty. *"NOW, I'M FREE, I'M FREE FALLIN!"* A bit of an oxymoron, but singing as loud as we could actually seemed to quiet our racing minds.

Parked in the dusty parking lot with the music turned off, we prayed for God to watch over us and keep us safe. After saying Amen, we looked at each other wide-eyed and opened the car doors. My adrenaline was already pumping as I checked us in, read a couple of papers on liability and potential risks, and then signed on the dotted line of the consent forms. There was nothing left to do now but wait for our turn.

Ryan and I sat on a bench out back watching a continuum of skydivers from start to finish. With anticipation, we would watch them load up in the small aircraft. The plane would take flight, and before long we would start to see a trace of movement way up in the sky. Those tiny specks would soon turn into skydivers getting closer by the second until they landed safely on the large grassy field. We stayed there watching all the activity until we were called inside and taken to a back room.

Colorful parachutes lined the floors as skydive instructors throughout the room were rolling them up to get ready for the next jump. Other people began entering the room with a similar newbie manner and vibe—the dozen or so of us were clearly student skydivers. A couple of men walked over to Ryan and me and introduced themselves as our tandem instructors—one standing close to Ryan, and the other standing close to me. Knowing we were first timers, they began walking us through the process, and teaching us some basics about skydiving. They assured us that they would take care of everything, and didn't waste any time by beginning to put our arms and legs through multiple taut straps. They mixed our jitters up with a bit of humor to downplay the fact that we were next up to jump out of the plane!

A couple of videographers came over and energetically greeted us with their cameras already rolling. They told us they would be with us to capture every minute of this amazing experience on film so we could always remember this day. "So tell us why you guys are doing this?!" one said. The videographers stood there ready to film our answer. "Are you celebrating something, like a birthday?" We kept it brief, but told them about Nate's passing, and tomorrow marking two years. I showed them the DA's T-shirt I was wearing in loving memory, and Ryan's blue wristband with Nate's initials—NAB—printed on it. He had been wearing it every day for two years now. Taken by surprise at our answer, both our tandem instructors and the two videographers took in our words with empathy. "We're going to take good care of you two," they assured us. "You guys are in for the thrill of your lives!"

I could hear the resonant rumble of the aircraft's engine fired up outside as the instructors double-checked our many black straps by pulling and tugging on them. "We're good!" Ryan's instructor called out with a thumbs up.

"Let's do this!" my videographer—who went by *Batman*—shouted with gusto!

Our group began walking the green mile toward the white plane and its spinning propellers. I pulled my long windblown hair back, and smiled with love at Ryan as we walked to our one-way flight and climbed in. The instructors showed each of us where to sit. I made my way to the back of the plane and sat down straddling the seat. My tandem instructor walked over and sat directly behind me. He patted me with assurance on the shoulders, and although I couldn't quite make out what he was saying due to the noise, his thoughtful gestures were enough for me to know what he meant. I leaned to the side and looked for Ryan. He was a few people ahead of me, closer to the front. With everyone on board, one of the instructors slid the oversized transparent door shut and the plane started moving forward.

Once airborne, I could feel the compression of my upper body increase as the instructor began connecting me to his harness. I held still, allowing him to do whatever he needed to do to keep us attached! While he did that, I looked out the windows taking it all in. I could see Highway 99, and all the traveling vehicles getting smaller as we ascended. Below us were vineyards spread over thousands of acres. All those grapes were destined for bottles of wine for the many wineries in the area.

At a much higher altitude, I couldn't see anything but the curve of the horizon through the blue summer sky. I heard Ryan call out to his instructor, "Looks like we're almost there."

"Not quite yet. We're only at two miles," he shouted back. "We're going up to 13,500 feet!" Ryan turned back around with a precarious look. Trying not to freak out, I contended with my fears by squinting my eyes together really tight.

"We got this, Mom!" Ryan called out with encouraging support. I nodded at him acknowledging his words of affirmation. My instructor began securing my safety goggles around my eyes which were almost as cumbersome as the harness itself.

A myriad of thoughts flashed through my mind as I saw the pilot give a hand signal to the instructors. My entire life began to play out on slow motion clips of black and white film. One of the videographers slid open the great big door causing brisk, whooshing wind to become a presence in the plane's cabin. I looked ahead to see the first tandem skydivers get to their feet. They got in position at the door. I watched ardently as they leaned back first and then, with forward momentum, were gone instantaneously. In a continuous sequence, it was one jump after the other. *Oh God!* I thought, as I saw Ryan with his instructor and videographer make their way to the opening. With my heart pounding, I stared at him intently. My son was at the precipice of his free fall. *God be with him,* I beseeched, and within seconds Ryan was out of sight. I was still straddling the bench in oneness with my instructor, who began scooting us forward as the trio in front of us stood at the doorway, and then they were gone, too.

Our threesome stood on the edge of the plane with nothing but wide-open sky in front of us. I was grasping onto the metal bar above me as my instructor got us in position at the threshold. Batman—ready to film—was right at the side of us and would be flying solo. With the howling wind whipping around us, Batman nodded at me and jumped! Everything was happening so fast! My body was vibrating with adrenaline! Trying my best to not look down, I took in a long, deep breath and let go of the bar. *"Oh God!"* I called out multiple times as I took the plunge! I screamed at the top of my lungs as we were free falling through the sky at well over a hundred miles per hour!

It didn't take long for me to realize that I couldn't even hear myself screaming. I could feel it, but all I could hear was the sound of rushing air. My cheeks fluttered uncontrollably as we fell through the sky. I caught a glimpse of Batman in front of us filming this breathtaking experience. He made his way over to us and took my hand. Our trio began whirling in the air together. I looked around in every direction taking in this very surreal sensory overload. This was unbelievable!

My instructor gave me a hand signal that he was going to release the parachute. Straightaway, I had an extreme and divergent sensation of soaring upward. This abrupt decline of speed left me feeling virtually disembodied, like I was defying the laws of gravity. As the bright teal parachute canopied above us, we stopped soaring—bringing us to a place of unexplainable peace and serenity as we glided through the air.

Great white, puffy clouds surrounded us, and my instructor pulled my arms out to the sides like wings of a bird. "This is my favorite part!" I heard him say from directly behind me. We weren't falling; we were flying through the air with a perception not fathomable from the ground. This was a level of tranquility only attainable from up high in the realms of the heavens.

I could see the panoramic landscape coming back into focus—appearing like a medley of a patchwork quilt. My instructor began guiding us to the drop zone of the large grassy field. Now

Ryan and I were the specks in the sky coming in for a landing. I wondered if he had already landed. We were still moving swiftly, but compared to that first minute of our high speed free fall, this juncture felt like nothing more than a joy ride to the finish line.

There he was! Ryan, in his blue shirt, was standing there on the grass. He was looking up at the sky watching us come in for a landing. I heaved a sigh of relief. "*Thank you, God!*" I said, overwhelmed with gratitude that he was in one piece. And just like that, my feet hit the ground. And so did my keister! Batman extended his hand, and I could feel my instructor from behind helping me back to my feet as well. We all high-fived each other, and with my deepest regards I thanked them for everything! Still a bit wobbly, but completely exhilarated, I wrapped my arms around Ryan and embraced my son!

This epic adrenaline rush caused me to lean forward and put my hands on my knees. My euphoric holler releasing all of the emotions it took to do something like this. There is *nothing* like the thrill of skydiving!!!

Chapter 13

"Home" by Chris Tomlin

RYAN RETURNED to SoCal the next summer with a high school diploma, and a decision to get his bachelor's degree in Film at California State University Long Beach. His senior year in Modesto was an active and good year for him. He played water polo, ran cross country, made films in video production, and was awarded the Nate Baker Scholarship for character at the Mock Trial Ceremony for his role as a prosecution attorney. I made frequent trips back and forth to Modesto, and was even asked to present the award to him, on his 18th birthday, in front of a room full of people who gave a standing ovation.

After the seniors threw their graduation caps up in the air, and we celebrated Ryan's graduation with a room full of family, friends, and sushi, the year ended just as it started—we went skydiving once again in loving remembrance of Nate. Except this time Ryan and I took friends with us—including the friends that Ryan stayed with for the year—and filled the whole plane!

Things were going well. While Ryan was starting college, Brittney was continuing her education at the Laguna College of Art and Design, and I was settled into my new dental offices—I had even reached the point where I recognized some of the patient's names on my schedule at work. We were experiencing Southern California living to its fullest—many trips to Disneyland, being in the studio audience for Dr. Phil and American Idol. Hiking Malibu. We had family all around us, and even Paul and Traci and the kids moved to nearby San Diego. It was great to have them close! Even though we had a good life and I was so thankful for our many blessings, my heart still hurt. I wondered if there would ever be a time when it didn't hurt so badly.

With a woeful sigh, I walked into the kitchen to make myself some breakfast before I left for work. Although I was making progress in my grief counseling, every few months the reality of losing Nate would become more than I could bear. I felt heavy— weighed down with sadness and the pain of heartbreak that was culminating from within. Much like magma starts rising from deep inside the earth resulting in a volcanic eruption, I had learned that grieving—at least for me—worked the same way.

As I waited for the bread to toast for my peanut butter and banana sandwich, I thought about this conundrum of life I was in. There were just no easy answers. My mind went back to that tragic phone call I received in the middle of the night that changed the trajectory of my entire life forever. I was now the single mom of two amazing kids who lost their *larger than life* father as teenagers. Never had I ever envisioned losing Nate when we were both forty-two. I continued waiting for the bread to brown, and pulled a banana off of the bunch.

Man, I grumbled, irritated with how long this toast was taking! If it doesn't pop up soon, I'm going to be late for work. *Forget it,* I thought, and leaned over the counter to stop the bread from toasting. Dumbfounded, I stood there staring at the empty slots of a cold toaster. With my mindset still in the depths of grief, it made even simple things difficult. Shaking my head, I grabbed a breakfast bar and the banana, and headed to work.

Jesus, please give me Your strength to get through the day. I have none. I pulled my distracted self together the best I could and walked into the dental office. On the outside, I looked normal as I said "*Good morning*" to everyone with a smile, but right beneath the surface I was coming undone.

God gave me the strength I needed to see my first few patients, but as soon as I got a break, I sent one of my 911 texts to Carrie.

Hi Carrie—I'm in the bathroom at work. I can feel the pressure building up again. As you know, there's no stopping it when it gets like this. It hurts Carrie. How am I ever going to live with this pain? It's not even lunch break yet, and I can barely control these emotions. I don't want to cry at work. Send me a prayer if you can. I really need one right now.

I pushed *send* and leaned my head against the bathroom wall. I closed my eyes for a minute. The slow accumulation of downright despair had been intensifying over the last few days. Some days my pain would stay dormant. Other days, however, my pressurized emotions would burst through to the surface spewing out tears of unbearable pain.

I washed my hands and glanced in the mirror. I barely recognized myself. Maybe it was the lighting, but my brown eyes looked different—an emptiness and vulnerability dwelled inside them. I remembered Chris's dad telling me the day of Nate's Memorial that the sparkle in my eyes was gone. His tears showed me how much it hurt him to see me like that, but he was right. I knew it to be true the second he told me. There was a colossal void in my soul. And now, almost three years later, that void was still there and the sparkle was still gone. Those sparkles are buried so deep under the heartache, it's unlikely I will ever see them again.

Sure, I had acquired a newfound resiliency on how to cope with the hurt while I was at work. I was really good at blinking back tears, or stepping outside for some fresh air, but on this day my strength was depleted. I splashed some cold water on my face and patted it dry. *God help me*, I whispered, and opened the bathroom door.

The receptionist caught sight of me as I stepped into the hallway. Walking toward me, she began apologizing because a couple had just called to reschedule their back-to-back appointments. With my normal lunch break, and now two hours of God-given time off, I told her it was totally fine. I would just return in a few hours to finish my day.

By the time I reached my car, I was already crying. I started the engine, but hesitated, unsure of where to drive. The kids might be home, and I didn't want them to see me like this. For the most part, I didn't hide my grieving from them, but somedays I felt it best to shelter them from my brokenness. I considered eating lunch at a restaurant, but I really wasn't hungry. And besides, I wasn't in any condition to be around people right then anyway. As my pain began to surface, I pulled into the back of a nearby shopping center and parked the car. I turned off the engine and raised my hands to cover my face. I felt myself falling into the same dark grievous hole. Time alone in the car gave me the space I needed to cry.

Saturated in anguish, I continued crying right there in the front seat until I heard my phone ding with a text message. It was Carrie. What would I do without Carrie? She was at work seeing patients herself, and here she was, bolstering me up once again. As usual, her heartfelt text was attached to a Bible verse and this one in particular was from Jeremiah. "For I know the plans I have for you," declares the Lord, "plans to prosper you and not to harm you. Plans to give you hope and a future.'" Jeremiah 29:11. Oh, how I needed those words from God. I sat there in the comforting warmth of the car, unblinking as I stared out the window at nothing in particular.

I soon realized that my solitary time of shedding tears in the car was truly the calm before the storm. My emotions began erupting, and I called Mary for a lifeline.

"Hi Shel," Mary answered, in her usual kindhearted tone. "I just pulled up to the grocery store," she informed me.

"Mom." And with that one word, Mary knew I was experiencing another meltdown.

"I can't do this, Mom! How am I supposed to live without Nate?! I love him! I'll spend the rest of my life missing him! I want him back!" I demanded, as if she had the power to snap him here with me. The car was getting too hot with the engine off, so I got out and began pacing under the parking lot's row of trees. The white lines blurred into the blacktop as I sobbed.

"Where are you, Shel? I'm coming to get you," Mary replied.

"No, I don't have time. I have to go back to work. I still have three patients to see," I sniffled.

"I'll call the office. They'll understand you need the rest of the day off," Mary urged, trying her best to help.

I ignored her offer and returned to my previous rant. "This pain is the worst, Mom! I can't do this!" I repeated, shaking my head back and forth.

"Yes you can, Shelley," she desperately tried convincing me.

I caught my breath for a moment, and replied apathetically, "I don't want to.

I hurt every day. I just don't want to do this anymore." And then I thought about the kids and how they mean the world to me. They need me and I need them too. "I'm lost between two worlds, Mom. The only way I can see Nate again is to die!" I yelled out in complete frustration. But if I die, the kids will hurt twice as much as they already are! How?! How am I supposed to figure all of this out?!"

"Shelley, you are so strong. Look at everything you have done. You can do this. God will help you, and so will I. We are all here for you, Honey." I listened to her affirming words of hope. It was a strong day for Mary. We often switched roles of being the strong one, taking turns holding each other up and giving reminders that we are all here for a purpose. Each of us being immortal until that purpose has come to fruition.

"I trust God," I said, with the phone pressed to my ear as I walked. "I just don't know what I'm supposed to do now. Nothing makes sense anymore. Life was so great. We were so happy. Why did this have to happen!?"

Mary listened to my rhetorical question that she couldn't answer. "I love God so much, and will do anything He wants me to do. I just don't know what that is," I conveyed. "I have told God over and over again that I am His willing servant. I just want some answers. Is that too much to ask?"

I sat down under a budding jacaranda tree behind the buildings and watched a delivery man carry in supplies through the back door as I continued talking. "Mom, I've been thinking about going to Israel," I said out loud for the first time. "I need to spend some one-on-one time with God." I caught sight of the clock on my phone and realized my time was about up. "Sorry, Mom, I need to get back to work."

"Are you sure you're okay?" she asked, concerned about me returning to work.

"Yeah, I'm alright," I assured her. "Thanks, Mom. I'll see you after work."

"Alright then, we can talk later." We exchanged I love you's, and hung up.

A hard cry always made me feel better. As I drove back to work, I no longer felt the emotional force of grief compressing my heart like a vise. The remainder of the day wasn't so bad. I left work feeling emotionally drained but accomplished. Neither my co-workers nor my patients had any idea of what kind of a day I had had.

I pulled up in front of Mary's house and smiled when I saw Dewey's sweet little face in the window eagerly waiting for me. Both dogs were barking with excitement as I walked up to Mary's front door. The pups greeted me with their tails fervently wagging back and forth. Dewey ran over to get a chew toy, and returned with his head lowered, enticing me to chase him. Mary sat comfortably on the couch watching us lap around the house, while Chloe barked as we ran. This had become our routine every time I returned for the day.

After the chase, I picked Dewey up and held him as I walked into the living room. "Thank you, Mom, for letting me vent with you today," I said, giving her a worn-out smile as I sat down.

"You're welcome, Honey. I'm glad I could be there for you," she said, returning a worn-out smile of her own. My sadness that day was exceptionally bad, but we had gone through similar scenarios many times together over the past couple of years. "After we talked," Mary said, "I left the grocery store to come home and cry."

I nodded, understanding how hard it is to watch a loved one hurting so deeply. The kids were each grieving in their own way, and it pained me to see their hurt. I felt helpless in being able to take their suffering away. We had learned in our GriefShare class that you can't jump over grief, nor can you go around it. The only way to deal with grief is to walk right through it. That's what we were all doing. We were walking through the valley of death—a valley filled with pits and thickets.

"Grieving is *so* hard," I sighed, my hand petting Dewey on my lap as we talked.

"Oh, that reminds me. I have something for you to read," Mary said, reaching for her phone. "A friend from church in Salinas sent me a Bible verse that I really liked. I think it'll help."

Leaning back in the recliner I asked, "It doesn't happen to be Jeremiah 29:11 does it?"

Mary stopped scrolling through her phone. "How did you know," she asked, with a look of confusion.

"That's the verse Carrie sent me after I sent her a text from the bathroom at work," I told her, somehow not surprised at all. That's how God works.

Mary shook her head with a smile. "...Tell me about this trip to Israel."

"Well, they've been advertising it for months on The Fish. I feel a calling to go, Mom," I shared. "I think about Israel a lot. I know that God is with me wherever I am, but I just feel like I need to be with Him up close and personal—in *His* land. I have so many questions about the future and my next step. I need to try to make some sense out of all of this," I looked over at Mary. "I pray that He will let me in on even a little bit of what He has planned for me. I'm so confused, and my active personality does not do well with being patient," I confessed. "I want to ask Him what He wants me to do."

"You're going to Israel," Mary smiled at me with a look of intent.

"I am?...But I would need to take time off work. It's expensive..."

"That will all work out. You are going to Israel. Say it. Say 'I am going to Israel,' " Mary said, with her eyes fixed on me.

I paused briefly, taken by surprise at how this conversation was transpiring. I looked right back at Mary in front of me, and took in a deep breath. "I'm going to Israel," I repeated at her request.

"Say it again!" Mary said eagerly.

Without hesitation this time, I expressed with absolute certainty, "I am going to Israel!"

Mary got up and left the room while I continued sitting there with Dewey resting on my lap. She returned from the kitchen with her cane in one hand, and an ivory soup tureen in the other. The tureen looked heavy. It was pressed against her body as she walked back into the room. I quickly sat up, and helped Mary set it down on the coffee table. "Let's start throwing all our loose change in here. We have over six months to save," she said, thinking out loud. "This tureen needs a name. What should we call it?"

"Jeremiah," I said instantly, thinking of the Bible verse that I had been given *twice* that day. Dewey jumped off the recliner and followed me as I walked over to get my purse. I lifted the rather weighty lid and emptied all the dollars and change from my wallet into the tureen. Mary, excited to help make this happen, did the same.

"Every month, we can count the money and make a payment," she said. "By the time October gets here, the trip will be paid for!" I wrapped my arms around Mary and hugged her tight. She is such a rock in my life. This epiphanic conversation left me feeling hopeful. With a genuine smile, I said goodbye and drove Dewey and me the one mile home for the night.

Back at the house, I told the kids about how my very grim day had transformed into plans of going to Israel in October. Bubs and Ryan both had concerns, but completely supported my solo trip to Israel. They understood how much I needed to get away and spend time with God. Although the news repeatedly warned of heightened acts of terrorism along the Gaza Strip, sporadic bombings, and other security risks regarding travel to the Middle East, there I was, online, placing my down payment towards Genesis Tours. My heart and mind were set—unless the trip was cancelled, Israel was my October destination. I opened my inbox and smiled at the sight of my confirmation number.

The pain never goes away, but my upcoming trip was a major and welcomed distraction for me. My tour of the Holy Land would be so much more than a sight-seeing getaway. It would be an experience—a pilgrimage with God that would bring scripture to life. I would have ten days to explore the same land where Jesus Christ lived out His human life.

As the days and weeks went by, I worked hard and regularly put money into Jeremiah. Mary did as well, and even my parents sent a contribution when I told them about my trip. This goal helped me stay focused, and that focus gave me not only something inspirational to think about, but something to look forward to as well. I scrolled through the packed itinerary over and over again with anticipation of all that awaited me. The trip would start in Tiberias where I would sail the Sea of Galilee on a wood boat—a replica of a wooden boat during Jesus' lifetime. I would stand on the Mount of Olives and take in the glorious view of Jerusalem, walk the fateful route of the Via Dolorosa, float in the salty Dead Sea, and be baptized—again, this time in the Jordan River. I would ride a cable car up to Masada, pray at the Wailing Wall, and walk into the Garden Tomb—where Jesus was buried, but didn't stay long. This guided tour would take me through the very sites written about on the pages of the Bible. From Jesus' first cry in Bethlehem, to His anguish upon the cross of Calvary, Israel was the land of miracles, and I prayed without ceasing for God to bless me with getting there.

Six months later my prayers were answered, and October 16, 2014, had soon arrived. I woke up to an early morning—the sun wasn't even awake yet. I finished getting ready, and double-checked my carry-on, making sure I had my passport, my Bible, a journal, and the itineraries for both my flight and the tour. The driver had arrived, and Brittney and Ryan got out of their beds to say goodbye with sleepy eyes. I hugged them both and told them how much I loved them—a love they would never completely understand until they had children of their own.

While the driver was putting my luggage in the car, I gave the kids another hug, and carried Dewey out to the car with me for the short drive to Mary's house. He was like a third child who was not only deaf, but also clueless regarding my ten-day absence that would be starting in a few minutes. Mary was already waiting for us on the porch when we arrived. She was wide awake, and excited for me and my hopes of finding answers and direction for this new life that I didn't ask for but was now living. I kissed Dewey before handing him over to Mary, and smiled at the newest pink lipstick mark on the top of his head—his white hair was often embellished with my kiss marks. I hugged them both, and with a deep breath, I said goodbye and got in the car that was waiting for me.

Just beyond all the red taillights blinking on and off from the braking drivers ahead, LAX was in sight. Before long, we were inching through departure gates until the driver pulled to the curb and announced, "Here we are."

In the faded sunlight of early dawn, I collected my things. I have traveled a lot in my life, but never had I flown across the Atlantic to the other side of the world. The excitement of the unknown left me feeling fearless—a security which came from knowing God was right there with me. I began rolling my luggage into the airport to embark on this trip of a lifetime.

Fueled with caffeine from a Starbucks inside the terminal, I made my way toward the departure gate. When I arrived, I scanned the crowd looking for a man in a red hat. The DJ from The Fish sent an email out a few days before saying he would be wearing a red hat so that he and his wife could easily be found. I took a seat knowing I was in the right place—I recognized the DJ's voice in the crowd even before I saw his red hat. For years now, I had listened to him broadcasting every morning as I drove to work.

As I sat there, I sipped on my warm latte and got my journal out—I wanted to remember everything about this trip, even if I was still at LAX. I continued writing until I heard the gate agents at the counter begin their boarding announcements. Passengers started forming a line, and I soon joined this group of complete strangers to board the Philadelphia-bound plane. Joy co-existed with pain as I thought about having a layover in yet another place with cherished memories. The last time I was at the Philadelphia Airport, I was having the time of my life with Nate. And now, six years later, all I had was the familiar voice of a radio personality, and a sought-after red hat.

I was assigned a middle seat for the five-hour flight, but it was all good. It turns out the passenger to my left was a lady approximately my age who was also part of The Fish's Holy Land tour. By the time the plane landed in Philly, we had gotten to know each other and decided to grab something to eat together. We had just met mere hours ago; nonetheless, our mutual Christian faith gave us an instant connection.

We finished eating our airport version of Philly Cheesesteak Sandwiches—they definitely didn't measure up to the ones served at The Swan—and left to find the boarding gate for our connecting flight. As we walked through the terminal, we stopped to check our flight status on the Departure Screen. Our 12-hour flight to

Tel Aviv was on time and would soon start boarding passengers. We navigated our way with excitement through luggage carts, families with kids, and business travelers. I caught the scent of the freshly painted walls and noticed the design of the new carpet as we walked—so much had been remodeled since the last time I was here. Following the signs, we turned the corner into a narrow, sloping hallway. Taken by surprise, I knew *exactly* where we were. Close enough to touch were those same old hallway chairs.

Noise from the bustling terminal all around me seemed to mute as I stared at the vacant chairs for a moment. I could almost see Nate and me sitting on them while waiting for our delayed flight back home from my 40th birthday. I felt a tug on my heart, remembering Nate talking like Rocky Balboa when he handed me a breakfast burrito. Out of the entire Philadelphia Airport, my flight to Israel was departing from a neighboring gate to these nostalgic chairs. The effortlessly magical love that Nate and I shared created memories everywhere we went. Even these old airport chairs evoked relished memories. With a bittersweet smile, I quickened my step and caught up with my new friend. As we walked to our nearby gate, I looked back over my shoulder at the vacant chairs one last time.

My carry-on knocked against the seats as I made my way down one of the aisles of the fuselage to my seat. Once again, my new friend was sitting next to me on the left, except this time, she was in the middle and I was in the aisle seat. As I fastened my seat belt, the red hat caught my attention. The DJ and his wife were sitting right next to me on the other side of the aisle. We talked briefly, and I told this well-known disc jockey that I recognized his voice back at LAX. With an early start to our day, a layover, and the three-hour time difference, many passengers, including myself, were settling into their seats and closing their eyes.

In a silent prayer, I prayed to God as the jumbo jet took flight…

Dear Lord, Thank you for allowing me to take this journey. I really need this. It seems impossible sometimes for me to survive losing Nate. With a physical pain in my heart, I continued. *I miss him so much, God.* Deep in thought, I paused. *But I have You, Lord, and if I have You, I have everything I need. Help me to learn how to hold on tight to the too many to count cherished memories I have with Nate, and at the same time look forward to my future. What is my future, Lord? Take my hand, Lord, and show me the way. I love You. You, Lord, are number one in my life. Amen.*

The wheels of the plane touched down at Ben Gurion International Airport twelve hours later. As we taxied the concourse, I looked out the sunlit window, and saw a grove of olive trees. I smiled, thinking about this quest with God that had only just begun. I gathered my things and waited in line to disembark. *Please bless this trip, Jesus,* I said, as I walked down the external staircase, and took my first step in Israel.

Photos

Dewey

Graduation Day with Marlisa and Kim

Ryan Skydiving!

Shelley Skydiving!

Always Remember Us This Way
by Lady Gaga

February 2010, our 22nd and last Anniversary

Dear Nate,

It took years for me to do it, but taking my wedding ring off was the most heartbreaking thing I have ever done in my life. Although I had to face the fact that we were no longer married, in my heart, I will always be married to you. The princess diamond solitaire from my wedding ring was made into a necklace that now hangs close to my heart.

Since the beginning of our relationship back in the summer of 1986, I have always felt so loved and cherished by you—so much so that I can still feel it to this day. We really did live a genuine love story, didn't we — right down to the tragic ending. Words could never suffice to explain the loss of you in my life, but your abiding love is with me forever.

Since you have been gone, I have learned that there is no marriage in Heaven. I was saddened to hear that, but nonetheless, our relationship is not over. We're simply on *pause* until I catch up with you on the other side. Someday, I will depart earth with a one-way ticket straight to Heaven. And when our blissful reunion happens, I don't think I will ever let go.

After all our conversations over the years about God and Heaven, you know all the answers now. You have met God face to face! For now, I can only imagine how incredibly paramount that was. I am so proud of you, Sweetheart. No doubt God told you, "*Well done, good and faithful servant!*"

I need to finish my life story and watch over our amazing children and grandchildren, but I know you are up in Heaven cheering us on. Thank you for all the years of *Happily*, Nate. Once God pushes *play*, our *Ever After* in Heaven will begin.

Until then, with all my love,
Shelley

I Can Only Imagine
by MercyMe

Dear Lord,

Over the past 10 years, I have witnessed Your Word and Your promises come to life like never before. In the throes of bereavement, I have come to know You in a way not possible to attain with an intact heart. Brokenness was my gateway to a front row seat of watching Your amazing love and miracles.

I want to thank You, Lord, for surrounding me with wonderful people in my life. I cherish each and every one of them—family and friends who literally carried me through the darkest days of my life, and still stand by my side to this day. I love them all, and could never have survived this without them.

In my despair, I traveled around the world in search of answers. My trip to Israel was life changing, and the most significant pilgrimage of my life. There, in the very places You lived out your human life, You put on my heart to write a book.

It took me seven years, but this letter to You, Lord, completes my book. The pages are filled with laughter and tears. Writing *The Gift* allowed me to hold on to Nate a little while longer—like I got to live the fun, twice. But then came Chapter 10. That chapter was so painful to write, I almost didn't finish the book. Thank you for giving me the strength, and for granting the prayers of family and friends to help me with that gut-wrenching chapter. Time alone writing has been cathartic and a huge part of my healing.

Thank you, Holy Spirit, for helping me write this book. For years, the very first thing I would do each time I sat down to write was to pray to You, and say, "I don't know how to write a book... but You do. I'm going to need Your help!" Only You, Lord, could take me, an amateur writer with not even a single writing class of experience, and make it so that the Oprah Winfrey Network designed a study for me to write in!

Chapter 1 starts with Nate about to hand me a gift for my birthday, but then throws it off the side of Jack's Peak, never to be seen again. That beautifully wrapped box was intentionally empty, but our marriage that ensued from that momentous night was overflowing with blessings. The meaning of the name Nathan is "Gift of God." Nate himself was *the gift*.

Amen

About the Author

PHOTO BY JEFF BRADSHAW

Shelley Baker is enjoying life in sunny Southern California. Her son, Ryan, and his beautiful wife of five years, Haziel, live next door with their Golden Retriever, Bo. And mother-in-law, Mary, lives just a mile away. Daughter, Brittney, relocated back to her hometown of Modesto when she married her husband, Chris, two years ago. Spending time with her grandson, Parker, (born 1-5-19) is one of the absolute highlights of Grandma Shel's life, and she can't wait for Brittney and Chris's second son, Adam, to arrive—he will be born by C-section on Sunday, December 6, 2020. Shelley continues to work as a Registered Dental Hygienist—her career of twenty-nine years—in Long Beach, California. She works for Dr. Laura Manuel D.D.S. where she has been for the last eight-plus years. The family is active in church and all pay it forward by co-leading GriefShare.

The **STANISLAUS FAMILY JUSTICE CENTER** opened its doors on November 1, 2010. In the 10 years since its opening, SFJC has served well over 10,000 victims of violence in their time of need. Adults and children of all ages are provided help and lifelong solutions to survive their specific abuse—domestic violence, sexual assault, child abuse, elder abuse, and human trafficking.

Although Nate passed away a few months before the Center's opening, he was an integral part of its planning and beginning. Ten percent of the proceeds from *The Gift* will go to the STANISLAUS FAMILY JUSTICE CENTER.

Mission Statement: "The Stanislaus Family Justice Center offers victims and survivors a path to safety and hope through compassion and coordinated services.

Vision Statement: "Together we break the cycle of violence."

RANCHO SANTA MARTA is a non-denominational Christian ministry located on the Baja California Peninsula, 130 miles south of San Diego. This Christ-centered Ranch provides housing for homeless, orphaned, and abused children. Their on-site school also provides education for children with learning disabilities.

Many missionaries over the years have provided much-needed dental work for those who reside and attend school—kindergarten through high school—on the ranch. The makeshift chicken-coup-turned-dental-office we once worked in has evolved into an actual dental office located right on the premises. An additional 10% of the proceeds from *The Gift* will go toward instruments and equipment for Rancho Santa Marta's dental office.

A faith statement from RANCHO SANTA MARTA: We believe "in the personal return of Jesus Christ. We believe that the hope of His coming again affects the personal life and service of all believers." (1 Corinthians 15:52-58)

Acknowledgments

First and foremost, I want to thank my adult children, Brittney and Ryan. The two of you mean the absolute world to me. I often catch physical resemblances, mannerisms, and characteristics of Dad in each of you that makes me smile. Through you, part of Dad lives on. As you build your lives with your individual families, these stories will always help you remember where you came from. When Dad passed away, you both could have turned to a life of making bad decisions to ease the intense pain a teenager should never have to experience. Instead, you made wise choices and I am so proud of you both. Our already close relationship grew even tighter as we became the *3 Musketeers*. Side by side, we faced the beast of grief together. Although always very different, you are both my favorite child and I love you beyond words...

My heartfelt thanks to you Bubs for your proficient help with story boarding, editing, and even writing a letter to Oprah. Getting a call from her network, OWN, was one of the biggest surprises of my life! I will always appreciate and fondly remember the time we spent together, and your support of helping my goal and dream of writing *The Gift* come true.

A big hug of gratitude to you Ryan for the many times you came over—all the way from next door :)—to listen to a story, make suggestions, enhance and send the chosen pictures, or to do something on the computer for me. I can always feel your love and protection.

Thank you Mary—aka Mom—for the hundreds of pages you have corrected for me over these last seven years. What a blessing to have a retired teacher as a mother-in-law to help me bring *The Gift* to fruition. I felt like a student waiting for a grade each time I dropped my papers off at your house. The markings of your red felt tip pen lessened over the years as my writing progressed. I have learned a lot from you, not only with correct grammar and punctuation, but also about kindness, humbleness, and a pure heart.

To Jon and Lisa—Jon, you are the best brother-in-law ever. We have sure been through a lot together over the years. I love watching your *Uncle*

Pups time with the kids. They really cherish you. And Lisa, thank you for all you did in helping with Nate's Celebration of Life video, helping us to find a new house, and even painting the front door red to make it feel more like home when we arrived. I love you both, and it's been so fun to watch our family grow!

To my best friend Carrie—or "Shoehorn" as Nate referred to you (maiden name Shehorn). Our friendship began over 30 years ago with test tubes, flasks, and beakers. Although our rock candy experiment in chemistry lab was a crystalized sugar flop—and we had to buy the class a new beaker—our friendship flourished. You are one of my life's greatest blessings, Carrie. You were a literal life vest for me when Nate died. By no exaggeration, I felt as if I, too, had died. You fed me God's Word daily. I found literal nourishment for my broken soul from the daily Bible verses you texted me. Grieving is a long journey of one step forward, and two steps back. But no matter if I was moving forward or falling into another pit, you were there. In your attempts to help me, you even took a 13 weeks GriefShare class at your church in Folsom so you could learn about ways to support me in my grieving. I wouldn't be where I am now without you. You were there from day one of this nightmare, and as I have healed, you are there to celebrate the victory. The idea of writing a book first came from you. And although I initially said no, God put it in my heart to write my story. I love you and thank you with all of my heart.

To Paul and Traci—It's been 10 years now, and you are always there—in person or by phone—to remember those annual dates that hurt a little more than the others. Our too many to count Scooby Doo toasts to Nate mean so much as we remember Nate together. Our shared faith strengthens our bond, and you both are more like family than friends.

To my dear childhood friend Flo—You just can't make old friends :)! Although the hustle and bustle of life separated us for many years, our rekindled friendship has been such a blessing. Thank you for the fun, laughter, prayers, a shoulder to cry on—and for putting up with my zest for long walks, haha. One of my favorite things about living in SoCal is having you near by!

To Pastor Cliff Sexton—I know it was in God's plan to have you there for the most excruciating days of my life. There was always something about you that made me feel God's help. You were the man with Biblical answers to all my questions, and above all, the hope that I desperately needed. I will never forget your enormous comfort as you bandaged my aching soul with God's Word.

To my patients, Carole Adams and Kathy Child—Thank you both from the bottom of my heart for all that you have each done to edit and make suggestions with my writing. The Gift is what it is today because of your considerate help.

Thank you Colleen Pak. It was you who suggested adding dialogue to my stories. You were my first editor who told me these stories would become a book someday. That day has arrived!

Thank you to the Oprah Winfrey Network's Home Made Simple for designing a beautiful study for me to write my book in. They even built a padded bench for Dewey right next to my desk. Our home was packed with producers, a film crew, contractors, interior designers, and the gregarious host Jeremiah Brent for a week. It was a fun and awesome experience the kids and I will always remember. The episode aired on May 23, 2015, and was appropriately named "It's a Novel Idea."

Made in the USA
Columbia, SC
12 May 2021